Cistercians, Heresy and Crusade in Occitania, 1145–1229

PREACHING IN THE LORD'S VINEYARD

YORK MEDIEVAL PRESS

Cistercians, Heresy and Crusade in Occitania, 1145–1229

PREACHING IN THE LORD'S VINEYARD

Beverly Mayne Kienzle

THE UNIVERSITY *of York*

YORK MEDIEVAL PRESS

First published 2001

A York Medieval Press publication
in association with The Boydell Press
an imprint of Boydell & Brewer Ltd
PO Box 9   Woodbridge   Suffolk IP12 3DF   UK
and of Boydell & Brewer Inc.
PO Box 41026   Rochester   NY 14604–4126   USA
website: http://www.boydell.co.uk
and with the
Centre for Medieval Studies, University of York

ISBN 1 903153 00 X

A catalogue record for this book is available
from the British Library

Library of Congress Cataloging-in-Publication Data
Kienzle, Beverly Mayne.
   Cistercians, heresy, and Crusade in Occitania, 1145–1229: preaching in the
Lord's vineyard/Beverly Mayne Kienzle.
      p.   cm.
   Includes bibliographical references and index.
   ISBN 1-903153-00-X (hardcover: alk. paper)
      1. Cistercians – France, Southern – History.   2. Albigenses.   3. Heresies,
Christian – France, Southern – History – Middle Ages, 600–1500.   4. France,
Southern – Church history.   I. Title.
   BX3432.S68 K54   2001
   271′.120448′09021–dc21
                                                                                00–063401

This publication is printed on acid-free paper

Typeset by Joshua Associates Ltd, Oxford
Printed in Great Britain by
St Edmundsbury Press Ltd, Bury St Edmunds, Suffolk

CONTENTS

List of Illustrations   vi

List of Abbreviations   viii

Chronology   xiv

Preface   xvii

Introduction   1

Appendix to Introduction
Deconstructing: Close Reading, Rhetorical Criticism, and
Historiography of Persecution and Heresy   16

1   The Lord's Vineyard in the Twelfth Century   25

2   Monastic Spirituality and Literature: the Domestic Vineyard   56

3   Bernard of Clairvaux, the 1143/44 Sermons and the 1145
   Preaching Mission: From the Domestic to the Lord's Vineyard   78

4   Henry of Clairvaux, the 1178 and 1181 Missions, and the
   Campaign against the Waldensians: Driving the Foxes from the
   Vineyard   109

5   Innocent III's Papacy and the Crusade Years, 1198–1229:
   Weeding the Vineyard   135

6   Hélinand of Froidmont and the Events of 1229: Planting Virtues
   in the Vineyard   174

   Conclusion   202

   Bibliography   219

   Index   239

ILLUSTRATIONS

Fig. 1. Map of Occitania, reproduced with permission from: Peter of les Vaux-de-Cernay, *The History of the Albigensian Crusade*, trans. W. A. and M. D. Sibly (Woodbridge, 1998).   26

Fig. 2. Cistercian Abbey of Villelongue (Aude) (photograph: Jean-Louis Gasc)   57

Fig. 3. The medieval quarter of Verfeil (Haute-Garonne) (photograph: Jean-Louis Gasc)   79

Fig. 4. Praemonstratenisan Abbey of Fontcaude (Hérault) (photograph: Jean-Louis Gasc)   111

Fig. 5. Cistercian Abbey of Fontfroide (Aude) (photograph: Jean-Louis Gasc)   137

Fig. 6. Eglise des Jacobins, Toulouse (photograph: Jean-Louis Gasc)   175

Fig. 7. Town of Fanjeaux (Aude) (photograph: Jean-Louis Gasc)   203

FOR LEWIS HENRY MAYNE,
MY FATHER,
LOVER OF HISTORY, INTELLECTUAL
FRIEND AND SUPPORTER,
WITH LOVE AND APPRECIATION

ABBREVIATIONS

Apocalypsim	Geoffrey of Auxerre, *Super Apocalypsim*, ed. F. Gastaldelli, Temi e Testi 17 (Rome, 1970).
Baldwin, *Masters*	J. W. Baldwin, *Masters, Princes and Merchants. The Social Views of Peter the Chanter and his Circle*, 2 vols. (Princeton, NJ, 1970).
Berman	*Medieval Agriculture, the Southern French Country-side, and the Early Cistercians. A Study of Forty-three Monasteries*, Transactions of the American Philosophical Society 76:5 (Philadelphia, 1986).
Biller and Hudson	*Heresy and Literacy, 1000–1530*, ed. P. Biller and A. Hudson, Cambridge Studies in Medieval Literature 23 (Cambridge, 1994).
Boswell, *Tolerance*	J. Boswell, *Christianity, Social Tolerance, and Homosexuality: Gay People in Western Europe from the Beginning of the Christian Era to the Fourteenth Century* (Chicago, 1980).
Brenon, *Cathares*	A. Brenon, *Les cathares. Vie et mort d'une Église chrétienne* (Paris, 1996).
Brenon, *Vrai visage*	*Le vrai visage du Catharisme* (Toulouse, 1990).
Caesarius, *Dialogus*	Caesarius of Heisterbach, *Dialogus miraculorum*, ed. J. Strange, 2 vols. (Cologne, 1851).
CaF	Cahiers de Fanjeaux (Toulouse, 1966–).
CCCM	Corpus Christianorum, Continuatio Mediaevalis (Turnhout, 1966–).
CCSL	Corpus Christianorum, Series Latina (Turnhout, 1953–).
Chanson	*La Chanson de la croisade albigeoise*, ed. E. Martin-Chabot, 3 vols. (Paris, 1931).
Châtillon	J. Châtillon, 'La Bible dans les écoles du XIIe siècle', in *La Bible*, pp. 163–97.
Chazan, *Stereotypes*	R. Chazan, *Medieval Stereotypes and Modern Anti-semitism* (Berkeley, CA, 1997).
Chenu, *Nature*	M.-D. Chenu, *Nature, Man and Society in the Twelfth Century*, ed. and trans. J. Taylor and L. K. Little (Chicago, 1968).
Cisterciens, CaF	*Les Cisterciens de Languedoc (XIIIe–XIVe s.)*, ed. M.-H. Vicaire, CaF 21 (Toulouse, 1986).

Cole, *Preaching*	P. Cole, *The Preaching of the Crusades to the Holy Land, 1095–1270* (Cambridge, MA, 1991).
Congar	Y. Congar, 'Henri de Marcy, abbé de Clairvaux, cardinal-évêque d'Albano et légat pontifical', in *Analecta Monastica*, Series 5, Studia Anselmiana 43 (Rome, 1958), pp. 1–90.
Constable, *Reformation*	G. Constable, *The Reformation of the Twelfth Century* (Cambridge, 1996).
Duvernoy, *Histoire*	J. Duvernoy, *Le Catharisme: l'histoire des Cathares* (Toulouse, 1979).
Duvernoy, *Religion*	J. Duvernoy, *Le Catharisme: la religion des Cathares* (Toulouse, 1976).
Evans, 'Crusade'	A. P. Evans, 'The Albigensian Crusade', in *A History of the Crusades*, ed. R. L. Wolff and H. W. Hazard, 4 vols. (Philadelphia, 1962), II, 277–324.
Exordium magnum	B. Griesser, *Exordium magnum cisterciense sive narratio de initio cisterciensis ordinis* (Rome, 1961), Series Scriptorum s. ordinis 2.
Fichtenau	H. Fichtenau, *Heretics and Scholars in the High Middle Ages 1000–1200*, trans. D. A. Kaiser (University Park, PA, 1998).
FIDEM	Fédération internationale des instituts d'études médiévales.
Grundmann, *Movements*	H. Grundmann, *Religious Movements in the Middle Ages: The Historical Links between Heresy, the Mendicant Orders, and the Women's Religious Movement in the Twelfth and Thirteenth Century, with the Historical Foundations of German Mysticism*, trans. S. Rowan, with an Introduction by R. Lerner (Notre Dame, IN, 1995).
Hamilton, 'Wisdom'	B. Hamilton, 'Wisdom from the East: the reception by the Cathars of Eastern dualist texts', in Biller and Hudson, pp. 38–60.
Hystoria	*Hystoria Albigensis*, ed. P. Guébin and E. Lyon, 3 vols. (Paris, 1926–39).
Interrogatio Iohannis	*Le livre secret des Cathares. Interrogatio Iohannis, apocryphe d'origine bogomile*, ed. and trans. E. Bozoky (Paris, 1980).
Inventer l'hérésie?	*Inventer l'hérésie? Discours polémiques et pouvoirs avant l'Inquisition*, ed. M. Zerner, Collection du Centre d'Etudes Médiévales de Nice 2 (Nice, 1998).
Kaelber, *Asceticsm*	L. Kaelber, *Schools of Asceticism. Ideology and Organization in Medieval Religious Communities* (University Park, PA, 1998).

Kaelber, 'Weavers'	L. Kaelber, 'Weavers into Heretics? The Social Organization of Early Thirteenth-Century Catharism in Comparative Perspective', *Social Science History* 21 (1997), 111–37.
Kienzle, 'Hugo Francigena'	B. M. Kienzle, 'The Works of Hugo Francigena: *Tractatus de conversione Pontii de Laracio et exordii Salvaniensis monasterii vera narratio; epistolae* (Dijon, Bibliothèque Municipale, MS 611)', *Sacris erudiri* 34 (1994), 287–317.
Kienzle, 'Mary speaks'	B. M. Kienzle, 'Mary Speaks against Heresy: An Unedited Sermon of Hélinand for the Purification, Paris, B.N. ms. lat. 14591', *Sacris erudiri* 32 (1991), 291–308.
Kienzle, 'Midi'	B. M. Kienzle, 'Hélinand de Froidmont et la prédication cistercienne dans le midi, 1145–1229', in *Prédication*, CaF 32, pp. 37–67.
Kienzle, 'Monastic Sermon'	B. M. Kienzle, 'The Twelfth-Century Monastic Sermon', in *The Sermon*, pp. 271–323.
Kienzle, 'Obedience'	B. M. Kienzle, 'Holiness and Obedience: Denunciations of Twelfth-Century Waldensian Lay Preaching', in *The Devil, Heresy and Witchcraft in the Middle Ages. Essays in Honor of Jeffrey B. Russell*, ed. A. Ferreiro (Leiden, 1998), pp. 259–78.
Kienzle, 'Touchstone'	B. M. Kienzle, 'Preaching as Touchstone of Orthodoxy and Dissent', *Medieval Sermon Studies* 42 (1999), 18–53.
Kienzle and Walker	B. M. Kienzle and P. J. Walker, *Women Preachers and Prophets through Two Millennia of Christianity* (Berkeley, CA, 1998).
La Bible	*Le Moyen Âge et la Bible*, ed. P. Riché and G. Lobrichon, La Bible de Tous Les Temps 4 (Paris, 1984).
Lambert, *Cathars*	M. D. Lambert, *Cathars* (Oxford, 1998).
Lambert, *Heresy*	M. D. Lambert, *Medieval Heresy. Popular Movements from the Gregorian Reform to the Reformation*, 2nd edn (Oxford, 1992).
Leclercq, *Learning*	J. Leclercq, *The Love of Learning and the Desire for God*, 3rd edn, trans. C. Misrahi (New York, 1982).
Letters	*The Letters of St Bernard of Clairvaux*, translated by B. S. James, with a new introduction by B. M. Kienzle (Stroud, 1998).
Little	L. Little, *Religious Poverty and the Profit Economy in Medieval Europe* (Ithaca, 1978).
Longère, *Prédication*	J. Longère, *La prédication médiévale* (Paris, 1983).

Maisonneuve	H. Maisonneuve, *Études sur les origines de l'inquisition*, 2nd edn (Paris, 1960).
McGinn, *Spirituality*	*Christian Spirituality. Origins to the Twelfth Century*, ed. B. McGinn, J. Meyendorff, and J. Leclercq (New York, 1988).
MGH	*Monumenta Germaniae historica inde ab a. 500 usque ad a. 1500*, G. H. Pertz *et al.* (Hannover, Berlin, etc., 1826–).
SS	*Scriptores* (in folio), 30 vols (Hannover, 1824–1924).
Models	*Models of Holiness in Medieval Sermons*, Proceedings of the International Symposium at Kalamazoo, 4–7 May 1995, ed. B. M. Kienzle, E. W. Dolnikowski, R. D. Hale, D. Pryds, A. T. Thayer, FIDEM Textes et Études du Moyen Âge 5 (Louvain-la-Neuve, 1996).
Monastic Preaching	*Medieval Monastic Preaching*, ed. C. A. Muessig (Leiden, 1998).
Moore, *Birth*	R. I. Moore, *The Birth of Popular Heresy*, Documents of Medieval History 1 (London, 1975).
Moore, *Formation*	R. I. Moore, *The Formation of a Persecuting Society. Power and Deviance in Western Europe, 950–1250* (Oxford, 1987).
Moore, *Origins*	R. I. Moore, *The Origins of European Dissent* (London, 1977).
Mundy, 'Urban Society'	J. H. Mundy, 'Urban Society and Culture: Toulouse and its Region', in *Renaissance and Renewal*, pp. 229–47.
Murphy, *Rhetoric*	J. J. Murphy, *Rhetoric in the Middle Ages. A History of Rhetorical Theory from St Augustine to the Renaissance* (Berkeley, CA, 1974).
Newman	M. Newman, *The Boundaries of Charity. Cistercian Culture and Ecclesiastical Reform, 1098–1180* (Stanford, 1996).
NJBC	*The New Jerome Biblical Commentary*, ed. R. E. Brown, J. A. Fitzmyer and R. E. Murphy (Englewood Cliffs, NJ, 1990).
Paix de Dieu, CaF	*Paix de Dieu et Guerre Sainte en Languedoc au XIIIe siècle*, ed. M.-H. Vicaire, CaF 4 (Toulouse, 1969).
Parole	*La parole du prédicateur Ve–XVe siècle*, ed. R. M. Dessì and M. Lauwers, Collection du Centre d'Études Médiévales de Nice 1 (Nice, 1997).
Paterson	L. Paterson, *The World of the Troubadours. Medieval Occitan Society, c. 1100–c. 1300* (Cambridge, 1993).

Perelman and Olbrechts-Tyteca	C. Perelman and L. Olbrechts-Tyteca, *The New Rhetoric. A Treatise on Argumentation*, trans. J. Wilkinson and P. Weaver (Notre Dame, IN, 1969).
Peters, *Inquisition*	E. Peters, *Inquisition* (Berkeley, CA, 1988).
PL	*Patrologia Latina Cursus Completus*, ed. J. P. Migne, 217 vols. (Paris, 1841–64).
Prédication, CaF 32	*La prédication en Pays d'Oc (XIIe–début XVe siècle)*, ed. J.-L. Biget, CaF 32 (Toulouse, 1997).
Puylaurens	Guillaume de Puylaurens, *Chronique, Chronica magistri Guillelmi de Podio Laurentii*, ed. and trans. J. Duvernoy (Paris, 1976).
Renaissance and Renewal	*Renaissance and Renewal*, ed. R. L. Benson and G. Constable with C. Lanham (Cambridge, MA, 1982).
Russell, *Dissent and Order*	J. B. Russell, *Dissent and Order in the Middle Ages. The Search for Legitimate Authority* (New York, 1992).
SBOp	*Sancti Bernardi Opera*, ed. J. Leclercq, H.-M. Rochais and C. H. Talbot, 8 vols. (Rome, 1957–77).
SC	Sources chrétiennes (Paris, 1940–).
SCH	*Studies in Church History*.
SCH S	*Studies in Church History. Subsidia*.
Sermons and Society	*Medieval Sermons and Society: Cloister, City, University*, ed. J. Hamesse, B. M. Kienzle, D. L. Stoudt and A. T. Thayer, FIDEM Textes et Études du Moyen Âge 9 (Louvain-la-Neuve, 1998).
Shirley	*The Song of the Cathar Wars*, trans. J. Shirley (Aldershot, 1996).
Sibly	Peter of les Vaux-de-Cernay, *The History of the Albigensian Crusade*, trans. W. A. and M. D. Sibly (Woodbridge, 1998).
Smalley, *Bible*	B. Smalley, *The Study of the Bible in the Middle Ages* (Oxford, 1952).
Smalley, Gospels	B. Smalley, *The Gospels in the Schools c. 1100–c. 1280* (London, 1985).
Song III	*On the Song of Songs, III*, trans. K. Walsh and I. M. Edmonds, Cistercian Fathers 31 (Kalamazoo, MI, 1979).
Stock, *Literacy*	B. Stock, *The Implications of Literacy. Written Language and Models of Interpretation in the Eleventh and Twelfth Centuries* (Princeton, NJ, 1983).
Strayer, *Crusades*	J. R. Strayer, *The Albigensian Crusades*, with a new Epilogue by C. Lansing (Ann Arbor, 1992).

Summer Season	Bernard of Clairvaux, *Sermons for the Summer Season. Liturgical Sermons from Rogationtide and Pentecost*, trans. with Introduction by B. M. Kienzle, additional translations by J. Jarzembowski, Cistercian Fathers 53 (Kalamazoo, MI, 1991).
The Sermon	*The Sermon*, ed. B. M. Kienzle, 2 vols., Typologie des sources du moyen âge occidental, 81–83 (Turnhout, 2000).
Thouzellier, *Catharisme et Valdéisme*	C. Thouzellier, *Catharisme et Valdéisme en Languedoc à fin du XIIe et au début du XIIIe siècle. Politique pontificale – Controverses*, 2nd edn (Paris, 1969).
Vauchez, *Laity*	A. Vauchez, *The Laity in the Middle Ages. Religious Beliefs and Devotional Practices*, ed. and intro. D. E. Bornstein, trans. M. J. Schneider (Notre Dame, IN, 1993).
Vicaire, 'Clercs'	M.-H. Vicaire, 'Les clercs de la croisade', in *Paix de Dieu et guerre sainte en Languedoc au XIIe siècle*, ed. M.-H. Vicaire, CaF 4 (Toulouse, 1969), pp. 260–80.
de Vogüé	Adalbert de Vogüé, *The Rule of Saint Benedict. A Doctrinal and Spiritual Commentary*, trans. J. B. Hasbrouck, Cistercian Studies 54 (Kalamazoo, MI, 1983).
Wakefield, *Crusade*	W. Wakefield, *Heresy, Crusade and Inquisition in Southern France, 1100–1250* (Berkeley, CA, 1974).
Waugh and Diehl	*Christendom and its Discontents. Exclusion, Persecution and Rebellion, 1000–1050*, ed. S. L. Waugh and P. D. Diehl (Cambridge, 1996).
WE	*Heresies of the High Middle Ages. Selected Sources Translated and Annotated*, ed. W. L. Wakefield and A. P. Evans, Records of Western Civilization Sources and Studies 81 (New York, 1991).
Zerner-Chardavoine, 'L'abbé Gui'	M. Zerner-Chardavoine, 'L'abbé Gui des Vaux-de-Cernay, prédicateur de croisade', in *Les Cisterciens de Languedoc (XIIIe–XIVe s.)*, CaF 21 (Toulouse, 1986), pp. 183–204.

CHRONOLOGY

1145	Bernard of Clairvaux's preaching mission to Occitania
1178	Preaching mission of Peter of St Chrysogonus and Henry of Clairvaux
1179	Third Lateran Council
1181	Henry of Clairvaux returns to Occitania and leads troops against Lavaur
1198	Innocent III elected pope
1200	Arnaud Amaury elected abbot of Cîteaux
1204	Arnaud Amaury commissioned legate; *Etsi nostra navicula*
1206	Fulk of Le Thoronet elected bishop of Toulouse; Diego of Osma and Dominic of Guzman join Cistercian legates; delegation of Cistercian abbots arrives to preach
1208	Assassination of Peter of Castelnau; Innocent III calls for crusade; Arnaud Amaury named chief legate; Guy of les Vaux-de-Cernay appointed master of preachers
1209	(May/June) Crusade departs and descends the Rhône valley (22 July) Sack of Béziers and massacre (July/August) Crusaders occupy towns including Montréal, Fanjeaux, Limoux (August) Siege of Carcassonne (August/September) Occupation of Mirepoix, submission of Pamiers, Saverdun, Lombers, Albi
1210	(April) Siege of Bram, mutilation of *c.* 100 prisoners to avenge that of two knights (June) Siege of Minerve, burning of 140 Cathars
1211	(April/May) Siege of Lavaur, execution of *c.* 80 *faidits* and burning of 300–400 Cathars (May) Siege of Les Cassès, burning of 60–100 Cathars (June) Failure to take Toulouse (August–October) Uprising in the Lauragais (November–December) Montfort winters at Fanjeaux, then Castres
1212	Widening of crusade to the north-west; Arnaud Amaury elected archbishop of Narbonne; Guy elected bishop of Carcassonne; battle of Las Navas de Tolosa
1213	(January) Crusade halted by Innocent III (May) Crusade resumed (September) Battle at Muret
1215	Fourth Lateran Council in Rome; Raymond VI deprived of land and rights
1216–17	Raymond VI regains ground
1218	Death of Simon of Montfort outside Toulouse
1219	Brief royal crusade undertaken by Prince Louis

1220–21 The future Raymond VII regains ground

1222–24 Raymond VI dies; peace efforts

1226   Louis VIII undertakes a crusade, is stalled at Avignon, returns home and dies in November

1226–28 Battles continue between royal army and supporters of Raymond VII

1229   (12 April) Public penance of Raymond VII before Notre-Dame of Paris; Treaty of Meaux/Paris (May) Opening of University of Toulouse (November) Council of Toulouse issues canons

1244   Siege of Montségur, burning of 205 Cathars

1255   Retaking of Quéribus

1318–25 Inquisitorial hearings conducted by Jacques Fournier

1321   Burning of the last Cathar perfect, William Bélibaste

PREFACE

Bernard of Clairvaux's use of the vineyard image to describe his turning from the monastery to the Church and the world inspired the organization of this book and its treatment of Cistercian preaching against heresy. While anti-heretical preaching constitutes the book's primary topic, it cannot be understood without an appreciation of monastic life and its inward-looking literature, more representative of the whole of monastic writing.

In the spring of 1995, I discovered the vineyard image in one of Bernard's letters while preparing an article on the abbot's preaching, but the initial research for this book dates back to the mid-1980s, after I began working on Hélinand of Froidmont's sermons. Hélinand's sermons represented a bridge for me to cross from the study of vernacular literature into the field of medieval Latin sermon studies. I discovered that Hélinand, the writer I first knew for his Old French poetry, had composed numerous Latin sermons, largely unexamined by scholars. I began to read them, to investigate the field of sermon studies, and to move, like Hélinand, from Old French poetry to Latin sermons. My first research explored the contemplative side of monastic literature with its richly imaged symbolism and experiential spirituality, a feature that still attracts me. As I explored these generally calm and meditative texts, I was jarred from time to time by the vehemence of the language used when monastic enemies came into play. I also found repeatedly that Hélinand's preaching had a polemical side to it, and my unravelling of his anti-heretical writing eventually led me to the Cistercian campaigns against heresy. It also brought me to heresiology and particularly to Cathar studies.

The journey involved in writing this book followed a path of change in professional direction and resulted in new areas of research, friendships, surprises and detours along the way. A lover of literature studied within its social and historical context, I was pulled towards the writings of moralists and eventually to religious literature. Dissatisfied with the detached literary criticism of the 1970s, I decided to explore Christian Latin writings in greater depth and to use my training in literature for historical research on literary texts. Sermon studies was just emerging as a field, and I was captured by its combination of literary, historical and theological approaches, and the challenge of reading large amounts of uncharted Latin. I found welcoming and encouraging communities among the sermonists of the International Medieval Sermon Studies Society, of which I am now President, and with the scholars in Cistercian studies. Many assisted my work and directed me to new projects that proved invaluable for learning about preaching and Cistercian monasticism and literature.

Yet the anti-heretical side of this otherwise beautiful and meditative literature was inescapable. As Augustine's beautiful *Homilies on First John* plunge into arguments against the Donatists, it seemed that each new text of Hélinand's that I edited dealt somehow with heresy. Guided by the works of Jean Duvernoy, I began to deepen my knowledge of Catharism, and with the help of R. I. Moore's *The Formation of a Persecuting Society*, the importance of Cistercian anti-heretical preaching for the history of persecution emerged clearly. My first publications in this area attracted the attention of Anne Brenon, then Director of the Centre d'Études Cathares in Carcassonne. Our professional relationship and eventual friendship opened the region of Occitania to me in an extraordinary way, making it come alive in its medieval history and seem like a sort of second home to me.

As my research on Hélinand and the Cistercians who preceded him began to accumulate, colleagues encouraged me to develop my conference papers and articles into a book. I struggled with how to put the two sides of monastic preaching together. How would I describe the Cistercians without making them into a sort of Dr Jekyll and Mr Hyde? I wondered whether the white monks could be described as medieval spiritual equivalents of the 1960s intellectuals whom David Halberstam called the 'best and the brightest'. Such a political perspective did not seem suitable for my work, and I continued to searched for a structure, ideally encapsulated by an image, that would achieve fairness and not resort to caricature. I hope that the result demonstrates how certain Cistercians transgressed from the monastic vocation during a specific period but does not seem to cast all the white monks as violators of their ideals.

While my method, all conclusions and shortcomings are ultimately my responsibility, I have benefited from the encouragement and guidance of many colleagues over the years of this research. While not all to be named here viewed the whole of this book, they have contributed in some fashion to its long gestation. Phyllis Roberts was a first and generous mentor in sermon studies. My early work on Cistercian spirituality and literature was supported by Fr Chrysogonus Waddell, E. Rozanne Elder, Brian Patrick McGuire, John R. Sommerfeldt, David Bell and other scholars who meet yearly at the Institute of Cistercian Studies in Kalamazoo, Michigan. Brian Patrick Maguire especially encouraged the writing of this book, and Martha Newman generously provided her photographs of a key manuscript. For heresiology, I am endebted to Jean Duvernoy, to Anne Brenon, who has helped to keep me abreast of European scholarship, and to Peter Biller. His extensive knowledge of Cathar and anti-heretical documents and his careful reading and insightful suggestions for this manuscript resulted in a much better book than the one first sketched. Colleagues at Harvard have contributed to the shaping of my ideas. Papers on this topic were presented at the Seminar on Medieval Culture organized by Jan Ziolkowski and Eckehard Simon. From the Divinity School, Clarissa Atkinson generously read the entire manuscript; François Bovon has given advice especially on exegetical questions as versions of the work were being written in article form; Elisabeth Schüssler Fiorenza's company and inspiration has sharpened my awareness of methodology and its implications. A semester of research leave from Harvard Divinity School in Fall 1998 allowed for completion of the manuscript. Kay Shanahan, Staff Assistant, editor, proof-reader, computer wizard, friend and fellow cat-lover assisted at so many stages of this work that it would be impossible to enumerate them all. Generous assistance from the Andover Library staff also allowed a swifter completion of the book than would otherwise have been possible. I am grateful to Clifford Wunderlich, Public Services Librarian, and especially to Gloria Korsman, Reference Librarian, who has helped at every stage in locating materials competently, swiftly and enthusiastically, saving me months of work. Student assistants have also helped over the years with collecting materials and scanning them, studying paleography from microfilms of Hélinand's sermons, and reading articles and chapters of the book in draft form. Susan Shroff, Pamela Lowe Dolan, Robert Canavello, Liza Burr, and Nancy Nienhuis all deserve acknowledgment, as does Jaehyun Kim, who read the whole manuscript with careful attention. Jean-Louis Gasc deserves heartfelt thanks for taking superb photos especially for the book.

Finally, I am grateful to my immediate family, Edward and Kathleen, who have supported, encouraged and celebrated the phases of this project for numerous years; our four cats, Walter, Basile, Athena and Tecla, who call me to rest and meditation; and my father, Lewis H. Mayne, always a lover of history and an enthusiastic supporter and believer in my work, to whom this book is dedicated.

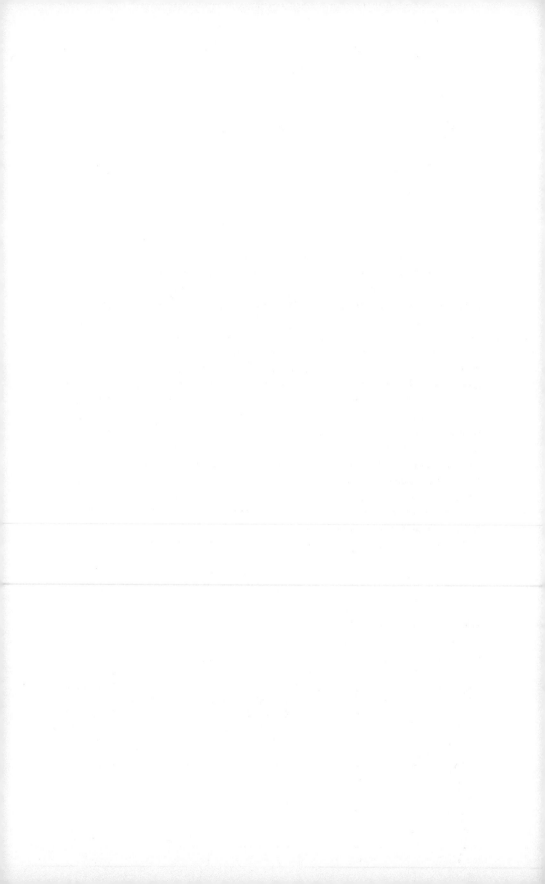

INTRODUCTION

Cistercians, Heresy, and Crusade, 1145–1229: Preaching in the Lord's Vineyard

From 1145 to 1229 Cistercian monks, respected as twelfth-century Europe's holiest and brightest men, embarked on preaching missions against dissident Christians in southern France. The twelfth century witnessed a remarkable upsurge of religious dissent, and preaching offered the medieval Church its most potent instrument of propaganda. Monastic preachers aspired to quell the opposition with words alone, but their sermons also roused recruits for the holy war of crusading on domestic soil as well as abroad. Public preaching was not at all customary for monks: in fact, ecclesiastical tradition and legislation prohibited it. Preaching was reserved instead to the secular clergy – the bishops and priests who espoused the active life in engagement with the world. In contrast, the monastic rule imposed a vow of stability, permanence within the monastery, as part of its design for a life centred on contemplation. Moreover, the Cistercian order established itself on a principle of withdrawal from the world and creation of a model Christian community isolated from the wickedness of society. Despite all this, some Cistercians served as itinerant preachers traversing city and countryside in anti-heretical campaigns. Others plunged even more deeply into the confrontation, accepting posts as bishops and papal legates who aided and even directed the Albigensian Crusade, one of the cruellest medieval wars, and who contributed to establishing procedures of inquisition, codified and expanded in the 1230s. Scholarship on the Albigensian Crusade (1209–29) and the development of the Inquisition has not yet centred on the crucial role of Cistercian prelates and preachers.[1] Neither has research delving into the gaps between Cistercian ideals and reality[2] focused on the monks' anti-

---

[1] The most useful sources on heresy and crusade that also include Cistercian preaching are: Moore, *Origins*; Moore, *Formation*; Lambert, *Heresy*; Lambert, *Cathars*; Wakefield, *Crusade*; Maisonneuve; Thouzellier, *Catharisme et Valdéisme*. Histories of the Albigensian crusade include: Evans, 'Crusade'; Strayer, *Crusades*; J. Sumption, *The Albigensian Crusade* (London, 1978); M. Costen, *The Cathars and the Albigensian Crusade* (Manchester, 1977). Sources on heresy and inquisition include E. Peters, *Inquisition*, and *Heresy and Authority in Medieval Europe* (Philadelphia, 1980); Russell, *Dissent and Order*; WE.

[2] Newman, *passim*, argues that the *Carta caritatis* approved in 1119 offers a focal point

heretical efforts.[3] Cistercian preaching against dissident Christians is too often neglected or overshadowed by preaching the Crusade to the Holy Land.[4] Furthermore, the thrust of scholarship on popular preaching against heresy generally leaves the Cistercians aside to focus on the Dominican and Franciscan orders, founded in the first quarter of the thirteenth century.

The present book examines this important but understudied aspect of Cistercian history to probe how and why the Order undertook endeavors that drew the monks outside their monastic vocation. While some of its members preached publicly against heterodoxy, a few rode at the head of armies like non-combatant knights. In contrast, some evidence also points to Cistercian monks who favoured the heretics and the *faidits*, the southern lords who fought against the northern French nobles and protected their persecuted compatriots. The Order eventually withdrew from popular preaching and military activities but retained a pro-French stance in Occitania, evidenced by collaboration with French lords in construction of new towns on Cistercian land. One Cistercian served as an inquisitor: Jacques Fournier, one time abbot of the powerful abbey of Fontfroide, and later bishop of Pamiers and Mirepoix. Fournier was subsequently elected pope, taking the name Benedict XII. He was responsible for the copious Inquisition records that have furnished material for researchers. In this volume we turn not to those Inquisition registers but to the lesser-known centuries preceding them, when the Cistercian presence was establishing itself in Occitania and laying the foundation for the Inquisition, which the papacy and the friars later developed into an elaborate structure.

How did a contemplative monastic order involve itself so intensely in public preaching against heresy? How did the Cistercians become embroiled in a situation that led some even onto the battlefield at the head of armies? The Albigensian Crusade exemplifies the abuse of power and force in a collaboration between Church and state which resulted in the systematic elimination of the Cathars and their sympathizers. Hysteria over heresy affected other areas of Europe during this period, but not with the same

---

for comprehending how the Order could have engaged itself so actively in the world. Newman's valuable demonstration of how *caritas* was turned outward with reforming zeal treats the campaign against heresy only briefly. Other studies on the Order begin with L. Lekai, *The Cistercians, Ideal and Reality* (Kent, Ohio, 1977), and include Berman on economic and agricultural history.

[3] An exception is the excellent article by Vicaire, 'Clercs'; however, he focuses on examples included in the *Hystoria Albigensis* and does not examine the entire period. After completing this manuscript, I received F. Neininger, 'Die Zisterzienser im Albigenserkreuzzug', in *Die rheinischen Zisterzienser. Neue Orientierungen in rheinischen Zisterzen des späten Mittelalters*, ed. N. Kuhn and K. P. Wiemer (Cologne, 1999), pp. 67–83. I am grateful to the author for sending it.

[4] Cole, *Preaching*, and the collection of articles, *The Second Crusade and the Cistercians*, ed. M. Gervers (New York, 1992) are valuable contributions to scholarship on this topic.

deadly alliance of papal urging and secular force. Historians have termed the Albigensian Crusade 'one of the most savage of all medieval wars' and 'one of the classic examples of repression of dissent and freedom of thought'.[5] To what extent did the Cistercians contribute to the propaganda that fuelled such barbarism? How did they perceive their roles and responsibilities when faced with heresy? What did they actually preach? Did they commit or order acts of violence? These are some of the questions the present book will address.

Among the Cistercians' opponents, we shall not treat 'intellectual' heresy and the disputes of theologians within the Church, but rather 'popular' or 'social' heresy,[6] chiefly the Cathar counter-church and the Waldensian movement. Both those dissident groups were strong in Occitania, the foyer of Catharism and the geographic scope of this study.[7] We also deal with neighbouring areas when pertinent, such as Gascony, where Bernard of Clairvaux preached in 1145, and Lyons, where the Waldensian movement began in 1173. Literature on heresy in the Rhineland, Italy and England appears when directly relevant to Occitania, but the abundant material from those areas warrants separate investigation.

In the summer of 1145, Bernard, abbot of Clairvaux and the most influential churchman of his day, departed from his native Burgundy to comb the countryside of southern France in search of the renegade monk, Henry, who had been condemned at the Council of Pisa (1135) for provoking the people of Le Mans and elsewhere to revolt against the authority of the clergy. Bernard was determined to persuade the region's inhabitants to reject that 'manifest enemy of the Church' who was irreverently denouncing its sacraments and ministers.[8] The spring of the same year, 1145, witnessed the passing of Halley's Comet, natural disasters that resulted in extensive famine, and the third death of a pope since 1143.[9] The apocalyptic fear that regularly haunted the medieval imagination was heightened during the twelfth century's middle decades.

---

[5] Sumption, *Albigensian Crusade*, p. 16; Strayer, *Crusades*, p. xii.

[6] Nonetheless, we bear in mind J. B. Russell's observation that orthodox writers often convert 'social' heresy into 'intellectual' heresy in order to argue against it. J. B. Russell, *Lucifer: The Devil in the Middle Ages* (Ithaca, NY, 1984), p. 184.

[7] Occitania is a region defined by linguistic criteria. See Paterson, pp. 1–9; Strayer, *Crusades*, pp. 1–3, 10–11. Historically the region also has been called Languedoc, but the term Occitania conforms to current usage in that area.

[8] The phrase, 'hostis Ecclesiae manifestus, irreverenter ecclesiasticis derogans Sacramentis pariter et ministris', appears in Geoffroy of Auxerre's account of the mission in chapter six of the *Vita prima*, the biography of Bernard, in *PL*, CLXXXV, 312–13. The mission is discussed in Chapter Three of this book.

[9] Innocent II died in 1143, Celestine II in 1144 and Lucius II in 1145. See the articles by G. Bounoure discussed in Chapter Three of this book: 'Le dernier voyage de saint Bernard en Aquitaine', *Bulletin de la Société Historique et Archéologique du Périgord* 115 (1988), 129–35; and 'L'archevêque, l'hérétique et la comète', *Médiévales* 14 (1988), 113–28; 15 (1988), 73–84.

Two years earlier in 1143, Everwin of Steinfeld, prior of a Premonstratensian community near Cologne, had written to Bernard requesting the
Cistercian's advice concerning the dissidents in the Rhineland, who, to
Everwin, bore the same marks as the false prophets denounced in the First
Letter to Timothy as harbingers of the last days. They were in fact adherents
of the Cathar movement which swept across Europe in the twelfth century,
establishing a counter-church that rivalled and challenged the authority and
practices of Rome. Three people were burned as heretics at Bonn in 1143, on
the authority of Count Otto.[10] In response to Everwin, Bernard wrote that
anxiety over the Lord's vineyard, the Church and the world, was moving him
towards affairs outside the domestic vineyard, the monastery.[11]

Twenty years later in 1163, the hysteria over heresy still pervaded the
Rhineland and reports of heresy had surfaced in France, Italy and England.
Four men and a girl were burned in Cologne by authority of a lay court, and the
Church's spokespersons hastened to preach against those they perceived as
false prophets, poisoning the people with an iniquitous doctrine that was
spreading like a cancer. Elisabeth of Schönau joined with the Benedictine
abbess Hildegard of Bingen to compose visionary treatises, denouncing the
Cathars and rebuking clerics who neglected to recognize the dangers of heresy.
In a situation most rare for a woman, even a religious, Hildegard of Bingen was
authorized to preach publicly against heresy and the clergy's failure to
eradicate it. Hildegard and Elisabeth influenced Elisabeth's brother, Eckbert
of Schönau, a black monk, to draft thirteen sermons against the Cathars.[12] The
Church hierarchy was waging war against heresy with pen and pulpit.

The Cistercians, also called the white monks because of the undyed cloth of
their habits, were summoned to lead the campaign. Their reputation for
austerity, their centralized governance, uniform dress, and recruitment of
intellectuals served them well as agents of reform and equipped them for
writing and preaching against heresy. Founded in 1098 by Robert of
Molesme, the Cistercian Order grew rapidly under the leadership of Bernard
of Clairvaux, who joined its ranks in 1113, becoming abbot of Clairvaux
within three years. After an initial period of concentration on the abbey's
affairs, Bernard began to widen the scope of his activities.[13] When papal

---

[10] Everwin's letter is found in *PL*, CLXXXII, 676–80, and translated into English in
Moore, *Birth*, pp. 74–8, with a short introduction.

[11] See below in this Introduction, pp. 8–9, and Chapter Three.

[12] For a discussion of Hildegard, Elisabeth and Eckbert, see A. Clark, *Elisabeth of
Schönau: A Twelfth-Century Visionary* (Philadelphia, 1992), pp. 22–5; B. M. Kienzle,
'*Operatrix in vinea domini*: Hildegard of Bingen's Preaching and Polemics against the
Cathars', *Heresis* 26–7 (1996), 43–56; B. M. Kienzle, 'Defending the Lord's Vineyard:
Hildegard of Bingen's Preaching against the Cathars', in *Monastic Preaching*, pp. 163–
81.

[13] For a biography of Bernard, see A. H. Bredero, *Bernard of Clairvaux: Between Cult and
History* (Grand Rapids, MI, 1996); and for biographical information: B. P. McGuire,
The Difficult Saint. Bernard of Clairvaux and his Tradition, CS 26 (Kalamazoo, MI,

schism threatened the Church in 1130, the abbot of Clairvaux defended the papacy of Innocent II and subsequently became Innocent's chief representative. Eugene III, a former Cistercian of Clairvaux, was elevated to the Holy See in 1145 and occupied it until 1153, the year that Bernard died. Eugene's brother and abbot at Clairvaux frequently gave him advice, preached the Second Crusade at his request, and composed for him the *Five Books on Consideration: Advice to a Pope*.[14] Cistercians after Bernard allied with the papacy as legates to southern France.

Following Bernard's abbacy, Henry of Clairvaux assumed his predecessor's charge with such adamant determination to avoid failure in the fight against heresy that he shifted the Cistercian role in Occitania radically, becoming in 1181 the first papal legate to raise an army and lead an expedition into a Christian land. Earlier, Henry played a key role in drafting legislation against heresy at the Third Lateran Council (1179), and in 1180, it was he who reportedly accepted the profession of orthodoxy made by Valdes,[15] who with his dramatic conversion at Lyons in 1173 had founded a lay apostolic movement so radical for its day that it advocated preaching by all believers, even women.

Other Cistercians also took a hand in suppressing the Waldensians. Some were bishops: Guichard, former abbot of Pontigny was archbishop of Lyons when the movement began; and Ponce, abbot of Clairvaux before his appointment as bishop of Clermont, banished women Waldensian preachers from that city.[16] Others not elevated to bishoprics took to pen and pulpit in the attack on the Waldensians and the Cathars: Geoffrey of Auxerre, for example, once secretary to Bernard and then abbot of Clairvaux himself; and Alan of Lille, a noted author and Paris master who joined the Cistercian Order later in his life.[17]

Henry of Clairvaux had at least one notorious successor who took to the battlefield during the Albigensian Crusade (1208/9–1229): Arnaud Amaury, one time abbot of Cîteaux and later papal legate (1204) and archbishop of Narbonne (1212–25). As legate, Arnaud Amaury recruited preachers but also appeared at the head of armies, notably in 1212 when he led about 100 knights from France into Spain to take part in the Battle of Las Navas de Tolosa. His fellow Cistercian, Caesarius of Heisterbach, years later attributed

---

1991); M. Casey, *Athirst for God. Spiritual Desire in Bernard of Clairvaux's Sermons on the Song of Songs*, CS 77 (Kalamazoo, MI, 1988), pp. 6–17.

[14] On Bernard, Innocent II and Eugene III, see E. T. Kennan's introduction to *Five Books on Consideration: Advice to a Pope*, CF 37 (Kalamazoo, MI, 1976), pp. 4–11. On the schism of 1130 and the Cistercians, see Newman, pp. 191–202.

[15] On Henry, see Chapter Four of this book and Congar.

[16] On Guichard of Pontigny and Ponce of Clairvaux, see Chapter Four of this book and the *Dictionnaire des auteurs cisterciens*, ed. E. Brouette, A. Dimier, E. Manning, La documentation cistercienne (Paris, 1979), cols. 310 and 576.

[17] Biographical information on these Cistercians is included in Chapter Four of this book, where their polemical works are discussed.

to Arnaud Amaury the infamous words uttered at the sack of Béziers in 1209. When asked to distinguish Christians from heretics, Arnaud Amaury reportedly replied: 'Kill them all; God will recognize his own.' Whether or not Arnaud Amaury spoke those words, which Caesarius did not flinch at reporting, there is no indication that he or anyone else tried to stop the massacre at Béziers.[18]

Still, some Cistercians like Guy of les Vaux-de-Cernay, later the bishop of Carcassonne, continued the preaching campaign, which had intensified in the early years of the thirteenth century under the Cistercian legates, Ralph of Fontfroide and Peter of Castelnau, whose murder precipitated the crusade. Moreover, Fulk, the abbot of Le Thoronet appointed bishop of the key city of Toulouse in 1206, endeavoured to strengthen the power of preaching. Fulk abandoned his life as a troubadour to become a Cistercian. He spent much of his controversial tenure as bishop in exile, but intervened with a corps of troops at the siege of Lavaur in 1211. Fulk established Dominic and his brothers as preachers in Toulouse, supporting their work from diocesan funds and appointing a master of theology to teach them at the cathedral.[19] When the university was founded in Toulouse in 1229 according to the provisions of the Treaty of Paris, a Cistercian abbot, Hélie of Grandselve, oversaw the appointing of the masters who were led by Dominicans, and another white monk, Hélinand of Froidmont, issued the academic charge to the new students and masters.[20] Thus the Cistercians passed the responsibility for public preaching against heresy to the new religious order of the Dominicans.

Although the Cistercians undertook extensive efforts against heresy in southern France, they repeatedly met with failure. From Bernard of Clairvaux's tour of the south in 1145 to the mission of a dozen abbots in 1206 and the signing of the Treaty of Paris in 1229, Cistercian preachers were bent on convincing the dissidents through preaching and debate that their beliefs were erroneous. The preachers' failures and frustrations are recorded in chronicles, letters, and even in epic poetry. The author of the first section of the *Canso de la Crozada*, William of Tudela, recounts that the Order of Cîteaux sent its monks to preach many times, but that the people paid no more attention to the sermons than they would have to a rotten apple. The crowds derided them and compared their voices to the buzzing

---

[18] See Chapter Five in this book.

[19] On Fulk, see Chapter Five of this book and the works cited there; also S. Stronski, *Le troubadour Folquet de Marseille, édition critique précédée d'une étude biographique et littéraire* (Cracow, 1910).

[20] On Hélinand of Froidmont, Hélie of Grandselve and the events of 1229, see Chapter Six of this book and the works cited there; also B. Kienzle, 'Education in the Late Twelfth and Early Thirteenth Centuries: The Witness of Hélinand of Froidmont', in *Faith Seeking Understanding: Learning and the Catholic Tradition*, Selected papers from the Symposium and Convocation celebrating the Saint Anselm College Centennial, ed. G. C. Berthold (Manchester, NH, 1991), pp. 77–88.

of bees.[21] Phrases such as these expressing the futility of the Cistercian preaching missions appear as formulae in this epic style poem. They capture the failure and frustration experienced by Cistercian preachers throughout this period, and indirectly, the resolute stance of Cathar believers. The few stories of success generally relate to preaching tours conducted in the north and aimed at bringing more recruits southward.

The Cistercians were the principal players in the drama staged in France, but they did not act alone. To some extent they continued an effort begun by the Cluniac Benedictines, particularly Peter the Venerable, who wrote and preached against the Petrobrusians.[22] Furthermore, Benedictines, regular canons, notably the Premonstratensians, and secular clergy, collaborated with the white monks.[23] The canons shared with the Cistercians an outward appearance of conformity in their standard, simple habits; this made them, particularly in the view of Innocent III, useful counter-models to the ideals of apostolic poverty espoused by the lay dissident movements.[24] In the early part of the thirteenth century, Cistercians preached alongside Dominic and supported the founding of the Dominican order. Nonetheless, for much of the twelfth century and into the early thirteenth, the white monks allied closely with the papacy, leading the effort against heresy and also preaching the crusade to the Holy Land.[25] Moreover, the Cistercian Order established itself internationally and developed a strong framework of governance, with an annual General Chapter and affiliations between mother and daughter houses that helped to ensure uniformity in strict observance of the Benedictine Rule and the Cistercian statutes. With such a concern for austerity and an efficient system of organization, Cistercian monks served well as agents of the papacy, or, as one historian puts it, 'the frontier guards of faith in all parts of Christendom and even beyond'.[26] Furthermore, Cistercians entered the monastery as adults; during the peak of the Order's growth, numerous new recruits had left behind academic careers. As the twelfth century's most successful 'textual community', the Cistercians produced copious works on monastic spirituality.[27] This common spiritual and literary culture also provided the springboard for a writing and preaching campaign against heresy. Some of the white monks assumed this work willingly, but overall the

---

[21] *Chanson*, I, pp. 12–13, 52–3, 110–13.

[22] Peter the Venerable, *Tractatus contra Petrobrusianos*, ed. J. Fearns, CCCM X (Turnhout, 1968). The prefatory letter is translated into English in Moore, *Birth*, pp. 60–2. See also D. Iogna-Prat, 'L'argumentation défensive: de la polémique grégorienne au Contra Petrobrusianos de Pierre le Vénérable (1140)', in *Inventer l'hérésie?*, pp. 87–118.

[23] On the Premonstratensians, see B. Ardura, *Prémontrés: Histoire et Spiritualité* (Saint-Etienne, 1995).

[24] On this point see B. Bolton, *Innocent III: Studies on Papal Authority and Pastoral Care* (Aldershot, 1995), chapter VI, p. 187.

[25] See Cole, *Preaching*.

[26] Bolton, *Innocent III*, chapter VI, p. 183.

[27] Stock, *Literacy*, pp. 403–54, esp. p. 405.

Order experienced tension over involvement in the active life. The correspondence between Innocent III and the Cistercians reveals their hesitations about departing from the life of contemplation.[28]

The vineyard image and monastic rhetoric

The scriptural image of the vineyard serves as a unifying motif for the various phases of Cistercian activity in Occitania and for the many texts that relate to it. At the opening of his Sermon 65 *On the Song of Songs*, Bernard of Clairvaux explains that it is necessary for him to preach a third sermon on Song of Songs 2. 15: 'Seize for us the little foxes that are destroying the vineyard.' The abbot expresses his anxiety about the Lord's vineyard and its vines, which are not secure. He feels that he must turn from inside to outside, away from domestic monastic matters in order to be of use in affairs of general concern.[29] Successive Cistercians and other ecclesiastical figures return to the vineyard image for capturing their vision of disorder in the Church and the world. Henry of Clairvaux praises the papal legate Peter of St Chrysogonus for exterminating 'the destructive little foxes from the Lord of Hosts' vineyard' as well as closing out 'the gnawing moths from the clothes-chest of Solomon'.[30] Innocent III enjoined the Cistercians in 1206 to eradicate the weeds harming the vineyard, and in 1208, upon demanding armed intervention in Occitania, he lamented the assassination of the legate Peter of Castelnau, describing him as a worker in the vineyard.[31] The 1213 sermon calling for the Fourth Lateran Council to be convened also grounds itself on the vineyard image: 'Vineam Domini Sabaoth. . .'.[32] Hélinand of Froidmont's opening sermon for the 1229 Toulouse Council describes God as *pater familias* who sends workers, namely the papal legate, into the vineyard to guard against thorny vines, nettles and vipers – symbols which, like the little foxes, represent heretics and their beliefs.[33]

---

[28] See Bolton, *Innocent III*, chapter VI, pp. 182–8.

[29] *Song*, III, pp. 179–80. *SBOp*, II, 172. The full text is cited and explicated in Chapter Three, pp. 78, 80, 85–90.

[30] *PL*, CCIV, 224C: 'ita de vinea Domini Sabaoth vulpeculas demolientes exterminat, ut de ipso quoque vestiario Salomonis tineas corrodentes excludat'.

[31] See Chapter Five, pp. 147, 150.

[32] *Ep*. 30, *PL*, CCXIV, 823–7.

[33] See Chapter Six of this book, pp. 188–9. The fox as embodiment of heresy appears consistently with the vineyard and dates back as far as Irenaeus's writing against the gnostics. See M. Scopello, 'Le renard symbole de l'hérésie dans les polémiques patristiques contre les gnostiques', *Revue d'Histoire et de Philosophie Religieuses* 71 (1991), 73–88. The fox as symbol of heresy also appears in Augustine and Jerome. See Congar, p. 13; and E. Mitre Fernández's overview of animals in medieval anti-heretical literature: 'Animales, vicios y herejías (sobre la criminalización de la disidencia en el Medievo)', in *Cuadernos de Historia de Espana LXXIV en memoria de don Claudio Sánchez-Albornoz* (Buenos Aires, 1997), pp. 257–83. I am grateful to the author for sending me his article.

The process of turning from inside to outside – from the monastery to the world, from the domestic vineyard to the Lord's vineyard – entails a shift from the interior and experiential spirituality of the monastery to a concern for the exterior world. There, the experiences of lay people in a changing society were leading to the development of a new spirituality, growing like monasticism from biblical and apostolic roots, but rejecting traditional expressions of piety and the obedience to hierarchical authority that underlay the monastic life, as set forth in the *Rule* of Benedict. When Bernard of Clairvaux directed his attention beyond the inner life and world of the monastery, he seemingly extended his abbatial charge over the souls of his monks to assume some responsibility for the salvation of the Church and thereby his society. His successors stepped even further outward, serving as bishops and papal legates in southern France. The Cistercians confronted the world in order to attack the heresy they felt threatened the existence of the Lord's vineyard and ultimately their own.

Just as the vineyard image encompassed the movement from inside to outside, so monastic literature, which cultivated rhetoric designed to edify the monks on their inward journey and to persuade others to join them, veered outward against opponents. From construction of the monastic ethos, the writers pivoted to destruction of dissident movements. The persuasive power of the biblical language that the monks aimed at extirpating vices, perfecting the soul, and fostering contemplation of the heavenly Jerusalem, shifted toward eradicating heterodox ideas, exposing doctrinal errors, and banishing heretics from the Babylons of the world. They applied the analytical reasoning of theological disputation to expositions of heretical beliefs. Sharpening the tools of exegesis long practised in monastic comment-aries on scripture, they opposed the dissidents' differing interpretations, bolstered orthodox views, and selected verses and images best suited to discredit their targets.

The white monks did not invent this polemical writing; they followed the doctors of the Church, notably Augustine and Jerome, who had employed exegetical weapons against their opponents. Patterns of rhetoric ranging from broad arguments to specific images like the little foxes constituted material for reappropriation and recycling centuries later. However, the medieval polemicists did not simply reproduce what they found in earlier literature; it influenced their perception, but they made choices and refashioned the older material, painting their own portraits of dissidents.

Methodology

For this volume, I combine literary and historical approaches into a methodology based on close textual analysis and committed to viewing texts within their historical, intellectual and cultural context. In my view, texts considered without their context hold value for their aesthetic or stylistic patterns but run the risk of being style without meaning, *forme* without *fond*. Likewise, mining sources for their reflection of events alone may neglect the writer's crafting of the argument and persuasive casting of the persons and events – all important keys to meaning. As a noted historian asserts, 'If the means by which actors interpret reality are ignored, the texts are effectively broken up into a junk heap of facts.'[34]

These aspects of my method can be termed reconstructive and deconstructive. The first phase entails retrieving the evidence for preaching and sermons available in extant sources and placing it in context; the second critiques it, demonstrating how preachers constructed their arguments and cultivated stylistic resources. I shall discuss both techniques briefly below. Because debates continue among historians over certain issues involved in my approach – the role of social structures versus the actions of individuals, the view of the majority versus the minority, and the text versus the sub-text – I include a more in-depth treatment of these points in an appendix to this chapter.

Reconstructing from available sources

Despite the repeated preaching expeditions carried out against the dissidents in 1145 and afterwards, few extant Cistercian sermons witness to these campaigns. For example, what Bernard of Clairvaux actually preached on his 1145 tour of the Midi can only be reconstructed, because no actual sermons from that mission have come down to us. Nonetheless, some of his letters were intended for public reading aloud, and his Sermons 65 and 66 in the collection *On the Song of Songs* must have provided resources for preachers. For Henry of Clairvaux, Arnaud Amaury, and the early thirteenth-century preachers, a single sermon survives, of uncertain attribution. The 1229 truce breaks this pattern; we possess four sermons of Hélinand of Froidmont, delivered at Toulouse in 1229. Still, Hélinand's sermons do not typify the preaching undertaken by groups of preachers travelling the countryside with the goal of refuting heterodoxy. For evidence of preaching in the field, other types of sources must be consulted.

For the most part, the history of Cistercian preaching in this period is reconstructed without actual sermon texts, by examining chronicles, treatises, letters, statutes, *exempla*, and other sources to glean information about preaching. Chronicles, for instance, trace the movements and confrontations of preaching missions, with occasional reported sermons. Treatises and letters demonstrate patterns of thought, argument, and language that

---

[34] B. Stock, *Listening for the Text. On the Uses of the Past* (Baltimore, 1990), p. 88. Stock argues for combining literary and historical, synchronic and diachronic perspectives: *Listening for the Text*, pp. 90–4. In *Implications*, p. 89, he advocates including literary analysis to gain benefits often overlooked by a strictly historical method.

correspond to the evidence recovered from chronicles. From the restrictions on preaching in statutes, we surmise that what they forbid must have taken place. Finally, some *exempla* (short anecdotes) are historical; these and others could have found a place in real sermons. The treatise against heresy, which crystallized as a genre in the late twelfth century, and the other types of sources aided prelates and preachers charged with examining, debating, and preaching against dissidents; such documents belong to the genre of polemical literature, writing that accuses and attacks its adversaries.[35]

To place sermons and other sources in the appropriate context, preaching outside the monastery, in the vineyard of the world, must be balanced with consideration of literature produced within the monastic environment, the spirit that animated it, the approach to the Bible that underlay it, and the themes and images that illustrated it. Understanding what happened when the monastic view turned outward requires familiarity with monastic culture; knowledge of monastic spirituality, exegesis, and language must ground the reconstruction from extant textual evidence.

Deconstructing the historical discourse of persecution

Both reconstruction of preaching and deconstruction of extant sources demand the discipline of close reading and the careful exercise of rhetorical criticism, which is explained further in the appendix to this chapter. Deconstructing entails working through certain variables, a process of sifting or filtering, what I called 'The Historical Filter' in a talk given at the Montaillou Medieval Festival in 1998.

To deconstruct controversial anti-heretical texts, I first distinguish the most frequent and overarching patterns of rhetoric used to describe dissidents. What impressions or fears do anti-heretical writers intend to create or evoke? In the texts examined for this book, four patterns emerge: (a) demonization, (b) pollution, (c) threat to the social order, and (d) apocalypticism. Authors return again and again to these rhetorical constructions. Demonization (a) constitutes the broadest and most frequent accusation, serving as a frame for the others. Medieval denunciations of heretics and other minorities cast them as allies of Satan, possessed by demons and never reasonable. Moreover, the humanization of Christ in twelfth-century culture has as a counterpart the closer identification of any given person with evil;[36] the ultimate good and the

[35] G. Dahan's discussion of anti-Jewish polemics proves helpful here. He distinguishes two feature of polemics: imprecation and attack. Anti-Jewish polemic appears also in anti-heretical polemics, in preaching, and in religious literature. Of the authors examined here, Alan of Lille also wrote against the Jews in his *Summa quadrapartita*. G. Dahan, *Les intellectuels chrétiens et les juifs au moyen âge* (Paris, 1990), esp. pp. 362–4.
[36] Russell discusses the demonization of minorities in *Lucifer*, pp. 184 and 190–2. He also points out that both saintly and demonic figures were increasingly humanized during the twelfth century. R. Chazan comments on this and anti-Jewish sentiment in *Stereotypes*, p. 93. G. Constable discusses the phenomenon in terms of Christian thought in *Three Studies in Medieval Religious and Social Thought* (Cambridge, 1995),

supreme evil were humanized. Pollution (b) refers to the tendency to construct dissidents as contaminated beings whose ideas and behaviour have the potential for corrupting others. Heresy is always seen as polluted, even if its adherents ascribe to rigorous asceticism grounded on ideals of purity.[37] Designating the rhetorical pattern of threat to the social order (c) characterizes the medieval view that non-conformity to ecclesiastical laws or disobedience of the hierarchy menaces the underpinnings of order and threatens to overturn the rightful disposition of Church and society. Heresy undermines authority and thereby social and divine order.[38] Apocalypticism (d), the belief that events of the last days are impending, extends in anti-heretical texts to the representation of contemporary events or conflicts as prototypes of the battle between good and evil at the end of time.[39]

These four rhetorical patterns encompass various specific accusations. Moreover, fear of one connects to fear of the others; and associations made in one pattern transfer to the others. Fear of threat to the social order, for example, covers accusations such as deceit, theft, or destruction, and connects to fear of the end times, sometimes expressed with language of pollution. For instance, an unauthorized preacher is often described as a thief; his corrupt doctrine pollutes those around him; and his disruption of the social order signals the end of time.[40]

The precise accusations connected to these general rhetorical patterns can be described as pairs of opposing elements. Borrowing from the language of statistics, I call these elements variables.[41] Opposing variables include:

pp. 143–217. In argumentation, Satan functions as the anti-model *par excellence*. See Perelman and Olbrechts-Tyteca, *Rhetoric*, pp. 366–8. J. B. Russell explores the New Testament association of Satan and demons with animals, many of which we shall see as types for heretics. J. B. Russell, *The Devil: Perceptions of Evil from Antiquity to Primitive Christianity* (Ithaca, NY, 1977), esp. pp. 243–6. E. Pagels also probes New Testament and early Christian associations between Satan and the Church's opponents in *The Origins of Satan* (New York, 1995).

[37] Here my analysis draws on Moore's *Formation* and his use of Mary Douglas, *Purity and Danger. An Analysis of the Concepts of Pollution and Taboo* (London, 1984).

[38] R. Girard's discussion of crimes against figures of authority in the context of crimes that attack 'the very foundation of cultural order' is useful here. R. Girard, *The Girard Reader*, ed. J. G. Williams (New York, 1966), p. 110. Medieval polemicists in our texts accuse heretics of not respecting the authority of the Church and perceive that as a powerful attack on the divine and social order. I credit here also E. Peters's insights on dissent and social order in *Inquisition*, pp. 40–1.

[39] On apocalypticism, see B. McGinn, *Antichrist: Two Thousand Years of the Human Fascination with Evil* (San Francisco, 1994) pp. 4–5; B. McGinn, *Visions of the End: Apocalyptic Traditions in the Middle Ages*, Columbia Records of Civilization Series (New York, 1979); and B. McGinn, *Apocalypticism in the Western Tradition* (Aldershot, 1994).

[40] In 'Obedience', pp. 259–78, I analyze these patterns in the polemical literature from the end of the twelfth century, not all of which is directly relevant to this book.

[41] I am grateful to Edward Kienzle, an Episcopal priest and economist, for helping me to bring together the realms of rhetoric, religion, and statistics.

(1) learning and ignorance: in the view of polemicists, heretics threaten the Church because they are either shrewd or ignorant, or both; (2) urban and rural: heretics pose dangers because they are city folk or peasants (the latter tied to being ignorant), and they threaten the cities or the countryside; (3) elite and popular: heretics adhere to restricted groups, or belong to popular movements, and in either category they risk infecting an entire population; for example, they penetrate the ranks of the clergy, or they push the people to rebel against the clergy; (4) public and private space: a heretic, especially a preacher, is dangerous for preaching in open air, and/or for delivering sermons in secret assemblies; (5) West and East: a heretical movement is polluted through filiation with earlier heresies known in the West, like Arianism, or/and through Eastern influence, notably that of ancient Greece. Sometimes West and East function as mutually exclusive (dichotomous) variables, the West harbouring right doctrine and the good, and the East, wrong teachings and evil.

What sets these rhetorical patterns and the related accusations in motion? It is the perception of heresy, perhaps construed for purely political purposes, but more often grounded on dissidents' beliefs or practices. Again a system of variables proves useful. Variables of belief and practice include ideas on: (1) the Trinity and the nature of Christ; (2) the role of sacraments; (3) the role of the saints and the dead; (4) ascetical practices; (5) the role of and responsibility for evangelism; and (6) morality and the interpretation of the virtues of poverty, chastity, obedience, and humility. Opinions frequently take their roots in varying interpretations of Scripture, with medieval dissident groups leaning toward a simple, more literal interpretation of Scripture and placing authority in New Testament texts, even to the exclusion of parts or all of the Old Testament.[42]

Medieval debates often take up issues that were controversial in other eras. Historically, Christians have differed in their interpretation of the Trinity and their weighing of Christ's humanity versus his divinity; they have debated the number and proper administration of sacraments; they have struggled over the meaning and recognition of sanctity, as well as over the role of saints as intercessors; the degree of asceticism required for clergy and laity has been the subject of much controversy; conflicts over who has the responsibility and the authority for evangelizing began early in the Church and continue. Finally, Christians have debated how to lead a moral life and how the principal virtues, concretized in monasticism, apply to lay people.

A few examples will illustrate briefly how these components of belief vary among the Waldensians and the Cathars. The Cathars leaned toward docetism, not accepting the human nature of Christ. They practised only one sacrament, the *consolamentum*, a laying-on-of-hands with precedents in

---

[42] See R. Lerner, 'Les communautés hérétiques (1150–1500)', *La Bible*, p. 597 and *passim*.

the book of Acts, while the Waldensians initially held that any believer could celebrate the Eucharist; both rejected any notion of the necessity of a priest's absolution for forgiveness of sin. The two groups rejected the idea that saints could serve as intercessors for directing prayers to God, or that prayers from the living could influence the lot of the dead. The Waldensians espoused the asceticism of absolute poverty for all, while the Cathars practised special dietary restrictions in addition to a generally austere way of life. The Waldensians, citing Mark 16. 15, saw preaching as the responsibility of all believers, including women; and the Cathars counted women *perfectae* among them, who performed evangelical, pastoral, and sacramental functions. Cathars and Waldensians alike refused obedience to Rome and the local clerical hierarchy. These and other related views spark the polemicists' attacks on twelfth-century dissidents and reappear in the later chapters of this book.[43]

Beliefs and practices that surface from anti-heretical texts can be compared with the portrait that emerges from the few extant texts emanating from dissident circles. After uncovering the rhetorical patterns in the polemical text, one seeks any traces of historical reality. For example, a statement such as 'the ministers of Antichrist are spewing their poison everywhere' possibly has at its core the historical reality of dissidents teaching or preaching in public. An assertion that the Cathars make petitions to the devil probably relates to the historical and textual reality that their myths represent Satan as the creator of the material world.[44] Other examples will surface in subsequent chapters. The appendix to this chapter surveys the current debate over searching for historical reality in anti-heretical texts.

In summary, Cistercians, led by the example of Bernard of Clairvaux in 1145, turned their attention outside the monastery to engage themselves in a world they viewed as threatened and threatening, a social order in danger of collapse because dissident Christians, particularly the Cathars, were undermining it. Cistercians and other intellectuals turned to pen, pulpit, and popular preaching in the hope of eliminating the danger from their midst. A few even took to the battlefield. The analysis of texts about the preaching campaigns and of their contexts seeks to retrieve the role of preaching and to reconstruct what was preached, in the light of its historical and specifically monastic context. It also aims to deconstruct the texts' rhetoric to determine the underlying patterns and how the writers characterized dissidents.

Monastic texts and their contexts furnish the keys to understanding how medieval monastic authors perceived heresy, preached, and wrote against it. Chapter One of the present book surveys the historical context for monastic writings against heresy, focusing on several elements: the ecclesiastical

---

[43] See Chapters Three to Six in this book.
[44] See Chapter Four, n. 51, for a similar statement on heretical preachers by Henry of Clairvaux, and Chapter Six, n. 47, for one by Hélinand of Froidmont on the Cathars.

reform movement; the flourishing of schools, monasteries, and literature; the expansion of cities and of literacy; the rise of lay apostolic movements; the tensions between popular religious movements and the hierarchy; and the development of the procedures for inquisition, a process termed the 'formation of a persecuting society'.[45] An overview of monastic culture follows in Chapter Two, which centres on the background and methods of exegesis and surveys the genres and techniques of medieval monastic literature, the well from which preachers tapped their themes and methods. Chapters Three and Four concentrate on monastic preaching against heresy in southern France from 1145 to the 1180s. Chapter Three deals with Bernard of Clairvaux, his 1143/1144 correspondence with Everwin of Steinfeld, and his 1145 preaching mission. Chapter Four shifts to Henry of Clairvaux/Albano and events from the 1160s through the 1180s, including the controversy over preaching by lay men and women in the Waldensian movement. Chapter Five covers the years of the Albigensian Crusade (1208/9–1229), the influence of Innocent III, and the roles of Arnaud Amaury, Guy of les Vaux-de-Cernay, and Fulk of Toulouse. Chapter Six looks at Cistercian involvement at the termination of the crusade, extending the book's boundaries to 1229, the signing of the Treaty of Paris with its provisions for founding the University of Toulouse. The Conclusion reflects on the whole of Cistercian engagement in the period studied, looks ahead to the later Middle Ages, and assesses the methodologies employed.[46]

---

[45] This phrase is borrowed from Moore's book: *The Formation of a Persecuting Society*.

[46] Two important studies appeared after this book had gone into production: C. Berman, *The Cistercian Evolution: The Invention of a Religious Order in Twelfth-Century Europe* (Philadelphia, 2000); and *The Medieval Church: Universities, Heresy, and the Religious Life. Essays in Honour of Gordon Leff*, ed. P. Biller and B. Dobson, SCH S 11 (Woodbridge, 1999).

APPENDIX TO THE INTRODUCTION

Deconstructing: close reading, rhetorical criticism, and historiography of persecution and heresy

The deconstruction of extant sources requires the discipline of close reading. Trained as a philologist, I retain the conviction that discourse in its written form must be scrutinized carefully in order to discover and uncover whatever historical reality it may contain. Discourse, as Emile Benveniste defined it, encompasses both an oral form and written manifestations which reproduce the oral.[1] This definition suits the analysis of preaching and the sermon quite well, since we are dealing with written vestiges of an oral genre. It also supports the view that the text or speech act is inseparable from the speaker/author, the speaker's intent, and the audience: discourse belongs to a social universe that it reflects. Analysis of discourse entails asking fundamental questions about the text[2] and rests on the close reading, which is often called the *explication de texte*.

Text and author
To search for the author's voice, the *explication de texte* provides a starting point: the in-depth analysis of a text directs the reader toward uncovering the writer's point of view, ideas, and intentions, and analysing how these are

---

[1] Benveniste defines discourse as: 'every utterance assuming a speaker and a hearer, and in the speaker, the intention of influencing the other in some way', and its written manifestations: 'every variety of oral discourse of every nature and every level . . . also the mass of writing that reproduces oral discourse or that borrows its manner of expression and its purposes . . . in short, all the genres in which someone addresses himself to someone, proclaims himself as the speaker and organizes what he says in the category of person'. E. Benveniste, *Problems in General Linguistics*, trans. M. E. Meek, Miami Linguistics Series 8 (Coral Gables, FL, 1971), p. 209.

[2] These questions are enunciated in the classical theory of *circumstantiae* and summarized in the brief formula: 'Who says what in which channel to whom with what effect?'; or: 'who?' 'what?' 'how?' 'to whom?' 'why?' The formula is cited and the factors discussed in J.-M. Schaeffer, *Qu'est-ce qu'un genre littéraire* (Paris, 1989), pp. 80–1. The 'who?' 'to whom?' and 'why?' concern the speaker, the audience, and the purpose for the discourse; the 'what?' and 'how?' concern its content and style. Two further questions – 'when?' and 'where?' – should be asked to elucidate the historical circumstances of the discourse, as far as possible. C. Delcorno, 'Medieval Preaching in Italy (1300–1500)', in *The Sermon*, pp. 449–560, discusses these criteria in the medieval *artes praedicandi* and employs them in his analysis of the sermon after 1200. He observes the difficulty of developing a general response to the questions: 'when?' and 'where?'

brought to light and emphasized. The methods of the *explication de texte*, like those of exegesis, generally employ contextual approaches of literary criticism which examine a passage with attention to its content, historical and literary context, genre, language, development and themes.

Analysis of the author's point of view is incomplete, however, if one does not look for what is omitted or subordinated or distorted in the text. One must seek out the sub-text. Such a search is crucial when evaluating anti-heretical writings, whose polemics sting the reader in their assault on adversaries and colour their targets with negatively charged language.

Text and audience

Not only does the text's meaning to its author interest the scholar, but also its impact on the immediate audience, that is, its reception among contemporary readers or hearers: the meaning a text assumes after it is written. That significance may not be what the author intended.[3] For example, we know that preaching against heresy generally failed, so that its reception was clearly not what the speakers intended.

Establishing the reception of discourse in a distant environment poses many challenges. In rare instances, sources report the live audience's reaction. Even so, the actual speech act and its impact on the audience are captured only imperfectly. The distance between the speech act and the report of it, or the written text of it, becomes all the more problematic to assess when we analyse rhetoric of violence. An extant written text may implicitly condone violence against heretics, for example, but to establish a cause–effect relationship, linking that written word to a sermon preached and then to subsequent actions, is very difficult. When sermons are not extant, we look to works written to aid preachers; they were transformed by clerical readers into the medium of the sermon and then preached. The audience's reaction can only be conjectured. A final problem to consider here resides in medieval authors' reception of sources written in an earlier age: does their recycling entail repetition or refashioning?

Text and meaning

A further consideration for evaluating medieval texts is the predominance of the figurative, spiritual meaning in their composition and interpretation. For a twelfth-century writer, any text, event or object of the exterior world had its true significance only through its connection to the divine. The Neoplatonism

---

[3] One thinks of Gregory the Great's *Dialogues*, for example; Gregory wrote the *Dialogues* for a monastic audience in the 590s, but after his death in 604 the work circulated widely to popular audiences, obscuring its original restricted purpose. See P. Meyvaert's review of F. Clark, *The Pseudo-Gregorian Dialogues*: 'The Enigma of Gregory the Great's Dialogues: A Response to Francis Clark', *Journal of Ecclesiastical History* 39 (1988), 377–81.

of earlier Christian authors, chiefly Augustine, exerted a formidable influence over medieval writers.[4]

Moreover, hidden meanings did not open themselves to just anyone. Bernard of Clairvaux, as Augustine before him, insisted on the necessity for right preparation of mind and soul before one could receive divine insights and serve as a vessel for understanding and interpreting the Scriptures. From the Cistercian perspective, interpretation of the Bible and the movement from contemplation to reformed experience and action, required the discipline of monastic life with its liturgical and contemplative immersion in the Scriptures. Brian Stock refers to this process for the Cistercians as a 'sensuous ritual' and 'paraliturgical experience'.[5] Hence grasping the real meaning of Scripture required membership in a spiritual elite, a notion already present in Augustine's views on the preparation necessary for a Christian exegete, and one that would clash with dissidents' claims to the right to read the Scriptures themselves and proclaim their meaning through preaching.[6]

The twelfth century's view of the relationship between the object (*res*) and the divine relates also to the predominance of typology as a mode of thought that extended beyond exegesis. Patristic and medieval exegetes searched everywhere in the Old Testament for the type of the New. Medieval writers in turn saw the events of their own day largely as antitypes,[7] the realization of the future happenings foreshadowed by the Scriptures. They extended the method of typology, based on the exegetical principle that the Old Testament texts prefigures the New, to find in the New foreshadowing of the events that swirled around them. They added another dimension as well, an apocalyptic one, seeing in current events prototypes of the last days. Thus they used Scripture for evaluating the present in terms of the past and the future.

The stance of the biblical text often suited their purposes perfectly, as when they adopted the prohibitions against women's speech, or judged dissidents as false prophets and harbingers of the end.[8] Frequently, medieval authors resorted to a use of typology that evidences their lack of any historical–critical concern. Contemporary figures appear as antitypes of New Testament persons or any number of biblical creatures: heretics as moths, or dogs, or little foxes, for example. To reconstruct or deconstruct what is meant by what is said in medieval texts of this sort, one must decode the symbols at work.

---

[4] See Chenu, *Nature*, pp. 50–78, esp. 50–1, 60–1, 65, 77–8, who cites several relevant examples.
[5] Stock, *Literacy*, p. 418.
[6] On Augustine, see Chapter Two, pp. 64–5.
[7] On type and antitype, see R. E. Brown, 'Hermeneutics', in *NJBC*, 71: 46–47, p. 1156.
[8] See Kienzle and Walker.

Rhetorical criticism

The basic assumptions of rhetorical criticism hold that texts disclose something about their author and their readers or hearers, and that they are intended to influence their audience. The classical study of rhetoric emphasized persuasion and argumentation along with the techniques that authors use in order to accomplish the desired effect: patterns of syntax and sound that contribute to conveying ideas and enhancing their expression.[9] At times the identification of techniques leans toward formalism, overshadowing elucidation of the text's basic aim to persuade and its purpose within its cultural context. Recent trends in rhetorical analysis re-emphasize the classical notion of rhetoric and its accentuation of the process of argumentation and the aim of persuasion.

Moreover, developments in twentieth-century literary criticism such as deconstruction, post-structuralism, and psychoanalytical criticism have led some literary critics to advocate a social–critical stance to texts. As Terry Eagleton states it, inquiring into the 'conventions and operations' of the literary institution or a mode of discourse without a 'critical attitude will certainly mean enforcing the power of the institution itself'.[10] Eagleton's assertion relates to the work of the present book and the analysis of texts of persecution: not to interrogate them leaves their message unchallenged.

The publication of *The New Rhetoric* of C. Perlman and T. Olbrechts-Tyteca[11] has influenced scholarship in biblical studies, offering parallels for examining medieval religious texts saturated with biblical allusions. The insights of social theory also have enhanced rhetorical criticism in the search to illuminate the social construction of a text by its author and readers, as well as its reception by the audience of the period. A greater awareness of cultural differences enlightens the diversity of interpretive strategies that contemporary scholars bring to bear on ancient texts in order to 'bridge the gap between a literature and its social history', to quote Burton Mack, a prominent biblical scholar. New Testament scholars have focused on the question of authority and the reconstruction of social implications and patterns.[12] These concerns relate closely to the biblically-based anti-heretical texts of the Middle Ages. The problem of authority in particular lies at the core of medieval conflicts over heresy, and rhetorical criticism aids in discerning the viewpoint of both sides.

[9] See Murphy, *Rhetoric*.

[10] See T. Eagleton, *Literary Theory* (Minneapolis, 1983), esp. pp. 194–217, and below for discussion of his critical stance.

[11] Perelman and Olbrechts-Tyteca, *Rhetoric*.

[12] B. Mack, *Rhetoric and the New Testament* (Minneapolis, 1990) reviews the modern hermeneutical methods of biblical scholars. See also the succinct summary by S. M. Schneiders, in 'Hermeneutics', in *NJBC*, 71:65, pp. 1159–60; the application of rhetorical analysis in A. C. Wire, *The Corinthian Women Prophets: A Reconstruction through Paul's Rhetoric* (Minneapolis, 1990); and the discussion of feminist rhetorical criticism in E. Schüssler Fiorenza's works, discussed immediately below.

Among the social interpretations of rhetoric, feminist rhetorical historiography, as forged by Elisabeth Schüssler Fiorenza,[13] offers arguments
pertinent to our analysis of discourse which attacks and aims to suppress
the voices of dissidents. Like gender identity, the identity of 'heretics' is
constructed linguistically and socially in the interest of those holding power.
One can apply Schüssler Fiorenza's approach, calling for understanding
history as 'the reality not only of Western elite men but also of the
subordinated and dehumanized others', to dissidents dehumanized by the
rhetoric of persecution. In fact, as I have argued elsewhere, within the
rhetoric of medieval anti-heretical texts, the person who suffers the most
vehemently negative rhetoric is the woman 'heretic' who dares to preach and
violate the social conventions of silence for women.[14] Clearly texts written
against dissidents, like those intended to suppress women's speech and
leadership, are inscribed with the 'rhetoric of otherness' and attempt to
silence their opponents' views and compel them to submission through
persuasion, or even violence. Schüssler Fiorenza's advocacy for a hermeneutics of suspicion that 'challenges the dichotomy between historical reality
and text' bears on the problem of approaching polemical literature which
overwhelmingly reflects the language of the persecutors and relegates the
reality of the dissidents to a sub-text. Schüssler Fiorenza argues that there is a
recoverable sub-text: feminist literary criticism, not accepting the stance of
literary criticism which claims that there is no historical reality behind the
text, takes instead 'a reading position different from that engineered by the
text'. The rhetoric of the text 'at once and displays and hides' a historical
reality. In my view, much polemical literature also holds some vestiges of the
reality of dissident movements. To find it, one must interrogate the text and
its rhetorical strategies.[15]

Different from feminist rhetorical historiography, this book is not written
from a social movement for change. However, I hope that the unveiling of
discursive patterns of persecution will alert readers to such discourse and its
dangers whenever and wherever they encounter them.

Historiography of persecution and heresy

The dangerous potential of preaching against heresy surfaces clearly when
we recognize that it belongs to a crucial period in the history of persecution.
The historiography of persecution and heresy shows the influence of
structuralism, that is the predominant role of social structures in identifying

---

[13] E. Schüssler Fiorenza, *In Memory of Her* (New York, 1983); E. Schüssler Fiorenza,
Bread Not Stone: The Challenge of Feminist Biblical Interpretation (Boston, 1984);
E. Schüssler Fiorenza, *But She Said. Feminist Practices of Biblical Interpretation*
(Boston, 1992), pp. 80–101. See also Kienzle, 'Touchstone'.

[14] Kienzle, ' Touchstone', pp. 35–40.

[15] Schüssler Fiorenza, *But She Said*, pp. 80–101; Schüssler Fiorenza, *Bread Not Stone*, pp.
93–115. See also Kienzle, 'Touchstone', pp. 20–1, 44–9.

targets for persecution and in elaborating the mechanisms of persecution. Robert Moore's highly influential book, *The Formation of a Persecuting Society*, exemplifies that approach. The structuralist view risks neglecting the roles of human agents, and historians, like social theorists, grapple with the problem of balancing the two forces.[16]

I consider in this book both individual Cistercians and their society, with the intent to highlight the Cistercians as agents, authors of texts and doers of deeds who influenced social structures. When Bernard of Clairvaux decided to move into the Lord's vineyard, he expressed himself clearly as an agent intending to have an impact on the Church and the world. Nonetheless, he and the Cistercians clearly felt the influence of both Church and society. The impact of both can be used to minimize Bernard's or the Order's agency, letting them 'off the hook', so to speak. Bernard was a product of his society, 'marked by the mentality of his time';[17] but various relationships were at work: the Cistercians influenced the Church; the Church influenced the Cistercians; and there was tension between the two.

Another risk may emerge from the emphasis on structuralist methodology and on the majority view: the role of dissidents, seen as a creation of their persecutors, may be reduced *ad nihilum*, which results in excluding the minority.[18] Intense debate on methodology surrounds the historiography of Catharism, perhaps more than other medieval heresies. Current trends of French historiography stress the 'invention' of heresy, emphasizing the roles of secular processes and/or the discourse of persecution and arguing that more research needs to be done from those perspectives. French historians such as Jean-Louis Biget and Monique Zerner-Chardavoine have contributed much valuable research on the political situations prevailing at crucial moments in the anti-heretical campaigns. Biget and others have also undertaken a careful analysis of rhetoric to emphasize the construction of heresy by orthodox writers. While I see the great merit of their research in these two thrusts, I do not agree with their tendency to regard anti-heretical texts as so distanced from historical reality that they do not serve for reconstructing the views held by dissidents, or that political situations invariably outweigh actual dissent in determining the identification of what is heresy. Even if

---

[16] On 'objectivism', its theoretical counter model: 'subjectivism', and the search for a middle ground, see A. Giddens, 'Hermeneutics and Social Theory', in *Hermeneutics: Questions and Prospects*, ed. G. Shapiro and A. Sica (Amherst, MA, 1984), pp. 215–30, who proposes a way of bringing together analyses of society and individual agency by what he calls 'structuration', the recognition of the duality and not the dualism of society and agent, that is, their complementarity. D. Nirenberg provides an excellent discussion of these issues for the historiography of persecution in his *Communities of Violence. Persecution of Minorities in the Middle Ages* (Princeton, NJ, 1996), pp. 4–7.

[17] J. Leclercq, 'St. Bernard's Attitude toward War', in *Studies in Medieval Cistercian History*, II, ed. J. R. Sommerfeldt, CS 24 (Kalamazoo, MI, 1976), p. 39.

[18] Chazan offers an excellent discussion on majority versus minority views in historiography in *Stereotypes*, pp. 77–88.

some accusations of heresy have been revealed as fabrications, this does not justify ending the search for real dissent in the Middle Ages. Nor do the distortions of polemical texts remove all reflections of historical reality.[19] As Carlo Ginzburg observes for the sources on which he draws in *The Cheese and the Worms*, 'The fact that a source is not "objective" . . . does not mean that it is useless.'[20]

There is a certain attitude in many anti-heretical texts that tends to reveal its own biases boldly, leaving the interpreter the job of sifting the plausible from the implausible. In my view, the accounts of mob violence analysed by René Girard resemble in important ways the polemical texts studied in this book, even though they generally do not relate mob actions. Girard underscores the textual naivety of testimony from medieval persecutors. By that he means that their certainty of being right kept them from covering up or censoring 'the fundamental characteristics of their persecution'. Focusing on Guillaume Machaut's account of the persecution of Jews accused of poisoning wells and bringing deaths that in reality resulted from the plague, Girard asserts that the text has various merits for research, among them: the accusations confirm the 'psychosocial context' of the violence; and the

---

[19] The trend is exemplified by the volume *Inventer l'hérésie?* It was set by G. Lobrichon's outstanding work on dating the polemical letter of the monk Heribert. That work is summarized in an article which probes the false accusations made in Arras in 1025: 'Arras, 1025, ou le vrai procès d'une fausse accusation', in *Inventer l'hérésie*, pp. 67–85. M. Zerner's earlier article, 'Question sur la naissance de l'affaire albigeoise', in *Georges Duby. L'Écriture de l'Histoire*, ed. C. Duhamel-Amado and G. Lobrichon, Bibliothèque du Moyen Âge 6 (Brussels, 1996), pp. 427–44, also exemplifies the trend. There (p. 427), Zerner argues that her findings 'relativize' the problem of heresy. In *Inventer l'hérésie*, M. Lauwers describes his work, here on the cult of the dead, much as I do: 'une sorte de déconstruction des textes anti-hérétiques' and then an effort to 'reconstituter l'entreprise de travestisement menée par les polémistes'. He concludes, however, that in the twelfth century, what polemicists describe is a generalized heresy, which leads him 'not to reconstruct the lost discourse of the heretics, in the philological-combinatory method denounced in the past by Arsenio Frugoni, but to follow the elaboration of an ecclesiastical discourse'. His remarks implicitly cast a negative light on such reconstructive work. His concluding sentence assesses polemical discourse positively, as contributing to the expression of doctrine and thus preparing the transformations of the thirteenth century: 'En se plaçant sur le terrain de l'Écriture Sainte, en s'attachant à la question du salut, le discours polémique a fait évoluer sinon la doctrine, du moins la manifestation de celle-ci, et de la sorte préparé les transformations du XIIIe siècle'. 'Dicunt vivorum beneficia nichil prodesse defunctis', Histoire d'un thème polémique (XIe–XIIe siècles)', pp. 158, 184–5, 187. J. L. Biget, 'Les Albigeois': remarques sur une dénomination', in the same volume, pp. 219–55, carries his methodology and the force of Cistercian rhetoric to the point of stating that heresy is 'the same, always and everywhere' in the polemical texts (p. 236), of minimizing the importance of Catharism in the Midi (p. 246), and of concluding that the discourse on heresy depended less on dissidence than on the general political context and particular situation of southern France (pp. 253–4).

[20] C. Ginzburg, *The Cheese and the Worms* (Baltimore, 1992), p. xvii.

'unreliable testimony' of persecution reveals more than reliable testimony because of its 'unconscious nature'. For such texts of persecution, Girard asserts: 'The fact that some of the details are imagined does not persuade us to consider the whole text imaginary.' One must deconstruct the text to sift the improbable from the probable, the real from the imaginary. Furthermore, Girard draws a conclusion for Machaut's text and other texts of persecution which recalls Eagleton's social stance as critic: 'one must either do violence to the text or let the text forever do violence to innocent victims'.[21]

Moreover, polemical texts contain not just common rhetoric of persecution but also observations on dissidents' beliefs which demonstrate consistency with other polemics and, in numerous cases, with texts from the dissidents themselves. To me, overemphasis on the 'invention' of heresy risks neglecting the voice and agency of dissidents and thus obscuring the diverse and dynamic character of medieval Christianity, such that the persecutors become the sole voices in the historical drama. My emphasis in this volume is not the reconstruction of dissident views from orthodox texts; first, the discourse of the orthodox texts themselves needs to be reconstructed from scarce sources or analysed – deconstructed when it appears in full textual form. Nonetheless, my analysis rests on the conviction that it is possible to uncover the sub-text and reconstruct the historical reality of dissidence beneath the language of the polemics attacking it. Most chapters of this book pay some attention to this sort of analysis.

[21] Girard, *Girard Reader*, pp. 102–6.

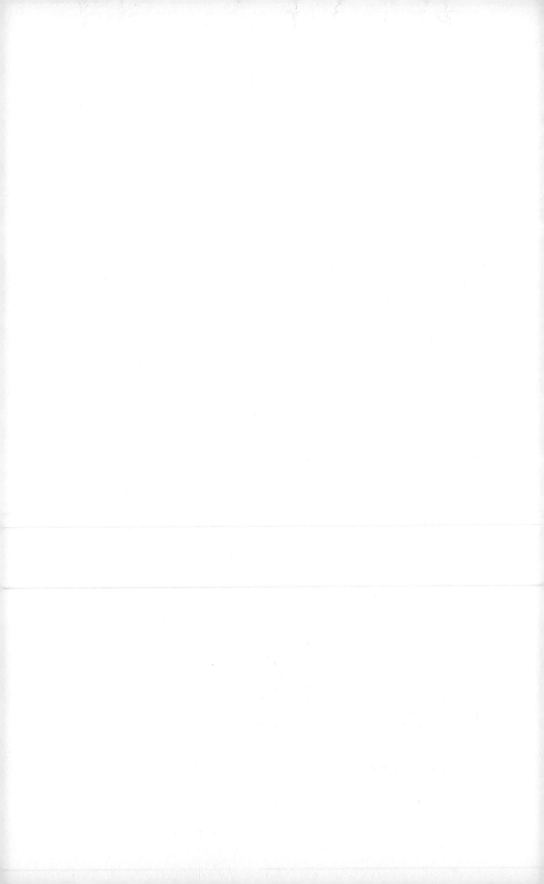

CHAPTER ONE

The Lord's Vineyard in the Twelfth Century

Cistercian preaching against heresy needs to be viewed within the general setting of twelfth-century France and the specific milieu of monastic culture. This chapter surveys several trends of the twelfth century that underlie the white monks' role as anti-heretical preachers in the Lord's vineyard. Chapter Two examines Cistercian writing and preaching against heresy as an outgrowth of monastic life and literature, a product of the domestic vineyard.

A period of transition between the patristic and the scholastic, the monks and the friars, the twelfth century witnessed economic, social, and religious ferment. Lay literacy and spirituality crystallized at the same time that new religious houses covered the landscape. The crucial elements in the backdrop of Cistercian preaching against heresy in Occitania belong to five important currents.[1] The Gregorian reform movement renewed and reformed religious and secular institutions, elevating monastic observance as the model for all Christians.[2] Schools multiplied and Latin literary culture flourished, secular and monastic, alongside the first vernacular literature.[3] Europe's economy

---

[1] Several important studies focus on the twelfth century. J. Le Goff, *The Birth of Purgatory* (Chicago, 1984) argues for a two-culture model of medieval society – clerical, learned vs. popular, oral. See J. H. Van Engen's critique of Le Goff, J.-C. Schmidt and B. Stock: J. H. Van Engen, 'The Christian Middle Ages as an Historiographical Problem', *American Historical Review* 91 (1986), 519–52. B. McGinn captures the century's pivotal role when he describes it as 'Janus-like', sitting 'astride the course of Christian spirituality with an ambiguous glance in two directions': McGinn, *Spirituality*, p. 194. B. P. McGuire and C. W. Bynum bring Cistercian spirituality to the fore in their respective studies on friendship and community, and authority and maternal imagery: B. P. McGuire, *Friendship and Community*, CS 95 (Kalamazoo, MI, 1988); C. W. Bynum, *Jesus as Mother: Studies in the Spirituality of the High Middle Ages* (Berkeley, CA, 1982). H. Fichtenau explores learning in the schools and monasteries in parallel with exegesis practiced by 'heretics' with the intent of investigating 'nonconformist' tendencies: Fichtenau, p. 2.

[2] Constable, *Reformation*, pp. 4–7. The reform's consequences ranged from promoting an ideal of apostolic life to developing the crusade ideology. See J. Riley-Smith, *The First Crusade and the Idea of Crusading* (Philadelphia, 1986).

[3] C. H. Haskins, *The Renaissance of the Twelfth Century* (Cleveland, 1963). For developments in biblical scholarship, see Smalley, *Bible*; Smalley, *Gospels*. Monastic culture is treated in Leclercq, *Learning*. On vernacular literature, see Paterson, pp. 90–119. French histories of Occitania include A. Armengaud and R. Lafont, *Histoire d'Occitanie* (Paris, 1979); P. Wolff, *Histoire du Languedoc* (Toulouse, 1967). On early

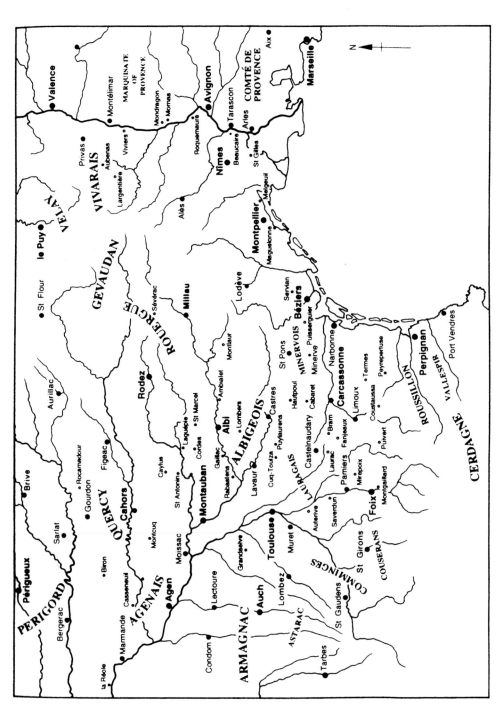

Fig. 1. Occitania in the early thirteenth century.

underwent transformation, and economic and social change provoked complex reactions from laity and clergy.[4] Clerical and lay 'textual communities' expanded, grounding their spirituality on the *vita apostolica* and a common interpretation of Scripture.[5] However, growth and centralization brought forth negative offshoots as well, notably the development of a persecuting mentality.[6] The nature of these trends and their significance for the Cistercians, heresy and Occitania are examined in more detail in the remainder of this chapter.

The impact of these currents on preaching manifests itself in a swirl of debates over propagation of the faith, waged within clerical ranks and between clerics and lay people. Sermons and polemical literature reflect this acute concern over preaching, which spurred exegetes and preachers to equip themselves through the burgeoning production of reference works. Preaching constituted the primary vehicle for disseminating the Church's teaching. Therefore, the papacy watched it with a careful eye; extensive legislation was devised to harness it; and controversies surrounded the authority and the authorization to preach.[7] These reached a high point in the late twelfth century when dissidents challenged the clergy's monopoly on preaching. In response, the Cistercians overstepped the bounds established for monastic preaching in order to denounce dissidents who defied the Church's opposition to lay evangelizing.

---

scholasticism, see R. Southern, *Western Society and the Church in the Middle Ages* (Harmondsworth, 1970), pp. 41–4.

[4] Little, *passim*.

[5] Stock, *Implications*. In my view, Stock exaggerates somewhat both the antithesis between Bernard and Abelard as Cistercian and scholastic and the unity of Cistercians, literate monks and illiterate lay brothers in Bernard's audience. *Implications,* esp. 406. On the search for the *vita apostolica*, see Grundmann, *Movements*.

[6] Moore, *Formation*. Secular power and popular hostility created a negative image of the Jews, and the crusades fomented violence against them. Chazan situates the creation of the 'broad ideational framework of the hostile and powerful Jew' in mid-twelfth-century northern Europe, and concludes that this area and era made not only positive contributions but at the same time left a 'legacy of hate-filled and hateful imagery that has inflicted incalculable harm': Chazan, *Stereotypes*, p. 140; see also R. Chazan, *The Year 1096 and the Jews* (Philadelphia, 1996).The late twelfth century marked a transitional point in the persecution of homosexuals as well: see Boswell, *Tolerance*, pp. 277–86.

[7] Until approximately the fifth century, preaching served principally as an instrument for catechesis. For the most part, sermons were delivered by bishops. After the sixth century, when the Council of Vaison (529) specified that priests should preach, and afterward during the Carolingian era, preaching remained catechetical but also, especially among travelling monks, took on a missionary purpose. See Longère, *Prédication*, pp. 31–6 and 48–52, on early medieval and missionary preaching. On medieval preaching, see *The Sermon; Sermons and Society; Monastic Preaching; Parole; Models*; and Longère, *Prédication*. On synodal statutes, see Longère, *Prédication*, pp. 82–4; and 'La prédication d'après les statuts synodaux du Midi au XIIIe siècle', in *Prédication*, CaF 32, pp. 251–74.

The Cistercians performed as key players in the twelfth century. They exerted a strong influence on the Church hierarchy, and some occupied powerful positions themselves, working as agents and models for reform. The Order's rapid expansion epitomized the drive to extend the *vita monastica* and live the *vita apostolica*. The white monks benefited from the growth of the schools by recruiting already educated men to their monasteries. They also spearheaded the campaigns against heresy, some transgressing their monastic vocation to adopt inappropriate roles of secular leadership. Occitania was a prime target for their efforts. Cistercian monasteries expanded there rapidly, and troubadours such as Bertran de Born and Fulk of Toulouse entered the order. Preaching missions began with Bernard of Clairvaux's in 1145, and later Cistercians continued to supply leadership and intellectual fuel to the campaigns.

The reform movement

Reform efforts from the mid-eleventh to the mid-twelfth century centred on the Church and the clergy and then shifted to the religious way of life, interpreted for communities and for individuals.[8] Gregory VII (1073–85) and his adviser, Humbert of Silva Candida, defined a hierarchical view of Christendom that fixed all lay persons below the ecclesiastical hierarchy, headed by the pope at Rome with all the bishops and Church leaders subordinate to him. This solidification of ecclesiastical organization followed upon the rebuilding of the empire under Charlemagne and the tenth-century Cluniac reforms.[9] The Gregorian reforms aimed to sanctify the world in order to gain salvation for as many souls as possible. Its programmes relied on developing more systematic statements of belief and rules for behaviour.[10]

Later twelfth-century intellectuals in Paris, who had close ties to the Cistercians, continued this effort to make society more holy, largely by urging the adaptation of monasticism to the lives of all Christians. At the end of the century, Pope Innocent III undertook a sweeping agenda for reform, concretized in the canons of the Fourth Lateran Council (1215). Innocent III's targets for reform included dissident movements, and preaching was the primary means for trying to persuade them to align with orthodoxy.[11] Preaching also propagated the call for crusades against heresy

---

[8] Constable, *Reformation*, pp. 4–5, 300–28.

[9] This hierarchical concept of the Church community had been developing at least since Jerome defined *christianitas* in the fourth century, but two models for the hierarchy were discernible afterwards: one, elaborated in the time of Charlemagne, accorded supremacy to the emperor, or to the emperor and the bishops; the other placed the pope in the predominate position. Russell, *Dissent and Order*, pp. 9–11, 3–4.

[10] Peters, *Inquisition*, pp. 40–1, speaks of a 'grand program of sanctifying the world'.

[11] On late twelfth century Paris intellectuals and the reform movement, see Baldwin,

in Europe and Muslim domination of the Holy Land, an element on the papal reform agenda since Urban V preached the First Crusade.[12] Cistercians, from Bernard of Clairvaux onward, aided in articulating the desire to convert dissidents and non-Christians.

The consequences of the eleventh- and twelfth-century reforms have caused much scholarly ink to be poured, as have their relationships to other developments in the surrounding culture. Historians generally agree that the reforms had extensive spillover effects. For example, the Church's attempt to free itself from secular control has been tied to the independent mentality of cities that demanded autonomy in governance.[13] Surely the reforms sharpened the distinction between clergy and laity, with a resultant hostility and mistrust toward the laity on the part of the Church hierarchy.[14] Correspondingly, the laity, persuaded by the importance of reform based on apostolic models, came to value those above obedience and to distrust the clergy, especially its upper ranks.[15] Finally, the reforms' solidification of a literate and elite clerical class led to the development of mechanisms of persecution.[16] The relationship of reform, heresy and persecution will be explored further below.

The Cistercian Order epitomized the spirit of reform through its emphasis on work, austerity, simplicity and withdrawal from the world. Cistercians raised the age for admission to the monastery, therefore not maintaining schools for the young and objecting to the Benedictine practice of receiving boys as oblates. The white monks also revised the daily schedule to allow more time for work and private prayer. Cistercians strove for greater simplicity in liturgy and architecture, and literature written from the Cistercian point of view reprehends Cluniac excesses in these and other areas.[17]

The Cistercians considered themselves an elite spiritual corps, ranking their members superior to other monks and provoking antagonism even in the early years, as evidenced in the Benedictine Rupert of Deutz's critique of various Cistercian practices, such as their insistence on manual labour. Cistercians accepted election as bishops from 1126 onward as part of their programme for reforming the Church; over sixty Cistercians served as bishops and cardinals between 1126 and 1180. Even before Bernard of

---

Masters. On the continuance of their work in the thirteenth century, see J. Bird, 'The Religious's Role in a Post-Fourth-Lateran World: Jacques de Vitry's *Sermones ad status* and *Historia occidentalis*', in *Monastic Preaching*, pp. 209–29. See also Chapter Four in this book.

[12] See Cole, *Preaching*, and Riley-Smith, *First Crusade*.

[13] Mundy, 'Urban Society and Culture', pp. 229–33.

[14] Constable asserts that the notion of a three-ordered society was replaced by a two-part model: clerical and lay. Constable, *Reformation*, p. 321.

[15] Russell, *Dissent and Order*, p. 22.

[16] Moore, *Formation*, p. 153.

[17] On the Cistercians, see Newman, *passim*; and M. Pacaut, *Les moines blancs. Histoire de l'ordre de Cîteaux* (Saint-Amand-Montrond, 1993).

Clairvaux's intense engagement in the 1130 schism, the order had established ties with bishops and princes. Nonetheless, through Bernard's activities in the world and during the papacy of Eugene III, formerly a monk of Clairvaux, the Cistercian Order moved to greater involvement in the world's problems. In the 1160s it divided within when faced with the 1159–77 papal schism and the controversy between Thomas Becket and Henry II.[18] Innocent III urged the Cistercians to embrace the active life even further by undertaking the pastoral work of preaching and leading papal reform efforts, notably the campaign against heresy in southern France. In that respect, the Cistercians assumed and expanded a role of leadership which had been played by Cluny before and would in turn be taken over by the Dominicans.

Bernard of Clairvaux's image of the inner and exterior vineyards captures the extension of Cistercian involvement in the world. In a well-known letter, Bernard described himself as a chimera, 'neither cleric nor layman' who kept the habit of a monk' but 'long ago abandoned the life' – an expression of the anxiety he apparently felt over his involvement in external affairs. In later chapters of this book, we shall see how the order itself became a chimera during its campaign against heresy.[19]

While Cistercian expansion touched many geographical areas, perhaps nowhere was it more evident than in Occitania, where the order's reforming zeal promoted the foundation of many new monasteries – twenty-four in Languedoc and neighbouring regions between 1135 and 1160.[20] Historians

---

[18] See Newman, pp. 129–30 on Rupert of Deutz's critique; p. 138 on elitism; pp. 142 and 148–49 on bishops, pp. 191–218 on the schism and Becket controversy.

[19] Bernard's description of himself as chimera appears in *Letters*, Letter 326, p. 402; Epistola 250, *SBOp*, VIII, 147: 'Clamat ad vos mea monstruosa vita, mea aerumnosa conscientia. Ego enim quaedam Chimaera mei saeculi, nec clericum gero nec laicum. Nam monachi iamdudum exui conversationem, non habitum.' C. Holdsworth offers an excellent analysis of this image in 'Bernard, chimera of his age', in *Essays in Honor of Edward B. King* (Sewanee, 1991), pp. 147–63. Holdsworth asserts that the image reveals the ambiguity and stress 'if not contradiction' in Bernard's life. Holdsworth connects this stress to the Martha and Mary theme, and he feels, as I do, that Bernard was well aware of the conflicts arising from his involvement outside the monastery: 'Bernard was conscious of tensions between the way he lived and acted and what he had originally professed when he fled the world for the cloister' (pp. 148 and 158–9). Constable, *Reformation*, p. 25, mentions the chimera image briefly, saying that for Bernard, it represented 'a sort of non-existence', that Bernard was 'neither one thing nor another'. Bernard also described the military orders' members in contradictory terms. He advocated an idealized union between the two paths of life, monk and knight, but he also sensed their fundamental incongruence. For Bernard's remarks on the Knights Templar, see *In Praise of the New Knighthood*, trans. C. Greenia, Bernard of Clairvaux: *Treatises III* CF 19 (Kalamazoo, MI, 1977); *Liber ad Milites Templi: de laude novae militiae*, 4.8, *SBOp*, III, 312–29. See also below, Chapter Three, pp. 106–7.

[20] M.-H. Vicaire, 'Introduction', *Cisterciens*, CaF, pp. 7–8; Paterson, p. 324. D. Baker has suggested that Bernard of Clairvaux and Eugene III collaborated on plans for expansion in an effort to improve the region by effecting the conversion of brigands

have explained this 'cistercianization', as well as the earlier ecclesiastical reforms effected in the region, in terms of rampant corruption among the southern clergy.[21] Some scholars, however, have questioned the negative characterization of the Occitanian Church. One French historian argues that heresy flourished in Occitania not because of the regional Church's long-standing instability and corruption but as a direct result of weakness caused by the Gregorian reforms.[22] The reforms undermined the laity's sense of having a secure place in the Church and further distanced them from the institution. Moreover, the separation of the upper clerical class from rural priests and ordinary people was exacerbated by the reform movement. The aristocratic life of the bishops opened the way for the common people to admire the asceticism lived by the Cathar clergy.

The 'Twelfth-Century Renaissance'

The monastic tradition viewed the monastery as the *schola Christi*, 'a school for the service of the Lord', with Christ as the master. As such it provided all the education necessary for attaining eternal life. Moreover, the Cistercians held as an ideal the *schola* of the early Church, a way of life rooted in the gospel.[23] Bernard of Clairvaux, in his sermons, holds up Christ as the greatest master *(magister)* and asserts that the virtues of the early Church are to be learned from the gospel.[24]

In the late eleventh century, however, the school of the monastery began to be overshadowed by cathedral schools. Their task had been training diocesan clergy in theology and canon law, but now increasing numbers of students sought education. Not intending to become monks, they gravitated toward the episcopal schools.[25] The Gregorian reforms also had an impact on the

---

like Pons of Léras, the robber-knight who founded the monastery of Silvanès, and by combatting the success of heretical movements. D. Baker, 'Popular Piety in the Lodèvois in the Early Twelfth Century: The Case of Pons de Léras', *SCH* 15 (1978), 39–46; Kienzle, 'Hugo Francigena', 287–317; and B. M. Kienzle, 'The Conversion of Pons of Léras and the True Account of the Beginning of the Monastery at Silvanès: Analysis and Translation of the Latin Text in Dijon, Bibliothèque Municipale, Ms. 611', *Cistercian Studies Quarterly* 30 (1995), 218–43.

[21] Paterson, p. 312, summarizes the predominant view of the pre-Gregorian reform Church in Occitania as an institution 'stagnated in material, institutional, and moral decadence'.

[22] Paterson, pp. 312–15 and E. Magnou-Nortier, *La société laïque et l'Eglise dans la province ecclésiastique de Narbonne (zone cispyrénéenne) de la fin du VIIIe à la fin du XIe siècle* (Toulouse, 1974), esp. 16–17, 447, 519.

[23] *Rule of Benedict*, Prologue, p. 45. See Chenu, *Nature*, pp. 273–4. Newman signals the military connotation of *schola* and its implications. Newman, pp. 21–2.

[24] *Summer Season*, Ascension 3.4, p. 39; Ascension 5, pp. 55–6; Peter and Paul 1, pp. 100–3; *SBOp*, V, 140–1, 149–50, 188–91.

[25] The cathedral clergy and schools gained strength during the earlier revival of

cathedral schools and on the canons who staffed them. New orders of regular canons were founded: the Victorines in 1108 and the Premonstratensians in 1120. The canons of the abbey of Saint Victor in Paris established a model for the new age, striving to be both monks and scholars.[26]

Twelfth-century scholars inherited the notion of the seven liberal arts and continued late antiquity's effort to balance Christian literature and the classics, the sacred and the profane.[27] The discipline of philosophy was also introduced into the curriculum, and theology gradually developed into a separate field. A new emphasis on dialectic (arguing both sides of a case) and rational argument emerged during the eleventh century and intensified in the twelfth. In the eleventh century, Berengar of Tours used these means to challenge teachings on the Eucharist,[28] and Peter Abelard's *Sic et non* exemplified the dialectical method's impact in the twelfth century.[29] By the thirteenth, theology and philosophy were pushing the study of literature into second place at

classical learning in the Carolingian era, often called the Carolingian Renaissance, and the extension of its impact on the courts of Otto I and his successors in Germany. Among the many works on the Carolingian Renaissance, see P. Riché, 'Instruments de travail et méthodes de l'exégète à l'époque carolingienne', in *La Bible*, pp. 147–61; and on the Ottonian courts, see C. Stephen Jaeger, *The Envy of Angels. Cathedral Schools and Social Ideals in Medieval Europe, 950–1200* (Philadelphia, 1994). Jaeger deals with three phases in the development of medieval learning: the Carolingian, the Ottonian and the twelfth-century, focusing on education in Germany and France.

[26] See B. McGinn, *The Presence of God: A History of Western Christian Mysticism*, 4 vols. (New York, 1996), II, 363–418; Longère, *Prédication*, pp. 63–8; Châtillon, pp. 179–86; N. M. Häring, 'Commentary and Hermeneutics', in *Renaissance and Renewal*, pp. 190–4; G. R. Evans, *The Language and Logic of the Bible. The Earlier Middle Ages* (Cambridge, 1991), pp. 28–9.

[27] The study of the classics and their 'christianization' lay at the heart of the medieval curriculum. See Murphy, 89–132; E. R. Curtius, *European Literature and the Latin Middle Ages*, trans. W. R. Trask, Bollingen Series 36 (Princeton, 1973), p. 37. In the late fourth and early fifth centuries, Augustine had endeavored to reconcile Christianity with classical rhetoric in his *De doctrina christiana*, and Martianus Capella dramatized the union of the seven liberal arts foundational for Roman education (grammar, dialectic, rhetoric, geometry, arithmetic, astronomy and music) in his *De nuptiis Philologiae et Mercurii*. The first three of the seven were grouped as the *trivium*, and the latter four were termed the *quadruvium*. On *De doctrina christiana*, see Murphy, pp. 43–88; Chapter Two in this book; and on Martianus Capella: Curtius, *European Literature, passim*; and Murphy, pp. 43–5. On the literature and authors of the curriculum, see Fichtenau, pp. 235–80; Jaeger, *Envy of Angels*, pp. 278–91; Curtius, *European Literature*, pp. 42–5 and 48–53. For a recent example of scholarly attempts to distinguish sacred and profane in medieval literature, see P. Dronke, 'Profane Elements in Literature', in *Renaissance and Renewal*, pp. 569–92.

[28] Berengar aroused hostility from monastic quarters and provoked Peter Damian's opinion that dialectic was not well suited for the study of Scripture: Châtillon, pp. 166–8. See also Fichtenau, 286–93.

[29] On dialectic, see Fichtenau, pp. 225–6, 234–48, 255–6; Stock, *Implications, passim*; Murphy, *Rhetoric, passim*.

Paris, which remained, even into the Reformation, the most important centre for the development of the university and for theological education.[30]

How did the Cistercians react to these changes? Bernard of Clairvaux's sharp opposition to Abelard is well known: the Parisian master was accused of heresy as vehemently as were the lay dissidents the abbot attacked. Gilbert of Poitiers also came under assault from the powerful clergyman and his secretary, Geoffrey of Auxerre. Bernard himself derided the dangers of the Parisian environment. Moreover, the Cistercians joined the new universities later than their mendicant confrères.[31] These tensions between monastic and scholastic learning will be examined in the later chapters of this book as the writings of individual monks are discussed.

Nonetheless, the Cistercians also gained from developments in the schools. One scholar even asserts that the Cistercians' advocacy of ecclesiastical reform made them 'intellectual precursors' to the school masters.[32] Bernard of Clairvaux, as we shall observe in Chapter Three, praises the value of reasoned arguments in defeating heresy. He and his successors in the anti-heretical campaigns must have learned their approach from the schools. As Ernaldus, one of Bernard's biographers observed, 'men of learning, masters of rhetoric and philosophy in the schools of this world, studied the theory of divine virtues' at the monastery of Clairvaux.[33] Certainly the intellectuals who influenced the preaching against heresy in the late twelfth and early thirteenth centuries were influenced by thinking that generated from the Parisian milieu, and some joined the Cistercian Order.

[30] The rivalries over the curriculum were reflected in literature: the English scholar John of Garland complained about the neglect of the *auctores* in his *Morale scolarium* (about 1241); and the French poet Henri d'Andelys composed the *Bataille des set arts* where the authors of the standard curriculum take the battlefield against Logic and her champions, including Plato and Aristotle. See Curtius, *European Literature*, p. 56. On the importance of Paris, see Haskins, *Twelfth-Century Renaissance*, p. 11. The history of Jesuit education departs from adoptions and modifications of the *modus parisiensis* in which Ignatius and others were schooled. J. O'Malley, *The First Jesuits* (Cambridge, MA, 1993), esp. pp. 215–17, 245–48. O'Malley notes that the so-called *modus parisiensis* was developed significantly in the Low Countries during the fifteenth century and cautions against over-simplified attribution of the method to the University of Paris alone.

[31] On Bernard, Abelard and Gilbert of Poitiers, see Newman, pp. 221–6 and 222–3; Fichtenau, pp. 283–5, 294–303. For Bernard's remarks on studying in the city, refer to *Epistolae* 2 and 106, *SBOp*, VII, pp. 12–22 and 265–7; *Letters* 2 and 107, pp. 10–18, 155–6. Cistercians and the universities are discussed in C. Obert-Piketty, 'La promotion des études chez les cisterciens à travers le recrutement des étudiants du collège Saint-Bernard de Paris au moyen âge', *Cîteaux* 39 (1988), 65–77; and C. Obert-Piketty, 'Benoît XII et les collèges cisterciens du Languedoc', in *Cisterciens, CaF*, pp. 139–150.

[32] Newman, p. 167.

[33] The late Edmé Smits' research was pursuing the links between the monastery and the schools, notably in his 'Hélinand of Froidmont, Science and the School of Chartres'.

Consider the following Cistercians who entered the order with experience as students or masters in the schools.[34] Bernard of Clairvaux was educated by the canons of St Vorles at Châtillon-sur-Seine.[35] Adam of Perseigne, famous as the chaplain to Countess Marie of Champagne, was probably educated at a cathedral school in Champagne, then served as a regular canon before becoming a Benedictine and finally a Cistercian and the abbot of Perseigne.[36] Odo of Ourscamp held the post of chancellor at Paris before entering the northern French house of Ourscamp in 1165.[37] Isaac of Stella (d. *c.* 1178), sometimes called Isaac Magister, probably left England to study in France. He may have studied under Abelard and at Chartres, where he later taught.[38] In contrast to Bernard of Clairvaux's professed anti-philosophical attitude, Isaac, also a Cistercian abbot, praised Plato as the 'great theologian of the gentiles'. Geoffrey of Auxerre, once under Abelard's tutelage, was swayed by Bernard's preaching in 1140 to follow him to Clairvaux, where he became the abbot's secretary.[39] Nicholas of Clairvaux, one of Bernard's secretaries, was versed enough in Platonism to correspond with the Benedictine Peter of Celle in a dispute over the Platonic primacy of unity and the Augustinian notion of simplicity. Peter the Chanter (*c.* 1130/40–1197), canon, master, chancellor of the cathedral school at Paris, and head of an influential circle of intellectuals, became a monk at Longpont. His predecessor in Paris, Peter Comestor (*c.* 1100–79), master and chancellor of the Paris cathedral school, became a canon of Saint Victor but probably had ties to the Cistercians.[40] Alan of Lille, on the other hand, spent the last years of his life at Cîteaux. The young Alan was a disciple of Gilbert of Poitiers (*c.* 1080–1154), one time master at Poitiers, Chartres, and Paris, then bishop of Poitiers, whose condemnation Bernard of Clairvaux strongly urged at the 1148 Council of Rheims. Alan composed masterpieces of medieval Latin literature, and devoted time to writing against heresy.[41]

---

[34] Similarly Bruno, founder of La Grande Chartreuse, was formerly a master at Reims. His commentary on the Psalms show the use of the *quaestio* and a commentary on Paul's epistles, from his school if not his hand, discusses for each epistle commented the *causa, materia* and *intentio*. See Châtillon, pp. 172–5.

[35] See Casey, *Athirst for God*, p. 7, n. 16.

[36] *The Letters of Adam of Perseigne*, trans. G. Perigo CF 21 (Kalamazoo, MI, 1976), pp. 4–9.

[37] Newman, p. 40.

[38] See 'Introduction', *Sermons*, I, ed. A. Hoste and G. Salet SC 130 (Paris, 1967), pp. 10–13.

[39] Newman, p. 38.

[40] On Peter Comestor, see J. H. Morey, 'Peter Comestor, Biblical Paraphrase, and the Medieval Popular Bible', *Speculum* 68 (1993), 6–35; and Smalley, *Gospels*, pp. 37–83. The Comestor's *Historia scholastica* (*c.* 1170) clearly influenced Hélinand of Froidmont's *Chronicon*, composed in the early part of the thirteenth century, and Hélinand could have met the master in Paris sometime before his death. See E. Smits, 'Editing the *Chronicon* of Hélinand of Froidmont: The Marginal Notes', *Sacris erudiri* 32 (1991), 269–89.

[41] On Alan of Lille and Peter the Chanter, see Pacaut, *Les moines blancs*, p. 224; Châtillon; and Chapter Five of this book, pp. 172–3. The definitive work on the Chanter is Baldwin, *Masters*.

Hélinand of Froidmont studied at the cathedral school of Beauvais under Ralph, an English pupil of Abelard, who was 'as learned in divine literature as in secular'.[42] Hélinand drew on his education to compose sermons and a chronicle that furnished references for preachers and served the anti-heretical campaigns.

The works of Alan of Lille, Peter the Chanter and Hélinand of Froidmont demonstrate the Cistercians' part in the growing emphasis on preaching evident in Parisian circles. Alan of Lille and Peter the Chanter counted among the first to write a collection of *distinctiones*, the predecessor of the verbal concordance, which provided figurative meanings for biblical words, illustrating each with a scriptural text. *Distinctiones*, while useful for exegetes, were produced primarily in response to demand from preachers for aids in compiling sermons. In contrast to their contemporaries, Alan and Peter alphabetized their collections, and in so doing, composed the first alphabetical tools for searching the Scriptures. At the end of the twelfth century, other Cistercians such as Garnier of Rochefort, later bishop of Langres, developed study aids with alphabetical indexing and reference systems.[43] Hélinand of Froidmont compiled extensive reference works: the *Chronicon* and a collection of sermons, many of which resolve thorny theological and exegetical questions. The compilation of such reference works involved Cistercians with the late twelfth century's schools' efforts to make information readily accessible to preachers, even before the canons of Lateran IV ordered expansion of popular preaching through the secular clergy and the nascent mendicant orders.

Occitania and the 'Twelfth-Century Renaissance'

Occitania did not experience such a flowering of learning in the schools, but effects of the 'Twelfth-Century Renaissance' were not altogether lacking, notably in scientific translations from Greek and Arabic, and in law and medicine. From its proximity to Spain and the Mediterranean, Occitania offered a point of contact for scientific texts and their translators, who disseminated materials from there, as from Italy, Sicily and Spain, to the rest of Europe.[44] The universities of southern France were influenced by the

---

[42] *Chronicon*, PL, CCXII, 1035D.

[43] On the development of study aids in general, see: R. and M. Rouse, '*Statim invenire*: Schools, Preachers, and New Attitudes to the Page', in *Renaissance and Renewal*, pp. 201–25. On the Cistercians, see: R. Rouse, 'Cistercian Aids to Study in the Thirteenth Century', in *Studies in Medieval Cistercian History* II, ed. J. R. Sommerfeldt, CS 24 (Kalamazoo, MI, 1976), pp. 123–34. On Garnier of Rochefort, see Pacaut, *Les moines blancs*, p. 224.

[44] See M.-T. d'Alverny, 'Translations and Translators', in *Renaissance and Renewal*, pp. 421–62, who updates Haskins's work in this area with copious references.

revival of the study of law. Legal experts, led by Bolognese scholars, returned to the sixth-century Justinian code, the *Corpus Juris Civilis*, and developed various types of glosses. This and Gratian's compiling of a compendium of canon law, the *Concordia discordantium canonum* (*c.* 1142), later simply called the *Decretum*,[45] prepared the way for the codification of legislation against heresy. The Occitanian universities of Toulouse and Montpellier[46] found models for faculties of law and medicine in the Italian schools of law at Bologna and medicine at Salerno. [47] Papal recognition was granted to the medical faculty of Montpellier in 1220, and after its founding in 1229, the University of Toulouse provided lawyers and judges for royal and ecclesiastical control of the region.[48] Faculties of theology were established from mendicant *studia* in both cities during the fourteenth and fifteenth centuries (Toulouse, 1360; Montpellier, 1421), although masters of theology came to Toulouse earlier, at the founding of its university in 1229, when the Cistercian Hélinand of Froidmont preached the opening address.[49]

In Occitania overall, vernacular literature with its extensive influence on European culture overshadowed the Latin writings produced there. Why troubadour poetry flourished in southern France has been the topic of scholarly debate for many years, as have possible connections among troubadours, Cathars and Cistercians.[50] Recent insights from social history clarify the backgrounds and contacts of the troubadours, their occupations and interaction with the courts. A survey of patronage in the courts of Occitania shows that the counts of Foix and those of Toulouse – Raymond V, Raymond VI and Raymond VII – figured among the troubadours' patrons. Raymond VI and VII received support for the Occitan cause from the political poems (*sirventes*) of the troubadours.[51] Evidence from the biographies of

---

[45] A single complete manuscript of Justinian's Digest (*Digesta seu Pandectae*) survived and was rediscovered about 1070. Canon law was probably taught at Oxford also at the turn of the twelfth century. On the Digest, the glosses, methods of the new jurisprudence, and the revival of the study of law in general, see S. Kuttner, 'The Revival of Jurisprudence', in *Renaissance and Renewal*, pp. 299–323.

[46] Evidence also points to the teaching of Roman law at Montpellier during the 1160s. See Kuttner, 'Jurisprudence', p. 319.

[47] On the development of Italian universities, see P. Roberts, 'Medieval University Preaching: The Evidence in the Statutes', in *Sermons and Society*, pp. 317–28.

[48] Paterson, pp. 196, 174.

[49] J. Verger, 'La prédication dans les Universités méridionales', in *Prédication*, CaF 32, pp. 275–76, 290, n. 2; and J. Verger, 'Jean XXII et Benoît XII et les universités du Midi', in *La papauté d'Avignon et le Languedoc (1316–1342)*, CaF 26 (Toulouse, 1991), pp. 199–219.

[50] Points of view on the origins of troubadour poetry are summarized by Pierre Bec in the introduction to his *Nouvelle anthologie de la lyrique occitane au moyen âge* (Avignon, 1972), pp. 35–60.

[51] The courts of Poitou, to the west, enjoyed stability earlier than those of Catalonia in the east, and Paterson dates signs of literary activity in Poitiers and the Limousin from the end of the eleventh century, in the Pyrenees from 1137, in Toulouse from

troubadours, compiled in the thirteenth century, concurs with the archives to demonstrate the average social location of the poets and entertainers (*joculatores*). Most troubadours were not patrons but instead practised various professions and depended on patrons for support. These findings indicate widespread literacy in the vernacular, a conclusion bolstered by records of legal transactions. J. H. Mundy assumes a 'vigorous growth' of legal Latin around 1200 and also brings to light the numerous village and small-town notaries in the areas outlying Toulouse. Thus literacy was not confined strictly to the cities, but even small villages had *scriptores* or *notarii publici*. In some cases, clerics functioned also as *scriptores*.[52]

At least two troubadours – Bertran de Born and Fulk of Marseille – aligned with the Church's cause, entering the Cistercian Order. Others, namely Bertran of Ventadorn and Raymond of Miraval, withdrew to Cistercian monasteries to spend their last days. The case of Raymond of Miraval illustrates the complexity in untangling allegiances: a supporter of the count of Toulouse, Raymond was deprived of his château by Simon of Montfort around 1209–11, and took refuge in the Cistercian monastery of Santa Clara, Lerida.[53]

Bertran de Born (*c.* 1150–1215) inherited in 1178 his family's land and castle at Hautefort in Périgord. He composed about thirty to forty extant songs of war from the 1180s to the mid-1190s, before he retired to the nearby Cistercian monastery of Dalon. Long-standing recipient of benefactions from Bertran's family, Dalon also sheltered the troubadour Bernard of Ventadorn. Two satirical poems from the period after Bertran's entrance into the abbey employ the language of love and war that marked his earlier poetry and could not have pleased his Cistercian superiors.[54] Fulk of Marseilles entered the Cistercian abbey of Le Thoronet about 1196 and became its abbot before being named bishop of Toulouse in 1206. Fulk and Bertran de Born knew each other, or at least of each other, for Fulk sent a vernacular poem to Bertran, urging that he devote himself to God. As bishop, Fulk reportedly so despised

the 1130s, in Catalonia from 1150, in the Auvergne before 1156, and in Provence from 1162. Paterson, pp. 90–100.

[52] Mundy, 'Urban Society', pp. 234–8; and J. H. Mundy, 'Village, Town and City in the Region of Toulouse', in *Pathways to Medieval Peasants*, ed. J. A. Raftis (Toronto, 1981), pp. 119–40 (p. 162).

[53] A. Brenon, 'Fin'amors et catharisme. L'exemple de Peire Vidal en Lauragais et de Raymond de Miraval en Carcasses, avant la croisade contre les Albigeois', in *Peire William de Luserna e lo tems dals trobaires*, ed. V. Cognazzo and G. M. di Coggiola, Atti del convegno Storico Internazionale, 4 e 5 maggio 1991 in Luserna San Giovanni (Cuneo, 1994), pp. 139–58 (p. 149).

[54] W. D. Paden, Jr, '*De monachis rithmos facientibus*. Hélinant de Froidmont, Bertran de Born, and the Cistercian General Chapter of 1199', *Speculum* 55 (1980), 669–85. Paden discusses an 1199 general chapter statute, concluding that it targets satirical poetry written by monks in the vernacular, and Bertran de Born and Hélinand of Froidmont in particular.

the songs written in his youth, that he would undertake a penance of bread and water when one of them was performed in his hearing.[55] Another Cistercian, the converted trouvère (the northern French equivalent of a troubadour) Hélinand of Froidmont, composed a lengthy poem, the *Vers de la Mort*, in which he sends death to warn those who sing about love and vanity that they should exhort instead to inspire fear of God.[56]

Fulk's attitude to his earlier poetry opens the question whether the Cistercians viewed the exaltation of adulterous love in troubadour poetry as a factor contributing to the growth of heresy. Certainly polemicists associated heresy with a general decline in morality and specifically with promiscuity. In northern Cistercian circles there is evidence of concern about popular literature: Hélinand of Froidmont wrote in his *Chronicon* that he intended to compose a version of the Grail story that conformed to Christian morality. He could have consulted the Grail romance at the abbey of Perseigne, whose abbot Adam was spiritual adviser to Marie of Champagne.[57] A more extensive study of Cistercian opinions on literature would perhaps provide answers to the question, which we shall revisit later in this chapter.

Economic growth

The flowering of troubadour poetry occurred during a period of economic growth in southern as well as northern France and other areas of Europe. The late eleventh century ushered in commercial and industrial expansion, the expanded use of money, and the growth of towns and cities and their populations. Spiritual reactions to this economic transformation divide into two broad categories: the attempt to avoid it, as monks and hermits did; and the desire to confront it, witnessed among the canons, certain lay people and then the friars.[58] When the Cistercians stepped into the world, they were caught in the midst of these tensions. Overall they were suspicious of urban centres but achieved remarkable economic success in the countryside, where they established a network of monasteries.

Cities, gaining in population and influence, began around 1100 to assert their autonomy against the authority of the landed nobility. This stemmed in part from the Gregorian reform's efforts at freeing the Church from domination by secular leaders. Furthermore, the eleventh-century Peace of God movement, which united Church and people in protest against feudal

---

[55] Paden, 'De monachis', p. 685.

[56] Hélinand chastized the clergy supporting Philip Augustus's desire to divorce Ingeburg of Denmark. See Paden, 'De monachis'; and *Les Vers de la Mort*, ed. F. Wulff and E. Walberg (Paris, 1905), II, 2.

[57] On Hélinand and the Grail, see Kienzle, *Midi*, pp. 37–67; and Chapter Six in this book.

[58] Little, *passim*; p. 218.

violence,[59] promoted associations by oath and provided a model for unification of citizens that altered distinctions of social location according to services provided. Town citizens became more equal under law and less bound by obligations of service for others. Assertions of urban autonomy were accompanied by bourgeois revolts in the communes of northern France, but in the south, the consulates established their freedom gradually.[60]

Occitania experienced a period of urban growth from the twelfth to the early fourteenth century, with increases in trade, construction and industry. Furthermore, a wide variety of groups inhabited Occitanian towns, resulting in fluid social boundaries. Social classes mingled more in southern than in northern France; unlike their northern French counterparts, southern knights lived in towns. In addition, Jewish communities and intellectual centres flourished in Narbonne and Montpellier, where Christian and Jewish scientists exchanged knowledge.[61] Jews were counted among the victims when some Occitanian cities fell to the crusaders.[62]

Economic change affected Toulouse profoundly before the devastation of the crusade. Late twelfth-century Toulouse achieved 'a modestly republican and patrician society', according to J. H. Mundy. Townsmen gradually usurped the count's prerogatives until 1189, when he capitulated. For about twenty years, the city was governed by a board of consuls, much like an Italian city state. Economic benefits accrued from the growing cloth and wine industries. Toulousans erected towers like wealthy citizens of northern Italy, although not to the same extent. In 1202 a new group of consuls coming to power moved the council toward expansion and waged war against neighbouring towns and villages in order to incorporate them into a large county. This expansion was cut short in 1209 by the crusade, and the towers of Toulouse attracted the resentment of the northern French conquerors who destroyed them.[63]

The European countryside also experienced population growth from

---

[59] See especially T. Head and R. Landes, ed., *The Peace of God: Religious Responses to Social Turmoil in France around the Year 1000* (Ithaca, NY, 1992).

[60] Mundy, 'Urban Society', pp. 229–33. See also below, n. 95.

[61] Paterson, pp. 151–3, 166, 175–6, 180–2.

[62] G. Dahan, Les *intellectuels chrétiens et les juifs au moyen âge* (Paris, 1990), pp. 362–3. Dahan also summarizes and discounts anything more than a common occurrence of some themes and motifs in Cathar writings and Jewish mysticism in southern France, p. 363. R. Chazan observes that the crusading spirit with its cry for revenge and evocation of negative stereotypes readily extended to attacks on Jews. Conflation of outgroups did not in Chazan's view lead from fear of one group to that of another, but it did strengthen the general sense of danger. Chazan, *Stereotypes*, pp. 5, 57, 92. Jews and heretics were depicted with similar motifs, including the cat, in the 'Bibles moralisées'. See S. G. Lipton, 'Jews, Heretics, and the Sign of the Cat in the Bible moralisée', in *Word and Image* 8 (1992), 362–77; and *Images of Intolerance. The Representation of Jews and Judaism in the* Bible moralisée (Berkeley, CA, 1999), pp. 83–111.

[63] Mundy, 'Urban Society', pp. 229–33.

around the mid-eleventh century onward. Areas of cultivable land were cleared and enlarged, and agricultural methods improved. These developments took place later in Occitania than in the north. Moreover, peasants in Mediterranean regions generally were unable to take advantage of the improved northern system of rotating crops triennially and could not afford the heavy, more effective plows used in the north. Still they cultivated cereals, vineyards and olives, and the population expanded, reaching a peak of growth around the mid-twelfth century. People settled in 'grouped habitats', hamlets or villages, and they populated towns more densely. The *castrum*, a fortified village built around a castle, became the typical Occitanian habitat. Various forms of exchange took place between town and countryside in fairs, markets and transport of raw materials for the cloth industry. The rural nobility, less prosperous and less military in character than their northern counterparts, lived in the *castrum* with members of other social classes.[64]

The population and cultivation of the countryside relates to both Cistercians and Cathars. The Cathars developed a strong network of household support in hamlets and villages where their adherents worked and worshipped together. These houses were integrated into their surrounding communities and open to visitors to come and go, learn a trade and discuss religious beliefs. The two functions of teaching religion and crafts were inseparable. Some of the Cathar houses were workshops where goods were traded and artisans worked. Apparently typical is an Inquisition witness's report that as a boy he sewed as a cobbler in the heretics' workshops, listened to their preaching and adored them (a ritual act of reverence to the perfects).[65] Thus it seems that as the population of rural hamlets and villages increased, so did the potential for adherence to Catharism.

The Cistercians meanwhile expanded their monastic network into uncultivated or under-cultivated lands. During the twelfth-century expansion, twenty-nine Cistercian monasteries were founded or affiliated to the order in Occitania, twenty-four, as we recall, from 1135 to 1160.[66] Bernard of Clairvaux's journeys were instrumental in promoting foundations and affiliations of existing monasteries. Two important Occitanian abbeys joined the order in 1145, the year of his journey to the Midi: Grandselve, near Toulouse, and Fontfroide, on the plain south-east of Carcassonne.

---

[64] Paterson, pp. 121–3, 140–2, 150–1; C. Higounet, 'Le milieu social et économique languedocien vers 1200', in *Vaudois languedociens et Pauvres Catholiques*, CaF 2 (Toulouse, 1967), pp. 15–9; Kaelber, *Asceticism*, p. 75.

[65] Toulouse MS 609, fol. 157r: 'Et tunc, cum esset puer, suebat in operatoriis eorum; et audivit predicationem eorum, et adoravit eos', cited by Kaelber, *Asceticism*, p. 207, to whom I am indebted for this view of the Cathar house, which he discusses on pp. 204–8.

[66] Vicaire, *Intro.*, 7–8; and B. Wildhaber, 'Catalogue des établissements cisterciens de Languedoc au XIIIe et XIVe siècles', *Cisterciens*, CaF, pp. 21–44.

Monks of both abbeys played a key role in the crusade years, as we shall see in Chapters Five and Six. Moreover, the abbeys benefited from the crusade in various ways, such as gifts, exemption from tolls and acquisition of lands belonging to heretics. The power and prestige of the order's abbots and bishops must have helped to obtain and protect property.[67]

The Cistercians' enormous success in agriculture is indisputable, although the extent to which the white monks opened up new lands for cultivation has been subject to scholarly debate. Cistercian monasteries obtained surrounding lands and covered them with granges, a central complex of buildings and fields organized into one agricultural unit. Granges varied widely in number and size, and monasteries owned other types of supporting property as well. Grandselve, for example, possessed lands in a relatively small area near the abbey, some subject to flooding from the Garonne and others not, and also owned olive groves and distant mountain pasture lands. The monks attracted workers for these properties by recruiting lay brothers, largely from the lands they acquired; they also employed labourers. Lay brothers previously had practised diverse occupations – peasant farmers, artisans and knightly estate managers – which they continued to exercise, adding to the granges' efficiency as an economic unit. They kept large flocks and herds, probably around 1000–1200 animals in a normal flock, which improved the land's fertility. Furthermore, Cistercians were able to purchase better tools and draft animals than the peasants could and were exempted from tithes and tolls to transport their goods. Productivity was impressive and led to investments in more land and construction, reaching a peak in the late twelfth century. Subsequently, the number of lay brothers declined and revolts occurred, fuelled no doubt by the gap between lay brothers and monks, who lived in the abbey, not in the granges, and came largely from the upper class.

The Cistercians' resolute acquisition of land contradicted the message of simplicity and austerity articulated in the order's founding and prompted satire of their greed from late twelfth-century writers such as Walter Map and Gerald of Wales, who cast the white monks as 'constantly on the look-out for rich lands and broad pastures'. This reputation for greed would do the Cistercians no good when they confronted the austere Cathars.[68]

---

[67] Berman, pp. 3–5, 124–8. See also C. d'Autremont Angleton, 'Two Cistercian Preaching Missions to the Languedoc in the Twelfth Century, 1145 and 1178', Ph.D. dissertation, The Catholic University of America, 1984, pp. 143–51.

[68] For this discussion of Cistercian agriculture, I am indebted to Berman, pp. 7, 74, 82–3, 96. See also Newman, pp. 67–82; C. Bouchard, *Holy Entrepreneurs: Cistercians, Knights, and Economic Exchange in Twelfth-Century Burgundy* (Ithaca, NY, 1991). On satire of the Cistercians, see Newman, pp. 79–81; Constable, *Reformation*, pp. 32–3; Little, p. 93.

Popular religious movements and tensions with the hierarchy

At the same time that the Gregorian reforms consolidated ecclesiastic order and power, avenues for expression of piety opened up to lay people.[69] The growth of towns, cities and literacy allowed for guilds and lay spiritual movements.[70] Similarly, urbanization may have contributed to the need for lay people to have simple, supportive, spiritual communities;[71] they found those increasingly outside the Church's complex structure and organization.

The Cistercians endeavoured to profit from the laity's fervour; among the conversions to the order were numerous men who became lay brothers. Stories of conversion include tales of such persons as Pons of Léras, who founded the monastery of Sylvanès in an area notorious for both heresy and everyday crimes of *routiers*. A converted brigand himself, Pons remained a lay brother all his life and was credited with the conversion of many *milites* to the Cistercian Order. His story illustrates how an illiterate knight could embrace poverty and transform the wilderness. Pons even delivers a simple but eloquent sermon to rouse his brothers to distribute their goods to their starving neighbours.[72]

Since Herbert Grundmann, historians have recognized that lay piety, like clerical, was marked with a veneration for the apostolic life that included ideals of both voluntary poverty and evangelism. André Vauchez notes that monastic reform and heresies of the year 1000 shared the view that the only hope for Christianity, and indeed for humanity, resided in separation from the material aspects of the secular Church and dedication by communities of faith to bring together believers in a reformed way of life.[73] Pursuing ideals of poverty and evangelism, however, brought some lay movements into conflict with the Church. Tension between the clergy and the laity existed for centuries before the Gregorian reforms, polarizing the clerical as good and the lay as evil.[74] However, once the Gregorian reforms had firmly fixed the clerical perspective, lay religious currents or movements that arose spontaneously and without the direction of the clerical hierarchy were likely to come under suspicion. The distrust with which the clergy regarded lay religion intensified sharply around the middle of the twelfth century when dissident movements gained strength.

The distrust was mutual. In contrast to the conversions of Pons of Léras

---

[69] Scholars are indebted to Grundmann's *Movements*, which provided the foundation for studying lay religious movements from the eleventh through the thirteenth centuries.

[70] Russell, *Dissent and Order*, p. 24.

[71] Russell, *Dissent and Order*, p. 26.

[72] On Pons of Léras, see articles cited in n. 20 above.

[73] Vauchez, *Laity*, p. 13.

[74] D. Bornstein aptly calls this 'Manichean rhetoric' and explains that it was transferred to historiography, resulting in a largely negative characterization of the laity. Bornstein, 'Introduction', in Vauchez, *Laity*, p. xvi.

and others, the new spiritual enthusiasm of the laity also resulted in resentment of the clergy. A strengthening sensibility developed among lay people in the twelfth century, an awareness of the contradictions they saw between the lives of the clergy, enriched by some of the reform measures, and the teachings of the Gospels.[75] Wandering preachers appeared who advocated the austerity of the apostolic life and relied on donations to make a living. Some like Robert of Arbrissel, who found patronage from Hildebert of Le Mans, were never condemned and eventually allied with the clergy.[76] Robert, who wandered through Brittany and Anjou in the 1090s, was commissioned with Bernard of Tiron to preach the First Crusade. Robert later established a new and influential double monastery at Fontevrault, and another itinerant preacher, Norbert of Xanten, founded the Premonstratensian Order.[77] Arnold of Brescia, on the other hand, carried his denouncement of clerical corruption and call for reform to the point that he started a popular uprising in 1146, drove the pope out of Rome, and declared a republic there. Condemned in 1139 by Innocent II at the Second Lateran Council and at the Council of Sens in 1140, he was finally excommunicated in 1148, arrested and executed in 1155 under orders of Hadrian IV.[78] Peter of Bruys (d. *c.* 1140) and Henry the monk (d. *c.* 1145) provoked the hierarchy's indignation[79] and aroused criticism from two of the most powerful figures in the Western Church: Peter the Venerable, abbot of Cluny, who attacked the Petrobrusians;[80] and Bernard, abbot of Clairvaux, who set out to capture Henry and dissuade his followers. The same Hildebert of Le Mans who was Robert of Arbrissel's patron had trusted Henry, even leaving the city in his charge, only to find that the popular preacher had so aroused the people against clerical authority that they greeted his return by pelting him with mud. Hildebert eventually excommunicated Henry, who reportedly was captured and died in prison.[81]

In the second half of the century, dissidents obtained even greater strength, denouncing clerical corruption, asserting differing beliefs and establishing a foothold throughout Europe. R. I. Moore suggests that between 1179 and 1215 there occurred 'the most rapid diffusion of popular heresy that Western

---

[75] Vauchez, *Laity*, pp. 19–20.

[76] Lambert, *Heresy*, pp. 40–2; Russell, *Dissent and Order*, p. 32; Moore, *Origins*, pp. 84–5.

[77] Grundmann, *Movements*, pp. 18–19; Lambert, *Heresy*, pp. 39–42; Moore, *Formation*, pp. 19–20; *Moore, Origins*, pp. 84–5, 89.

[78] Lambert, *Heresy*, pp. 52–3; Russell, *Dissent and Order*, p. 35; Moore, *Origins*, pp. 115–36.

[79] Lambert, *Heresy*, pp. 44–50; Russell, *Dissent and Order*, p. 32; Moore, *Origins*, pp. 82–114.

[80] See Moore, *Formation*, p. 25; D. Iogna-Prat, 'L'argumentation défensive', in *Inventer l'hérésie?*, pp. 87–118.

[81] Lambert, *Heresy*, pp. 47–8; Russell, *Dissent and Order*, pp. 32–3; Moore, *Formation*, pp. 20–1; Moore, *Origins,* pp. 82–114, and Moore, 'Literacy and the making of heresy', in Biller and Hudson, pp. 29–31.

Europe had yet experienced'.[82] Among the movements that arose, the Waldensians and especially the Cathars aroused the greatest suspicion of heresy and consequently were the primary targets of Cistercian preaching missions.

The Waldensians, followers of the converted merchant Valdes of Lyon, grew into a strong apostolic movement that survives today. Valdes had the Scriptures and some patristic works translated into the vernacular. For all believers including women, he advocated a life devoted to preaching and supported by donations. Waldensians gathered in houses to preach and teach to one another about the Scriptures; and preachers, apparently bare-foot at first and then recognizable by their sandals, travelled in pairs evangelizing. In 1179, Pope Alexander III approved the Waldensians' voluntary poverty but refused to allow them to preach without their bishop's permission. That refusal alienated the group from the hierarchy; they continued to preach, nonetheless, and in 1184 the Waldensians along with the Humiliati, the Arnoldists and the Patarenes were condemned in *Ad abolendam*, a decree issued at Verona by Pope Lucius III and backed by the Emperor Frederick I.[83] Most Waldensians then dispersed to the north and east. Innocent III sent Cistercian abbots to Metz in 1199 to investigate their use of vernacular texts.[84] The Waldensians developed strongholds and eventually bishoprics in sites north of the Alps, such as Besançon, Mainz and Regensburg, as well as in some Italian cities, notably Milan, where the movement became more radical. Occitanian Waldensians were numerous enough to draw the ire of polemicists and the condemnation of the archbishop of Narbonne sometime between 1185 and 1187. Interrogations of Waldensians appear in Occitan inquisition records in the 1230s and 1240s. However, the numbers of Waldensians in Occitania were far less than the Cathars and their influence smaller. They received less support from the nobility than the Cathars.[85]

Although later Waldensians developed their own church, the early fol-lowers of Valdes differed from Rome not because of doctrine, but primarily over the question of obedience, brought to a head in the controversy about

---

[82] Moore, *Formation*, p. 23.

[83] Lambert, *Heresy*, pp. 5–78; Russell, *Dissent and Order*, pp. 44–7; Peters, *Inquisition*, pp. 47–8. On the Waldensians, the Cistercians and the late twelfth-century lay preaching controversy, see also Chapter Four in this book.

[84] Kienzle, 'Obedience', p. 265. On the texts of the Waldensians, see A. Patschovsky, 'The Literacy of Waldensianism from Valdes to c. 1400', in Biller and Hudson, pp. 112–36; and A. Brenon, 'The Waldensian Books', in Biller and Hudson, pp. 137–59.

[85] On the later Waldensians, see Lambert, *Heresy*, pp. 149–71; P. Paravy, 'Waldensians in the Dauphiné (1400–1530): From Dissidence in Texts to Dissidence in Practice', in Biller and Hudson, pp. 160–75; P. Biller, 'What *did* Happen to the Waldensian Sisters? The Strasbourg Testimony', in *Studi in onore del Prof. Jean Gonnet (1909–1997)*, ed. F. Giacone, *Protestantesimo* 54 (1999), 222–33.

preaching. Lay preaching obviously posed a threat to the ecclesiastical hierarchy. Dissidents travelled widely, advocating apostolic poverty, and also met in private residences. Waldensians met and preached in the homes of their patrons, as did the Cathars, whose bishops were accompanied by assistants who set forth their doctrines. The count of Toulouse, for example, reportedly invited Bishop Fulk to his castle to hear the 'preaching of the heretics'.[86] Reacting to dissident preaching, Alan of Lille, who composed one of the first *artes praedicandi* in about 1200, states that preaching is very dangerous (*periculosissimum*) for the uneducated, who do not know what should be preached, nor to whom, how, when and where preaching should be done.[87] Moreover, monks generally were not authorized to preach. A monk preaching without authorization was subject to discipline. The notorious Ralph, a Cistercian who incorporated anti-Jewish propaganda into his crusade sermons, was rebuked for unauthorized preaching and sent back to his monastery. Another monk was recalled from preaching the Albigensian Crusade, apparently for usurpation of the preaching office.[88] Alan of Lille's remark that even very holy men who understood the Scriptures, as did many Cistercians, were nonetheless not commissioned as preachers, encapsulates the clerical resentment felt over claims by the Waldensians and others to the right to preach publicly.[89]

[86] On dissident preaching, see W. L. Wakefield, *Heresy, Crusade, and Inquisition*, p. 32; J. Duvernoy, 'La prédication dissidente', in *Prédication*, CaF, pp. 111–24. The *Hystoria Albigensis* reads: 'Dixit etiam comes dicto episcopo Tolosano ut veniret de nocte in palatium ejus et audiret praedicationem haereticorum: unde perpenditur quod saepe de nocte audiebat eos'. I. 34, p. 34.

[87] *Summa quadrapartita (Summa contra haereticos)*, *PL*, CCX, 379CD: 'Quomodo etiam praedicabunt illitterati qui scripturas non intelligunt? . . . Si sapientibus et sanctis periculosum est praedicare, periculosissimum est idiotis, qui nesciunt quo praedicandum, quibus praedicandum, quomodo praedicandum, quando praedicandum, ubi praedicandum'. See also Chapter Four in this book.

[88] On Ralph, see Cole, *Preaching*, p. 44; for the other example, see J. Canivez, *Statuta Capitulorum Generalium Ordinis Cisterciensis ab anno 1116 ad annum 1786, I (1116–1220)* (Louvain, 1933), 1212.50, p. 400.

[89] On the prohibition against monastic preaching, see: *Summa quadrapartita*, *PL*, CCX, 379D: 'Videmus etiam sanctiores iis non praedicare, qui intellectum sacrae Scripturae habent, ut multos Cistercienses, quia nimirum missi non sunt'; G. Constable, 'The Second Crusade as Seen by Contemporaries', *Traditio* 9 (1953), 276–8, and *Reformation*, pp. 227–8, on prohibitions against monks preaching. The *Decretum* of Gratian specifies that a monk must have permission from his bishop and consent from his abbot to preach, that is, publicly: 'Nullus monachus preter Domini sacerdotes audeat predicare. Monachi autem, et si in dedicatione sui presbiteratus (sicut et ceteri sacerdotes) predicandi, baptizandi, penitenciam dandi, peccata remittendi, beneficiis ecclesiasticis perfruendi rite potestatem accipiunt, ut amplius et perfectius agant ea, que sacerdotalis offitii esse sanctorum Patrum constitutionibus conprobantur; tamen executionem suae potestatis non habent, nisi a populo fuerint electi, et ab episcopo cum consensu abbatis ordinati.' *Decretum Magistri Gratiani*, ed. E. Friedberg (Corpus Iuris Canonici I; Leipzig 1879), Dictum post c. 19, C. XVI, q. 1 (coll. 765–6).

Early thirteenth-century events, namely the Fourth Lateran Council (1215) and the approval of the mendicant orders (Dominicans, 1216; Franciscans, 1220), expanded the scope and frequency of orthodox preaching to the people, partly in response to the threat that the Church perceived in dissident preaching. Papal concern for undertaking crusades to the Holy Land also had an impact on the history of preaching. Diocesan clergy had insufficient training for widespread propagation of the papal agenda. First the Cistercians, then the friars were enlisted as preachers in service of the papacy. Both the Dominicans and the Franciscans received training in the art of preaching and developed extensive manuals and preaching aids. Neither group took a vow of stability as did the Cistercians and Benedictines; on the contrary, itinerant preaching figured as a key element of the friars' vocation. In some locales, early mendicant preachers were barely distinguishable from their dissident predecessors and counterparts, and the populace accepted them only after confirmation of their orthodoxy. In the case of the Dominicans, the mission of public preaching was conceived as a response to and against the dissemination of heterodox ideas; the order was founded specifically to teach correct doctrine and preach against heresy. From the thirteenth century onward, the friars furnished the Church with a clergy trained in theology and preaching who assumed the campaign against heresy from the Cistercians.[90]

The clerical hierarchy's suspicion of apostolic movements like the Waldensians and its concern for controlling the authorization to preach were sharpened by the growth of Catharism and its ecclesiastical structure: a real counter-church that shared certain basic elements of belief, organization, and ritual with the Bogomils who emerged in Bulgaria in the early tenth century.[91] References in the West to groups with Cathar-like beliefs appear sporadically in the eleventh century and increase from the 1140s onward, from England to Germany, northern Italy and Occitania. Those reports are discussed in later chapters of this book. Occitanian Catharism surfaces clearly in the 1140s, and by 1167 an international Bogomil-Cathar council was taking place in the Lauragais to confirm the boundaries of four Cathar bishoprics. Catharism remained strong in Occitania until the crusade and tenacious even afterwards.[92]

The Cathars called themselves simply 'good Christians'. Their church consisted of believers, clergy and bishops. They advocated an austere

---

[90] On mendicant preaching, see Longère, *Prédication*, pp. 93–122; D. d'Avray, *The Preaching of the Friars. Sermons Diffused from Paris before 1300* (Oxford, 1985); C. Maier, *Preaching the Crusades. Mendicant Friars and the Cross in the Thirteenth Century* (Cambridge, 1994), pp. 4–5; and Grundmann, *Movements*, pp. 66–7, on distrust of the mendicants in France and Germany.

[91] On the Bogomils, see Lambert, *Cathars*, pp. 23–37; Hamilton, 'Wisdom'; Duvernoy, *Histoire*, pp. 13–76; M. Loos, *Dualist Heresy in the Middle Ages* (Prague, 1974).

[92] Later chapters of this volume will deal with the history of Catharism as relevant. Extensive coverage is provided by Lambert, *Cathars*, pp. 60–80, 131–41, 165–70, 215–39, and 256–71.

manner of life and engaged their believers in some form of work such as weaving or cobbling.[93] Differences from Rome centred primarily on the nature of Christ, the structure and role of the church hierarchy, the number and function of the sacraments, the source of evil in the world, and the possibility of salvation for all believers. For the Cathars, Jesus was not truly human; they objected that a good God would not send his son to earth for crucifixion. Moreover, the only sacrament necessary for salvation was the *consolamentum*, a laying-on-of-hands modelled on the imposition of hands described in the New Testament. It served as baptism, confirmation, ordination, forgiveness of sins, and extreme unction. Neither marriage nor the Eucharist was considered a sacrament, but the Cathars shared a symbolic breaking of bread. Cathars and Bogomils held the belief that matter was created by the rebellious angel Lucifer and that the last fallen soul would be saved at the end of this world. Their myths, recounted in the *Interrogatio Iohannis*, describe Satan's creation of the visible world and humankind. Furthermore, both groups rejected icons and practised a simple repetitive liturgy emphasizing the Lord's Prayer, an *Adoremus* formula, and multiple genuflections. The relationship between the Bogomils and the Cathars and the history of Catharism itself have been reevaluated extensively in recent years.[94]

Why did these dualist beliefs implant themselves so successfully in Occitania? In contrast to Italy, where Catharism assumed a strongly urban base, Occitanian villages provided the principal stronghold for Cathar believers. Certainly Toulouse, which Cistercian preachers decry as the *caput erroris*, represented a centre for heresy and resistance to the Roman Church. The invaluable research of J. H. Mundy has illuminated the socio-historical background of Catharism in that comital city and helped to establish that Cathar believers belonged to all social classes. Mundy has also brought to light the attacks on heretics and usurers waged by the White Confraternity

---

[93] See Kaelber, 'Weavers', pp. 111–13.

[94] B. Hamilton suggests that dualist religion spread from East to West with the travels of various groups of people, such as orthodox monks and crusaders. Hamilton, 'Wisdom', pp. 38–60. Hamilton offers an excellent analysis of Cathar spirituality in 'The Cathars and Christian Perfection', in *The Medieval Church : Universities, Heresy, and the Religious Life. Essays in Honour of Gordon Leff*, ed. P. Biller and B. Dobson, SCH S 11 (Woodbridge, 1999), pp. 5–23. P. Biller calls attention to the neglected role of northern Catharism in 'Northern Cathars and Higher Learning', in *The Medieval Church*, ed. Biller and Dobson, pp. 25–53. On the Cathars and Bogomils, see also Lambert, *Cathars*, pp. 23–59; A. Brenon, 'Les hérésies de l'an mille', *Heresis* 24 (1995), 21–36; J. Duvernoy, 'Le Catharisme: l'unité des églises', *Heresis* 21 (1993), 15–27; Y. Hagman, 'Le catharisme, un neo-manichéisme?' *Heresis* 21 (1993), 47–59; Y. Hagman, 'Le rite de l'initiation chrétienne chez les cathares et les bogomiles', *Heresis* 20 (1993), 13–31. From the point of view of the history of the laity, A. Vauchez also points out that the mentality of the masses was already 'spontaneously dualist' and that the apparent simplicity of Cathar beliefs and their sober liturgy, part of what he terms their 'exacerbated spiritualism' had appeal. Vauchez, *Laity*, pp. 20 and 44.

under Bishop Fulk of Toulouse in the early thirteenth century. Although earlier research sought explanations for the success of Catharism in Occitania among these and other economic factors, they do not appear to provide a solid explanation.[95]

The *castrum*, the fortified village or town organized around a castle, and not the city, offered Catharism its most frequent foyer and the path for its dissemination from household to household. The Occitanian system of partible inheritance probably accounts for the representation of all social classes among the Cathars. Southern nobles, many of whom were impoverished as individual land holdings diminished because of repeated subdivisions, often lived among their subjects in the *castra*. Some famous *castra* were hill or mountain-top villages, although those developed later than the villages built near rivers or at lower elevations. Ruins of various villages are now being excavated, notably the *castrum* at Montségur.[96] Three important centres of Catharism – Verfeil, Lombers and Fanjeaux – were inhabited by numerous nobles. Catharism was perhaps introduced by the upper class and then filtered down to other classes, but it also spread horizontally, from one family to the next. Villages allowed extraordinary freedom for Cathars to teach, worship and live together in community, and some families passed between city and country in search of refuge.[97] Cathar houses played a religious and socio-economic role, as we have seen; people were welcomed there for instruction in trades and religion.[98]

Recent research has explored the evidence for literacy among the Cathars. Although the language of Catharism was predominantly the vernacular,[99] its scholarly leaders composed treatises and other documents in Latin. Peter Biller, surveying the use of written materials among the Cathars, underscores the evidence for formal correspondence among Cathar leaders. Letters

---

[95] The Cathar religion placed no economic restrictions on believers and its churches exacted no tithes from their adherents. See Mundy, 'Urban Society', pp. 240–2; and Kaelber, 'Weavers', pp. 112–13, on the Marxist view that the textile industry produced a gap between wealthy merchants and impoverished weavers, leading to the workers' protest through heretical beliefs.

[96] See Kaelber, 'Weavers', pp. 113–15; Grundmann, *Movements*, pp. 14–17. Lambert, *Cathars*, pp. 67–8 ; Paterson, p. 141, who uses the term 'castelnaux' instead of *castra*. On the excavations at Montségur, see A. Czeski, 'Aspects de la vie quotidienne à Montségur, révélés par les témoins archéologiques', in *Montségur: La Mémoire et la Rumeur 1244–1994*, ed. C. Pailhes (Saint-Girons, 1995), pp. 65–86.

[97] Lambert, *Cathars*, pp. 68–9; Brenon, *Cathares*, p. 54.

[98] M. Roquebert, 'Le catharisme comme tradition dans la 'familia' languedocienne', in *Effacement du Catharisme (XIIIe–XIVe s.)*, CaF 20 (Toulouse, 1985), pp. 221–42; Kaelber, 'Weavers', pp. 117–22; and Kaelber, *Asceticism*, pp. 204–8. See n. 65 above.

[99] B. Hamilton argues that Cathar liturgical texts were first translated into Latin and raises the question of what the language of worship was before the availability of vernacular translations: 'Wisdom from the East', pp. 48–58. Lambert, *Cathars*, p. 193, asserts that there 'is little doubt' that a Latin archetype existed for the extant Occitan and Latin rituals.

conveyed between Occitania and Lombardy must have been written in Latin. Liturgical texts in Occitan contain headings and some prayers in Latin; extant theological works were written in Latin, and references are made to others composed in Latin or in a mixture of Latin and vernacular. Furthermore, there are numerous references to Cathars reading and commenting on books, and also to learned Cathar *perfecti*.[100]

The fact that Catharism flourished in Occitania at the same time as troubadour poetry has provoked much speculation on possible causal relationships. The notion that troubadour songs, particularly the hermetic genre of *trobar clus*, constituted encoded statements of Cathar beliefs and thereby a type of mysticism has been refuted resoundingly by historians of Catharism and romance philologists.[101] The connections that historians of Catharism have established between Cathar followers and poets of courtly love are primarily political.[102] It was logical for the poets to favour the cause of Catharism, a product of their native soil, while the crusaders were considered foreigners whose invasion devastated Occitan society.[103]

What intrigues us is the possibility that medieval clerics perceived a link between courtly love and heresy which parallels the opinion now refuted by historians. René Nelli asserted that the friars disapproved of the courtly love

---

[100] P. Biller, 'The Cathars of Languedoc and Written Materials', in Biller and Hudson, pp. 48–58. Lorenzo Paolini focuses on Italian sources to examine contradictory accusations that the Cathars were illiterate, on the one hand, and that they were wise and learned, on the other. Some of Paolini's observations apply generally to Catharism and thus to Occitania as well, while others are limited to Italy whose Cathar scholars, Paolini concludes, 'exercised a kind of intellectual and religious leadership in western European Catharism'. Clearly Cathar *perfecti* viewed themselves as learned (*sapientes*), and they became well known for skill in public debate. L. Paolini, 'Italian Catharism and Written Culture', in Biller and Hudson, pp. 83–103.

[101] D. de Rougement popularized this notion. De Rougemont, accepting the argument that the idealized love of *cortezia* did not reflect the reality of women's low status in society, looked for another source for *cortezia* and found it in Catharism. Drawing on the ideas of others who hazarded such a view, de Rougement drew parallels between Cathar beliefs, albeit misunderstood, and passages taken from troubadour poetry, twelfth-century Neo-Platonism, Dante, and even Wagner, Manes and the gnostics. Sweeping across time and space in his thought, de Rougement states: 'All this leads me to assert confidently now . . . that courtly lyrical poetry was at least inspired by the mysticism of the Cathars.' D. de Rougement, *Love in the Western World*, trans. M. Belgion (Greenwich, CN, 1956), pp. 77–105 (quote at p. 105).

[102] A recent study by A. Rigier points to the possibility of encoded politics in a song by the *trobairitz* Lombarda. Rigier claims that a discussion of political alliances during the Albigensian Crusade appears disguised under the language of courtly love. A. Rigier, *Trobairitz. Der Beitrag der Frau in der altokzitanischen höfischen Lyrik. Edition des Gesamtkorpus* (Tubingen, 1991), pp. 243–54; cited by Paterson, p. 262.

[103] A song composed by Raymond of Miraval in 1213 links his hope for the reestablishment of Catharism with that for the return of the world of *fin'amors* and the departure and defeat of the French crusaders. Brenon, *Vrai visage*, pp. 200–4; and Brenon, 'Fin'amors et catharisme', p. 140.

poetry of the Midi because of its exaltation of adulterous relationships and considered it responsible for the lax morality that fostered heresy. Romance philologists have shared this view to explain the eventual shift in troubadour lyrics from praise of the lady to that of the Virgin.[104] To what extent the friars' unedited writings such as sermons reflect such notions and whether Cistercians shared the same suspicions constitute interesting questions for further research.

Certainly Cathar beliefs and the courtly love of the troubadours were tolerated in the same milieu, even though they did not proceed from the same principles. Some Occitanian nobles protected both Cathars and troubadours.[105] Moreover, the Cathar perfects probably tolerated the sensual love praised by the troubadours at least as much as the institution of marriage, although they opposed both in theory.[106] Such attitudes certainly would have provoked the anger of the orthodox clergy, who routinely denounced the Cathars for their opposition to marriage and for feigning chastity.[107] If

---

[104] According to René Nelli, the poetry of courtly love was doomed by the Inquisitor's suspicions, and the troubadours of the 1240s–1260s lamented its passing and its golden age, preceding the crusade. Due to the Inquisition's disapproval, poets were forced to rethink the ethics of *fin'amors*, developing a deeper interpretation of love than that of the earlier 'classical' troubadours, and advocating a purified carnal love that valued the teaching of charity and compassion. Nelli, p. 163, cites J. Coulet, stating: 'C'étaient maintenant les 'valeurs' de l'érotique provençale qui devenaient suspectes à l'Église. Celle-ci, comme le dit J. Coulet, "condamnait les pratiques de l'amour courtois, l'amour en dehors du mariage, comme les agents de la dissolution des moeurs grâce à laquelle l'hérésie s'était propagée." [*Le Troubadour Guilhem Montanhagol*, Toulouse, 1898, p. 46] Et la chanson d'amour, désormais tenue pour immorale et dangereuse, devait fatalement disparaître: "Au siècle suivant il n'y a plus de chanson d'amour; le seul amour qu'il est permis de chanter, c'est l'amour de Dieu et de la Vierge Marie" (Coulet, p. 46).' R. Nelli, 'Introduction', *Le roman de Flamenca. Un art d'aimer occitanien du XIIIe siècle* (Centre National d'Etudes Cathares, 1966), pp. 163–81. See also Bec, *Nouvelle anthologie*, pp. 79–80 and 269, where he explains: 'Cette assimilation progressive [de la chanson d'amour vers la chanson à la Vierge] . . . s'explique en second lieu par une recrudescence, après la croisade des Albigeois, de l'orthodoxie catholique: les troub. [sic] sont plus ou moins mis à l'index, et il ne leur reste plus, par une lente déviation dont ils ont parfois conscience, qu'à transcender leurs louanges en les adressant à la Dame par excellence, c'est-a-dire la Vierge.'

[105] Brenon surveys the history of the debate in *Vrai visage*, pp. 197–204. Also significant for the connections between Catharism and *fin'amors* are the Cathar matriarchs, who found few outlets for the religious life and turned to Cathrarism in their later years. Lady Garsende, for example, was a Cathar believer and the mother of the five co-lords of Mas-Saintes-Puelles. Brenon, 'Fin'amors et catharisme', p. 156. See also A. Brenon, *Les femmes cathares* (Paris, 1992); A. Brenon, *Les Cathares. Pauvres du Christ ou apôtres de Satan?* (Paris, 1997), pp. 50–2. For a recent view of research on Cathar women, see Lambert, *Cathars*, pp. 148–52; and P. Biller, 'Cathars and Material Women', in *Medieval Theology and the Natural Body*, ed. P. Biller and A. J. Minnis, York Studies in Medieval Theology 1 (Woodbridge, 1997), pp. 61–108.

[106] See the arguments of R. Nelli, *Le phénomène cathare* (Toulouse, 1964), pp. 150–61.

[107] See the critiques of Bernard of Clairvaux in Chapter Three, below; Hildegard of

the Cistercians connected Cathar practices to troubadour poetry, Bishop Fulk would have had strong reason to be embarrassed by his youthful poetry.

Development of processes for inquisition and persecution

Clerical opposition to Cathars, Waldensians and other dissidents rested on the centralized structure directed from Rome and solidified during the Gregorian reforms.[108] The clergy concentrated religious functions in their hands and were often openly hostile towards unlearned people, especially the heretics they denounced as unlettered.[109] Moreover, dissenters from prescribed beliefs or behaviour were suspected of trying to undermine the whole reform programme, and therefore to overturn the social order.[110]

This mentality spurred the establishment of the process of inquisition, when teaching and preaching no longer proved effective in persuading dissenters to conform.[111] Cistercians played key roles in the development of the inquisitorial process and in forming and disseminating the ideas necessary to sustain it. The lands of Occitania were the proving ground for

Bingen in Kienzle's articles cited above, Introduction, p. 4 n. 12; and Hélinand of Froidmont in Chapter Six.

[108] This analysis draws primarily on the views of three historians who work from a sociological perspective: J. B. Russell speaks in terms of the tensions between order and dissent; E. Peters stresses the shift from persuasion to coercion over the course of the eleventh and especially the twelfth century; R. I. Moore underscores the development of a persecuting attitude among those in power in twelfth-century Europe, who sought increased control at a time of social change. See also Introduction, pp. 20–3; and Chazan's critique that Moore's use of Weber and Durkheim does not apply strictly to the Jews. Chazan, *Stereotypes*, pp. 82–3.

[109] Moore, *Formation*, pp. 134, 139–40, 70. Moore asserts that that the learned (*literati*) felt fear for the unlearned (*rustici*), and that persecution assisted the 'cohesiveness and confidence' of the persecutors. Nonetheless, Moore also accords a role to the centralization of the hierarchy in the definition of heresy, stating that when one compares heresy in the earlier versus the High Middle Ages, one 'must make a substantial allowance for the greater sensitivity of the more centralized structure to the manifestation of dissent'. On *literati* vs. *rustici*, see Grundmann, *Movements*, pp. 14–16, and 'Litteratus-illiteratus. Der Wandel einer Bildungsnorm vom Altertum zum Mittelalter', *Archiv für Kulturgeschichte* 40 (1958), 1–65; Stock, *Implications*, pp. 26–30.

[110] Peters, *Inquisition*, pp. 40–1, observes that the growing view that dissent was heresy 'shaped the long transition from persuasion to coercion'. On the view that reform gave rise to both heresy and its prosecution, see Russell, *Dissent and Order*, p. 22. On the theme of persuasion vs. coercion, see also R. Manselli, 'De la *persuasio* la *coercitio*', in *Le* Credo, *la Morale et l'Inquisition*, CaF 6 (Toulouse, 1971), pp. 175–97.

[111] Peters, *Inquisition*, pp. 40–1, argues that 'ecclesiastical and lay leaders turned to coercion, and as part of that process of coercion they revived and transformed the older *inquisitio* legal procedure and created a new office, that of inquisitor'.

the developing machinery of inquisition, and the dissident movements that flourished there, particularly the Cathars, became its victims.

Socio-political changes and the codification of laws facilitated persecution. Gratian's *Decretum* combined Roman and canon law in an organized system that allowed for enforcing order.[112] Collections of canon law, the product of renaissance and reform, included provisions for the definition and suppression of heresy and were developed for local use. Incidents of persecuting heresy increased and the persecuting process gained strength, in a sort of snowball effect. The third canon of the Fourth Lateran Council (1215) established the mechanisms for persecution, but it was preceded by a series of landmarks: (1) Chapter 21 of the Assize of Clarendon in 1166, the first secular legislation against heresy;[113] (2) the Third Lateran Council in 1179; (3) *Ad abolendam* in 1184, the first joint (secular and spiritual) condemnation of heresy since the Theodosian code; (4) Innocent III's 1199 decree *Vergentis in senium* equating heretics with traitors before the law. Other important steps in the development of persecution in the mid-twelfth century include Peter the Venerable's intervention in diocesan affairs and his call for the use of secular power in dealing with the Petrobrusians; and Bernard of Clairvaux's intervention in the Count of Toulouse's territory. Bernard's mission was aimed not only at Henry the monk but also at his followers, and Bernard achieved a judgment from the citizens of Toulouse that ostracized the heretics and their sympathizers and deprived them of legal rights.[114]

Edward Peters points out that the rift between the Emperor Frederick Barbarossa and the papacy accounted for a delay in the formulation of a universal policy against heresy. That period of schism – 1159–77 – corresponded with the spread of Catharism in the Rhineland and the visionary writing and preaching of Hildegard of Bingen who accused the clergy's negligence for the growth of heresy. The schism was followed by the Third Lateran Council and *Ad abolendam*, which accorded importance to the defiance of authority (*contumacia* in Latin), a matter of no small import in the discussion of polemics against the Waldensians. With it secular authorities were bound to cooperate with the Church and to prosecute heretics according to local law. Innocent III continued and intensified his predecessors' efforts against dissidents, issuing strong condemnations of heresy such as *Vergentis in senium* in 1199. Henceforth, heresy was seen not simply as a

---

[112] Russell, *Dissent and Order*, p. 23. On eleventh-century heresy and persecution, see Lambert, *Heresy*, pp. 9–32, 36–7; Russell, *Dissent and Order*, pp. 27–31; Moore, *Formation*, pp. 13–9. Stock focuses on the Patarenes in *Implications*, pp. 151–240.

[113] Moore, *Formation*, pp. 6–9. For Moore, Arnold of Brescia's execution and the 1148 burning of Eon de l'Étoile, who had looted and burned monasteries in Brittany, mark a 'very clear watershed in the history of the Church' that demonstrated the episcopal resolve to treat heresy severely. *Formation*, pp. 24–5.

[114] See Moore, *Formation*, p. 25.

sin, but as a crime against Christian society just as treason was a crime against the Roman Empire.[115] Moreover, Innocent III issued in 1207, just prior to the Albigensian Crusade, *Cum ex officii*, which provided for the delivery of heretics to secular courts, the confiscation and sale of their possessions, destruction of their homes, and penalties imposed on their followers or supporters.[116] Investigation took on a greater role in the identification of heretics: as they were forced to hide their activities from the authorities, lay and ecclesiastical powers undertook greater efforts to discover them. The twelfth-century legal revolution lent much to the new procedure for dis-covering and trying heretics.[117]

The severity of measures against heresy is clear in the canons of the Council of Toulouse in 1229, at the close of the Albigensian Crusade. Those canons extend the provisions against heresy to include the power to search out heretics, to require that the repentant heretics live in orthodox locations and wear coloured crosses on their clothing, and to bar even suspected heretics from certain professions.[118] Cistercians were involved in negotiating the Treaty of Paris/Meaux in 1229, and a Cistercian – Hélinand of Froidmont – preached at both the opening and closing of the Toulouse Council.[119] Thus we see a Cistercian presence at the close of the crusade and the transition to the Inquisition.

Conclusion

The twelfth century prepares the transition between the intellectual and religious domination of the monks and that of the friars. The foundation of the Cistercian order and its extensive growth during the second half of the century reflect the various societal transformations underway. Generally, the Cistercian anti-heretical campaigns that will be the focus of this book stem from the reform efforts of the Church and clash with the increasing spiritual independence of lay people.

At the founding of their order, the Cistercians epitomized the reform

---

[115] Peters, *Inquisition*, pp. 47–8, notes that *Ad abolendam* was the 'most elaborate juridical statement concerning the treatment of heretics made to that date by the Latin Church', and that it has been called 'the founding charter of the inquisition'. Manselli, 'De la *persuasio* à la *coercitio*', pp. 185–6, stresses the importance of the years between 1179 and 1184 for the Church's shift in position and the passage from persuasion to coercion.

[116] Peters, *Inquisition*, pp. 47–8.

[117] Peters, *Inquisition*, p. 52. See Chapter Six of this volume, where the 1229 synod is discussed in greater detail.

[118] The secular powers also strengthened their hand against heresy the following year, 1230, when Louis IX issued *Cupientes*, a law that committed royal officials to searching for heretics in the lands under their jurisdiction. Peters, *Inquisition*, p. 51

[119] On the events of 1229, see Chapter Six in this book.

movement with the emphasis on austerity and withdrawal from the world. By the 1140s, under the leadership of Bernard of Clairvaux, the white monks began to direct their attention to society's problems. During the middle decades of the century, the Cistercians founded many new monasteries in Occitania, and then in the late twelfth and early thirteenth centuries, they began accepting election to important sees in the region. Under pressure from Innocent III, the monks expanded their work in the world even further, directing the campaign against heresy. Expansion, ecclesiastical administration and popular preaching were key elements of the Order's reform programme in Occitania. However, the Gregorian reforms had produced a gap between ecclesiastical leaders and ordinary clergy and people, and the Cistercians probably widened it by their leadership of the anti-heretical campaigns.

The intellectuals who preached and directed the preaching drive formed their ideas in northern French circles, at the cathedral schools and the nascent university at Paris. Among them figured the prominent Paris master Alan of Lille and his mentor, Peter the Chanter, who both joined the Cistercians at the end of their lives. Poets too entered the order and enlisted in the anti-heretical endeavours: Fulk the troubadour and Hélinand the trouvère both experienced conversions and expressed regret for their earlier follies, possibly contributing to the attitude linking courtly love and heretical ideas. Both turned their talents to preaching and writing against heresy; Fulk was elected a bishop. Fulk, Abbot Arnaud Amaury and the legate Peter of Castelnau were apparently from the Midi, but other white monks, as we shall see later in this book, had ties of family and friendship to the crusaders.

Despite advocating a wilderness ideal of spirituality, the Cistercians contributed to and benefited from economic growth. Cultivating new and neglected lands, they expanded into the Occitanian countryside, reaping enormous success in agriculture with the efficient system of grange farming. Land acquisition, new construction and segregation of the lay brothers who tended the granges provoked resentment, which fomented revolts. By the end of the twelfth century the white monks had become targets of satiric literature, and criticism for their excessive building programmes came even from within the order's ranks.

At the same time that the Cistercians tilled uncultivated land, the Cathars established a network of houses in villages and hamlets, teaching religion and trades to their visitors. Their simple way of life rivalled the Cistercians' reputation for austerity and clashed with the visible signs of the white monks' growing prosperity. Cathars and especially Waldensians established houses in cities as well, and their presence in urban centres concretized the Cistercians' rhetorical and ideological scorn for the Babylons of the world. The Waldensians came into conflict with the hierarchy on the questions of obedience and authorization for preaching. We shall see in Chapter Two the centrality of obedience for monastic spirituality. The Cathars, like their

Eastern counterparts, the Bogomils, held a dualist doctrine and developed their own ecclesiastical structure: a counter-church that quietly but decisively opposed the leadership of Rome.

The stage was set for conflict. Step by step, between the Third and the Fourth Lateran Councils, papal decrees cemented an alliance between secular and ecclesiastical authorities for the prosecution of heresy. Cistercians played roles in developing the inquisitorial process and disseminating the ideas that sustained it. The examination of their activities outside the monastery in the Lord's vineyard begins in Chapter Three with the mission of Bernard of Clairvaux to the Midi. First we shall look into the domestic vineyard, the contemplative silence of the monastery, to explore how deeply dissident beliefs and practices clashed with monastic spirituality.

CHAPTER TWO

Monastic Spirituality and Literature:
the Domestic Vineyard

When the Cistercians stepped into the Lord's vineyard, they carried with them patterns of monastic thought, writing and preaching. Immersed in the Scriptures and the *Rule of Benedict*, the white monks viewed the surrounding world through the lens of the domestic vineyard, its spirituality and symbolist mentality. Imbued with reforming zeal, the Cistercians sought to bring dissident Christians into conformity with the monastic vision of the proper arrangement for society: to convert dwellers in the spiritual Babylon of the world into aspirants toward a heavenly Jerusalem where monks occupied the highest ranks.

Two types of sources inform our study of monastic spirituality: religious experience and written texts.[1] One section of this chapter will be devoted to religious experience as prescribed in the *Rule of Benedict*, and two to dealing with written texts: first, exegesis, and second, other monastic literature. To comprehend monastic exegesis and literature, one must first understand the precepts of the *Rule of Benedict*, which represents the culmination of oral and written monastic tradition and provides the experiential program for the monastic life. From the experience prescribed in the *Rule*, we shall turn to the genres of monastic literature, inseparable from oral tradition and lived experience.

The Rule of Benedict

The *Rule of Benedict*, attributed to Benedict of Nursia (*c.* 480–*c.* 550),[2] came to dominate Western monasticism during the Carolingian era.[3] The Cistercian

---

[1] Leclercq, *Learning*, p. 53.

[2] The *Rule of Benedict* depends on the earlier *Rule of the Master*, which also appeared in the sixth century and probably derived from the influence of John Cassian (*c.* 360–435). Less particular in its stipulations than the *Rule of the Master*, the *Rule of Benedict* continues to be praised for its practical wisdom, even by lay people who find inspiration in its establishment of a rhythm for work and prayer. See for example, E. de Waal, *Seeking God. The Way of St Benedict*, forewords by Archbishop R. Runcie and Basil Cardinal Hume (Collegeville, MN, 1984).

[3] During the reign of Louis the Pious, councils of 816 and 817 prescribed the *Rule* of

Fig. 2. The Cistercian abbey of Villelongue (Aude), founded in 1149.

Order aspired to return to the purity of Benedict's *Rule*, which they felt had been lost with the growth of Cluniac monasticism. The twelfth-century *Dialogue between a Cluniac and a Cistercian* reflects the white monks' reproaches of their Benedictine brothers' indulgence in practices from fine eating to teaching poetry.[4] The *Rule* draws a theology and spirituality from the Bible and prescribes a way of life rooted in a simple reading of the Scriptures. In that sense, the *Rule* grounds a lived exegesis, that is, the integration of the Bible's meaning into every possible aspect of daily life. The *Rule* also rests on the writings of the early monastic Fathers[5] and so reflects the patristic tradition.

The Prologue and seventy-three chapters of the *Rule* set forth prescriptions for community living such as: the positions of authority in the monastery and the responsibilities for each; procedures for correction and discipline, including cases where the *Rule* should be modified; schedules for the liturgy, meals, manual labour and sleeping; the programme of readings to be done in the divine office; procedures and limitations on contact with the world, including the ministry of hospitality; and discourses on the virtues essential to the monastic life, chiefly obedience and humility. Scripture inspires and animates every section. Monastic life appears throughout as a struggle – a battle of moral and experiential dimensions within the soul and a fight to persevere in the harsh observance of monasticism. As the Prologue reads: 'monks must prepare [themselves] in body and soul, to fight under the commandments of holy obedience'.[6] Understanding the moral qualities necessary for perseverance in the monastery proves vital for comprehending how monks regarded outside events.

The *Rule* mandates prayer in the divine office seven times during the day and once at night.[7] The entire Psalter is to be recited each week, beginning

Augustine for canons, and for monks the *Rule of Benedict*, as it was interpreted by the reformer Benedict of Aniane during the late eighth century. For a concise discussion of the *Rule* and the beginnings of western monasticism, see J. Leclercq, 'Monasticism and Asceticism II. Western Christianity', in *Spirituality*, pp. 113–24.

[4] Idung of Prufening, *Cistercians and Cluniacs: The Case for Cîteaux. A Dialogue between Two Monks, An Argument on Four Questions*, trans. J. O'Sullivan, J. Leahey and G. Perrigo, CF 33 (Kalamazoo, MI, 1977). A brief account of the birth of the Order and the importance of the *Rule* is found in B. Pennington, 'The Religious World of the Twelfth Century III. The Cistercians', in *Spirituality*, pp. 205–8. See also Newman, and Pacaut, *Les moines blancs.*

[5] See de Vogüé, pp. 2–4. De Vogüé speaks of a 'continuous chain that binds our Rule, through the writings of the Fathers, to the teaching of the New and Old Testament'.

[6] *The Rule of St Benedict*, trans. with intro. and notes by A. C. Meisel and M. L. del Mastro (New York, 1975), p. 45. Subsequent references will indicate chapter numbers in parentheses.

[7] 'Seven times daily I have sung your praises' (Psalm 119. 164). The seven services were: Lauds, at daybreak; Prime, at about 6 a.m.; Tierce, at approximately 9 a.m.; Sext, at about noon; None, at approximately 3 p.m.; Vespers, which was timed to end at sundown and the rising of the evening star; and Compline, which ended the Day

every Sunday at the night office (*RB* 18). The Scriptures and patristic texts reflecting on them are also read in the office: sermons, for example, during the night office, in each of the divisions – called nocturns – of Matins (*RB* 9).[8] In addition to the *opus Dei*, the work of God through community prayer (*RB* 16), the monks were expected to read daily, together and silently (*RB* 42, 48).[9] Approximately three quarters of the day were for work and one for reading. Furthermore, meditation, which involves recitation, continued the work of reading and the two were reciprocal.[10] Meditation was not limited to the hours of community worship, but as one scholar asserts: 'the monk ate to the sound of reading, just as he worked while reciting texts, and what he did while eating and working, he continued at the work of God'.[11]

The highest form of reading was to devote oneself to the *lectio divina*, the sacred text of the Scriptures.[12] The aim of all reading, individual or communal, silent or aloud, was to inspire prayer and meditation, and thereby achieve contemplation – mystical union with God. Meditation centred on the Scriptures, the life of Christ and images from both. With certain images such as that of the heavenly Jerusalem, several aspects of monastic culture intersect: the sacred text, the liturgy, the process of meditation and the eschatological focus of monastic theology. The paradise of the afterlife was envisioned as the city of the heavenly Jerusalem and the vision of peace, *urbs Ierusalem beata/dicta pacis visio*, in the words of the hymn.[13] Citizenship among the number of the chosen within its confines symbolized the attainment of salvation.

Furthermore, in monastic thought the heavenly city's closest earthly parallel was the monastery. In so far as possible for a terrestrial place, the monastery contained the dignity and spiritual benefits of the supernal city.

Office when darkness fell. The psalmist or prophet also said: 'I arose at midnight to confess to you' (Psalm 119. 62). Therefore, the office of Matins served as an eighth call to prayer, taking place at around 2 a.m. The exact hours of the offices varied of course according to the seasons and the time of daybreak and sunset. These prescriptions are contained in the Rule, chapter 16, and discussed in de Vogüé, pp. 127–72.

[8] During the short nights of summer, a brief lesson from the Old Testament, which was to be recited by heart, was substituted for the three readings of the night office (*RB* 10).

[9] During Lent, an extra hour of reading was assigned. Also for the Lenten season, each monk was issued a book for individual reading (*RB* 48).

[10] de Vogüé prefers to expand the traditional description of the monastic life: *ora et labora*, to a four-part formula: *ora, labora, lege et meditare*. de Vogüé, pp. 241–2. Meditation, often described with eating metaphors and the word *ruminatio*, represents not a work of silence but one of recitation: an exercise of total memorization, pronouncing aloud the sentence read by the eyes and hearing with the ears what is said and read. Leclercq, *Learning*, pp. 72–3.

[11] de Vogüé, pp. 135–6.

[12] de Vogüé, p. 245, defines *lectio divina*, which 'designates the divinely inspired text'.

[13] *Urbs Ierusalem beata* is included in *The Twelfth-Century Cistercian Hymnal*, ed. C. Waddell, 2nd edn, CLS 2 (Trappist, KY, 1984), pp. 232–3.

There one lived as near as possible to the mountain where Christ is to return at his second coming. Bernard of Clairvaux described the monk as a dweller in Jerusalem; he also defined Jerusalem as those who lead the religious life in this world and thereby imitate the way of the heavenly Jerusalem. When speaking of Clairvaux, he states that in that abbey could be found a Jerusalem 'associated with the heavenly one through the heart's complete devotion, through the imitation of its life, and through real spiritual kinship'.[14]

This identification of the monastery with the heavenly city had both positive and negative results. Monasticism had a formative influence on the urban model. The city's ideal purposes were kept alive in the monastery, and practical inventions such as the clock, the account book and a schedule for the day were passed on to medieval towns.[15] However, the association of the heavenly Jerusalem and the monastery as a blessed earthly city cast the secular terrestrial city in the role of Babylon. Echoing Augustine's antinomy of Jerusalem and Babylon, Bernard of Clairvaux speaks even of warfare between the two cities, the Babylon that is the present life and the Jerusalem that is Heaven: 'Between Babylon and Jerusalem there is no peace, but continuous war.'[16]

This extension of the inner battle in each monk's soul to a larger combat between Jerusalem and Babylon shaped the thought and imagery that animated the campaign against heresy. Military imagery figures prominently in monastic literature.[17] For a few Cistercians, it was played out at the head of armies. Furthermore, monastic writers coupled the monastery and the Church in a sort of reciprocal mirroring: one reflected the other and both were idealized. Exegesis of the bride's body in the Song of Songs envisioned groups within the monastery and various parts of the Church, all united by charity.[18] This close identification of monastery, Church, and heavenly Jerusalem placed any who resisted or differed with monastic values in a state of profound separation and rejection. Using the body imagery in a sermon at the 1163 Council of Tours, Geoffrey of Auxerre stated:

> Monastic society, by which we live for God and vow to keep the hard ways, produces nothing for the eternal salvation of souls if there is not ecclesias-

---

[14] *Song*, III, Sermon 55.2, p. 84; *SBOp*, II, 112; Ep. 64, *SBOp*, VII, 157–8; *Letters*, 67, pp. 90–2. See also the discussion by Leclercq, *Learning*, p. 55, and by Casey, *Athirst for God*, pp. 219–24.

[15] The monastery was the closest link between the classical and medieval cities. See L. Mumford, *The City in History* (New York, 1961), pp. 246–7.

[16] 'Inter Babylonem et Ierusalem nulla est pax sed guerra continua.' *Parabolae* 2.1; *SBOp*, Vib, 267.4. See also Casey, *Athirst for God*, pp. 219–20.

[17] See Newman, pp. 21–36.

[18] On this exegesis, see Newman, p. 107. On the background for interpretations of the Church in the Song of Songs, see E. A. Matter, *The Voice of My Beloved: The Song of Songs in Western Medieval Christianity* (Philadelphia, 1990), pp. 86–122; and for Cistercian interpretation of the Song, pp. 123–50.

tical unity. Without a doubt, it is impossible for a limb to be part of a body if it does not wish to be under a head.[19]

The head and body imagery represents powerfully the bond between unity and obedience to authority and the nature of the consequent threat to order that monasticism perceived in dissidence.

While the monastery provided its monks the path to attaining the reward of eternal salvation, the road was not easily travelled. Perseverance in the monastic life required discipline: obedience to the *Rule* and to the abbot (or abbess) who governed in accord with its precepts. The *Rule* demanded of each follower the humility to surrender his own will in favour of that of the community as represented by the abbot.[20] The abbot in turn stood accountable before God at the judgment for his teaching and for the obedience shown by his disciples.[21] The heavy accountability enjoined on the abbot helps to understand how Bernard of Clairvaux and other Cistercian abbots viewed their role in the world when they extended their notion of responsibility outside the monastery.

Hence the supreme and inseparable monastic virtues are obedience and humility. The opening of Chapter Five in the *Rule* advises that the 'first degree of humility is obedience without delay', explaining that such obedience is

> the virtue of those who hold nothing dearer to them than Christ; who, because of the holy service they have professed, and the fear of Hell, and the glory of life everlasting, as soon as anything has been ordered by the Superior, receive it as a divine command and cannot suffer any delay in executing it.[22]

Chapter Seven of the *Rule* represents the twelve steps of humility with the well-known image of Jacob's ladder; striving to reach the highest degree of humility is compared to ascending the ladder. Numerous works of monastic literature echo that theme, and our discussion here is but a scant reflection of

---

[19] The passage, from *PL*, CLXXXIV, 1101, is cited and translated by Newman, p. 242 and p. 346, n. 19.

[20] The abbot 'is believed to hold the place of Christ in the monastery, being called by a name of His, which is taken from the words of the Apostle: 'You have received a spirit of adoption as sons, by virtue of which we cry, "Abba – Father!"'' (*RB* 2).

[21] 'And let the Abbot be sure that any lack of profit the master of the house may find in the sheep will be laid to the blame of the shepherd'. Yet he could be acquitted for the wanderings of an 'unruly flock' if he had given 'all his pastoral diligence' and 'tried every remedy for their unhealthy behaviour' (*RB* 2).

[22] The desire to attain eternal life motivates the monks' choice of 'the narrow way', that is, the monastic life as defined in Jesus' words: 'Narrow is the way that leads to life', and explained as 'not living according to their own choice nor obeying their own desires and pleasures but walking by another's judgment and command'. See de Vogüé, pp. 91–111 on obedience, and pp. 117–26 on humility.

the presence of the themes of humility and obedience in the *Rule* and in monastic spirituality.[23]

A final key component of the monastic life is activity, the activity of work. Praying and manual labour were both considered work: prayer in the divine office is termed the *opus Dei*, the work of God. This notion of work's importance derives from Pauline texts and the early fathers of monasticism: Christians should earn their own bread and also earn through their work the wherewithal to help the needy. Monks were taught to follow in the footsteps of Paul, who not only devoted himself to the ministry, but also worked voluntarily to set an example for others.[24]

Given the crucial role assigned to humility, obedience and work in monastic life, it is not surprising that dissidents were criticized for disobedience and lack of humility when they refused to comply with the Church's regulations on lay preaching, or, in the case of the Cathars, totally refused obedience to the Roman Church. Moreover, when the Waldensians believed that evangelizing was their most important activity, one that precluded working and required them to accept bread from others, the monks not unforeseeably opposed that point of view.

Monastic exegesis and its background

Monastic rhetoric and literature have their sources first in the Bible; second in the patristic heritage, which likewise drew on the Scriptures and also transmitted the classics; and third in the classical learning taught in the schools.[25] Therefore, exegesis clearly dominates other monastic writing, but it is influenced by patristic writings and the liberal arts.[26]

The patristic tradition distinguished between the letter and the spirit, the literal and the spiritual, making the analogy between body and soul, between the word-text and the Word-God, incarnate in Jesus Christ.[27] Numerous images describe the relationship of letter and spirit, the latter always superior to the former. Paul's statement in II Corinthians 3. 6, 'the letter kills, but the spirit gives life', was taken to designate the two meanings of Scripture. Bernard of Clairvaux refers to 'the surface meaning of divine Scripture, which the Apostle calls the written letter that kills'.[28] Images like the kernel of

---

[23] See especially Bernard of Clairvaux, *Treatises II: The Book on Loving God*, trans. M. A. Conway, and *The Steps of Humility and Pride*, trans. R. Walton, CF 13 (Kalamazoo, 1980). For further discussion, see de Vogüé, pp. 91–111 on obedience, and pp. 117–26 on humility.

[24] de Vogüé, p. 240.

[25] Leclercq, *Learning*, p. 71.

[26] Smalley, *The Bible*, p. xv.

[27] See H. de Lubac, *Medieval Exegesis, I*, trans. Mark Sebanc (Grand Rapids, MI, 1998), pp. 3–8; Smalley, *The Bible*, pp. 1–2.

[28] Bernard states earlier in the same sermon: 'Now we must consider who this Goliath

wheat convey the notion that the letter is exterior and the spirit interior. One must strip away the exterior in order to arrive at the interior, hidden meaning. The process of removing or seeing through the outer literal sense in order to arrive at the hidden inner meaning constitutes exegesis in the patristic tradition and for the most part remains the exegetical task in the twelfth century.

The roots of this method are Eastern, going back to ancient Alexandria and especially to Origen, the most influential scholar of the Alexandrian school (*c.* 185–*c.* 254).[29] Western monks incorporated the readings of the Eastern Fathers into their own, as recommended in the *Rule of Benedict*. Early Christian exegetes found models in Paul's usage of rabbinical techniques of interpretation, such as attaching meaning to isolated words. From Paul and other New Testament sources, they adopted the method of typological interpretation.[30] Romans 5. 14 uses the term *typos* (Latin: *figura*) in identifying Adam as the type of Christ; as does I Corinthians 10. 6, interpreting events of the exodus as types for Christians.[31] Both the study of words and the usage of typology became favourite techniques of patristic and medieval exegetes.

Origen developed the idea of the three senses of Scripture: literal or historical; typological, pertaining to moral application; and spiritual, corresponding to the old covenant's prefiguring of the new.[32] Medieval scholarship

seems to be, if we are not unaware that the law is spiritual, according to the Apostle's testimony, and was written for us, not only to please us with the appearance of its outer surface, but also to satisfy us with the taste of its inner meanings, as with a kernel of wheat [Deuteronomy 32. 14].' *Summer Season*, Fourth Sunday after Pentecost, 2–3, pp. 115–16; *SBOp*, V, 202–3. In *De doctrina christiana*, Augustine speaks of figurative things, whose 'secrets are to be removed as kernels from the husk as nourishment for charity'. 3.XII.18, *On Christian Doctrine*, trans. D.W. Robertson, Jr (Indianapolis, 1958), p. 90.

[29] de Lubac devotes a chapter and much more to Origen in *Medieval Exegesis, I*, pp. 142–72 and *passim*. E. A. Matter explores Origen's influence on medieval exegesis of the Song of Songs in *Voice of My Beloved*, pp. 20–48. A recent and excellent study of Origen's exegesis is B. Daley, 'Origen's *De Principiis*. A Guide to the Principles of Christian Scriptural Interpretation', in J. Petruccione, ed. *Nova et vetera* (Washington, D.C., 1998), pp. 3–21. Also see R. D. Crouse, 'Origen in the Philosophical Tradition of the Latin West: St Augustine and John Scotus Eriugena', in *Origeniana Quinta*, ed. R. Daly, (Leuven, 1992), pp. 564–9. I am grateful to A. van den Hoek and N. Constas for assistance on Origen and his works.

[30] For a succinct account of early Christian exegesis, see S. M. Schneiders, 'Scripture and Spirituality', in *Spirituality*, pp. 5–9.

[31] Other examples not using the term *typos* include interpreting Jonah or the paschal lamb as types of Christ (Matthew 12. 40; John 1. 29). See Brown, 'Hermeneutics', *NJBC*, 71:46–7, p. 1156.

[32] In *De principiis*, Origen relates these three senses respectively to the human body, soul and spirit, although in his influential *Commentary on the Song of Songs* and elsewhere, the spiritual sense is applied to the soul. Origen distinguished four kinds of types in the Old Testament and two in the new, and his method is sometimes categorized as typology rather than allegory. See *De principiis* 4.1–3, H. Crouzel and

reflects his method, attitude and limitations.[33] These were transmitted through the works of the Latin Fathers and through translations of the Alexandrian's own works. The writings of Ambrose, Augustine, Jerome and Gregory the Great all reveal the influence of Alexandrian exegesis, as do the works of many others[34] such as the late eleventh-century compilers of the *Glossa ordinaria* who used translations of Origen's homilies.[35] Bernard of Clairvaux drew from them to such an extent that he was accused of having plagiarized the Alexandrian's commentary when writing his own sermons *On the Song of Songs;*[36] and Hildegard of Bingen's homilies show some striking parallels with Origen's *Homiliae in Genesim*, translated into Latin by Rufinus.[37]

Ambrose, Jerome, Augustine and Gregory the Great all had an impact on medieval commentators, who cited their works frequently.[38] Augustine set forth clearly the principle for typological analysis of the Old Testament: 'The New Testament lies hidden in the Old; the Old Testament is enlightened through the New.'[39] In *De doctrina christiana*, a work directed to the Christian exegete and presenting 'precepts for treating the Scriptures', Augustine develops his theory of signification and programme for the Christian exegete.[40] These strengthened the importance given to the alleg-

---

M. Simonetti, *Origène: Traité des principes, I*, SC 252 (Paris, 1978). See Daley, 'Origen's *De Principiis*', p. 16; K. J. Torjesen, ' "Body", Soul and "Spirit" in Origen's Theory of Exegesis', *American Theological Review* 67 (1985), 17–30; and for a brief summary, Schneiders, 'Scripture and Spirituality', pp. 11–12.

[33] Smalley, *The Bible*, p. 13.

[34] On Origen's influence on these and other writers, see de Lubac, *Medieval Exegesis, I*, pp. 150–9; Smalley, *The Bible*, pp. 20–24, and Schneiders, 'Scripture and Spirituality', pp. 13–14. B. Daley links Origen's plan for *De principiis* to the first part of *De doctrina christiana*, 'Origen's *De Principiis*', p. 18.

[35] See Smalley, *The Bible*, p. 13.

[36] See Leclercq, *Learning*, pp. 94–7, on Origen's influence on Bernard.

[37] See B. M. Kienzle, 'Hildegard of Bingen's Gospel Homilies and Her Exegesis of the Parable of the Prodigal Son', in *Im Angesicht Gottes suche der Mensch sich selbst* (forthcoming).

[38] A survey of the history of Western exegesis is beyond the scope of this book. See: Schneiders, 'Scripture and Spirituality', pp. 8–10, on the Alexandrian school; on the Antiochene, Smalley, *Bible*, pp. 14–19, and Schneiders, 'Scripture and Spirituality', p. 13. On John Cassian and his *collationes*, see Smalley, *Bible*, pp. 27–8; and pp. 41–2 on J. S. Eriugena and Angelom of Luxeuil. Gregory the Great's famous letter to bishop Leander of Seville appears in *S. Gregorii Magni Moralia in Iob Libri I–IX*, ed. Marcus Adriaen, *Ad Leandrum* 3, CCSL CXLIII (Turnhout, 1979), pp. 4–7. On Gregory's exegesis, see de Lubac, *Medieval Exegesis, I, passim*; R. A. Markus, *Gregory the Great and His World* (Cambridge, 1997), pp. 46–7. On Paul the Deacon's homiliary, see R. Grégoire, *Homéliaires liturgiques médiévaux. Analyse de manuscrits* (Spoleto, 1980). For the Carolingian period, see P. Riché, 'Instruments de travail et méthodes de l'exégète à l'époque carolingienne', in *La Bible*, pp. 147–58.

[39] *Quaest. in Heptateuchum* 2.73, *PL*, XXXIV, 625; cited by Brown, 'Hermeneutics', 71:38, p. 1154.

[40] *On Christian Doctrine*, Prologue, p. 3; 2.I.1–II.3, pp. 34–5; 2.VI.8, p. 38. Augustine

orical interpretation of the Scriptures and stressed the necessity of extensive preparation for the work of exegesis, a task to which only an intellectual elite could aspire.

The twelfth-century renaissance had an impact on exegesis, preceded by developments at the cathedral schools, which, as we observed in Chapter One, began to assume more importance than monastery schools during the eleventh century.[41] At the turn of the twelfth century, scholars at Laon under Master Anselm (d. 1117) and his brother Ralph laid the foundation for what would become in the Paris schools the textbook known as the *Glossa ordinaria*, a biblical commentary in the form of marginal and interlinear glosses. Its format and development were influenced by parallel works written on Roman and canon law, such as the *Decretum* of Gratian. The *Glossa ordinaria* became the standard reference for biblical study, just as Peter Lombard's *Sententiae*, completed around mid-century, served as the book for teaching doctrine.[42] Its usage was so widespread and its prestige so great that Pope Alexander III, when approached in 1179 about allowing lay people to preach, prohibited teaching the Bible without it; moreover, the Waldensians were reported to have it in translation.[43]

Cistercians participated in the revival of biblical scholarship during the twelfth century, principally through the numerous commentaries they composed, notably on the Song of Songs. Moreover, among the evidence of contact between Christian and Jewish scholars in the schools and in monastic circles, we find that Stephen Harding, abbot of Cîteaux, sought the help of Jews to correct the text of the Old Testament. Another Cistercian, Nicholas of Trois Fontaines, compared the three Latin translations of the Psalms and preferred Jerome's from the Hebrew, describing it as closest to the 'Hebrew truth'.[44]

Trends in twelfth-century exegesis intersected and took new directions at

---

explains in 2.IX.14, p. 42, that teachings about faith, the mores of living, hope and charity are stated openly in Scripture. See esp. pp. 38–40, 43–67, 79.

[41] Nonetheless, the monastic school at Bec with the great teachers Lanfranc (1005–89) and Anselm (d. 1109) placed the foundation for a new approach to Scripture that underlay the methods solidified by thirteenth-century scholasticism. See Châtillon, pp. 169–72.

[42] Châtillon, p. 193, nn. 71–5 cites the work of I. Brady and his 1971 edition of the *Sententiae* of P. Lombard. Brady, pp. 122–8, dates the *Sentences* around 1155–57.

[43] On the school at Laon, its achievements and the development of the *Gloss* at Paris, see G. Lobrichon, 'Une nouveauté: les gloses de la Bible', in *La Bible*, pp. 103–11; Châtillon, pp. 175–7. Lobrichon points out that the Waldensians, according to Walter Map, had translations of the *Gloss*; 'Une nouveauté', p. 111: 'librum . . . lingua conscriptum gallica, in quo textus et glossa psalterii plurimorumque legis utriusque librorum continebantur' (*Monumenta Germaniae Historica*, SS, 66). The background on Alexander III's 1179 pronouncement is found in: B. Bolton, 'Poverty as Protest: Some Inspirational Groups at the Turn of the XIIth Century', in *The Church in a Changing Society* (Uppsala, 1978), pp. 28–32.

[44] See Smalley, *Bible*, pp. 78–80.

the Abbey of St Victor in Paris, which had close ties to the Cistercians. Bernard of Clairvaux composed an Office for the feast of St Victor.[45] The Victorines, whose order combined aspects of the monastic and the secular, correspondingly incorporated developments from both schools and monasteries in their biblical exegesis. They too, especially Andrew of St Victor (d. 1175), were in contact with Jewish biblical scholars.[46] Hugh of St Victor's *Didascalion*, advised a special course of studies necessary before investigation of each of the three senses of scripture he distinguished: geography and history for the historical-literal; doctrine for the allegorical; and a broad sense of virtue and vice and of God's presence in nature for the tropological. Hugh's three-part division enhanced the importance of the historical sense and reflected his own interest in history and an historical view of the sacraments.[47] Thus, like Augustine before him, Hugh of Saint Victor emphasized the arduous preparation necessary for undertaking the work of exegesis.

The Victorine tradition was continued in the Paris schools under three famous masters: Peter Comestor, Peter the Chanter and Stephen Langton.[48] The Comestor and the Chanter both served as Chancellor of the University at Paris, and both had ties to Cistercian colleagues. The Chanter, introduced in Chapter One, will be discussed again in Chapters Four and Five. Less is known about the Comestor's circle and influence, but his *Historia scholastica* (*c.* 1170), using the historical-literal method of St Victor, presents biblical history in an accessible and simplified form that assured its success as a manual for understanding the Scriptures.[49] Hélinand of Froidmont's extensive use of the *Historia Scholastica* has been demonstrated.[50]

Despite the increased importance accorded to the historical-literal sense in the early Victorine school, the twelfth-century exegete inside and outside the monastery remained largely an uncoverer of allegories, an interpreter of symbols who revealed to his or her audience the hidden and most important meaning of the Scriptures. The exegete shared in the 'symbolist mentality' of

---

[45] Founded in 1108 by William of Champeaux, a dialectician who had studied at Laon and who was elected bishop of Châlons. See Châtillon, p. 178. Bernard describes the writing of the Office in Letter 398, *SBOp*, VIII, 377–9; *Letters* (430), pp. 501–2. See also *Ep.* 369, *SBOp*, VIII, 328; *Letters* (402), p. 474.

[46] Smalley discusses Andrew at length in *Bible*, pp. 112–95. See also Châtillon, pp. 183–4.

[47] Smalley, *Bible*, p. 103, and pp. 83–106 on Hugh of St Victor.

[48] Châtillon, pp. 194–5, notes that some of the Chanter's criticisms of commentators apply to the Victorines' methods, but that he differs from the Victorines more with respect to his view of the purpose of studying theology. The Chanter observed that the study of Scripture involved *lectio, disputatio* and *praedicatio*; distinct from Hugh of St Victor's more monastic statement that *lectio* should lead to *meditatio, oratio* and *contemplatio*. Langton is discussed on p. 196. See also. Smalley, *Bible*, pp. 178–80 (on their familiarity with Andrew of St Victor's work) and pp. 196–7 on these points; and Smalley, *Gospels*, pp. 37–84, 101–17.

[49] Châtillon, p. 195.

[50] See Chapter One, p. 34 n. 40, and E. Smits, 'Editing the *Chronicon*', pp. 269–89.

the twelfth century.[51] Medieval authors combed lapidaries and bestiaries for clues to the hidden meaning in the elements and creatures of nature. Colours, numbers, names, individual words, even the alphabet were considered signs that revealed spiritual realities. Myths were christianized by allegorical interpretation, and Christian scholars drew moral lessons from ancient authors through the method of *integumentum* or *involucrum*, enclosing the text in a wrapping of truth.[52]

Metaphor was also developed into analogy and used as a means to perceive spiritual reality. Cîteaux and St Victor, albeit in different styles, mastered this use of symbolism. The word *speculum* came to refer to the world and the elements therein as a mirror or reflection of God. History too had a spiritual meaning, and Alan of Lille wrote:

> Omnis mundi creatura
> Quasi liber et pictura
> Nobis est et speculum.
>
> (Every creature of the world is as a book or picture, and
> also a mirror for us.)

Finally, in the symbolism of the sacraments nature and history came together. Following Augustine's *De doctrina christiana*, everything was considered a sign or a figure, and the transference of words from the literal to the figurative sense was an essential operation for explaining the Scriptures. In short, the Alexandrian method dominated the twelfth century as it did the earlier Middle Ages, and Origen, as Chenu states, 'became, under cover of Augustine's prestige, the inspirer of the symbolist mentality of the Middle Ages'.[53] We shall see that the allegorical complexity of medieval exegesis and its insistence on the necessity for proper academic and spiritual preparation inevitably clashed with dissidents' claims to access to the Scriptures.

Since the hidden spiritual meaning of scripture was seen as the manifestation of eternal truths, medieval scholars of the Bible generally were not concerned in the sense of historicity that characterizes modern exegesis. Typology, 'something real and historical which announces something else that is also real and historical',[54] was pursued without a sense of history and became a predominant mode of medieval thought extending into politics and

---

[51] Chenu, *Nature*, p. 102: 'the conviction that all natural or historical reality possessed a *signification* which transcended its crude reality and which a certain symbolic dimension of that reality would reveal to man's mind. . . . Giving an account of things involved more than explaining them by reference to their internal causes; it involved discovering that dimension of mystery.'

[52] Chenu, *Nature*, pp. 104–11.

[53] Chenu, *Nature*, p. 123; earlier references in this paragraph are to pp. 113–17. Alan of Lille's lines are from *Rhythmus alter*, PL, CCX, 579A.

[54] E. Auerbach, 'Figura', in *Scenes from the Drama of European Literature* (New York, 1959), p. 29.

daily life. The influence of familiar types could be beneficial or harmful, as when the opposition of the synagogue and the church as darkness and light became associated with the Jewish people and contributed to anti-Jewish feeling.[55] Such typology was employed commonly by medieval Christian intellectuals writing against the Jews.[56]

The lack of a sense of history meant that resemblances between contemporary events and those narrated in the Bible were interpreted without regard to the changing circumstances of the thousands of intervening years. Moreover, twelfth-century polemicists extended typology to make analogies between texts and events rather than between one text and another. The usual pairing of the type, generally a person or thing in the Old Testament, and the antitype, the person or thing foreshadowed in the New Testament by the Old, was stretched into contemporary time; a current event then became the antitype or thing foreshadowed by its New Testament type. Commentators interpreted the lived text of the present according to the past text of Scripture: a twelfth-century dissident was considered the antitype of a New Testament false prophet, and the anxiety and warnings present in the New Testament text were transferred to the twelfth century. Identifying contemporary persons as dangerous, with biblical precedent, worsened the negative reaction against them. Similarly, finding antecedents for heretics in patristic literature or antiquity augmented the perception of threat.[57] In addition, medieval writers manipulated typology by apocalyptic thinking, interpreting the present occurrence or person as both antitype, foreshadowed by scripture, and prototype, harbinger of the end of time. Thus present was read in terms of both past and future, intensifying the danger that any symbol viewed this way could represent. The false prophet typified a double menace, pointing perilously backward and forward at the same time.

Scholars of both the Bible and the Middle Ages have commented on the dangers of typology, and the peril of overusing it. One medievalist observes the risks of Bede's extension of typology:

> For all of its effectiveness in bridging the gap between the world of the gospel story and the world of the listener, this extension of typological thinking into the present existential situation of the Christian is a risky business, for it presents a real danger to the essential basis of typology . . .

While typological exegesis may be based on historical reality, allegorical exegesis often ignores historical context and one biblical scholar warns that allegorizing of this type can lead to the treatment of events as 'ordained

---

[55] See Smalley, *Bible*, pp. 25–6.

[56] Dahan, *Les intellectuels chrétiens et les juifs*, p. 368. See also Chazan, *Stereotypes*, p. 47.

[57] This is similar to the transition that Chazan observes from traditional Christian imagery of the Jew as enemy to more dangerous stereotyping of a contemporary Jew as an enemy. *Stereotypes*, p. 52.

merely to teach moral lessons'.[58] Another biblical scholar states that, 'good typology does not stress continuity between the Testaments at the price of obliterating important aspects of discontinuity'.[59] Medieval exegetes showed not only little awareness of historical context; they also seemed at times oblivious to any notion of discontinuity in the parallels they wished to establish. Hélinand of Froidmont, for example, unflinchingly compared the Virgin Mary to an elephant in one sermon and to an ox in another when he sought to praise the chastity represented by the pachyderm and the diligence embodied in the ox.[60] Extending the similarities perceived between twelfth-century dissidents and New Testament false prophets is hardly surprising when one considers the leaps taken by the twelfth-century imagination.

The untangling of complicated symbolism fell to the educated. Within the monastic community, it was the special responsibility of the abbot to interpret the hidden meaning of the Scriptures. The abbot-interpreter combined the apostolic authority and responsibility of his teaching office with the sacramental authority of his ordination. The *Rule of Benedict* held him accountable to God for his teaching (*RB* 2). Many of Bernard of Clairvaux's sermons contains digressions or reflections on his responsibilities as abbot and in particular as interpreter of the scriptures.[61]

In the monastic view, understanding of the Scriptures came to a but a few through revelation. Bernard of Clairvaux describes the text and the world as tied closely to the work of divine creation. He states that whatever Christ said or performed or suffered was deliberate and that Christ's words and deeds are 'filled with hidden meanings, filled with salvation'. Thus, if we learn that something comes from Christ, we should 'attend to it not as if we are bringing forward a sort of improvisation, but as something which would not have happened without some reason, even if we do not know it before-hand'. God's disposition of Christ's work is analogous to the writer's arrangement of a text:

> For just as a writer arranges everything for specific reasons, so the things that are from God are appointed; and especially those performed by [his] majesty present in the flesh.[62]

---

[58] L. T. Martin, 'The Two Worlds in Bede's Homilies: The Biblical Event and the Listener's Experience', in *De Ore Domini: Preacher and Word in the Middle Ages*, ed. T. L. Amos, E. A. Green and B. M. Kienzle (Kalamazoo, MI, 1989), pp. 34–5; and G. W. H. Lampe, 'The Exposition and Exegesis of Scripture: To Gregory the Great', in *The Cambridge History of the Bible, II: The West from the Fathers to the Reformation*, ed. G. W. H. Lampe (Cambridge, 1969), pp. 165–6.

[59] Brown, 'Hermeneutics', 71:46, p. 1159.

[60] See Kienzle, 'Mary Speaks', 292–3.

[61] See, e.g., *Summer Season*, Ascension 4.2, p. 45; *SBOp*, V, 139; and Sixth Sunday after Pentecost 2.1, p. 123; *SBOp*, V, 209. In the latter, Bernard employs eucharistic metaphors for biblical interpretation. Stock devotes attention to this type of physical imagery in Bernard's sermons *On the Song of Songs*, *Implications*, pp. 413–14.

[62] *Summer Season*, Ascension 4.2, p. 45; *SBOp*, V, 139.

Hence for Bernard, text and events concealed meanings appointed or arranged intentionally by their creators, whether God, Christ, or a writer. Only a few, the literate in positions of recognized authority, could unravel such profound meaning.

Monastic literature

Monastic literature springs from the routine of monastic life, its interpretation of and permeation with the Scriptures, and its integration of the oral, aural and written word. Recitation, listening and reading were all key parts of the Cistercian day and all involved the Scriptures or scripturally based texts. Monks recited the office that incorporated much of the Scriptures. They listened to talks on the *Rule* with its strong scriptural base, to sermons – both read in the office and delivered – that commented on Scripture; and to readings from the lives of saints who lived out the Scriptures. Monks also read the Scriptures, sermons, commentaries, saints lives, and so on. Hence the vital place of the Scriptures in everyday life explains the primary influence of the Bible on monastic writing, its genres, themes and language.

Genres

A few literary genres, but with rich variations, dominate monastic writing: letters, sermons, exegetical commentaries, *florilegia* or collections of sayings and stories, and histories including saints' lives and chronicles.[63] Letters, sermons and exegetical commentaries interest our study the most. The techniques as well as the function of the three genres overlapped and their boundaries proved fluid, so that one often substituted for the other. The predominantly oral genre of the sermon took written form as a letter or a commentary. A letter could even contain a sermon, or letters and sermons could be sent together to a correspondent.[64] All three genres could be used to persuade their audience, whether a congregation or an individual reader. For example, one of the most stinging critiques of the late twelfth-century Waldensians is found in Geoffrey of Auxerre's commentary on the book of Revelation.[65] Although preceded with a salutation and introduction, letters frequently contained commentary on Scripture or were composed in the form of sermons.[66] Sermons were structured around scriptural verses like com-

---

[63] Leclercq reviews genres of monastic literature in *Learning*, pp. 153–72.

[64] See Kienzle, 'Monastic Sermon', p. 299.

[65] See Chapter Four, where *Apocalypsim* is discussed in more detail.

[66] See, for example, the commentary on Luke 10. 38 addressed from Ralph d'Escures (bishop of Rochester 1108–14, archbishop of Canterbury 1114–22) to William (abbot of Fécamp, c. 1078–1107) and Arnulf (abbot of Saint Martin of Troarn, c. 1088–1112), written between 1088 and 1107 and probably while Ralph was abbot of Sees, c. 1089–1104), when he fled to England. This homily is edited in B. M. Kienzle,

mentaries and often were exchanged between correspondents like letters.[67] The scholar relies on the salutation to signal a letter while indications of orality such as plural direct address or exhortations serve as hallmarks of the sermon.[68]

Consider the example of a community that receives a letter from a Bishop in response to their questions about the Scriptures. The letter substitutes for the bishop's physical presence to address them on the same issues. The Cistercian Hugh of Francigena, monk at Sylvanès, sent at least two letters to Gaucelin, bishop of Lodève (1161–87).[69] Hugh's two letters, probably composed around 1165, speak for the entire community and ask for clarification on passages of Scripture tied to doctrinal issues debated by orthodox and heterodox Christians. Bishop Gaucelin must have been considered an authority on such matters, for he questioned the Cathars at the 1165 Council of Lombers. Hugh's second letter describes how his brother monks received the bishop's letter with keen interest, reading silently but mouthing the words:

> It was snatched, stolen and taken by everyone and whoever was able to get it would read and reread it, sitting motionless, hidden from others in a corner of the cloister, opening his mouth like a pauper eating in secret.[70]

Hence Gaucelin's letter, directed in part against heterodoxy, functioned both as exegetical commentary and sermon within the silence of the monastery.

Letters

Monastic communication often took place through letters: exchanged between members of the same community, or sent over long distances from one monastery to another and at times circulated within the walls

---

'Exegesis on Luke 10:38 around 1100: Worcester MS F.94, f.1r–2r, A Tribute to James E. Cross', *Medieval Sermon Studies* 40 (Autumn 1997), 22–8. It was also translated into Old English and edited by R. D. N. Warner, *Early English Homilies from the Twelfth Century Ms. Vesp. D XIV*, EETS OS 152 (1917), pp. 134–9; printed as Anselm, Hom. 9, *PL*, CLVIII, 644–9 (with prologue as in ms., and in *PL*, CXCV, 1505–8 (without prologue). See A. Wilmart, 'Les homélies attribuées à S. Anselme', *Archives d'histoire doctrinale et littéraire du moyen âge*, 2 (1927), 5–29, 339–41.

[67] Peter of Celle's letter contain passages saying he hasn't had time to finish his sermons to send. See Kienzle, 'Monastic Sermon', p. 274, and *Ep.* 167, *PL*, CCII, 610.

[68] This problem is discussed in further detail in Kienzle, 'Monastic Sermon', pp. 291–8.

[69] The two letters and a reply to the first are edited in Kienzle, 'Hugo Francigena', pp. 273–311. An earlier article co-authored with Susan Shroff discusses the doctrinal issues: 'Cistercians and Heresy: Doctrinal Consultation in Some Twelfth-Century Correspondence from Southern France', *Cîteaux* 41 (1990), 159–66.

[70] 'De epistola quam misistis nobis quo gaudio, quanta laeticia, quanta devotione, et exultacione mentis a fratribus suscepta fuerit; possibilitatis meae non est edicere nec . . . memorare valebo, quo legendi studio, quo videndi desiderio rapiebatur ab omnibus, furabatur, tollebatur, et quicumque eam habere poterat in angulum claustri secedens semotus a ceteris legebat atque relegebat adaperiens os suum quasi pauper edens in occulto.' Kienzle, 'Hugo Francigena', p. 309, ll. 26–33.

like Bishop Gaucelin's letter to the monks at Sylvanès. Monastic correspondence substituted for conversations, involving messages of friendship,
advice, consolation or inspiration for someone dying, providing encouragement to persevere in the monastic vocation, or persuading someone to
undertake it. Letters of recommendation have been found as well as
business letters and others.[71] Monastic letters also served as position
papers in ecclesiastical disputes, and writers honed their persuasive and
combative rhetoric during quarrels over specific tithes or the superior way
to lead the monastic life.[72] Indeed, the eleventh and twelfth centuries
represented a sort of Golden Age of letter-writing in which textbooks on
the epistolary art were developed.[73]

   When read publicly, letters resembled the sermon in their hortatory
features and had the strong potential for persuasion. Most letters were
probably read aloud when received,[74] but important persuasive letters
could be addressed to a whole community or to the people of a region.
Moreover, we recall that sermons were at times recorded as letters. For
example, Hildegard of Bingen's 1163 public sermon at Cologne against
heresy has come down to us in the form of a letter, requested by the cathedral
clergy after her visit there.[75] Many congregations must have heard Bernard of
Clairvaux's crusading letters read, although only ten are extant.[76] Evidence
points to the public reading in the cathedral at Prague of Bernard's letter to
Duke Wadislaus of Bohemia; and following the Second Crusade, a chronicler
denounced the ecclesiastical drive for crusading, including the proclamation
of letters in churches.[77] One can readily imagine Bernard's letters on heresy in

---

[71] See Leclercq, *Learning*, pp. 176–81; Kienzle, 'New Introduction', *Letters*, pp. viii–xi.
[72] M. Newman discusses letters arguing the position of Cluny vs. that of Cîteaux,
   pp. 132–6. A classic model of persuasion is Bernard of Clairvaux's Letter 64 to
   Bishop Alexander of Lincoln, which utilizes forceful rhetoric to persuade the bishop
   to follow a certain course. That letter takes up the cause of a certain Philip who
   decided to become a monk at Clairvaux and was concerned that his family in
   England not suffer financial loss because of his decision. In three short sections, the
   letter employs fourteen direct scriptural citations and more allusions as it describes
   Philip's new life at Clairvaux with the image of his becoming a citizen of the
   heavenly Jerusalem. Bernard then makes a direct request of the bishop and finally
   exhorts him not to love the things of this world because death may catch him
   unprepared. *SBOp*, VII, 157–8; *Letters*, pp. 281–3.
[73] See G. Constable, *Letters and Letter Collections*, Typologie des sources du moyen âge
   occidental 17 (Turnhout, 1976), pp. 31–9.
[74] G. Constable, 'Papal, Imperial and Monastic Propaganda in the Eleventh and
   Twelfth Centuries', in *Preaching and Propaganda in the Middle Ages: Islam, Byzantium,
   Latin West.* Penn-Paris-Dumbarton Oaks Colloquia III, Session of October 20–5 1980,
   ed. G. Makdisi, D. Sourdel, J. Sourdel-Thoumine (Paris, 1980), pp. 181–2.
[75] Hildegard's 1163 Cologne sermon is in *Epistolarium* I, ed. L. Van Acker, CCCM XCI
   (Turnhout, 1991). XVr, pp. 34–44 plus two additional passages in appendixes.
[76] G. Constable, 'The Second Crusade as Seen by Contemporaries', *Traditio* 9 (1953),
   213–79 (p. 245).
[77] Cole, *Preaching*, pp. 47–8, 55.

southern France serving a similar purpose of propaganda. The public letter from his 1145 journey to Toulouse will be examined in the next chapter.

Sermons

While both sermon and letter were woven into the fabric of monastic life, the sermon played an even more integral role, because its preaching and reading aloud figured in the liturgy mandated by the *Rule*. Accordingly the monastic sermon genre encompassed the informal talks given at the community's gathering in the chapter house (after Prime in the Cistercian usages), the formal sermons delivered on feast-days, and the patristic sermon texts read for the nocturns of Matins, for edification in the refectory and for private meditation. Written evidence of this genre ranges from complete, stylistically polished texts such as many of Bernard of Clairvaux's sermons, to brief reports of what was preached on a given occasion, to short summaries or outlines of sermons, either written by the author before delivering a sermon or taken down by a secretary while the sermon was being preached.[78]

Sermons, like letters, were diffused by courier through the network of monastic houses. Furthermore, sermons counted among the books necessary for founding a new house and conducting its liturgy: homiliary, office and refectory lectionaries, and books for daily reading. A manuscript from the Swiss Benedictine abbey in Engelberg, obviously French Cistercian in its script and decoration, demonstrates something about how sermons were acquired and propagated. The initial rubric reads: 'Holy father Bernard spoke these sermons to his pupils, but his secretary Geoffrey of Auxerre endeavoured to propagate them with his stylus.' Hence at Geoffrey's instigation the manuscript had travelled from France to Switzerland through the monastic network, perhaps as a gift.[79]

With respect to content, the monastic sermon generally looks inward at life within the monastery and at the spiritual journey of the community and its individual members. Sometimes it provides a glimpse of problems in observing the *Rule*, such as snoozing or snoring during sermons, and occasionally biographical information can be gleaned from its pages. Seldom, however, does it incorporate information from the outside world. Studies of Bernard of Clairvaux's sermons show that the more he revised his sermons, the less they reflect concrete details of daily life, even within the monastery.[80] Bernard is not unique in that regard. Julien of Vézelay's sermons, for example, were collected during the period when pilgrims flocked there to see the veil of Mary Magdalene, yet his texts reflect almost

---

[78] Kienzle, 'Monastic Sermon', pp. 273–8.

[79] J. Leclercq and H. Rochais, 'La tradition manuscrite des sermons liturgiques', *Scriptorium* 15 (1961), 240–84 (p. 267).

[80] Kienzle, 'Monastic Sermon', pp. 290–1, 312–16. On the specific case of Bernard's Circumcision sermon, see J. Leclercq, 'Etudes sur S. Bernard et le texte de ses écrits', *Analecta Cisterciensis* 9 (1953), 55–62.

nothing of those events. He apologizes for a seeming transgression of the *Rule* when he announces in one sermon an important victory for the Christian armies in the Holy Land.[81] These examples reflect a general characteristic of monastic literature to look inward. Indeed, Bernard's model of the revised literary sermon became the standard for later Cistercian sermon collections.

Overall then, the focus of monastic sermons, as one would expect, is monastic culture and particularly its strong scriptural grounding. Generally, therefore, we turn in vain to monastic sermon collections when seeking information about heresy in the world. This tendency of monastic sermons to centre exclusively on monastic theology or spirituality explains in part the notable lack of sermons preserved from the campaigns against heresy. Events in the world entered more often into letters than into sermons. While monastic sermons are a rich source for monastic culture, rarely do they transport our view outside the cloister. We recall that for the Second Crusade, Bernard's letters remain but his sermons do not. This adds to the difficulty of reconstructing preaching against heresy from sermon texts.

Sermons and commentaries

The link between sermon and commentary grows from the community interpretation of the Scriptures and of the *Rule*, charged to the abbot but sometimes delegated to others. It has roots also in the patristic tradition. Augustine and Gregory the Great composed works that established patterns for writing commentaries in sermon form, with collections such as Augustine's *In epistolam Joannis ad Parthos tractatus X*[82] and Gregory's *Homiliae in Hiezechihelem prophetam* and *Homiliae XL in evangelia*.[83] Bede continued Gregory's work with numerous commentaries and two collections of homilies that resemble commentaries.[84] The influence of Augustine, Gregory and Bede on monastic exegesis extended to the choice of the genre employed for written reflection on the Scriptures.

Twelfth-century monastic writers gathered sermons into collections that were often organized like commentaries and served a similar function: to assist the *lectio divina*, the meditation on the Scriptures. Hildegard of Bingen's nuns preserved the texts of her talks or sermons to them on the Gospels, the *Expositiones evangeliorum* that constitute a running commentary on each

---

[81] Kienzle, 'Monastic Sermon', pp. 306–12 and for Julien of Vézelay specifically, *Sermons*, ed. D. Vorreux, 2 vols., SC 192–3 (Paris, 1972), I, S9, pp. 208 and 210.

[82] Augustine, *Commentaire de la Première Epître de S. Jean*, trans. P. Agaësse, SC 75 (Paris, 1984); *PL*, XXXV, 1977–2062; Abridged English version in *Love One Another, My Friends. St Augustine's Homilies on the First Letter of John*, trans. J. Leinenweber (San Francisco, 1989).

[83] *Homiliae in Hiezechihelem prophetam*, ed. M. Adriaen CCSL 142 (Turnhout, 1971); *Homiliae XL in evangelia*, *PL*, LXXVI, 1075–1312; English translation: *Forty Gospel Homilies*, trans. D. Hurst CS 123 (Kalamazoo, MI, 1990).

[84] *Bedae Homiliae evangelii*, ed. D. Hurst, CCSL 122 (Turnhout, 1955); *Homilies on the Gospels*, trans. L. T. Martin and D. Hurst, 2 vols., CS 110–11 (Kalamazoo, MI, 1991).

phrase of the Gospel text for the day. At least two of those concern Catharism.[85] Bernard of Clairvaux composed several series of sermons, many of which are grouped according to a structure or link based on Scripture. While the most notable examples of these series are Bernard's and other Cistercians' commentaries on the Song of Songs, Bernard and his successors composed sermons on other texts.[86] These scripturally linked and organized sermons underscore the fusion of preaching and exegesis. Sermons from Bernard of Clairvaux's series on the Song of Songs and Geoffrey of Auxerre's on Revelation provide anti-heretical material that our study will examine.

Themes and the power of words

The themes of monastic literature like its forms derive from the experience of living according to the *Rule of Benedict*. Its vocabulary is predominantly scriptural; accordingly, key words and images from Scripture are repeated to develop a motif or a theme. The word *castellum*, for example, in the Latin translation of Luke 10. 38, 'Jesus entered into a certain city' (*castellum*), sparks the monastic writer's imagination to describe the process of preparing a place for God in the heart in terms of constructing a spiritual castle in the soul.[87] Bernard of Clairvaux, in two sermons on Mark 8. 1–9, interprets the seven loaves with which Jesus fed the crowd as seven elements necessary for salvation. He also views the crowd's three-day wait as fear, holiness and reason, and as the journey into the desert that his listeners must undertake to offer a pleasing sacrifice to God.[88]

In the emotive flow of words intended for inspiring meditation, all saturated with the language and imagery of the Bible, monastic authors move from one image to the next, building associations. Various mental processes of association have been discerned in their writing, including reminiscence, the phenomenon whereby verbal echoes stir the memory and evoke phrases from Scripture that in turn suggest other biblical allusions. A word functions like a hook, as Jean Leclercq explains: 'it catches hold of one or several others which become linked together and make up the fabric of the exposé'. This phenomenon repeats itself as motifs are created and themes developed. The hook-words form groups of quotations, 'like variations on the

---

[85] 'Expositiones evangeliorum', ed. J.-B. Pitra, in *Analecta S. Hildegardis*, Analecta sacra 8 (Rome, 1882), pp. 245–327. A new edition is in preparation by B. M. Kienzle and C. Muessig for CCCM.

[86] Bernard wrote homilies on the *Missus est* and on the psalm *Qui habitat*. Sermons on the Song were composed by Bernard (86 in number), Gilbert of Hoyland (148) and John of Ford (120). Other series include exegetical commentaries such as Ogier of Locedio's on chapters 13–15 of the Gospel according to John. See Kienzle, 'Monastic Sermon', p. 300.

[87] See Kienzle, 'Monastic sermon', pp. 282–3; and 'Exegesis on Luke 10:38', pp. 22–8.

[88] Sermons One and Two for the Sixth Sunday after Pentecost, *Summer Season*, pp. 119–27; *SBOp*, V, 206–13.

same theme'. Hearing the sound of a word therefore sets off a sort of 'chain reaction of associations' that unites words connected to one another merely by chance.[89]

At the same time that words appear in the streams of associations produced in the memory and imagination, they also reflect stylistic patterns cultivated by Christian writers since the patristic era. Monastic writers, like their patristic predecessors whose writings drew on patterns of classical authors, were fond of parallel constructions that highlight key words and phrases, all the more so when those words or phrases are antithetical. Bernard's style illuminates the patterns of Christian Latin writers who followed Augustine and were influenced by his strong taste for parallelism and antithesis. It also reveals a clearly Cistercian pattern, as Christine Mohrmann observes: 'a principle of order and an austere and rigorous structure appear under the surface of sonorous words; [that structure and order] recall the architecture inspired by the Cistercian movement and their *compositio*, an harmonious arrangement balanced in all parts, is an essential element'.[90]

Austerity, structure, harmony; these are the characteristic elements of Cistercian architecture discernible beneath the antithetical pairings and the richly figurative and sonorous words of Bernard's writing. While not always in agreement with modern taste, all these features of monastic writing taken together produce a rich and beautiful literature, which at its best leads the mind to prayer and meditation and thus to peaceful contemplation.

Austerity, structure and harmony also characterize the Cistercian world-view and confident belief in a right social and ecclesiastical order, where each member of society belongs to the body, the image for the Church extended to the world, and performs a specific function. Bernard of Clairvaux's description of the writer's work and its connection to divine order demonstrates how closely knit in his thinking were the patterns of human and divine creation and order. Moreover, monastic life and work, a concept unified in and by the *Rule of Benedict*, was subject to the abbot's authority. Exegesis of images like the bride's body in the Song of Songs, illustrated above in a sermon of Geoffrey of Auxerre, connected the monastery and the Church, which was the frame for viewing the world. Challenges to the Church's authority threatened to disrupt the entire order, human and divine. Harmony depended on structure and imbalance destroyed it.

Furthermore, some of the elements of monastic literature – its taste for symbol and allegory, disregard for the historical-literal sense of the text, reverence for the Fathers, skill at persuasive writing, and patterns of word association – could serve a purpose other than inspiring contemplation, but

---

[89] Leclercq, *Learning*, pp. 73–4.
[90] C. Mohrmann, 'Observations sur la langue et le style de S. Bernard', Introduction to *SBOp*, II, xi–xii.

also within the confines of scriptural genre and language: the denunciation of what was seen as false doctrine and behaviour, and the persuasion against allying with it. Underneath the stylistic and exegetical techniques lay the monastic principle of order, which dissidents defied. The next chapter, focusing on Bernard of Clairvaux and events from the mid-twelfth century, begins our examination of monastic preaching and writing against heresy: the clash of differing views of the Church and the religious life.

CHAPTER THREE

Bernard of Clairvaux, the 1143/44 Sermons and the 1145 Preaching Mission: From the Domestic to the Lord's Vineyard

At the opening of his Sermon 65 *On the Song of Songs*, Bernard of Clairvaux explains to his audience that it is necessary for him to preach a third sermon on Song of Songs 2. 15: 'Seize for us the little foxes that are destroying the vineyard'. His first sermons, he explains, gave sufficient warning to his brothers so that they could guard against the three sorts of foxes who might ravage their vineyard, interpreted as the vices that could lead them astray on their spiritual journey in the monastic life. However, the abbot expresses his anxiety about the Lord's vineyard and its vines, which are not so secure. He feels that he must turn from inside to outside, away from domestic monastic matters in order to be of use in affairs of general concern.

> I have examined one verse for you in two sermons; I am preparing a third on the same verse if listening will not be tiresome [for you]. And I consider the third necessary. For I think that what I have done in the two sermons is adequate for our domestic vineyard, which you are, for protecting it against the snares of three sorts of foxes . . . who are skilled and practised at representing evil things under the appearance of the good. Truly the Lord's vineyard is not so [well protected]. I speak of that vineyard which has filled the earth, of which we too are part: an exceedingly great vineyard, planted by the Lord's hand, redeemed by his blood, watered by his word, increased by grace and fertilized by the Spirit. Therefore caring more for [our] particular property, I have been less useful to the universal [vineyard]. For its sake I am troubled by the hoard of those demolishing it, the scarcity of its defenders, and the difficulty of its defence.[1]

[1] *SBOp*, II, 172: 'Duos vobis super uno capitulo disputavi sermones; tertium in eodem paro, si audire non taedeat. Et necessarium reor. Nam quod ad nostram quidem spectat domesticam vineam, quae vos estis, satis me arbitror in duobus fecisse sermonibus pro munimento illi adversus insidias tripertiti generis vulpium . . . gnari et assueti mala sub specie boni inducere. Verum dominicae vineae non ita. Illam loquor, quae implevit terram, cuius et nos portio sumus: vineam grandem nimis, Domini plantatam manu, emptam sanguine, rigatam verbo, propagatam gratia, fecundatam spiritu. Ergo plus proprii curam gerens, incommune minus profui. Movet me autem pro ipsa multitudo demolientium eam, defensantium paucitas,

Fig. 3. The medieval quarter of Verfeil (Haute-Garonne), the town that Bernard of Clairvaux cursed as the 'seat of Satan'.

This process of turning from inside to outside – from the monastery to the Church in the world, and in Bernard's imagery, from the domestic monastic vineyard to the Lord's vineyard – brings us to examine the role of Bernard of Clairvaux, his deeds and his works, in setting patterns of Cistercian involvement in the world that would last into the early thirteenth century.

Bernard entered Cîteaux in 1113, along with a group of around thirty men, including four of his brothers. He came from a noble family and persuaded some of his brothers to take on a higher calling than arms, the *militia Christi*, and become spiritual soldiers for Christ. Bernard quickly distinguished himself, becoming abbot of the new foundation at Clairvaux in 1115. At first involved in exterior affairs through letter writing, Bernard began to engage himself more extensively outside the monastery during the 1130s. His pursuit of Abelard and his support of Pope Innocent II against the antipope Anacletus (Peter Leonis) are well documented. Likewise history remembers his justification for the order of the Knights Templar, espoused in the treatise, *In Praise of the New Knighthood*. The introduction to the rule for the Knights Templar, whose formation was approved in 1129, credits Bernard's advice for its composition. In relation to the crusade to the Holy Land, the second of which he preached at Vézelay in 1147 after his 1145 preaching mission against heresy, Bernard advocated an ideal knighthood, a harmonious union of spirituality and chivalry tied together by the willingness to undertake penitential service and become a martyr to protect the Holy Land.[2] The Cistercians followed the Cluniac efforts to control knights' behaviour but added this inner goal and also encouraged knights to fight for causes the monks advocated.[3] The ideal knighthood was doomed to failure, however, an 'irreconcilable contradiction', as one scholar puts it,[4] but one that reflected the views on employment of 'restricted violence' developed during the Gregorian Reform, that is, justifying violence under certain conditions, according to the goal, means, and intentions.[5]

These ideas brewed in Bernard's mind during the 1130s, before he was

---

difficultas defensionis.' Translation is mine. The text is also translated in: *Song*, III, 179–80.

[2] For Bernard's biography, see sources cited in the Introduction at n.13; and on Bernard and the Second Crusade, see G. Constable, 'The Second Crusade as Seen by Contemporaries', *Traditio* 9 (1953), 213–79 (pp. 276–8); and various articles in *The Second Crusade and the Cistercians*, ed. M. Gervers (New York, 1992).

[3] See Newman, p. 183.

[4] R. J. Zwi Werblowsky, 'Introduction', to 'In Praise of the New Knighthood', in Bernard of Clairvaux, *Treatises III*, CF19 (Kalamazoo, MI, 1977), p. 117.

[5] J. Leclercq discusses the development of theories on restricted violence, notably the work of Anselm of Lucca, who attempted to maintain a balance between violence and charity: 'Saint Bernard's Attitude toward War', in *Studies in Medieval Cistercian History, II*, ed. J. R. Sommerfeldt, CS 24 (Kalamazoo, MI, 1976), pp. 7–10.

writing and preaching against heresy outside the Church.[6] The contradiction that emerges from his writing about the new knighthood stands in parallel to the ambiguities in his thought about dealing with heresy. While opposing the use of force to compel orthodox belief, he nonetheless intervened in the affairs of another region of France, and his example led other white monks to engage in the active life, as they confronted the heresy that they perceived as a threat to the existence of the Lord's vineyard and ultimately their own. Bernard experienced tensions over his pursuit of the active life: he described himself as a chimera, as we have seen, and Brian P. McGuire points to the possibility of seeing 'two Bernards': the abbot and the 'ecclesiastical politician'.[7]

The investigation of Bernard of Clairvaux's role in the campaign against heresy focuses on his works, highlighting the patterns of rhetoric and thought that demonize heretics and associate heresy with pollution, threat to the social order and apocalypticism. Sources include Bernard's sermons *On the Song of Songs* 63–66, his letters (especially 241 and 242), accounts of his 1145 journey in the chronicle of William of Puylaurens, the *Vita prima* (a hagiographical text), and the *Exordium magnum*, a laudatory account of the Cistercians' beginnings.[8] The sermons, the *Vita prima*, and the *Exordium magnum* would have been read in Cistercian houses and influenced the monastic community confronting dissidence around them. They could have also provided material for preachers. The sermons *On the Song of Songs* circulated quickly and extensively, even as Bernard was composing them.[9] The letters were assuredly disseminated even more broadly, by public reading. Letter 242, addressed to the people of Toulouse, resembles others of Bernard's letters that were read publicly, such as those urging the Second Crusade. One of Bernard's letters describes a process of dissemination that could apply in a localized fashion to letter 242. Letter 394 (dated to 1147) advocating an expedition against the Wends, who posed a possible obstacle to the Second Crusade, alludes to the decree made in Frankfurt that 'a copy of this letter should be carried everywhere and that the bishops and priests should proclaim it to the people of God'.[10] In that respect, the

---

[6] A. Bredero dates the *Liber ad Milites Templi de laude novae militiae* between 1128 and 1138: *Bernard of Clairvaux*, p. 145.

[7] McGuire, *Difficult Saint*, p. 17. On the chimera image, see p. 30.

[8] An earlier version of this chapter appears as 'Tending the Lord's Vineyard: Cistercians, Rhetoric and Heresy, 1143–1229. Part I: Bernard of Clairvaux, the 1143 Sermons and the 1145 Preaching Mission', *Heresis* 25 (1995), 29–61; sections of it are reused here with the editor's permission.

[9] J. Leclercq, C. H. Talbot and H. Rochais, 'Introduction', in *SBOp*, I, xv, n. 6; xviii; xx, n. 1; xxiv, on the manuscript tradition of the *Sermones super Cantica Canticorum*.

[10] Kienzle, 'New Introduction', in *Letters*, p. xi; and Letter 394, p. 467; Ep. 457, *SBOp*, VIII, 432–3. The expedition against the Wends is discussed by Leclercq, 'Bernard's Attitude toward War', pp. 20–2.

letter functioned as a sermon, and its reading aloud as the equivalent of preaching.

The 1143/44 sermons and the 1145 preaching mission

Bernard of Clairvaux's personal and direct intervention in the Midi began in 1145, when the Cistercian abbot participated in a mission led by the papal legate Alberic of Ostia. However, Bernard's attitude toward heresy is already apparent in some of his sermons *On the Song of Songs*, probably written in 1143/44. Those sermons elucidate patterns of thought and rhetoric that should be examined before moving to the 1145 documents.

Before his journey to Occitania in 1145, Bernard was also aware of the heresy that would be labelled as Catharism around twenty years later. In 1143, Everwin of Steinfeld, prior of a Praemonstratensian community near Cologne, requested that Bernard speak out against groups of heretics in the Rhineland.[11] Sermons 65 and 66 *On the Song of Songs* constitute Bernard's reply and the most frequently discussed sources for his views on the treatment of heresy and heretics.[12]

Everwin opens his letter with praises of Bernard's eloquence, especially his interpretation of the Song of Songs. Clearly aware of the Cistercian's work in progress, the Praemonstratensian casts the abbot of Clairvaux as the bridegroom having wine poured (John 2. 10) from successive jugs but saving the best for last. The time has come, says Everwin, to draw from the fifth jug, against the heretics who, in the words of I Timothy 4. 1–3, will come at the end of time.[13] Clearly for Everwin, the signs distinguishing those heretics in

---

[11] Everwin's letter, *PL*, CLXXXII, 676–80, is discussed by A. Brenon, 'La lettre d'Evervin de Steinfeld à Bernard de Clairvaux de 1143: un document essentiel et méconnu', *Heresis* 25 (1995), 7–28. English translation of the letter in WE, pp. 127–32.

[12] Sermons 65 and 66 are in *Song*, III, 179–206, and *SBOp*, II, 172–88. G. Cracco argues that Sermon 65 should be dated after Bernard's 1145 journey; Cracco emphasizes the lack of correspondence between Sermon 65 and Everwin's letter, saying that only Sermon 66 replies to Everwin. He also feels that Sermons 63 and 64 do not deal strictly with heresy. G. Cracco, 'Bernardo e i movimenti ereticali', in *Bernardo Cistercense: Atti del XXVI Convegno Storico Internazionale, Todi, 8–11 ottobre 1989*, ed. E. Menesto, Academia Tudertina. Centro di studi sulla spiritualità medievale dell'università degli Studi di Perugia 3 (Spoleto, 1990), pp. 165–86, esp. pp. 179–80. However, Sermon 64's treatment of unauthorized preaching and persuasion of heretics contradicts his view, in my opinion. As for Sermons 65–66, my analysis will underscore points the two have in common. I do not find Cracco's arguments strong enough to reverse prevailing scholarly opinion on dating the letters.

[13] Epistola CDXXXII, *PL*, 182, 676B–677A: 'Laetabor ego super eloquia tua, sicut qui invenit spolia multa, qui nobis memoriam abundantis suavitatis Dei eructare in omnibus dictis et scriptis vestris soletis, maxime in Cantico. De hydria quantum, sanctissime pater, habes nobis modo propinare! De . . . quinta, contra haereticos circa finem saeculi venturos, de quibus per Apostolum manifeste Spiritus dicit: 'In novissimis temporibus . . .' Jam tempus est ut de quinta haurias, et in medium

the Pauline epistle (attention to the teachings of demons, hypocrisy, opposition to marriage and abstinence from certain foods) also mark the people he
observes before him in the region of Cologne. He claims that the 'new
heretics' are emerging everywhere and in nearly all churches, rising up
from the pit of the abyss, that is from Hell. Everwin requests that Bernard
explicate Song of Songs 2. 15: 'Seize for us the little foxes that are destroying
the vineyards', a verse that he finds appropriate for the problem and for
Bernard's fifth jug. He appeals for the Cistercian to distinguish all the
elements of the heresy and provide arguments and authorities from the
orthodox faith to combat them. The latter phrase ('ut omnes partes haeresis
illorum . . . distinguas, et contrapositis rationibus et auctoritatibus nostrae
fidei, illas destruas')[14] summarizes succinctly the method used to some
degree throughout the literature against heresy: clarify what the errors are
and destroy them by counter positing arguments and authorities from the
faith. That method, a reflection of the disputations taught in the schools,
provided an outline that debaters and preachers could adapt and employ
when they confronted dissidents who frequently evidenced confident knowledge of the Scriptures. Bernard's usage of the techniques of disputation has
been minimized or denied by some scholars, but we shall see that he echoes
these words of Everwin's and views his own writing as appealing to reason
(*ratio*).[15]

After making his request of Bernard, Everwin turns to an exposition of the
heresy and a narrative of the events that have transpired in his region: the
public examination of a group of heretics; the burning of three, which was
opposed by Everwin, even though he associates them strongly with the
Devil;[16] a reported statement of their apostolic faith and disdain for the

proferas contra novos haereticos, qui circumquaque jam fere per omnes Ecclesias
ebulliunt de puteo abyssi, quasi jam princeps illorum incipiat dissolvi, et instet dies
Domini.'
[14] *PL*, CLXXXII, 677B.
[15] On Bernard's lack of disputation skills, see D. Iogna-Prat, 'L'argumentation
défensive', in *Inventer l'hérésie?*, pp. 87–118 (pp. 91–4, 117), where Iogna-Prat
concludes that: 'le discours de Bernard de Clairvaux relève exclusivement de
l'imprécation. Pour lui, l'hérésie est sans contenu; c'est une abomination qu'il
convient de mettre au jour et de dénoncer, l'acte de langage ayant le pouvoir
sacramental de réprimer.' In my view, Bernard resorts to both imprecation and
reasoning, responding to Everwin amidst and in spite of his denunciations. Iogna-
Prat relies to some degree on Fichtenau's synchronic juxtaposition of the growth of
heresy and the development of procedures based on reason; Iogna-Prat places
Bernard outside this emphasis on reason in the schools. See Fichtenau, pp. 105–7.
M. Newman, in contrast, argues that differences between the Cistercians and the
schoolmasters have been exaggerated and points to the use of scholastic arguments
by Bernard of Clairvaux, Geoffrey of Auxerre, and others. Newman, pp. 38–40. See
also below, p. 86, and Chapter One, pp. 33–5, of this book on the schools.
[16] *PL*, CLXXXII, 677C: '. . . rapti sunt a populis nimio zelo permotis, nobis tamen
invitis, et in ignem positi, atque cremati . . .'; 'Hic, sancte pater, vellem, si praesens

world, a summary of their practices, especially baptism, and of their quarrels with other heretics in the area. One group rejects baptism by water in favour of the imposition of hands (early Cathars) while the other rejects infant baptism but apparently not the then traditional administration of the sacrament with water (proto-Waldensians).[17]

Everwin's closing appeal urges Bernard to take up his pen against the 'wild beasts' (*feras*), later called monsters (*haec tot monstra*). Some who are reconciled to the Church report that they are a world-wide movement and the three who were burnt even professed a faith which had remained hidden in Greece and other lands since the times of the martyrs. They call themselves apostles and have their own pope. Their opponents, the other group of heretics Everwin distinguished above, reject the Roman pope's authority but have no pope of their own.[18]

The last section of Everwin's letter to Bernard completes the impression of fear that encircles the two popular movements he describes. The one group is reported as widespread, threatening and having ancient roots; the other defies the authority of the Church. The language with which he describes both groups reflects the danger he perceives. He dehumanizes and demonizes his adversaries, especially those 'apostles of Satan' whom he views as offending conventional sexual morality by modelling themselves on the apostles and 'having women among them'.[19]

---

essem, habere responsionem tuam, unde istis diaboli membris tanta fortitudo in sua haeresi, quanta vix etiam invenitur in valde religiosis in fide Christi.'

[17] *PL*, CLXXXII, 678CD: 'Et talem baptismum per impositionem manuum debere fieri conati sunt ostendere testimonio Lucae, qui in Actibus Apostolorum describens baptismum Pauli, quem ab Anania suscepit ad praeceptum Christi, nullam mentionem fecit de aqua, sed tantum de manus impositione: et quidquid invenitur tam in Actibus Apostolorum, quam in Epistolis Pauli, de manus impositione, ad hunc baptismum volunt pertinere.' Everwin goes on to distinguish the 'electi' who have received the baptism by laying on of hands and can thus baptize others, the 'credentes', and the 'auditores' who can be received among the 'credentes', also by the imposition of hands.

[18] *PL*, CLXXXII, 679CD–680A: 'Contra haec tam multiforma mala rogamus, sancte pater, ut evigilet sollicitudo vestra, et contra feras arundinis stilum dirigatis. . . . Sed volumus, pater ut haec armatura propter nos simpliciores et tardiores, vestro studio in unum collecta, contra haec tot monstra ad inveniendum fiat paratior, et in resistendo efficacior. Noveritis etiam, domine, quod redeuntes ad Ecclesiam nobis dixerunt, illos habere maximam multitudinem fere ubique terrarum sparsam, et habere eos plures ex nostris clericis et monachis. Illi vero qui combusti sunt, dixerunt nobis in defensione sua, hanc haeresim usque ad haec tempora occultatam fuisse a temporibus martyrum, et permanisse in Graecia, et quibusdam aliis terris. Et hi sunt illi haeretici, qui se dicunt apostolos, et suum papam habent. Alii papam nostrum annihilant, nec tamen alium praeter eum habere fatentur. Isti apostolici Satanae habent inter se feminas (ut dicunt) continentes, viduas, virgines, uxores suas, quasdam inter electas, quasdam inter credentes; quasi ad formam apostolorum, quibus concessa fuit potestas circumducendi mulieres.'

[19] The language distinguishing the two groups at the end of the letter is somewhat

Bernard's reply in the sermons *On the Song of Songs*

In response to Everwin of Steinfeld, Bernard reflects on Song of Songs 2. 15 in Sermons 65 and 66, usually cited as the Cistercian abbot's reply to the Praemonstratensian prior. Bernard's exposition of Song of Songs 2. 15 begins earlier, however, with Sermon 63, where he interprets the vineyard generally as the spiritual person and the foxes as those who undermine the person's effort to bear the fruits of salvation. He then views the passage in a more strictly monastic context. In Sermon 64 he first continues the monastic interpretation undertaken in 63, explaining the foxes as temptations. In section 3 of the former sermon (64), he takes up the topic of unauthorized preaching by monks, which relates to the non-commissioned preaching by heretics that he will denounce in his Epistle 242. Citing Hebrews 5. 4, Romans 10. 15 and Jerome's assertion that the duty of monks is 'not to teach, but to weep',[20] Bernard states that these sources 'make it clear that it is not expedient for a monk to preach in public, nor is it seemly for a novice, nor proper for anyone unless he is expressly sent'. The temptation to preach publicly is thus a fox, evil disguised as good,[21] as is the excessive abstinence discussed in section 5 of this same sermon. Section 8 continues the allegory, but turns sharply to consider the foxes as heresies or heretics, who like the temptation-foxes must be caught. Here Bernard makes it clear that he is not advocating the use of force: heretics should be captured by arguments and not by arms: *capiantur, dico, non armis, sed argumentis.*[22] The abbot also

ambiguous in its use of demonstrative pronouns. The referential pattern of 'alii . . . istis . . . Isti' used in 678D refers to early Cathars ('alii') and then proto-Waldensians ('istis', 'Isti'). In 679D the pattern is reversed. 'Illi', 'hi', ad 'illi' clearly refer to early Cathars (having roots in Greece, calling themselves apostles and having their own pope); 'Alii' denotes the proto-Waldensians (who deny the Roman pope but do not have another); and 'Isti', which might seem to refer to the proto-Waldensians as in 678D, designates the heretics who are organized into 'electi' and 'credentes'. clearly a mark of the Cathars. A. Brenon argues convincingly that 'Isti apostolici Satanae' applies to the early Cathars and not to the second group of proto-Waldensians. 'La lettre d'Evervin', pp. 18–28.

[20] Jerome, *Contra Vigilantium* 15; *PL*, XXIII, 367A.

[21] *SBOp*, II, 168: 'Ex his nempe claret et certum est, quod publice praedicare nec monacho convenit, nec novitio expedit, nec non misso licet. Porro contra haec tria venire, quanta conscientiae demolitio est? Ergo quidquid tale animo suggeratur, sive sit illud tua cogitatio, sive immissio per angelum malum, dolosam agnosce vulpeculam, id est mal sub specie boni.' *Song*, III, 172. See also Constable, 'The Second Crusade', pp. 276–8; and J. Brundage, 'St. Bernard and the Jurists', in *Second Crusade and the Cistercians*, pp. 25–34 (p. 29).

[22] *SBOp*, II, 170: 'Simplex est sensus, ut haeretici capiantur potius quam effugentur. Capiantur, dico, non armis, sed argumentis, quibus refellantur errores eorum; ipsi vero, si fieri potest, reconcilientur Catholicae, revocentur ad veram fidem. Haec est enim voluntas ejus qui vult omnes homines salvos fieri et ad agnitionem veritatis venire (I Timothy 2. 3) . . . Quod si reverti noluerit, nec convinctus post primam jam

specifies the method a churchman should employ for persuading a heretic: 'convincing him of the error in such a way as to convert him', and later, when he asserts the importance of refuting a heretic:

> Let it not be supposed, however, that it is a small and unimportant thing for a man to vanquish a heretic and refute his heresies, making a clear and open distinction between what is true and what seems true, and exposing the fallacies of false teaching by plain and irrefutable reasoning in such a way as to bring into captivity a depraved mind which had set itself up against the knowledge revealed by God.[23]

Like Everwin of Steinfeld's request for clear exposition of error supported by arguments and authorities, Bernard's view on how to debate or preach to heretics supposes that clear reasoning furnishes the best method to achieve a heretic's conversion. Bernard will however contradict himself in Sermon 66.12, where he claims that heretics cannot understand logical argumentation. This refusal and its rhetorical articulation ground in part the assertion that Bernard was not skilled in the art of disputation.[24]

In Sermon 64.8, Bernard considers what to do when a heretic does not bend to clarity:

> But if he will not be converted or convinced even after a first and second admonition, then, according to the Apostle, he is to be shunned as one who is completely perverted. Consequently I think it better that he should be driven away or even bound rather than be allowed to spoil the vines.[25]

Here the abbot leaves the door open for shunning, banishing or arresting heretics who do not respond to arguments grounded on orthodox reasoning.

In Sermons 65 and 66 Bernard identifies the foxes directly with the 'new heretics', seeming to combine the two groups that Everwin of Steinfeld differentiated: those with ancient roots who practice the laying-on-of-hands

---

 et secundam admonitionem, utpote qui omnino perversus est, erit secundum Apostolum (Titus 3. 10) devitandus. Ex hoc jam melius, ut quidem ego arbitror, effugatur, aut etiam religatur quam sinitur vineas demoliri.' *Song*, III, 175–6.

[23] I have modified the translation from *Song*, III, 175–6. *SBOp*, II, 170: 'Itaque homo de Ecclesia exercitatus et doctus, si cum haeretico homine disputare aggreditur, illo suam intentionem dirigere debet, quatenus ita erratem convincat, ut et convertat, cogitans illud apostoli Iacobi . . . (James 5. 20). Nec propterea sane nihil se egisse putet qui haereticum vicit et convicit, haereses confutavit verisimilia a vero clare aperteque distinxit, prava dogmata, plana et irrefragabili ratione prava esse demonstravit, pravum denique intellectum, extollentem se adversus scientiam Dei, in captivitatem redegit.'

[24] See Iogna-Prat, 'L'argumentation défensive', p. 93 ('refus rhétorique de toute confrontation') and n. 15 above.

[25] Sermon 64.8, *SBOp*, II, 170: 'Quod si reverti noluerit, nec convictus post primam iam et secundam admonitionem, utpote qui omnino subversus est, erit, secundum Apostolum, devitandus. Ex hoc iam melius, ut quidem ego arbitror, effugatur, aut etiam religatur, quam sinitur vineas demoliri.' *Song*, III, 176.

as their sacrament and live openly with women (early Cathars); and those who reject infant baptism and ecclesiastical authority (proto-Waldensians). Sermon 65 refers to the weaver men and women (*textores et textrices*), as will Geoffrey of Auxerre in the *Vita prima*, possibly designating early Cathars.[26] Bernard denounces the heretics' secrecy, likening them to snakes creeping in hiding because they keep their teachings secret, and to the hind parts of foxes, because they supposedly practise unspeakable obscene acts in private (Sermon 65.2). It is to God's glory to reveal teaching (Proverbs 25. 2), and the gospel, he says, orders that the truth be revealed (Matthew 10. 27).[27] Appeals to secrecy occur frequently in anti-heretical literature and function to support accusations of suspicious and reprehensible behaviour, even when dissidents reportedly do no more than discuss the Scriptures together. More examples of this will appear in Chapter Four.

Bernard assails the dissidents' view of the apostolic life, asserting in Sermon 66.8 that they are unable to show any signs of their apostolate.[28] He further criticizes them for rejecting the Church's authority, its teaching on purgatory and its practice of infant baptism (Sermon 66.9,11).[29] He refutes their claim to follow the gospel and asserts that the heresy deceives with both tongue and way of life (Sermon 65.4).[30] Animal metaphors convey the notion of deceit when Bernard compares the dissidents to the wolves in sheep's clothing who come to prey on the flock (Matthew 7. 15, John 10. 12): sheep in appearance, foxes in deceit, but wolves in action (Sermon 66.1). He also calls them dogs (Sermon 66.9).[31]

The Cistercian abbot demonstrates particular anger at the dissidents' living

---

[26] *PL*, CLXXXV, 411–12. 'Paucos quidem habebant civitas illa, qui heretico faverent; de Textoribus, quos Arrianos ipsi nominant, nonnullos; ex his vero, qui favebant heresi illi, plurimi erant et maximi civitatis illius.' See Grundmann's reading of this statement, *Movements*, pp. 260–1, n. 35, and n. 54 below.

[27] *SBOp*, II, 173: 'Quid faciemus his malignissimis vulpibus, ut capi queant, quae nocere quam vincere malunt, et ne apparere quidem volum, sed serpere . . . "Non", inquiunt, "sed ne mysterium publicemus." Quasi gloria Dei non sit revelare sermonem. An Dei invident gloriae? Sed magis credo quod pandere erubescant, scientes inglorium. Nam nefanda et obscena dicuntur agere in secreto: siquidem et vulpium posteriora foetent . . . Stat nempe Scripturae veritas: "Gloriam regum celare verbum, gloria Dei revelare sermonem" . . . Respondeant proinde Evangelio: "Quod dico", ait "in tenebris, dicite in lumine, et quod in aure auditis, praedicate super tecta" [Matthew 10. 27].' *Song*, III, 182–3.

[28] *Song*, III, 199; *SBOp*, II, 183: 'Nempe iactant se esse successores Apostolorum, et apostolicos nominant, nullum tamen apostolatus sui signum valentes ostendere.'

[29] *Song*, III, 199–203; *SBOp*, II, 183–5.

[30] *Song*, III, 185; *SBOp*, II, 175: 'Quod signum dabitis, ut palam fiat pessima haeresis haec, docta mentiri non lingua tantum, sed vita?'

[31] *Song*, III, 191 and 199; *SBOp*, II, 178: 'Hi sunt qui veniunt in vestimentis ovium, ad nudandas oves et spoliandos arietes . . . Hi oves sunt habitu, astu vulpes, actu et crudelitate lupi'; *SBOp*, II, 183: 'Videte detractores, videte canes.' Iogna-Prat cites this last statement as the example of invective in the sermon. 'L'argumentation défensive', p. 92.

with women and he casts doubt on their chastity. The latter prompts his often quoted remark: 'To be in a woman's company all the time and not have carnal knowledge of a woman – is this not more [a miracle] than raising the dead?' (Sermon 65.4).[32] Furthermore, those who maintain that marriages may take place only between virgins are said to exercise poisoned fangs in their attempt to tear apart the sacraments (Sermon 66.4).[33] Earlier in Sermon 66.3, he rails even more harshly against their disregard for the Church's views on marriage, exclaiming in another often-quoted line:

> Take away from the Church honourable marriage and the pure marriage-bed: Will you not fill it with takers of concubines, committers of incest, masturbators, the effeminate, men who lie with men, in point of fact, with every sort of impure person.[34]

Here Bernard starts from the heretics' rejection of marriage to associate heresy with sexual activity he viewed as impure: fornication, incest, masturbation and homosexuality. Bernard's successor, Henry of Clairvaux/Albano, also would make charges of sexual depravity against dissidents in southern France, and we shall see in Chapter Four that he probably contributed to the Third Lateran Council's canon against homosexuality.

Bernard asserts to some degree the continuity of the new heresy with the old. He states that it is 'taught by the examples of the old' (Sermon 65.2), that what the new heretics say is merely what was already trite and vented among the old heretics (Sermon 65.8).[35] Yet he adds that these new heretics have no professed leader, which for him makes them more dangerous, in the line of the hypocrites denounced in I Timothy 4. 1–3, a passage that he cites as did Everwin. Even the Manicheans, he says, had leaders, as did other groups of early heretics (Sermon 66.2).[36] In accord with I Timothy 4. 1–3, he also assails

---

[32] *SBOp*, II, 175: 'Cum femina semper esse, et non cognoscere feminam, nonne plus est quam mortuum suscitare?' The translation is mine. (*Song*, III, 184.) On the history of polemics against the chaste cohabitation of men and women (syneisacticism), see J. McNamara, *Sisters in Arms. Catholic Nuns through Two Millennia* (Cambridge, MA, 1996), pp. 56–57 and *passim*.

[33] *Song*, III, 194; *SBOp*, II, 180: 'Quidam tamen dissentientes ab aliis, inter solos virgines matrimonium contrahi posse fatentur. Verum quid in hac distinctione rationis afferre possint, non video: nisi quod pro libitu quisque suo sacramenta Ecclesiae, tamquam matris viscera, dente vipereo decertatim inter se dilacerare contendunt.'

[34] *SBOp*, II, 179–80: 'Tolle de Ecclesia honorabile connubium et thorum immaculatum: nonne reples eam concubinariis, incestuosis, seminifluis, mollibus, masculorum concubitoribus, et omni denique genere immundorum?' The translation is mine. (*Song*, III, 193.)

[35] *Song*, III, 181 and 188; *SBOp*, II, 173: 'Docta, credo, exemplis veterum . . .'; *SBOp*, II, 177: 'Nec enim in cunctis assertionibus eorum – nam multae sunt – , novum quid aut inauditum audisse me recolo, sed quod tritum est et diu ventilatum inter antiquos haereticos a nostris autem contritum et eventilatum.' *Song*, III, 188.

[36] *Song*, III, 192; *SBOp*, II, 179: 'Quaere ab illis suae sectae auctorem: neminem

the dissidents' abstinence, and he compares them directly to Manicheans who in their 'insane manner' find God's creation unclean. While the dissidents reject foods that they consider unclean, for Bernard, they themselves are unclean like vomit, and he denounces them directly: 'But it is you, polluted and unclean, who are spewed out by the Body of Christ, which is the Church' (Sermon 66.7).[37] Again the image calls at a minimum for casting out dissidents from the Church.

Bernard derides the heretics for their lack of learning as he calls them 'a base sort [of people] and rustic, or unlettered, and in short, cowardly' (Sermon 65.8), and again, 'rustic, unlettered and in a word, contemptible' (Sermon 66.1).[38] For Bernard, orthodox theologians 'crush and explode' the heretics' teachings (Sermon 65.8), surpassing them by far in theological proficiency.[39] Here Bernard exploits the notion that those who disagree with orthodoxy are ignorant, associating a claimed lack of learning with cowardice.

Bernard, like Everwin, paints the rapidly increasing heretics in a sort of crescendo:

> Women have left their husbands, and husbands their wives, to join these people. Clerks and priests have left their people and their churches, the untonsured and the bearded have been found there among the weaver men and women. Is this not great havoc? Is this not the work of foxes? (Sermon 65.5)[40]

In Sermon 66.1, he threatens that they must not be dealt with negligently, for their evil will escalate and grow like gangrene or a cancer (II Timothy 2. 16).[41]

---

hominem dabunt. Quae haeresis non ex hominibus habuit proprium haeresiarcham? Manichaei Manem habuere principem et praeceptorem . . .'

[37] *Song*, III, 198; *SBOp*, II, 182–3: 'At si de insania Manichaei praescribis beneficentiae Dei . . . Vae qui respuistis cibos quos Deus creavit, iudicantes immundos et indignos quos traiciatis in corpora vestra, cum propterea vos corpus Christi, quod est Ecclesia, tanquam pollutos et immundos expuerit.'

[38] *SBOp*, II, 177: 'Vile nempe hoc genus et rusticanum, ac sine litteris, et prorsus imbelle'; *SBOp*, II, 179: 'Rusticani homines sunt et idiotae, et prorsus contemptibiles . . .' The translations are mine. (*Song*, III, 188 and 191.)

[39] *Song*, III, 188; *SBOp*, II, 177: '. . . quod tritum est et diu ventilatum inter antiquos haereticos, a nostris autem contritum et eventilatum.' On the prejudices of the intellectual elite, see P. Biller, 'Heresy and Literacy: Earlier History of the Theme', in Biller and Hudson, pp. 1–18; and Moore, 'Literacy and the Making of Heresy, c. 1000–c. 1150', in Biller and Hudson, pp. 19–37.

[40] *Song*, III, 186; *SBOp*, II, 176: 'Mulieres, relictis viris, et item viri, dimissis uxoribus, ad istos se conferunt. Clerici et sacerdotes, populis ecclesiisque relictis, intonsi et barbati apud eos inter textores et textrices plerumque inventi sunt. Annon gravis demolitio ista? Annon opera vulpium haec?' Translation of the second sentence is mine. The reference to weavers men and women appears frequently; see Chapter One, pp. 47–8, on the social location of dissidents.

[41] *SBOp*, II, 179: '. . . sed non est, dico vobis, cum eis negligenter agendum: 'Multum enim proficiunt ad impietatem, et sermo eorum ut cancer serpit.' *Song*, III, 191.

Accusations in Sermon 65 that the growth of heresy is reversing the social order and menacing the overturn of established relationships point implicitly to the need for stopping its advance. Sermon 66, moreover, warns explicitly that heresy, like the contamination of gangrene, must be stopped before it overcomes society. All these statements evoke strong feelings of fear.

Despite the emphasis in Sermon 65 on the method for refuting heretics, Bernard observes in Sermon 66.12 that since the heretics are perverted, they cannot be convinced by logical reasoning, because they do not understand it. Neither can they be won over by reference to authorities which they do not accept, nor by persuasive arguments. They prefer to die rather than to convert. Proof of the heretics' adherence to error resides in the reported reaction of those who defend their faith even during trial by water and who provoke violent reaction from the onlookers. Bernard condemns the murder by mob actions, asserting in an often quoted sentence that faith is to be persuaded and not forced: *fides suadenda est, non imponenda* . . . Nonetheless, he says that he applauds the zeal of the mob and adds:

> It is better for them to be restrained by the sword of someone who bears not the sword in vain than to be allowed to lead others into heresy. One who avenges a wrong-doer for wrath is the servant of God [Romans 13. 4].[42]

The final section of Sermon 66 restates the measures for trapping the foxes: separate the men from the women, he says, and then expel them if they don't comply.[43] The ending of Sermon 66 recapitulates the sermon's most important points. While Bernard condemns a mob's violence against accused heretics, he applauds their zeal and thus leaves a contradictory message. His reference to Romans 13. 4, that restraint by the sword is preferable to further dissemination of heresy, leaves the door to violence at least ajar.

The 1145 mission

The sermons we have just analysed were written sometime after 1143, the date assigned to Everwin of Steinfeld's letter to Bernard, and probably in that year or in 1144. In 1145 Bernard himself set out for southern France to preach

---

[42] *Song*, III, 203–4; *SBOp*, II, 187: 'Approbamus zelum, sed factum non suademus; quia fides suadenda est, non imponenda. Quamquam melius procul dubio gladio coercerentur, illius videlicet qui non sine causa gladium portat, quam in suum errorem multos trajicere permittuntur. Dei enim minister ille est, vindex in iram ei qui male agit [Romans 13. 4].' Translation of the last sentence is mine.

[43] *Song*, III, 205; *SBOp*, II, 187: 'quamobrem ut deprehendantur, cogendi sunt vel abicere feminas, vel exire de Ecclesia . . . Hoc solo, etiamsi aliud non esset, facile deprehendis si, ut dixi, viros et feminas, qui se continentes dicunt, ab invicem separes, et feminas quidem cum aliis sui et sexus et voti degere cogas, viros aeque cum eiusdem propositi viris.'

against heresy. The dates for the journey have been the topic for scholarly debate. Gilles Bounoure has proposed the following chronology: Bernard was in Bordeaux on 2 July 1145; from that city he went to Toulouse, travelling along the Dordogne through Bergerac, Sarlat, and Cahors; the group traversed Verfeil and Saint Paul-Cap-de-Joux before reaching Albi on 31 July.[44] Bounoure also describes the apocalyptic atmosphere of 1145: famine and severe weather conditions, the appearance of Halley's comet from 15 April to 9 July 1145, and the deaths of three popes (Innocent II, Celestine II, Lucius II) in the brief period from 1143 to 1145, before Eugene III's elevation to the papacy.[45]

The motive for Bernard's journey was clear; he set out to preach against Henry the monk and his followers.[46] The abbot was accompanied by Bishop Geoffrey of Chartres, who worked with him during the 1130 schism as well as against Abelard, and travelled with him to Pisa in 1135 and to southern France in 1134 to persuade William of Poitiers to support Innocent II.[47] The sources for Bernard's intervention in Occitania include two letters by the abbot himself as well as the *Chronicle* of William of Puylaurens, two accounts of the mission from the *Vita prima* and one from the *Exordium magnum*.[48] These sources stand out from others pertaining to later Cistercians involved in the preaching mission in Occitania, because they provide details which allow for a partial reconstruction of the sermons delivered and of the circumstances under which the preaching was done.

Bernard's adversary in 1145 was Henry the monk, whom R. I. Moore terms 'the first heresiarch' in modern European history.[49] Henry was perhaps a renegade Benedictine monk[50] who began his preaching career in Lausanne and appeared in Le Mans about 1116, where he provoked a revolt against the local clergy. In 1135 the Archbishop of Arles brought him before Innocent II at the Council of Pisa, where he was condemned. Bernard attended that council with Geoffrey of Chartres, who joined his Cistercian friend again on

[44] Bounoure, 'Le dernier voyage', p. 133.
[45] Bounoure, 'L'archevêque', 113–28, 73–84; G. Bounoure, 'Saint Bernard et les hérétiques du Sarladais', *Bulletin de la Société Historique et Archéologique du Périgord* 116 (1989), 277–92 (pp. 287–8).
[46] Bernard doubtless took advantage of the journey to promote Cistercian expansion in Occitania and from there to New Catalonia. See C. d'Autremont Angleton, 'Two Cistercian Preaching Missions to the Languedoc in the Twelfth Century, 1145 and 1178' (unpublished Ph.D. dissertation, Catholic University of America, 1984), pp. 143–51; and Berman, pp. 3–5, 124–8.
[47] Newman, p. 196.
[48] In the *Vita prima*, these are a letter of Geoffrey of Auxerre (*PL*, CLXXXV, 410–16) and parts of chapter 6 (*PL*, CLXXXV, 313–14), as well as chapter 17 of the *Exordium magnum* by Conrad of Eberbach. *Exordium magnum*, pp. 110–11 (excerpted in the *Vita prima*, *PL*, CLXXXV, 427–8).
[49] Moore, *Origins*, p. 83; see also Moore, 'Literacy and the Making of Heresy', pp. 29–31.
[50] Fichtenau, p. 59 disputes that view.

the 1145 journey to Occitania, when Henry resurfaced. The Cistercian abbot followed his path from Poitiers to Bordeaux to Cahors, Périgueux and Toulouse. After Bernard's departure, Henry was reportedly captured, chained and led to the bishop.[51] Henry's teachings are preserved in manuscripts of a debate held with and recorded by a monk named William. The renegade clearly challenged the authority of the Church and of the priesthood in the area of the nature and the administration of the sacraments.[52]

Bernard's secretary, Geoffrey of Auxerre, writing the biography of Bernard, the *Vita prima*, distinguishes Henry's followers from those he calls Arians, used vaguely to designate those with heretical views on the nature of Christ, or perhaps specifically any who espoused Cathar beliefs. One scholar asserts that during the Middle Ages, Arianism was 'a generic name for any heresy touching even indirectly on the divinity of Christ . . . it is the archetypal heresy, and Arius the archetypal heretic'. The term 'Arian' is often joined with 'Manichean' to designate Cathars.[53] Geoffrey's comment implies that he and others called those heretics 'weavers', whereas they called themselves 'Arians'. Moreover, the Arians, who could have been early Cathars, were more numerous than Henry's followers and counted leaders of that prosperous city among them.[54]

---

[51] Moore, *Origins*, pp. 83–136, esp. pp. 83–101.

[52] For a recent study of this document, see M. Zerner-Chardavoine, 'Au temps de l'appel aux armes contre les hérétiques: du Contra Henricum du moine Guillaume aux Contra hereticos', in *Inventer l'hérésie?*, pp. 119–56. Moore, *Origins*, pp. 93–7.

[53] On Arianism as the 'archetypal heresy', see M. Wiles, *Archetypal Heresy. Arianism through the Centuries* (Oxford, 1996), pp. 53–4. Bounoure, 'Saint Bernard et les hérétiques du Sarladais', p. 286, points out the importance of Geoffrey's testimony and that the Cathars would not have supported Henry's tolerance for eating meat, even on Fridays, nor other aspects of his character: 'Au demeurant, pour s'en tenir au témoignage de Geoffroy, il n'est guère concevable que des "arriens" de doctrine cathare aient pu rallier l'hérétique Henri qui tolérait la consommation de viande y compris le vendredi, ni que les autres cathares présumés aient toléré à leurs portes des hérétiques aussi sataniques que les Henriciens . . .' Bounoure also points out (p. 286) a range of meanings in the term 'Arian'.

[54] *PL*, CLXXXV, 411–12: 'Paucos quidem habebat civitas illa [Tolosa], qui haeretico faverent; de textoribus, quos Arianos ipsi nominant, nonnullos; ex his vero qui favebant heresi illi, plurimi erant et maximi civitatis illius . . . Fugas Henrici, et Arianorum latibula longum est enarrare.' This passage is taken from the Letter to Master Archenfred that Geoffrey includes in the *Vita prima*: *Epistola Gaufridi, PL*, CLXXXV, 410–16. My literal translation: 'That city held few who favoured the heretic; [it held] some of the weavers, whom they themselves call Arians. Among those who favour that heresy, there were many and the foremost of the city. . . . The flights of Henry and the hiding-places of the Arians are long to recount.' Moore, *Birth*, p. 43, translates the first part of the passage with no differentiation between *haeretico* and *heresi*: 'There were only a few in the city who favoured the heresy, some of the weavers [*de textoribus*], whom they called *Ariani*. A great many of these supported the heresy in the city, including some of its most prominent citizens . . .' Grundmann, *Movements*, pp. 260–1, n. 35, differs from Moore on this, and I agree with Grundmann. Manselli, 'De la *persuasio* la *coercitio*', p. 182, also sees two groups:

Geoffrey of Auxerre's references to Henry in the *Vita prima* employ themes and images that we observe in Bernard's own writings. In Chapter 6 of the *Vita prima*, Geoffrey casts Henry as an apostate, a man of very bad life, pernicious doctrine, and persuasive speech, like those whose deceit and hypocrisy Paul foretold in I Timothy 4. 2. Both Everwin of Steinfeld and Bernard use that same passage. Furthermore, Geoffrey writes that Henry, an obvious enemy of the Church, irreverently denounces the sacraments and ministers of the Church.[55]

Bernard's 1145 letters

Bernard himself wrote two letters related to the Toulouse tour: numbers 241 and 242.[56] Letter 241, written prior to the journey, addresses Hildefonsus, count of Saint Giles and Toulouse. Letter 242, composed after Bernard's return home, is addressed to the people of Toulouse. These letters do not say much about Bernard's preaching, but they set a persuasive and emotive tone and establish a complex pattern of biblical imagery and language that continues throughout the texts we examine.

To summarize the content of the letters briefly, Letter 241 deplores the state of the Church in the region, denounces Henry the monk, and announces the mission. Bernard asks Hildefonsus to receive favourably Alberic of Ostia and the other bishops. Letter 242, written late in 1145 upon Bernard's return,[57] provides a motive for his failure to make a second tour of the region; it also reveals the threat that the abbot sees in rival preachers. In that letter, Bernard says that he would like to make another trip to Toulouse, even though he is ill and weak.

Letter 241 describes Henry in the language of Matthew 7. 15, as a *lupus rapax* or ravenous wolf in sheep's clothing. The first part of the letter accumulates the evil fruits of his activity in a crescendo recalling that of Sermon 65.5: churches lack people; the people lack priests; the priests are not shown respect; Christians are without Christ; the sacraments are not revered – neither confession, nor the eucharist, nor baptism.[58] Bernard attacks

followers of Henry and Arians or Cathars ('. . . *Arriani*, les Cathares, dirions-nous') On the economic development of Toulouse, see Moore, *Origins*, pp. 110–11, and Mundy, 'Urban Society', pp. 229–47.

[55] *PL*, CLXXXV, 312–13: 'In partibus Tolosanis Henricus quidam, olim monachus, tunc apostata vilis, pessimae vitae, perniciosae doctrinae, verbis persuasibilibus gentis illius occupaverat levitatem, et, ut praedixit apostolus de quibusdam, in hypocrisi loquens mendacium (I Timothy 4. 2), fictis verbis de eis negotiabatur. Erat autem hostis Ecclesiae manifestus, irreverenter ecclesiasticis derogans Sacramentis pariter et ministris.'

[56] *SBOp*, VIII, 125–9. *Letters*, 317 and 318, pp. 387–91.

[57] *SBOp*, VIII, 128, n.1.

[58] *SBOp*, VIII, 125: 'Quanta audivimus et cognovimus mala, quae in ecclesiis Dei fecit,

Henry's reported position toward baptism with particular attention, lamenting that this sacrament is denied to children, the very ones whom Christ favoured. Bernard finds such behaviour, which he attributes to envy, diabolical and he claims that it denies the value of Christ's incarnation, passion and crucifixion.[59] In short, for Bernard the rejection of infant baptism undermines the core of christological beliefs.

In Part Two, Bernard speaks directly to the people in the second person plural, asking how they can believe such a man. The abbot describes Henry as 'either envying or not seeing the truth, with Jewish-like blindness', a conventional motif of anti-Jewish literature that Bernard uses to place Henry outside Christianity.[60] Bernard also demonizes Henry, claiming that he uses 'diabolic skill to influence the foolish and senseless people'. Animal imagery here casts Henry as a wild beast or boar (*ferus*), with no one to resist him or save the people from his ravages, and the shrewd serpent (*serpens callidus*), capable of deceiving even the count of Toulouse.[61] Hence Bernard's analogies and imagery locate Henry outside Christian society, as a threat to the social order through his deceit and destruction, as well as his alliance with Satan.

Part Three of the letter describes Henry directly – an apostate who has polluted himself by re-entering the world and the flesh, and in the language of II Peter 2. 22, a dog returning to its own vomit. Furthermore, Bernard accuses Henry of preaching to earn money to live and of squandering that money by gambling or more foul pastimes. Bernard asserts that Henry, sarcastically called the noteworthy preacher (*praedicator insignis*), often would spend the day with the people and at night frequent prostitutes and some-

---

et facit quotidie Henricus haereticus? Versatur in terra sub vestimentis ovium lupus rapax; sed ad Domini designationem, a fructibus eius cognoscimus illum. Basilicae sine plebibus, plebes sine sacerdotibus, sacerdotes sine debita reverentia sunt, et sine Christo denique christiani. Ecclesiae synagogae reputantur, sanctuarium Dei sanctum esse negatur, sacramenta non sacra censentur, dies festi frustrantur solemniis. Moriuntur homines in peccatis suis, rapiuntur passim animae ad tribuna terrificum, heu! nec paenitentia reconciliati, nec sancta communione muniti.' *Letters*, p. 388.

59   *SBOp*, VIII, 125–6: 'Parvuli christianorum Christi intercluditur vita, dum baptismi negatur gratia, nec saluti propinquare sinuntur, Salvatore licet pie clamitante oro eis: "Sinite", inquit, "parvulos venire ad me." . . . Quid, quaeso, quid invidet parvulis Salvatorem parvulum, qui natus est eis? Invidia haec diabolica est . . . An putat parvulos Salvatore non egere, quia parvuli sunt? Si ita est, ergo gratis magnus Dominus factus est parvus, ut omittam quod flagellatus est, quod sputis illitus, quod cruci affixus, quod denique mortuus est.' *Letters*, p. 388.

60   On this stereotype of Jewish blindness, see Dahan, *Les intellectuels chrétiens et les juifs*, pp. 400, 475–81.

61   *SBOp*, VIII, 126: 'Quam certe manifestam omnibus veritatem solus iste stupenda, et prorsus Iudaica caecitate, aut non videns, aut invidens adimpletam, simul nescio qua arte diabolica persuasit populo stulto et insipienti . . . Nec mirum tamen si serpens ille callidus decepit te [principem illustrem], quippe speciem pietatis habens, cuius virtutem penitus abnegavit.' *Letters*, p. 388.

times even married women.[62] The summary image for Henry's character is the bad tree (Matthew 7. 18): not only does it not bear good fruit; it also pollutes the land in which it grows and sends forth a foul odour everywhere.[63] Thus Henry as heretic constitutes a pollutant that threatens his surroundings.

In the fourth part of the letter, Bernard returns to his motives for the journey and, echoing the theme if not the exact language of the Parable of the tares (Matthew 13. 24–30, 36–43), he employs the traditional image of clearing a field, the Lord's field, for the work of eliminating heretical ideas. The Church has called him to have Henry's works eradicated, he asserts, and to rely on the bishops with him to uproot the thorns and evil deeds of the heretics from the Lord's field while they are still small.[64] Agricultural imagery, used traditionally for constructing a community ethos,[65] serves the seemingly constructive endeavour of clearing the field. But the process of clearing implies destroying the weeds, human ideas at the least, if not human beings. The imagery suggests the presence of a potentially uncontrollable power that threatens to overtake the established order.

In Letter 242, Bernard demonstrates concern about unauthorized preaching

---

[62] *SBOp*, VIII, 126–7: 'Homo apostata est, qui relicto religionis habitu, – nam monachus exstitit –, ad spurcitias carnis et saeculi, tamquam canis ad suum vomitum, est reversus . . . Cumque mendicare coepisset, posuit in sumptu Evangelium, – nam litteratus erat –, et venale distrahens verbum Dei, evangeliabat ut manducaret. Si quid supra victum elicere poterat a simplicioribus populi vel ab aliqua matronarum, id ludendo aleis aut certe in usus turpiores turpiter effundebat. Frequenter siquidem post diurnum populi plausum, nocete insecuta cum meretricibus inventus est praedicator insignis, et interdum etiam cum coniugatis.' *Letters*, p. 389. Henry undertook a programme to convert prostitutes and find husbands for them. See Lambert, *Heresy*, p. 45; Moore, *Origins*, p. 109; Fichtenau, p. 60; and the account in WE, p. 112.

[63] *SBOp*, VIII, 127: 'Tu de tali arbore tandem bonos sperabas fructus? Terrae profecto in qua est, fecit foetere odorem in universa terra, quia "non potest", iuxta sermonem Domini, "arbor mala fructus bonos facere" [Matthew 7. 18].' *Letters*, p. 389.

[64] *SBOp*, VIII, 127: 'Haec . . . causa adventus mei. Nec a meipso venio, sed vocatione pariter et miseratione Ecclesiae trahor, si forte spina illa et prava ipsius, dum adhuc parva sunt, germina de agro dominico extirpari queant, non mea, qui nullus sum, sed sanctorum, cum quibus sum, episcoporum manu, tua quoque potenti dextera cooperante.' *Letters*, p. 389. The Parable uses the word 'zizania' for the tares; the verb 'eradicare' as does Bernard; and speaks of tying and burning the tares. The Parable of the sower (Matthew 13. 3–8, 18. 23; Mark 4. 3–8, 13–20; Luke 8. 5–8, 11–15), which follows the second portion of the Parable of the tares, speaks of thorns ('spinae') as Bernard does. On the interpretation of the Parable of the tares against heresy, see S. L. Wailes, *Medieval Allegories of Jesus' Parables* (Berkeley, CA, 1987), pp. 105–8. Smalley discusses Peter Comestor and Peter the Chanter's views on the treatment of heretics in connection with the Parable of the tares (Matthew 13. 24–30) in *Gospels*, pp. 109–10.

[65] On agricultural imagery in Hellenistic culture and its influence on the New Testament, see B. Mack, *A Myth of Innocence: Mark and Christian Origins* (Philadelphia, 1988), pp. 159–60.

and fear for its influence on the people of the region. While Letter 241 focuses on Henry himself, Letter 242 treats heretics in general. Bernard viewed his own mission as a success: it deterred the wolves in sheep's clothing (Matthew 7. 15) devouring the people and the little foxes destroying the Lord's vineyard (Song of Songs 2. 15). Here the Lord's vineyard, in grammatical apposition with the city of Toulouse, has a context smaller than the outside world; it refers to the one city (*pretiosissimam vineam Domini, civitatem vestram*) which was later and often seen as the foyer of heresy.[66] Despite the claimed success of the mission, the work was not finished, according to Bernard, and he exhorts the people to continue the effort until their territory is wholly rid of the heretics, for it is not safe to sleep near serpents (Psalm 9. 29). In referring to a group of heretics, Bernard might have transferred to a poorly-defined plurality of people the questionable evil attributed to Henry; or he might have had two groups in mind: Henry's followers and the 'Arians', numerous in Toulouse and possibly early Cathars.[67] The dissident Toulousans, demonized as serpent-like heretics, are also compared to highly dangerous thieves who sit in waiting to kill the innocent, a potent menace to the social order. Bernard likens their words to a cancer or gangrene, as in II Timothy 2. 17,[68] again conveying the notion that their deceitful and polluted actions were consorting to threaten the social order.

In section two of Letter 242, the abbot expresses his desire to return to the region, while lamenting his own physical weakness. He then admonishes the residents of Toulouse to obey their bishops and other Church leaders and to extend hospitality to pilgrims. In section three, however, he warns them to be wary of any foreign or unknown preacher unless that person has been sent by the pope or authorized by their bishop.[69] False preachers, he says, mix poison with honey, introducing new profane ideas with words from Heaven. Before

[66] See Chapter Four in this book, on the mission of Henry of Clairvaux/Albano; and on how Toulouse came to be known by metonymy as the city of the Albigensians, J.-L. Biget, '"Les Albigeois": remarques sur une dénomination', in *Inventer l'hérésie?*, pp. 219–55, esp. p. 255.

[67] I am grateful to P. Biller for this suggestion. See nn. 26 and 54 above.

[68] *SBOp*, VIII, 128–9: '. . . deprehensae vulpes, quae demoliebantur pretiossimam vineam Domini, civitatem vestram; deprehensae sed non comprehensae. Propterea, dilectissimi, "persequimini et comprehendite" eos [Psalm 70. 11], et nolite desistere, donec penitus depereant et diffugiant de cunctis finibus vestris, quia non est tutum dormire vicinis serpentibus. Sedent "in insidiis cum divitibus in ocultis, ut" interficiant innocentes. Fures sunt et latrones, quales in Evangelio Dominus notat. Subversi sunt et parati ad subvertendum, plane maculatores famae vestrae, corruptores fidei vestrae. "Corrumpunt bonos mores colloquia mala"; praesertim talum "sermo", sicut dicit beatus Apostolus, "serpit ut cancer" [I Corinthians 15. 33; II Timothy 2. 17].' *Letters*, p. 390.

[69] Ep 242, *SBOp*, VIII, 129: 'ut nullum extraneum sive ignotum praedicatorem recipiatis, nisi qui missus a summo seu a vestro permissus Pontifice praedicaverit.' *Letters*, p. 390.

closing the letter, Bernard again draws on the image of wolves in sheep's clothing (Matthew 7. 15). The unknown or unauthorized preacher, like the wolf, should not be trusted or welcomed.[70] The abbot implies, therefore, that preaching without authority bears a polluted and potentially deadly message. The potential threat that such a preacher poses emerges clearly from the biblical imagery and the abbot's stern warnings.

Sarlat, a sermon and a bread miracle

Following the itinerary suggested for Bernard's journey, we begin with his preaching at Sarlat (Gascony). In the sixth chapter of the *Vita prima*, a sermon preached at Sarlat is followed by a reinforcing miracle, which strengthens the sermon's message and demonstrates the authentic holiness of its preacher. According to Geoffrey of Auxerre's account, when the sermon was completed, the people brought several loaves of bread to be blessed and gave them to Bernard. As he made the sign of the Cross over the loaves, Bernard blessed them and said,

> If the infirm among you return to health after tasting these loaves, then by this sign you will know that the true things are from us and false ones are argued by the heretics.

The bishop of Chartres (Geoffrey), who accompanied Bernard, asked him to clarify the point. Surely, he thought, Bernard meant that the people had to eat the bread in good faith. Bernard replied that he did not say that, but simply that, if the people tasted it, they would be healed and would know that he and his companions were truthful messengers of God. Geoffrey reports that the infirm ate and were healed, and that the news of the miracle spread through the region.[71]

---

[70] *SBOp*, VIII, 129: 'Ipsi sunt qui, induentes sibi formam pietatis et virtutem eius penitus abnegantes, profanas novitates vocum et sensuum, tamquam melli venenum, verbis caelestibus intermiscent. Cavete proinde eos tamquam beneficos, et cognoscite in vestimentis ovium lupos rapaces.' *Letters*, p. 390.

[71] *PL*, CLXXXV, 313–14: 'Est locus in regione eadem, cui Sarlatum nomen est, ubi sermone completo plurimos ad benedicendum panes, sicut ubique fiebat, Dei Famulo offerebant. Quos ille elevata manu et signo Crucis edito in Dei nomine benedicens: "In hoc," inquit, "scietis vera esse quae a nobis, falsa quae ab haereticis suadentur, si infirmi vestri gustatis panibus istis adepti fuerint sospitatem." Timens autem venerabilis episcopus Carnotensium magnus ille Gaufridus (siquidem praesens erat et proximus Viro Dei); "si bona," inquit, "fide sumpserint, sanabantur." Cui Pater sanctus de Domini virtute nil haesitans: "Non hoc ego dixerim," ait, "sed vere qui gustaverint, sanabantur: ut proinde veros nos et veraces Dei nuntios esse cognoscant." Tam ingens multitudo languentium gustato eodem pane convaluit, ut per totam provinciam verbum hoc divulgaretur, et Vir sanctus per vicina loca regrediens ob concursus intolerabiles declinaverit, et timuerit illo ire.' Bounoure

Based on this account, we know nothing for certain about the content of Bernard's sermon, only that he delivered one. If the blessing scene is thematically related to the preaching that precedes it, then one can imagine a sermon drawn from one of the many references to bread in the New Testament that could have provided a thematic link between the sermon and the miracle: John 6, for example, where Jesus feeds the crowd from five barley loaves and two fish and then distinguishes the true bread that comes down from Heaven from other bread; or one of the stories of the miracle of the loaves and fishes in the synoptic gospels; or I Corinthians 11. 27–30, where Paul associates eating the bread and drinking the cup of the Lord's supper with self-examination, proclaiming that many are weak and ill while others have died because they have eaten and drunk without discerning the sacredness of the actions. Since Bernard's words of promise refer to discerning the true from the false, he probably structured the sermon to emphasize such a discernment, and what the words expressed the blessing, eating, and healing actualized. However, Bernard's personal holiness, as revealed in the blessing and miracle, serves as the point of the story and the deciding factor in the events that the chronicler reports.

Since Geoffrey aimed to enhance Bernard's holiness by telling the miracle story, he did not care to specify the beliefs of the heretics in Sarlat. G. Bounoure has addressed the problem of their identity, asking if they were followers of Henry, of his predecessor, Peter of Bruys, or 'crypto-Cathars'. He suggests that they could have been Petrobrusians who did not accept the new leadership of Henry. Bounoure also offers various reasons for the presence of heresy in Sarlat in 1145, as observed above. Among these, famine holds an evident link to the telling and the power of bread miracles.[72]

Verfeil: a failed sermon

The *Vita prima* tells us of Bernard's successes. In contrast, William of Puylaurens, a later chronicler in the service of Bishop Fulk of Toulouse, opens his chronicle with a tale of Bernard's failure in the town of Verfeil. In the church there, Bernard began to direct his sermon against the nobles, who left the church, followed by the people. Bernard went after them and began to preach outside in the square, but the nobles obstinately entered their houses, still refusing to listen to the visiting preacher. Bernard continued preaching to the people standing around outside, but those inside pounded against their doors and made such a racket that the people outside could not hear the abbot preaching. Finally, Bernard 'shook the dust from his feet' and cursed

argues that the exchange between the bishop of Chartres and Bernard reveals Geoffrey's concern to portray the abbot of Clairvaux as a defender of transubstantiation: 'Saint Bernard et les hérétiques du Sarladais', p. 282.

[72] Bounoure, 'Saint Bernard et les hérétiques du Sarladais', pp. 287–8. See n. 45 above.

the town as he left, saying: 'Viridefolium, desiccet te Deus' ('Greenleaf, may God dry you up').

The chronicler interprets the action of Bernard's shaking dust from his feet as a reminder that the inhabitants of Verfeil were dust and would return to dust. He does not allude, as a hagiographer might, to any parallels with Jesus's advising his disciples that they should shake the dust from their feet when they encountered unmovable hostility in the towns they visited (e.g., Mark 6. 11, Matthew 10. 14, Luke 9. 5, Acts 13. 51). The chronicler emphasizes Bernard's power to place a curse on the town, and he asserts that the town remained cursed until Simon of Montfort delivered it to Bishop Fulk of Toulouse.[73] Although Bernard's curse was powerful in this case, his preaching was not.

In contrast to William of Puylaurens's account, the *Vita prima* mentions the town of Verfeil only briefly, saying that Bernard healed someone there and describing the town as the seat of Satan (*ubi sedes est satanae*).[74] It reports no failure there; generally its stories concern Bernard's miracles and the signs of his astuteness. Receiving much more attention in the text than his sermons, the miracles purportedly had a greater impact on the people of the region. The *Vita prima*, at least one of its versions, was written to support the case for Bernard's canonization, and its clear hagiographic intent largely explains its emphasis on miracles. The first attempt to canonize Bernard failed in 1162 and the revision of the *Vita* was then charged to Geoffrey of Auxerre, who prepared the text as part of the successful canonization attempt in 1174.[75]

An additional factor relating miracles to preaching also comes to mind: the literary and theological model of the apostle who preaches and performs miracles on his journey. Related to this apostolic model is the insistence on the value of miracles to confirm holy and valid preaching.[76] Rooted in the accounts of Jesus's ministry in the gospels, the model of the holy apostle appears also in the apostles' evangelizing journeys in the book of Acts. It also figures prominently in the apocryphal tales of the *Virtutes apostolorum*,[77] the

---

[73] Puylaurens, I, 26–9. A. Picard and P. Boglioni cite this tale from Verfeil in the context of the importance accorded to Bernard's touch by his contemporaries: 'Miracle et thaumaturgie dans la vie de Saint Bernard', in *Vie et légendes de Saint Bernard de Clairvaux, Création, diffusion, réception (XIIe–XXe Siècles). Actes des Rencontres de Dijon, 7–8 juin 1991*, ed. P. Arabeyre, J. Berlioz and P. Poirrier, Cîteaux: Commentarii Cistercienses, Textes et Documents 5 (Cîteaux, 1993), pp. 36–59 (p. 44).

[74] *PL*, CLXXXV, 414B: 'Quintum mancum sanavit in castro quod dicitur Viride-Folium, ubi sedes est satanae.'

[75] A. M. Piazzoni, 'Le premier biographe de Saint Bernard: Guillaume de Saint-Thierry', in *Vie et légendes de Saint Bernard de Clairvaux*, pp. 7–8.

[76] On the role of miracles in the early Church, with a connection to preaching, see Gregory the Great, Homily 29, *Forty Gospel Homilies*, trans. D. Hurst, CS 123 (Kalamazoo, MI, 1990), p. 229 (*PL*, LXXVI, 1213–20). The necessity for miracles to confirm the validity of preaching appears in the literature against unauthorized preaching. See Chapter Four, pp. 130–2 in this book.

[77] The dating (late sixth century) and principal manuscripts of the *Virtutes apostolorum*,

collection of stories about the apostles' lives and passions which were rendered in Latin around the sixth century and had their place in medieval monastic libraries. Not only was the claim to an apostolic life style a key issue for both dissidents and orthodox clergy during the twelfth century, but the necessity for miracles to validate the holiness of preaching also figured as a salient argument in the polemical tracts and papal letters written in the latter part of the century. Those are largely concerned with the problems that the Church perceived in unauthorized Waldensian preachers. Defenders of orthodoxy claimed not only that valid preachers must be sent by a higher authority, but also that their preaching, just as that of the apostles, must be confirmed by the working of signs and miracles.[78]

Albi: a sermon on the Parable of the tares

While the content of Bernard's preaching at Sarlat is difficult to reconstruct with certainty and that at Verfeil can not be reconstructed, one can find an actual reported sermon at Albi in Geoffrey's letter to Master Archenfred, the most important source in the *Vita prima* for Bernard's preaching in the region in 1145. Bernard preached to a large crowd in the church at Albi on the feast of Saint Peter, which occurred the day after his arrival there. According to Gilles Bounoure's chronology, Bernard arrived in Albi on 31 July 1145 and the date of the sermon was Wednesday 1 August 1145 the Feast of St Peter in Chains.[79] Bernard said that he had come to sow, Geoffrey tells us, but he found the field already sown with wicked seed. Here the abbot, as in an earlier instance, was drawing on the Parable of the tares (Matthew 13. 24–30, 36–52), a Matthean text that was also used by Augustine of Hippo against the Donatists.[80] Assuring the audience that the field was human reason and that they were God's husbandry, Bernard explained that he would show them both the good and the wicked seed and let them decide which to choose. Bernard then expounded various points one at a time, beginning with the sacrament of the altar, and explained what the heretics were preaching in contrast to what the true faith said. When the abbot asked his listeners to choose, so Geoffrey reports, they chose the true faith and began to despise the heretics' beliefs.

---

also known as the pseudo-Abdias collection, are discussed in E. Junod and J.-D. Kaestli, *Acta Iohannis*, Corpus Christianorum Series Apocryphorum (Turnhout, 1983), pp. 750–7, 790–5.

[78] Kienzle, 'Obedience', pp. 263–4.

[79] Bounoure disagrees with E. Griffe's chronology here and explains his argument in 'Le dernier voyage', p. 131.

[80] On the usage of the Parable of the Tares in texts against heresy, see Wailes, *Medieval Allegories*; and U. Luz, *Das Evangelium nach Matthäus 2, Mt 8–17* (Zürich, 1990), pp. 343–8.

Finally, at Bernard's request, they raised their right hands to Heaven as a sign of unity.[81]

Judging from Geoffrey's account of the sermon, we can assume that Bernard based his preaching on the Parable of the tares and used a debate-like structure, raising a point of doctrine and then explaining the positions of each side, with emphasis on orthodox beliefs. In this case, unlike the preceding story of the bread at Sarlat, Bernard's preaching itself reportedly moved the audience; there was no divine intervention.

A sermon and a swan-like neck

A passage from the *Exordium magnum*[82] demonstrates how even a sermon that had proceeded well could be followed by a confrontation. The episode again suggests a debate type of structure, and it confirms that Bernard's actions and personal holiness again proved more powerful than his preaching.

The author carefully set the stage for the arrival of his main character. Bernard journeyed to the region of Toulouse with the papal legate and some bishops in order to refute the opposition, identified as the heresy of Manicheans. Because of the difficulty of the journey, the brothers prepared a better mount than usual for the abbot of Clairvaux. The chief adversary was Henry, the former black monk who became, in the author's words, a vile apostate and leader of the heretics. Knowing that he could not stand up to either Bernard's wisdom or the power of the spirit within him, Henry had already fled and could not be found. In contrast, Bernard, the heroic figure, performed signs and wonders in the sight of all on a daily basis. Innumerable crowds flocked to him throughout the day, beseeching him to bestow the signs of his holiness: erudition and the power of healing.

On a certain day, after Bernard had admonished a very large crowd on preserving the catholic faith and avoiding impure association with heretics

---

[81] *PL*, CLXXXV, 414D–416A: 'Sequenti vero die, cum beati Petri solemnitas esset, tanta ad audiendum verbum Dei multitudo convenit, ut non caperet eos grandis ecclesia. Quos allocutus dominus Abbas: "Seminare, inquit, veneram, sed praeoccupatum a semine pessimo agrum inveni. Verumtamen, quia rationalis et ager, Dei enim agricultura vos estis, ecce ostendo vobis semen utrumque, ut sciatis quid eligere debeatis." Et incipiens a Sacramento altaris per singula capitula, quid haereticus praedicaret, quaeve esset fidei veritas, diligentius exponebat. Demum interrogavit eos quid eligerent: et respondens omnis populus coepit abominari et detestari haereticam pravitatem, et cum gaudio suscipere verbum Dei, et catholicam veritatem. "Poenitemini, inquit, igitur quicunque contaminati estis, redite ad Ecclesiae unitatem. Et ut sciamus quis poenitentia agat et suscipiat verbum vitae, levate in coelum dextras in signum catholicae unitatis." Factum est ergo, ut levantibus omnibus dextras in coelum cum exsultatione, ipse sermoni finem imponeret.'

[82] *Exordium magnum*, chapter 17, pp. 110–11.

(*de immunda haereticorum societate vitanda commonuisset*), he was challenged by one heretic, described as seemingly stronger and more intelligent than the others. Irked at the veneration the crowd showed towards Bernard, the fellow wanted to obfuscate and stain the abbot's glory. Compared by the author to a twisted snake with head upright (*coluber tortuosus erecto capite*), the heretic came up to Bernard and, crying out to all present, said that his teacher's horse was not so thick-necked and fat (*cervicosus et pinguis*) as Bernard's noisy-footed nag (*sonipes*). Bernard, 'meek and patient', replied with all tranquillity (*tranquillo vultu et animo*) that God was not offended nor was justice harmed by the horse's desire to eat and get fat. The abbot asserted that neither he nor the heretic's teacher would be rebuked for their horse's necks, but each would be judged concerning his own neck. Bernard challenged the heretic, saying: 'Now then, if it pleases you, look at my neck and see if it is fatter than your master's neck, and from that perhaps you may be able to reprove me justly.' The abbot then pulled back his hood, baring his head down to the shoulders, and showed a long and graceful neck which shone bright with whiteness like a swan's even though it was thin and emaciated. The people all rejoiced at Bernard's response and blessed the Lord who gave his servant a response suitable to confound and silence the mouth of one speaking iniquities (Psalm 62. 12).[83] Thus the abbot of Clairvaux foiled the man of Sarlat who must have intended to undermine Bernard's teaching, challenging him about the expense and attention evidently given to his beefy mount. Here the sight of Bernard's lean and shining neck, proof of his austerity and purity, preserved the impact of his sermon.

The scope of Bernard's activity appears succinctly in the prelude to the following episode in the *Exordium magnum*, where a blind man is restored to sight by the dust containing the print of Bernard's feet.[84] This story probably derives from an oral tradition that circulated at Clairvaux around 1180–90, perhaps told by men who had accompanied Bernard on the journey southward.[85] Likened to one of the apostles, Bernard is described in this episode as travelling through villages and cities preaching the gospel and curing illnesses, reproaching the very foul ravings of the heretics, persuading and

[83] *Exordium magnum*, p. 111, ll. 27–34: 'Nunc igitur, si placet, respice collum meum et vide, et si grosius est collo magistri tui, inde me forsitan iuste reprehendere oteris. Hoc itaque dicto capitum exuit et capite denudato usque ad humeros apparuit ipsius collum, ut erat productum et gracile; quod quamvis esset carnibus exesum et tenue, erat tamen ex dono caelesti pulchrum et candidum nimis sicut collum oloris. Quod cum viderent universi, qui aderant, laetati sunt laetitia magna benedicentes Dominum, qui dedit in ore famuli sui tam paratum et conveniens responsum, unde confunderetur et obstruetur os loquentis iniqua.'

[84] *Exordium magnum*, chapter 18, p. 112.

[85] B. P. McGuire, 'La présence de Bernard de Clairvaux dans l'*Exordium magnum cisterciense*', in *Vies et légendes de Saint Bernard*, p. 74. McGuire agrees with C. Griesser that Conrad of Eberbach is the author of the *Exordium magnum*.

refuting.[86] Hence preaching goes hand in hand with healing, and persuading crowds to the true faith balances the refutation of heretics' errors. The summary following the miracle story indicates the instruments of Bernard's success in similar terms and describes the errors of heresy with vivid language of pollution and damnation. Conrad of Eberbach, probable author of the *Exordium magnum*, affirms that with the word of his preaching and his wondrous signs and miracles, Bernard called the region's people back from the jaws of uncleanliness (*de faucibus putidissimae*) and from the belly of Hell (*de ventre inferi*).[87]

Conclusion

Bernard of Clairvaux established a powerful model for Cistercian engagement against heresy, one that entailed writing and public preaching. Upon Everwin of Steinfeld's request, Bernard took up his stylus against heretics in the Rhineland, primarily those who evidenced beliefs associating them with the dissidents whom Eckbert of Schönau labelled Cathars in the 1160s. Bernard used Song of Songs 2. 15 as his point of departure, incorporating anti-heretical material into an exegetical sermon cycle and falling back on the centuries old association of heretics with foxes in the vineyard. A year or two later (1145), the influential abbot embarked on a preaching mission to Occitania. His targets were Henry the monk and his followers, and another group of heretics called 'weavers' and 'Arians', who held power in Toulouse and may have been early Cathars.

A corpus of extant texts provides evidence for Bernard's preaching and his denunciations of heresy. The abbot's attacks sound particularly vehement against the dissidents' abstinence, whether dietary or sexual. His anger emerges most strongly when dissidents lay claim to religious practices that were the special reserve of monks. The concept of 'mimetic rivalry' comes to mind.[88] Adapting René Girard's concept, I suggest the following process was at work. Both dissidents and Cistercians viewed themselves as imitators of the apostles. Within the Church, the Cistercians considered themselves the superior imitators of the apostles, notably because of their rigorous asceticism. For the Cistercians, adherence to a strict ascetic model required life in community and close observance of the Benedictine *Rule*. When dissidents

---

[86] *Exordium magnum*, p. 112: 'Dum adhuc in eadem regione reverentissimus pater moraretur et tanquam ex apostolis unus circuiret per castella et civitates evangelizando et curando omnes languores, haereticorum quoque turpissima delireamenta redarguendo, convincendo, confutando . . .'.

[87] *Exordium magnum*, pp. 112–13: '. . . certe ii ipsi Gasconiae populi, quos de faucibus putidissimae haereseos pater sanctus verbo praedicationis, signis etiam et prodigiis admirandis tanquam de ventre inferi revocabat . . .'.

[88] Girard, *Girard Reader*, pp. 9–14.

held to sexual and dietary abstinence, especially in communities of mixed gender, they were claiming to be monks of a sort but practising accepted monasticism and violating its norms for separate living quarters for men and women. Thus they asserted themselves to some degree as rivals of the Cistercians, thereby challenging the girdings of monasticism and provoking outrage from Bernard, his contemporaries and their successors.

In Bernard's letters and sermons, he weaves a polemical web employing rhetoric and scriptural passages that forcefully connote demonization, pollution, threat to the social order, and apocalypticism. A brief recap of the scriptural passages that Bernard employs will clarify the construction of his arguments and provide a guide for subsequent chapters. Key scriptural elements stock his verbal arsenal: foxes spoiling the vineyard (Song of Songs 2. 15); wolves in sheep's clothing (Matthew 7. 15) and preying on a flock (John 10. 12); a dog returning to its vomit (II Peter 2. 22); evil spreading like gangrene (II Timothy 2. 17); the deceit and danger of serpents (Psalm 9. 29); the bad tree producing bad fruit (Matthew 7. 18); the characteristics of hypocrites who announce the coming of the last days (I Timothy 4. 1–3); the tares to be pulled and burned (Matthew 13. 24–30, 36–43); avenging a wrong doer making one a servant of God (Romans 13. 4). The anti-heretical association of these passages takes root in patristic exegesis; and the pastoral epistles originally belong to a controversial period in early Christianity.[89] Bernard moulds them around contemporary events, and the same reshaping will appear in the polemical writing and preaching of his successors.

Thus the abbot solidifies a composite portrait of the heretic, one that adapted the writings of the Church Fathers to the twelfth-century crisis, and he transmitts it to later authors.[90] Moreover, the stereotype of the heretic belongs to wider patterns of preconceived ideas about heresy that we shall trace in later chapters. J. B. Russell distinguishes three such currents of thought, namely that heresy was: (1) an unchanging phenomenon or 'Platonic reality'; or (2) an evil like the Devil with an unchangeable essence

---

[89] For a summary of research on the pastoral epistles, see R. P. Martin, '1, II Timothy and Titus', in *Harper's Bible Commentary*, ed. J. L. Mays (San Francisco, 1988), pp. 1237–44: and R. A. Wild, 'The Pastoral Letters', in *NJBC*, pp. 891–902; L. M. Maloney, 'The Pastoral Epistles', in *Searching the Scriptures, II: Feminist Commentary*, ed. E. Schüssler Fiorenza (New York, 1994), pp. 361–80.

[90] Stock, *Implications*, pp. 152–3, states that the reformers' demand to return to earlier Christian roots prompted intellectuals to expand their knowledge of patristic sources. There they found not only material on the early Church and the *vita apostolica* for imitation, but also denunciations of ancient heresy. We see this process at work in Bernard, Eckbert of Schönau, and other writers to be examined later. Peters situates the development of a 'type' of the heretic in the late twelfth century. Peters, *Inquisition*, p. 42: 'a certain kind of person, one whose curiosity was not disciplined by reason and revelation, whose will was stubborn, refusing to bow before superior wisdom and legitimate authority, and whose pride was so great as to require that others validate his own opinion by following him as a leader.'

that took different forms and appearances in various times; or, (3) the 'mirror image of the orthodox Apostolic Succession' which saw a series of heretical leaders beginning with Simon Magus who mirrored and opposed the orthodox succession beginning with Simon Peter.[91] Bernard saw strands of continuity in heresy, seemingly following the first or second current of thought above; however, he implied that the new heretics were worse than the old. The new heretics, he claimed, had no leaders and were inclined to secrecy, while the old ones sought to achieve victory in public debate. Since the new heretics took their name and therefore their ideas from no one leader, their beliefs must have originated with demons.[92] Thus the abbot did not stop short at a simple comparison of likeness; instead he highlighted a difference to demonize contemporary dissidents and accentuate their potential danger.

From the accounts of Bernard's impact on various towns or villages in southern France, we obtain some evidence specifically about his preaching. In Sarlat, a sermon, which receives little attention in Geoffrey of Auxerre's account, is followed by a miracle of healing. In Verfeil, William of Puylaurens's *Chronicle* reports that the local nobles caused such a commotion that Bernard's sermon could not be heard, and the abbot left the town in anger, shaking the dust from his feet. This offers a rare glimpse of failure for Bernard and a hint at the sort of resistant confrontation a preacher could meet in a hostile milieu. An actual report of a sermon at Albi records that Bernard preached on his coming to sow and his finding the field already sown with wicked seed, a probable reference to the Parable of the tares (Matthew 13. 24–30, 36–52). The structure for the abbot's sermon can be imagined from Geoffrey's observation that the abbot showed the crowd the good and wicked seed, expounding various points one at a time and explaining both the orthodox and the heterodox teaching on each. Such a structure corresponds to the reasoning Bernard advocated for persuading heretics of their errors, and since it comes from Geoffrey's pen, it probably represents the way Bernard wanted his preaching remembered. Nonetheless, Bernard does not follow such a plan strictly in his extant writings. Furthermore, his sermons must have contained other features for filling out the structure which would have appealed to a popular audience. The vituperative rhetoric of his anti-heretical letters and extant sermons must have played a role in the sermons he delivered. *Exempla* such as those described from the *Vita prima* and the *Exordium magnum* which demonstrate the worth of orthodoxy most likely formed a part of Bernard's sermons also. Similarly, the miracles recorded brought vitality and force to his preaching and can be considered performative aspects of his sermons. The final account of the abbot's preaching,

---

[91] Russell, *Dissent and Order*, p. 4. Also relevant is Chazan's observation that medieval people held the assumption that human character did not change, and therefore that medieval Jews 'shared the same propensities as those who had called for the crucifixion of Christ a millennium earlier.' Chazan, *Stereotypes*, p. 15.

[92] *Song*, III, 192; *SBOp*, II, 179.

reported in the *Exordium magnum*, captures an instance of performance. Like the report from Albi, it refers to Bernard's admonishing a crowd on the preservation of orthodox faith and the avoidance of the heretical. In this case, Bernard wins over the crowd with the sight of his emaciated but shining white neck.

Bernard's own evaluation of his preaching effort has been illumined to some extent by the sources analysed above, as have the views of others. His letters (241 and 242) express his sense of the necessity of preaching missions and his regret that he could not return himself. His biography depicts him as the inheritor of a crucial and apostolic mission, travelling the heathen countryside, preaching and performing miracles. Reports of his audiences' reception of his preaching include enthusiastic support, awe at miracles performed, clamorous confrontation, and direct verbal challenge.

Contemporary scholars have debated at length Bernard's views on war, the crusades, and to a lesser extent, on the use of force against heretics. The question of clerics' participation in military action constitutes one aspect of the issue; their advocacy of the secular recourse to violence represents another. On the former, Bernard's views remain clear; on the latter, his writings held ambiguities and contradictions.

Bernard's position on clerics and the use of force is examined by James Brundage: Bernard felt that a cleric should be a prophet and not a general, that the pope could advise secular rulers to use force when it was morally justified, but that the pope and clerics in general had no right to declare war or to take up arms. In no way should clerics participate in war-making, whether to declare it or direct it. Bernard's Letter 544 declares that any Cistercian monk who would embark on a crusade was to be excommunicated. Moreover, Bernard also advised Eugenius III in 1150 that he agreed with the proclaiming of a new crusade but that the pope should not be involved directly in its conduct.[93]

The same letter from 1150 grounds Brenda Bolton's analysis, further clarifying Bernard's position on clerics and the use of force. In May of 1150 at the Council of Chartres, Bernard was nominated as spiritual and military leader of a proposed Third Crusade. Bernard objected strongly to that role, and in Letter 256 addressed to Eugenius III[94] he states: 'Who am I to lead an army into battle, to march at the head of the troops? What could be further from my profession, even if the strength and necessary skills were not lacking in me?'[95]

While Bernard's view on clerics' participation in military action is clear, his

---

[93] Brundage, 'St Bernard and the Jurists', pp. 25–33. *SBOp*, VIII, 511–12, *Ep*. 544 from 1147; *Letters*, 396, pp. 468–9. *Ep*. 256, *SBOp*, VIII, 163; *Letters*, 399, pp. 470–2.

[94] Bolton, B. M., 'The Cistercians and the Aftermath of the Second Crusade', in *The Second Crusade and the Cistercians*, ed. M. Gervers (New York, 1992), pp. 131–40, esp. p. 137.

[95] *Ep*. 256, *SBOp*, VIII, 163–5; *Letters*, 399, p. 472.

writings on the secular employment of force remain ambiguous. Bernard's position holds contradictions: he judged heretics incapable of persuasion by reasoning but asserted that logical argument, not force, was the way to persuade them to change. On the one hand, he opposed the use of force against heretics; on the other, he denounced heresy with virulence and allowed for the sword to punish heretics.[96] Moreover, he articulated a vision for uniting the spiritual and the military in the Knights Templar. It is altogether possible that these contradictions reflect Bernard's uncertainties over the appropriate course for the Church to follow when confronting heresy, which he considered one of the three great historical trials to afflict the Church (along with persecution and clerical corruption).[97] Bernard's uncertainties probably relate as well to his inner conflict over engagement in the Lord's vineyard and his use of the chimera image to reflect the different directions in which he was drawn.

The 1145 expedition into Occitania had profound consequences. R. I. Moore signals it as a significant step in the development of inquisitorial processes. The mission represented an advance in the centralization of responsibility for dealing with heresy and in the securing of outside intervention for quelling heresy in Occitania. In addition, it established a precedent for depriving heretics and their supporters of legal rights. Moore cites as evidence for his opinion the judgment that Bernard obtained from the citizens of Toulouse: 'the heretics, their supporters and all who gave them any help would not be eligible to give evidence or seek redress in the courts, and nobody would have any dealings with them, either socially or in business'.[98]

Scholars attempt to separate the strands of Bernard's thoughts and deeds; his contemporaries tended to seize the elements that suited their goals. Bernard's views may be sufficiently nuanced for scholars to disculpate him from advocating violence; however, some of his successors did not grasp the contradictions. We may consider a parallel here with Bernard's stance to protect the Jews from violence during the Second Crusade. While Bernard

---

[96] Manselli, 'De la *persuasio* à la *coercitio*', p. 181, states that Bernard's reference to bearing the sword does not seems to indicate any systematic persecution of heretics but 'une légitime défense' against heretical preaching and activity. He concludes (p. 182): 'Même le caractère batailleur du grand cistercien se refusait à l'idée d'une véritable persécution proprement dite de l'hérétique: essentiellement il lui semblait plus important de faire connaître qui ils étaient et ce qu'ils voulaient plutôt que de les frapper.'

[97] See J. Leclercq, 'L'hérésie d'après les écrits de S. Bernard de Clairvaux', in *The Concept of Heresy in the Middle Ages (11th–13th C.). Proceedings of the International Conference, Louvain, 13–16 May 1973*, ed. W. Lordaux and D. Verhelst (Leuven, 1976), pp. 12–26. J. Leclercq surveys Bernard's writings against Abelard, the Cathars and Gilbert of Poitiers and treats the abbot's images of heresy and darkness and preaching as archery against heresy.

[98] *PL*, CXCV, 412. Moore, *Formation*, p. 25. See also Maisonneuve, pp. 125–6, and Newman, pp. 226–7.

showed concern for protecting the Jews, a feeling of hostility remains in his rhetoric. David Berger concludes that, although Bernard's arguments did not lead him to violence, 'the hatred which he preached was fanning the flames of violence in lesser men'.[99] Lesser men were to succeed Bernard and attain positions of leadership as abbots of Clairvaux and Cîteaux, whom we discuss in Chapters Four and Five.

There has been scholarly speculation on whether the abbot of Clairvaux's ideas would have evolved in the 1150s and 1160s, when the problem of heresy appeared increasingly urgent to the Church, and whether the seeds for trying to justify the extermination of heretics were already present.[100] While Bernard's statement in Sermon 66.12, that it is better for a heretic to be restrained by the sword than to lead others into error, does not directly advocate the use of force against heretics, it is certainly shaded enough to lay the groundwork for armed intervention by secular forces.

[99] Chazan, *Stereotypes*, p. 42, comments on D. Berger, 'The Attitude of St Bernard of Clairvaux toward the Jews', *Proceedings of the American Academy for Jewish Research*, 40 (1972), 89–108.

[100] See Leclercq on the Wends, for example, and the many references he includes in his 'Saint Bernard's Attitude Toward War', pp. 20–2. Congar, pp. 16–18, also deals with this issue.

CHAPTER FOUR

Henry of Clairvaux, the 1178 and 1181 Missions, and the Campaign against the Waldensians: Driving the Foxes from the Vineyard

Henry – abbot of Hautecombe (1160–76) and then of Clairvaux (1176–79), named cardinal bishop of Albano in 1179 and papal legate in 1181 – did not have the same reservations about leading troops as did his predecessor Bernard of Clairvaux.[1] Under Henry's leadership, the Cistercian posture in Occitania shifted radically and set an unfortunate pattern. Bernard's sixth successor as abbot of Clairvaux was deliberately trying to avoid the failure that his predecessor encountered. Furthermore, Henry extended Bernard's justification of using force in Jerusalem to the campaign against heretics in Occitania. As Yves Congar concluded: 'La croisade s'est transposée en guerre sainte contre les hérétiques.'[2] He placed the blame squarely on Henry of Clairvaux and the evolution of his thinking during the two years preceding the Third Lateran Council. Accepting that conclusion, we shall extend it by examining more sources, looking for evidence of Henry's preaching, and analysing his language with a view to the rhetorical patterns of demonizing heretics and evoking pollution, threat to the social order, and apocalypticism.

A short overview of events in the 1150s and 1160s in France, the Rhineland and England will chart the heightening sense of alarm over heresy during the years that preceded and coincided with the beginnings of Henry of Clairvaux/ Albano's involvement as a leader in the affairs of the Cistercian Order and the Church.

---

[1] An earlier version of this chapter was published as 'Henry of Clairvaux and the 1178 and 1181 Missions', *Heresis* 28 (1997), 63–87; sections are reused here with the editor's permission.

[2] Bernard's immediate successor, Gerard, died after being wounded by a crazed monk. See Congar, p. 5. On Henry and Bernard, Congar cites two similar passages, one from Bernard in 1128 about the threat to Jerusalem: 'Dissipentur gentes quae bella volunt et abscindentur qui nos conturbant, et disperdantur de civitate Domini omnes operantes iniquitatem'; and the other from Henry of Clairvaux about the heretics in the area of Toulouse: 'Persequantur interim, peccatores Amalech, et de civitate Domini veteres exterminent Jebusaeos . . .' Congar, p. 18. The passage quoted from Bernard is in *Ad milites Templi*, c. 3. n. 5, *PL*, CLXXXII, 824–5; the passage from Henry is in *PL*, CCIV, 224–5. See p. 115 below for further discussion.

In 1153, reports of heresy surfaced in the northern French city of Arras, followed in 1157 by a council at Rheims that attacked dissidents loosely called 'Manicheans'. In 1162/63, another group of 'Manicheans' was discovered in Arras,[3] and around the same time, dissidents called *Publicani* appeared in England. Assumed to have come from Germany, the dissidents reportedly numbered sympathizers in France, Spain and Italy. The chronicler William of Newburgh recorded the events, employing the imagery of little foxes and the Lord's vineyard and praising England's freedom since Pelagius from the 'germ of heretical infection'. A synod at Oxford, called by Henry II, proclaimed the people heretics and ordered them to be branded and expelled to die in the winter cold. The first secular legislation against heresy followed in the 1166 Assize of Clarendon, which ordered anyone who sheltered heretics to be expelled and have their homes burned.[4]

Cologne saw the escalation of violence against accused heretics in 1163, when a group of people was burned there. This incident marked the initiation of collaborative efforts against heresy by Hildegard of Bingen, Elisabeth of Schönau, and her brother, Eckbert of Schönau, who composed an important series of sermons against the Cathars, applying that name for the first time to the dualistic dissidents who rejected the authority of Rome and its sacraments.[5]

In France, the Council of Lombers, presided over by Gaucelin of Lodève in 1165, interrogated a group of 'good men' (*boni homines*), what so-called Cathars named themselves, and compelled them to make a statement of belief in response to various charges, including those that they accepted only the New Testament, and opposed marriage, oath-taking and the power of unworthy priests.[6] Two salient events occurred in 1167: accused heretics were reported in Vézelay, and an important meeting of Cathar bishops took place at St Félix de Caraman, although it provoked no confrontation or extant polemical

---

[3] On the events in Arras and Rheims, see the texts in Moore, *Birth*, pp. 80–2.

[4] An English translation of the relevant passage from William of Newburgh's chronicle appears in Moore, *Birth*, pp. 82–4. P. Biller examines the episode, the one woman heretic mentioned, and the connections between the campaigns against heresy in England and France in 'William of Newburgh and the Cathar Mission to England' in *Life and Thought in the Northern Church c. 1100–1700. Essays in Honour of Claire Cross*, ed. D. Wood, SCH S 12 (Woodbridge, 1999), pp. 11–30. R. I. Moore emphasizes how Henry II's desire to seem strong in religious matters at the time he was involved in struggles with Thomas Becket motivated him to identify the common enemy of heresy. 'À la naissance d'une société persécutrice: les clercs, les cathares et la formation de l'Europe', in *La persécution du Catharisme. Actes de la 6e session d'histoire médiévale, 1er–4 septembre 1993*, Heresis 6 (hors série) (Carcassonne, 1996), pp. 11–37 (pp. 28–9).

[5] The events are reported in a contemporary chronicle (see Moore, *Birth*, pp. 88–9) and in Caesarius, *Dialogus*, translated in WE, pp. 243–5. See Kienzle, '*Operatrix in vinea domini*' and 'Defending the Lord's Vineyard' cited in Introduction, n. 12.

[6] On the Council of Lombers, see Moore, *Birth*, pp. 94–8. On Gaucelin of Lodève and his interaction over doctrinal questions with the monks at the Cistercian abbey of Sylvanès, see Kienzle and Shroff, 'Cistercians and Heresy: Doctrinal Consultation'.

Fig. 4. The Praemonstratensian abbey of Fontcaude (Hérault), whose abbot
Bernard composed a treatise against the Waldensians *c.* 1190

literature. The people who were sentenced to the stake in Vézelay reportedly
espoused some Cathar-type beliefs, namely the rejection of traditional
sacraments.[7] A group of dissidents, including a woman learned in the
Scriptures, was persecuted in Rheims around 1176–80; their ideas clearly
matched those associated with the Cathars, including rejection of traditional
sacraments and food resulting from procreation, and belief in an apostate
angel who presides over material creation.[8]

---

[7] On the persecution at Vézelay, see Moore, *Birth*, p. 85. The events at St Félix have
caused much scholarly debate. A summary can be found in Lambert, *Cathars*,
pp. 45–59.
[8] On the persecution at Rheims, see Moore, *Birth*, pp. 86–8. Cathar and Bogomil beliefs
on the creation of matter by Satan appear in the myths of the *Interrogatio Iohannis*,
brought to Italy by the Cathar bishop Nazarius of Concorezzo around 1190.
Interrogatio Iohannis, p. 27. This reference from a decade earlier is quite interesting.

These and other events produced an atmosphere of increasing alarm and provoked the widespread engagement of Church leaders against a perceived common enemy: the Cathar Christians they cast as inheritors of Manicheanism.

Against this background of widespread alarm over heresy, Henry commonly called 'of Marcy', entered the Cistercian order at Clairvaux in about 1155. He was elected abbot of Hautecombe in 1160, then abbot of Clairvaux in 1176. Controversy within the order over sheltering Thomas Becket and then about reprisals against Henry II after Becket's 1170 murder had caused strife at Clairvaux and brought the resignation of Geoffrey of Auxerre in 1165. After Bernard's canonization, it was Henry of Clairvaux who endeavoured to patch up relations with King Henry II of England by sending him a relic of Bernard's finger.[9] In 1178 Henry of Clairvaux participated in a preaching mission led by the legate Peter, cardinal of St Chrysogonus. Subsequently the Cistercian exerted a strong influence at the Third Lateran Council in 1179, then accepted Valdes's profession of faith in 1180,[10] and returned to Occitania in 1181 as papal legate. Thus he was at the forefront of the Church's campaign against heresy. He also became involved in the diffusion of propaganda for the crusades to the Holy Land. Following his presence in Occitania, Henry preached the crusade and wrote his *De peregrinante civitate Dei* – a manifesto of crusade ideology – sometime before 1 January 1189, when he died, never having reached the Holy Land as he had hoped.[11]

Sources for Henry of Clairvaux/Albano's role in the preaching campaign against heresy include: some chronicle accounts and miscellaneous sources that mention him; three of his own letters from 1178 (nos. 28, 11 and 29); and Canon 27 of the Third Lateran Council, which he probably helped to draft. On the whole, these sources tell us more about his ideology than about his sermons. A few *exempla* not related to Henry's involvement in preaching against heresy stress his humility, even as cardinal bishop.[12] A letter from Peter of St Chrysogonus speaks of the debate in 1178 that took place in the church of St Etienne in Toulouse, followed in the church of St Jacques by a public profession of faith and accusations from witnesses who charged the two heretics under interrogation with preaching doctrine contrary to what they had just professed. That episode is also included in Roger of Howden's

[9] Newman, pp. 213–16.

[10] See Congar, pp. 28–9, 31–3; Thouzellier, *Catharisme et Valdéisme*, pp. 25–5.

[11] Congar, p. 43. According to Congar, Henry had begun the text at the Curia between 1185 and 1186. P. Cole also reviews Henry's crusading ideas and activities in *Preaching*, pp. 65–71.

[12] Other stories about Henry emphasize aspects of monastic humility in the face of his elections as cardinal and bishop. In two chapters (30 and 31) of the *Exordium magnum*, he is praised for his faithfulness to monastic humility even after his election as a cardinal. *Exordium magnum*, pp. 137–8. He also appears in the *Dialogus miraculorum* of Caesarius of Heisterbach. See nn. 5 and 99 in this chapter. I am grateful to Jessalyn Bird for reference to these *exempla* from Caesarius.

Chronicon.[13] Geoffrey of Auxerre provides an account of the success of Henry's preaching, which reportedly influenced two noteworthy conversions on 15 September 1181.[14] Geoffrey's praise for Henry's effective preaching is echoed by the chroniclers Robert of Auxerre and William of Puylaurens.[15] The chronicles and miscellaneous sources will be included with the letters and Canon 27 of the Third Lateran Council and commented upon chronologically as we assess Henry's role in the Church's campaign.

1178, the preaching mission and prior letters

From the year 1178, Henry's three letters, with the letter from Peter of St Chrysogonus, describe the events around the preaching mission and also reveal the attitudes of the two men towards the situation facing the Church. Two of Henry's letters (28 and 11), written in the spring of 1178, precede the preaching mission and one (29), written in the autumn, follows it, as does the letter from Peter of St Chrysogonus. Henry's writings demonstrate a strong conviction that ecclesiastical and secular forces should collaborate to stamp out heresy.

The two letters written in the first five months of 1178 show a change in Henry's position toward the appropriate means for combating heresy: a shift from reliance on preaching alone to the conviction that a preaching mission should be reinforced by the secular authorities.[16] In the autumn of 1177, Louis

---

[13] The 1178 debate is described in a letter written by Peter of St Chrysogonus, the papal legate leading the preaching mission. Two heretics, Raymond of Baimac and Bernard Raymond, were granted a hearing and safe passage for eight days afterwards. They were excommunicated and the legate's letter appeals to his audience to reject their false preaching and to drive them away as heretics and forerunners of the Antichrist. *PL*, CXCIX, 1119–24. Peter's letter is translated in Moore, *Birth*, pp. 113–16. The letters of Peter Chrysogonus and Henry of Clairvaux were the source for Roger of Howden's narrative in his chronicle. A translation of his entry for 1178 appears in WE, no. 29, pp. 195–200.

[14] The text from *Apocalypsim*, p. 210, reads: '. . . duos haeresiarchas . . . in partibus Tolosanis . . . ab exercitu zelo fidei congregato comprehensos novimus et oblatos venerabili patri nostro domino Henrico Albanensi episcopo, apostolicae sedis in Aquitania tunc legato. Quibus astantibus, dum idem pontifex ad copiosissimam multitudinem diversae conditionis et diversi ordinis adversus eamdem haeresim sermonem faceret, prout Spiritus Sanctus dabat eloqui illi, praedicti haeresiarchae in verbis gratiae quae procedeant de ore eius Domino inspirante usque adeo sunt compuncti ut secretas haeresis illius blasphemias et exsecrandas abominationes cum multis lacrimis, audientibus omnibus, non distulerint confiteri.'

[15] Robert of Auxerre, *Chronicon* (MGH SS SSVI, p. 245.40), '. . . missus est ab Alexandro papa vir linguae diserte Henricis, ex abbate Clarevallis episcopus Albanensis, qui predicationis verbo militum peditumque copias undecumque contraxit, prefatos hereticos expugnavit.' Puylaurens, p. 28, includes the conversion episode. See also Thouzellier, *Catharisme et Valdéisme*, p. 39, nn. 95–6.

[16] *Ep.* 28, *PL*, CCIV, 234–5, written in the spring of 1178 and *Ep.* 11, *PL*, CCIV, 223–5,

VII and Henry II of England had met with Peter of St Chrysogonus on 21 September and decided to back an expedition to southern France but not to lead it themselves, as requested by Raymond V; instead they advocated that Peter of St Chrysogonus lead the mission. Raymond V had supported the collaboration of spiritual and secular powers, as evidenced in his letters to the 1177 General Chapter at Cîteaux, sometime after 13 September, and to the two kings. Raymond's letter to Cîteaux brings the vineyard image into play.[17] During the last months of 1177, Henry of Clairvaux, according to Congar, was won over to the view of the necessity for ecclesiastical and secular collaboration, and that point of view is reflected in his spring 1178 letter to Louis VII.

In that letter (28), Henry of Clairvaux describes the king as the propagator of the faith and the vanquisher of the infidels, and he promises him the prayers of the monks. Henry states that he had intended to go to the south himself and visit Cistercian monasteries, but decided that his admonitions might forwarn the heretics and make them more cautious. The victory would be better as the king's, for he would return the heretics to the bosom of the Church or cast them out of the kingdom for their defiance.[18]

In another letter – from May of the same year, 1178 – Henry entreated Pope Alexander III to extend Peter of St Chrysogonus's charge as legate and to entrust him with the fight against heresy. Peter had been in France and England since 1174 trying to reconcile Louis VII and Henry II.[19] In this May 1178 letter (11), Henry describes papal intervention as the only effective remedy against heresy and widespread moral corruption. The letter uses imagery of bride and bridegroom and figures from the Hebrew Scriptures to assert that the pope should avenge the wrongs done to the bride:

written in May of 1178, according to Congar, p. 14. The two letters and background are discussed on pages 10–18 of the same article.

[17] Raymond's letters are discussed in Congar, pp. 10–12. Biget, partly because of the vineyard image, argues for the influence of Cistercian advisors on Raymond V in 'Les Albigeois', p. 238.

[18] *PL*, CCIV, 234CD: 'Non ergo cessamus pauperes vestri de Claravalle, sedulo pro vobis orantes ad Deum, ut vestrae magnanimitatis vota grata, rata et acceptabilia faciat, et omnes regiae dispositionis adnisus ad gloriam suam et salutem vestram promoveat, ordinet et disponat; specialiter autem in hoc opere Christianae religionis et fidei copiam vobis gratiae coelestis impendat, per quam dignus inveniamini corona justitiae, tam propagator fidei, quam victis infidelibus triumphator. Et nos quidem nuper ire ad partes illas pro visitandis nostris domibus disponentes, decreveramus faciem vestram etiam in hoc ipsum praecedere, ut possemus aliquos ex infidelibus illis prius ab erroribus suis, deinde ab ore imminentis gladii liberare. Habita tamen deliberatione nobiscum, praesensimus melius esse nobis omnino desistere, ne ipsi forsitan ex monitis nostris in sua redderentur perfidia cautiores. Vobis melius decernitur hujus pugnae victoria, per quam favente de supernis Altissimo, vel faciatis eos ad Ecclesiae sinum reduces, vel a sinu regni propulsabitis contumaces.' Congar, p. 12, comments on Henry's change of opinion and part of this passage.

[19] See Congar, p. 13 on Peter's mission.

It is time that the bridegroom's friend avenge the wrongs to the bride, and the sword of the priest Phinehas be drawn against the incest of the Israelite and the Midianite.

Henry continues, stating that Alexander III had reconciled the schismatic, obviously referring to the schism with Frederick Barbarossa that ended in 1177, and now the pope must put heresies to sleep.[20] The allusion to Phinehas combines notions of sexual impurity, faithlessness and punishment by violent death: Phinehas in Numbers 25. 6–9 slays an Israelite man who has sexual relations with a woman from the Midianites, worshippers of Baal, who were corrupting the Israelites.

A key passage in Letter 11 – the symbol of the two swords, temporal and spiritual – illustrates how the crusade ideology had been extended to the notion of a holy war against heretics:

> Truly it is necessary and in accordance with the word of the Gospel that there be two swords here [Luke 22. 38]; we believe it worthy and honourable for you that your striving for the good (*aemulatio*) be joined to the zeal of the secular princes. . . .[21]

Besides this advocacy of a holy war to be waged by ecclesiastical and secular forces, the letter reveals an intense concentration of highly charged rhetoric. The letter is structured with Henry's request at its centre; approximately forty-four lines introduce the specific request, painting a picture of the evil and corruption wrought by heresy;[22] another forty lines or so state the letter's goal, to extend Peter of St Chrysogonus's term as legate in France and to charge him with fighting heresy;[23] a third, closing section of 25–30 lines urges the collaboration of secular and ecclesiastical

---

[20] *PL*, CCIV, 224A: 'Tempus est ut amicus sponsi sponsae ulciscatur injurias, et gladius Phinees sacerdotis in incestum Israelitae et Madianitidis exeratur. Ecce in diebus vestris, auctore domino, sedata sunt schismata; euge pastor bone, facite ut et haereses sopiantur.'

[21] 'Verum, quia necesse est, ut juxta Evangelii verbum sint gladii duo hic (Luc, XXII, 38), dignum credimus et honorificum vobis, ut zelum saecularium principum vestra quoque aemulatio comitetur, ne pia eorum intentio sumat ex occasione defectum, si oportunum non acceperit ex vestra cooperatione subsidium. Expedit igitur ut praedicto cardinali congruas prorogantes inducias, detis ei specialiter in mandatis, ut contra hostes charitatis et fidei magnanimiter accingatur . . . Persequantur interim, ut optime coepit, peccatores Amalech, et de civitate Domini veteres exterminet Jebusaeos . . .' Congar emphasizes this passage, *PL*, CCIV, 224–5, in his article, and compares it to a statement by Bernard written in 1128 to the Templars about the threat to Jerusalem: 'Dissipentur gentes quae bella volunt et abscindentur qui nos conturbant, et disperdantur de civitate Domini omnes operantes iniquitatem.' *Ad milites Templi*, c. 3. n. 5, *PL*, CLXXXII, 824–5. Congar, p. 16.

[22] *PL*, CCIV, 223B–224AB.

[23] *PL*, CCIV, 224B–D.

forces and uses the image of the two swords.[24] Congar focused his study on the ideas of the third section; here the language and imagery of the first will be scrutinized, with some additional examples from the second and third parts.

Henry begins with the assertion that the Gallic Church has been soiled by many evils, among them the fall of virtue and the overthrow of faith. Shameful people rush in from all sides to defile the pure chastity of the simple, and the chaste simplicity of devout belief is shut out. In short, there are ruinous portents (*prodigia funesta*) and papal intervention offers the only remedy. Thus Henry uses elements of evil, pollution and threat to the social order to characterize the direness of the situation he describes. The repetition of word groups that suggest sexual pollution – *pudicitiae lapsum*; *casta simplicitas . . . excluditur*; *candida simplicium castitas . . . inquinatur* – deserves special attention, for the suggestion of sexual immorality will be reiterated more strongly in this same section of the letter.

The image of Joseph's coat is introduced next: offended doubly, by filth and by error, the coat represents the Church and serves to bring to focus the twin motifs of pollution and division. Made without stain or tear, it is now being spotted and rent in Gaul. Henry further links heresy and pollution with another two-part image, that of a two-forked river where heresy and disgrace flow together, as the cloak is soiled by impurity and rent by the laceration of treachery. The last expression, *laceratione perfidiae*, brings to mind the legal equation of heresy and treason (*laesa majestatis*) that was to be formulated in Innocent III's 1199 *Vergentis in senium*. In this 1178 letter Henry of Clairvaux already envisages heresy as a divisive and treasonous offence. He uses the word *perfidia* here, not the legal term *laesa majestatis*, and *perfidia* appears also in Letters 28 and 29.[25]

After exploiting the image of Joseph's coat, Henry accumulates more biblical allusions. A snake, called the serpent of ancient lust (*antiquae libidinis vermis*), rises from the ashes of the Sodomites and from the lake of damnation. Through the reference to the Sodomites, Henry associates the heretics not only with the pollution of sin, but with the East, for he has the snake breathing out foulness and infecting the West. The link between the East and heresy surfaces again when Henry states: 'Arius has come back to life in the West.'[26] Moreover, Henry, like Geoffrey of Auxerre in the *Vita prima*,

---

[24] *PL*, CCIV, 224D–225A.

[25] *PL*, CCIV, 234D: '. . . ne ipsi forsitan ex monitis nostris in sua redderentur perfidia cautiores'; and *PL*, CCIV, 238D: 'Venit . . . veteris exuens perfidiae pravitatem.' In that same letter Henry tells of excommunicating Roger II of Béziers publicly as a traitor, heretic and perjurer: 'proditorem, haereticum, et . . . perjurum . . .', *PL*, CCIV, 240C.

[26] *PL*, CCIV, 223D: 'Surrexit enim de cineribus Sodomorum antiquae libidinis vermis, qui post ignis pluvias imbresque sulphureos de lacu damnationis emergens, fetoris sufflatibus occiduas inficit regiones. Revixit et Arius in partibus Occidentis, qui ab orientali judicio in propia persona damnatus, nunc in successoribus suis fines

uses Arius and Arianism as the archetypal heretic and heresy.[27] When we recall that some medieval writers envisaged a line of heretical leaders starting with Simon Magus who opposed the orthodox succession beginning with Simon Peter,[28] it seems that Henry's attitude could be characterized that way. Indeed, in his view, the lineage of immorality that he links with heresy extends back to the cities of Sodom and Gomorrah. He refers to the infamous towns again, linking their sins to the shameful secret deeds of the heretics, which offend or betray (*laederet*, the verb used for treason) the decency of the reader and the shame of the writer. Apparently this latter phrase serves to apologize for the shameful acts he describes in the following sentence. 'Like Sodom[ites], the heretics preach their sin and they call forth guests, as if they resided near Gomorrah, to the sin of [unnatural] lust (*convivas libidinum provocant ad peccandum*), that is, into Gomorrah itself.'[29]

Henry apparently wishes to implicate the heretics in behaviour beyond what he views as general sexual immorality; that is, he specifically implicates them in homosexual acts. The recurrence of vocabulary with sexual connotations, the allusions to Sodom and Gomorrah, and the strong language Henry uses, namely that the secret actions of heretics offend both the one who writes about them and the one who reads about them, create that impression.

While vague accusations of sexual morality appear commonly against heretics, the last decades of the twelfth century also witnessed specific attacks against homosexuality. According to John Boswell, Peter the Chanter (d. 1197) was the first influential scholar to associate homosexual acts with biblical prohibitions against sodomy and the Third Lateran Council was the first general council to issue legislation against homosexual acts.[30] Boswell situates

---

    ultimos occupavit.' Henry uses the word 'vermis', usually a worm, but it is unlikely that the worm would describe suitably this threatening creature, breathing out venom.

[27] See Chapter Three in this book, pp. 92, 96.

[28] Russell, *Dissent and Order*, p. 4.

[29] 'Nam et haeretici in publico disputant contra fidem; et quod multi in occulto faciunt, et scribentis verecundiam, et legentis laederet honestatem. Sed quid dicimus in occulto? Peccatum suum sicut Sodoma praedicant, et velut in suburbanis Gomorrhae convivas libidinum provocant ad peccandum. Numquid super his non indignabitur zelus vester, aut impune peccabunt, et vos tacebitis?' 'Convivas . . . peccandum' could read: 'call forth guests of lust for sinning'; or 'call forth guests for the sin of lust'. The latter seems a better interpretation to me; the guests, dwellers near Gomorrah, would be called to lust, or into the city of Gomorrah itself.

[30] Moore, *Formation*, p. 92, reads Peter Comestor, referring to Boswell who cites P. Cantor on p. 277 of *Tolerance*. Boswell's remarks (p. 277): 'As if in direct response to Peter's urging, Lateran III of 1179 became the first ecumenical ('general') council to rule on homosexual acts.' The remarks of the Chanter that Boswell cited are found in the *Verbum abbreviatum*, which Baldwin dated from 1191 to 1192 in his

this council's ruling in the context of the increasingly intolerant attitude towards all types of nonconformity. He does not bring to light J. Baldwin's observation that parts of the *Verbum abbreviatum*, the work of the Chanter's that he cites, contain 'vivid and detailed accounts' of the Third Lateran Council and that Peter the Chanter could well have attended the council, although there is no 'positive evidence'.[31] It is important to add to Boswell and Baldwin's observations the possibility of Henry of Clairvaux's influence at the Third Lateran Council. Henry was a driving force at the council, and the allusions he makes to Sodom and Gomorrah in the 1178 letter predate the council's canon. It is thinkable then that the Chanter was influenced by the council and by Henry.

The ruling from the Third Lateran Council remains somewhat vague about the specific acts it targets, but makes a clear reference to the destruction of the cities by fire:

> Whoever shall be found to have committed that incontinence which is against nature, on account of which the wrath of God came upon the sons of perdition and consumed five cities with fire, shall, if a cleric, be deposed from office or confined to a monastery to do penance; if a layman, he shall suffer excommunication and be cast out from the company of the faithful.[32]

Despite the vagueness of the council's wording, the allusion to the burning of Sodom and Gomorrah, when juxtaposed with the preoccupation with homosexuality during this period, argues that homosexual acts were the target of the decree. As Boswell concludes:

Although the literal tenor of this canon could be interpreted as referring to all non-procreative intercourse, and during the transition period which followed it was often so construed, its social context suggests strongly that

---

Masters, I, 13. Still Baldwin considers it likely that the Chanter collected notes for the *Verbum abbreviatum* while he was composing his commentaries and lectures. Baldwin, *Masters,* I, 5–6.

[31] See Baldwin, *Masters,* I, 9; II, 212, n. 5. Baldwin cites a passage in *Masters,* I, 315, from the *Verbum abbreviatum (PL,* CCV, 235C) in the context of views expressed at Lateran III. Baldwin also treats the Chanter's views on homosexuality in *The Language of Sex. Five Voices from Northern France around 1200* (Chicago, 1994), pp. 43–7, where he concludes: 'Peter the Chanter played an important role in the revival of homophobia at the end of the twelfth century.' Appendix 2 to the volume, pp. 247–50, contains the long version of Chapter XLVI of the *Verbum abbreviatum,* 'Contra sodomiticam turpitudinem'.

[32] The translation is from Boswell, *Tolerance,* p. 277. He cites the Latin in pp. 277–8, n. 26: 'Quicumque in incontinentia illa quae contra naturam est, propter quam venit ira Dei in filios diffidentiae, et quinque civitates igne consumpsit, deprehensi fuerint laborare, si clerici fuerint, ejiciantur a clero, vel ad poenitentiam agendam in monasteriis detrudantur; si laici, excommunicati subdantur, et a coetu fidelium fiant prorsus alieni.'

it was aimed at homosexual practices, and it passed into the permanent collections of canon law compiled in the thirteenth century . . .[33]

Returning to Henry of Clairvaux's Letter 11 and its implications, Henry's presence and influence at the Third Lateran Council, the sexual language he uses, and the fact that he writes this letter to Alexander III in May of 1178, or less than a year before the council, together suggest that he is associating heresy with homosexual acts. The tie that he makes predates other signposts in the history of this connection. The word 'bougre' from Bulgar (Bogomil) used as a synonym for Cathar gave rise to 'bougrerie', which was used in thirteenth-century northern France to denote heresy as well as sodomy and bestiality. Alan of Lille, the Paris master who spent the end of his life in a Cistercian monastery, accused the Cathars of bestiality and derived the name 'Cathar' from the heretics' practice of kissing the hind parts of a cat as part of their ritual. One reference from the Anonymous of Passau (*c.* 1260–66) describes such a ritual followed by homosexual acts among the men and the women.[34] Henry of Clairvaux's relatively early insinuations of homosexual acts among the heretics may indicate that his opinion played a decisive role in formulating this unfortunate association at the Third Lateran Council.

Following these accusations against the heretics, Henry calls for the man of the hour, Peter of St Chrysogonus, to be retained as a legate in France, now for the purpose of fighting heresy. With his praise of the legate, the abbot of Clairvaux adds more scriptural analogies to describe Peter's merits and typify his adversaries. Peter is said: 'to fight steadily against the beasts of Ephesus'; to don Simon Peter against Simon the Magician; and to display a new Elisha to the lepers of Syria.[35] The first reference echoes I Corinthians 15. 32, where Paul asks, 'What . . . if . . . I fought with beasts at Ephesus?' The second alludes to Simon Peter's defeat of Simon Magus. The latter appears in Acts 8. 9–24, but Peter's spectacular victory over him is found in the apocryphal *Acts of Peter*, where the magician's flying machine crashes to the ground at the apostle's word.[36] The third characterization is drawn from II Kings 5 where Naaman, the commander of the Syrian army suffering from leprosy, is healed by Elisha, and Gehazi is struck with the disease. Thus the

---

[33] Boswell, *Tolerance,* p. 278.

[34] Duvernoy, *Religion*, pp. 255–7, on accusations of immorality, and pp. 309–11 on the word 'bougres'. The passage from Alan of Lille is in *PL*, CCX, 366.

[35] *PL*, CCIV, 224C: 'Pugnat constater ad bestias Ephesi, Simonem Petrum contra Simones magos induens et leprosis Syriae novum exhibens Eliseum . . .' The legate is also described with the set of four verbs that becomes formulaic for a legate's work: 'evellit et destruit, aedificat et plantat' (*PL*, CCIV, 224C). See Congar, p. 30, n. 99, on the use of this formula in another text.

[36] *Acts of Peter*, in The *Ante-Nicene Fathers*, ed. A. Roberts, J. Donaldson, A. C. Coxe (Grand Rapids, MI, 1951), vol. 8. Bernard of Clairvaux was familiar with that text and refers to Simon being in the air when Peter's word reaches him. Sermon One for the Feast of Peter and Paul, *Summer Season*, p. 101.

analogies to biblical models – Paul, Peter and Elisha – compare Peter of St Chrysogonus with a prophet and with the foremost of the apostles. Furthermore, the adversaries juxtaposed with these holy men – beasts, Simon Magus and lepers – all designate heretics in other contexts. The threat posed by heretics is often compared to that of wild beasts; the heretics may be viewed as successors of Simon Magus; and heresy is compared to the contagion of leprosy.

In the third reference, the one to Naaman, the association between heresy and leprosy brings to mind R. I. Moore's assertion that:

> For all imaginative purposes heretics, Jews and lepers were interchangeable. They had the same qualities, from the same source, and they presented the same threat: through them the Devil was at work to subvert the Christian order and bring the world to chaos.

Although I do not accept the notion of interchangeability, I do recognize the similarities that Moore points out.[37] He signals Raymond V's use of the phrase 'the putrid sore of heresy' in his 1177 letter where he describes the extent of heresy and asks for the kings Louis VII and Henry II to intervene in his lands. The putrid sore (*tabes*) of a leper was viewed as a sign that death was inevitable. Furthermore, Henry, in his references to the breathing that infects the West, demonstrates another notion of this period: that heresy could be spread like leprosy through the poisoned breath of the diseased person, which infected the air. That notion partially explains the use of fire to kill heretics and to destroy the possessions of the dead leper, as Moore comments: 'Against so insidious an infection nothing less than fire was effective.'[38] Hildegard of Bingen also described evil as being carried through the winds, although her writings against the Cathars do not make reference to leprosy.[39]

Following the praises of Peter just analysed above, the abbot of Clairvaux returns to the traditional figure of the heretics as little foxes, while adding the image of moths gnawing (*tineas corrodentes*) in Solomon's wardrobe chest:

> Thus he exterminates the destructive little foxes from the Lord of Hosts' vineyard, so that he also closes out the gnawing moths from the clotheschest of Solomon.[40]

---

[37] Chazan persuasively rejects this notion of interchangeability in *Stereotypes*, pp. 80–3, and 'The deteriorating image of the Jews – twelfth and thirteenth centuries', in *Christendom and its Discontents*, p. 224.

[38] Moore, *Formation*, pp. 63 and 63–65. Moore also suggested that both heresy and leprosy were believed to be spread through seminal fluid. R. I. Moore, 'Heresy as Disease', in *Concept of Heresy*, pp. 1–11 (pp. 5–6).

[39] See Kienzle's articles on Hildegard cited in n. 5 above, and Introduction, n. 12.

[40] *PL*, CCIV, 224C: 'ita de vinea Domini Sabaoth vulpeculas demolientes exterminat, ut de ipso quoque vestiario Salomonis tineas corrodentes excludat.'

The lowly moth, found in several books of the Bible, was associated commonly with heretics by patristic writers because of its destructive capabilities. It appears less frequently in the twelfth century and not at all in the other sources scrutinized for this book.[41]

Before Henry's final call for the two swords, discussed by Congar, he makes brief references to the 'aforesaid plagues' and the care needed for the 'aforesaid wounds', and to the fact that God has touched the hearts of the kings who have made peace and agree to pursue the 'heretical multitude' after putting on the breast plate of faith (*lorica fidei*, I Thessalonians 5. 8).[42] Thus Henry brings to conclusion the preceding impressions of disease and pollution, the implications of sexual impurity, and the widespread threat he sees posed by hoards of heretics. He calls for all of this to be remedied by force.

The 1178 letters of Henry of Clairvaux and Peter of St Chrysogonus after the preaching mission

Following the the 1178 mission, which took place between the beginning of August and October,[43] Henry composed his Letter 29, *Audite coeli*,[44] a summons to engage in a holy war against heresy, and Peter of St Chrysogonus addressed a letter *Ad universos fideles*.[45] The audiences designated for both indicate that they were probably intended for some form of public reading aloud, just as was Bernard of Clairvaux's letter to the people of Toulouse.[46] Hence they functioned like sermons. The events recounted in Henry's letter

[41] The 'tinea' appears in Ecclesiastes 42. 13; Isaiah 14. 11; 50. 9; 51. 8; Proverbs 25. 20; Job 4. 19; 13. 28; 27. 18; Matthew 6. 19; Luke 12. 33; James 5. 2. Ambrose of Milan links the moth to the heretic and specifically the Arian (*Expositiio Evangelii secundum Lucam*, Lib. 1, *PL*, XV, 1538–9; *De spiritu sancto* I.16; *Expositio psalmi cxviii*, littera 12, cap. 4). Gregory I echoes this (*Moralia in Job*, *PL*, LXXVI, 51; *CCSL* 143A, Lib. 18.17); and Rabanus Maurus takes it up in *Allegoriae in universam sacram scripturam* (*PL*, CXII, 1067 *et al.*). Bernard of Clairvaux links the moth with the Devil and Hell (*SBOp* VI, 1, p. 259).

[42] *PL*, CCIV, 224C: 'Hunc itaque vobis contra praedictas pestes prolixiori temporum spatio petimus indulgeri . . . ut cita exhibitam praedictorum vulneram curam, non sit iste vir nostris regionibus subtrahendus . . . cum tetigerit corda regum, qui . . . in nullo melius sanctiusque conveniunt, quam ut induti lorica fidei haereticam multitudinem persequantar.'

[43] Congar, p. 20. Also participating were two others with Cistercian ties: Garin of Bourges (d. 1180) and John Bellesmains, bishop of Poitiers and eventually monk at Clairvaux. Some temporal lords accompanied the group but Congar observes (p. 19) that they did not seem to exceed the numbers of a usual escort.

[44] Henry's *Epistola* 29 is in *PL*, CCIV, 235–40. An English translation is found in Moore, *Birth*, pp. 116–22.

[45] See n. 13 above for location of sources.

[46] See Chapter Three of this book, pp. 81–2, 93, 95–7.

precede the public debate discussed in Peter's letter. Specifically we learn that Henry, who left Toulouse before Peter, was responsible for sending two heretics back to Toulouse for the debate and interrogation by Peter. Furthermore, Henry's letter describes the conversion of Peter Maurand and Peter's does not. The two letters do not overlap and one has the impression that the men could have agreed on what events each would narrate.

Henry's Letter 29, *Audite coeli*, opens with highly emotional apostrophes, beginning 'Listen, Heaven, to what we lament!', and asserts that there is a general subversion of order. Martial references from the Scriptures set the parameters of the current battle: the order of heretics, an army of the perverse, constitutes a new Philistine, a new Goliath standing against the ranks of Israel, reviling God's troops and blaspheming against the Lord (I Samuel [I Kings] 17). Henry exhorts David directly to take up his sling and stone, to strike the blasphemous Goliath on the forehead and to remove his wicked head with his own hands but with Goliath's sword.[47] The triumph over Goliath will be a victory for Christ, not to be denied to the champion who will fight in Christ's love.

Here in Henry of Clairvaux's letter, the threat of violence is no longer implicit or ambiguous, as it was in Bernard of Clairvaux's writing. This abbot of Clairvaux calls directly for combat and the death of the Philistine, whose signification in Christian literature as the enemy to be slain is decidedly clear.[48]

Henry follows the David against Goliath paradigm with agricultural imagery, calling for the aid of labourers to reap Christ's harvest. He appeals to 'husbands, fathers, leaders of nations and princes of peoples', exhorting them to rise up and drive away the wild beasts or at least to put to flight the little foxes.[49] The heretics are also compared to new monsters hidden in the labyrinth of their deceit and to lesser creatures that are hard to catch: the little

---

[47] *PL*, CCIV, 235AB: 'Audite coeli, quod plangimus, sentiat terra gemitum cordis nostri. Doleant vices Christi catholici Christiani, et ad detrimentum fidei fidelis populus ingemiscat. Quique terrigenae et filii hominum humanae salutis damna deplorent et generalis vitae suae subversio ab omnibus viventibus generaliter lugeatur. Stat contra phalangas Israel novus nostri temporis Philisthaeus, haereticorum ordo, exercitus perversorum, qui agminibus Dei viventis irreverenter exprobat, et Dominum majestatis impia praesumptione blasphemat. Quid dubitas, o David? quid trepidas, vir fidelis? Sume tibi fundam et lapidem, percutiatur protinus in fronte blasphemus, et caput nequam, quod impudenter erigitur, suo tuis manibus mucrone tollatur.'

[48] Goliath (I Samuel 17) represents the vice of pride, to be slain by David's stones and his own sword, in Bernard of Clairvaux's Sermon for the Fourth Sunday after Pentecost, *Summer Season*, pp. 115–18. Bernard of Fontcaude refers to Goliath in his *Adversus Waldensium sectam*, *PL*, CCIV, 819.

[49] 'Surgite, inquam, surgite, viri Patres [sic], duces gentium, principes populorum. Abigite feras pessimas quas vidimus, quas monstramus, vel saltem vulpes parvulas effugate.' *PL*, CCIV, 235CD. The text probably should be amended to read 'viri, patres . . .' or 'viri Patris'.

fallow-deer and the snake. Chasing away the heretics is feasible, Henry observes, although not as desirable as capturing them.[50] A narrative section follows the letter's highly charged beginning and recounts the mission's entrance into Toulouse, *mater haeresis et caput erroris* (mother of heresy and head of error). The habitants of that city, which is described as 'diseased from the soles of its feet to the top of its head', greeted the mission with scorn. The heretics, like serpents in hiding places, dominated the people, so much that the orthodox preaching was ineffective, as summarized in these straightforward sentences: 'The heretics were speaking and all were marvelling. The Catholic was speaking and all were saying: "Who is this?"' The heretics were so powerful, Henry remarks, that they had their own bishops, priests, and evangelists who preached to the deceived people.[51]

According to the abbot, the preaching of orthodoxy forced the heretics into hiding, causing the foxes to metamorphose into moles and go underground where they could gnaw and destroy the roots of holy plants.[52] Subsequent animal images characterize the heretics as leopards, attempting to hide their true colours by their spots; wild beasts; and loathsome reptiles, retreating into the depths of the earth.[53] Henry's observations hold potential interest for

---

[50] *PL*, CCIV, 235D: '. . . et in quodam suarum fraudium labyrintho monstra novissima reconduntur. Tanquam damula de manu diffugiunt, et instar colubri tortuosi quo eos plus astrinxeris facilius elabuntur. Deo autem gratias, quia etsi capi nequeunt, fugari possunt; ut cum prodiderint quod demoliebantur in nobis confundantur et pereant in seipsis.' The snake image needs no comment. The fallow-deer is noted for its ability to escape. Isidore of Seville explains: 'Dammula vocata, quod de manu effugiat' *PL*, LXXXII, 427; *Etymologiarum sive originum Libri XX*, ed. W. M. Lindsay (Oxford, 1911), vol. 2, XII.1.22. Walafrid Strabo associates the creature with the Devil and perverse doctrine, *PL*, CXIII, 1252.

[51] *PL*, CCIV, 236A–C: '. . . ita etiam dicebatur mater haeresis et caput erroris . . . Et ecce inventa est plaga ejus magna nimis, ita ut a planta pedis usque ad verticem non esset in ea sanitas . . . Locum in ea sibi abominatio desolationis invenerat, et propheticorum similitudo reptilium in latibulis ejus domicilium obtinebat. Ibi haeretici principabantur in populo, dominabantur in clero; eo quod sicut populus, sic sacerdos; et interitum gregis ipsa configurabat vita pastoris. Loquebantur haeretici, et omnes admirabantur. Loquebatur Catholicus et dicebant: Quis est hic? . . . Interim praevaluerat pestis in terra, quod illi sibi non solum sacerdotes et pontifices fecerant, sed etiam evangelistas habebant: qui corrupta et cancellata evangelica veritate, nova illis Evangelia caderent, et de corde suo nequam recentia dogmata seducto populo praedicarent.'

[52] *PL*, CCIV, 236–7: 'Habito sermone orthodoxae praedicationis ad plebem, conterriti sunt in Sion peccatores, possedit tremor hypocritas, ut qui prius obstruebant ora loquentium, jam apparere coram loquentibus non auderent. Audires illico vel videres vulpes transfiguratas in talpas, ut quae prius in publico discurrebant, jam terrarum latebris, jam sese cellulis immergerent cavernosis; et plantaria sacra, quae jam non audebant in aperto commandere, infra terrae viscera corroderent et necarent.' Rabanus Maurus associates the mole (Isaiah 2. 20) with heretics or false Christians in *De universis*, *PL*, CXI, 226.

[53] *PL*, CCIV, 237A–B: 'Ne autem pardus ille discolor pellis suae varietate se proderet, sermonem sibi nequam callidis adinventionibus firmaverunt . . . Ex

---

heresiologists. The forcing of heretics into hiding implies that Cathar perfects were involved in public preaching before the 1178 mission, whereas historians generally agree that Cathar preaching took place in the households of supporters and not in a public venue.[54]

Henry then tells one famous tale of success: the discovery, interrogation, confession and public repentance of Peter Maurand, a chief of the heretics who had held meetings at his castle.[55] His heresy is described as Arian, and he too is cast as a mole led out from his treacherous hole and transformed from a rapacious wolf into a sheep of Israel.[56] Hence the characteristic action or role of the animals representing the heretics is inverted as the heretic is converted: moles are brought above ground and the wolf is tamed to become a sheep. Moreover, a sort of triple metamorphosis takes place as Peter Maurand heretic turns from mole to wolf to sheep.

Henry left Toulouse early in order to attend the General Chapter meeting, which began around 13 September. The cardinal legate granted him permission to do so, provided that the abbot of Clairvaux pass through the diocese of Albi, which Henry describes as a 'very depraved region' and the 'filthy conflux of heresy' with the 'bilge-water of all wickedness' flowing into it.[57] The abbot aimed to secure the bishop of Albi's release from Roger of Béziers and to drive out the heretics.[58] Roger, soundly demonized in Henry's letter as an 'agent of evil who hated the light of truth' and who retreated to the 'works of darkness', [59] left his castle. Its inhabitants, including his wife, gave no reply to the preachers. In the absence of Roger and a reply from the household, Henry and company condemned Roger as a traitor, a heretic and a perjurer,

---

illa ergo die dominus legatus, et nos alii, qui feris bestis congredi putabamus, ad perscrutandos eos, quos timor et confusio tanquam ignobile reptile in ima terrae detruxerant . . .' Many authors comment on the leopard (Ecclesiastes 28. 27; Is 11. 6; Jeremiah 13. 23, Habakkuk 1. 8). Hugh of St Victor links the leopard with heresy in *De amore sponsi ad sponsam*, *PL*, CLXXVI, 989; as does Gilbert of Hoyland in his *Sermones in Canticum*, *S. 29*, *PL*, CLXXXIV, 152; and Peter Comestor, *Sermones*, *PL*, CXCVIII, 1788.

[54] See Kienzle, 'Touchstone', pp. 41–3.

[55] *PL*, CCIV, 239C: '. . . jussus est . . . et castrum quoddam suum, quod hereticorum conventiculis profanarat, ab ipsis fundamentis evertere'.

[56] *PL*, CCIV, 237CD: It is said to Peter: '. . . in Arianae haeresis deveneris pravitatem . . .'; *PL*, CCIV, 239C: 'cum de caverna perfidiae talpa talis educitur, et in Israeliticam ovem lupus rapacissimus reformatur'.

[57] *PL*, CCIV, 240A: 'illam perditissimam regionem, quae velut totius sentina malitiae totam in se colluvionem haeresis illuc defluentis excepit . . .'.

[58] *PL*, CCIV, 239D: 'Nos autem vix tandem extorta cum lacrymis licentia revertendi, pro eo quod instantia capituli nostri jam reditus exigebat: petita licentia sub ea novis est exceptione concessa, ut Albiensem diocesim intraremus, commonituri principem terrae . . . ut Albiensem episcopum, quem sub custodia haereticorum in vinculis tenebat, absolveret, et universam terram suam juxta domini legati praeceptum eliminatis haereticis emundaret.'

[59] *PL*, CCIV, 240AB: 'Oderat enim lumen veritatis actor malitiae, nec sustinere poterat nostrae collocutionis accessum, qui totus recesserat in opera tenebrarum.'

and publicly excommunicated him.[60] They also managed to send two Cathars, Raymond de Baimac and Bernard Raymond, back to the legate still in Toulouse.[61] The closing of Henry's letter mixes the proclamation of success in the city of Toulouse, manifested through the count's oath not to favour heretics in any way,[62] with a call for revenge on Roger. The abbot proclaims:

> It is very apparent that a great and manifest door is open to Christian princes, that they may avenge the offences to Christ and establish the Lord's garden in that desert and the delights of paradise in that wilderness.[63]

Henry himself would return to take his own revenge with the siege of Roger's castle at Lavaur in 1181.

The second source recounting events of the 1178 mission is Peter of St Chrysogonus's letter, which opens with a statement on the strength of the faith, then identifies the attackers, describes the circumstances of the public interrogation, the attendees, the content of the debate and its outcome: the excommunication of Raymond de Baimac, Bernard Raymond and their associates. Before the hearing, the two were granted safe passage for eight days following it. The debate took place in the church of St Etienne, followed in the church of St Jacques by a public profession of faith and accusations from witnesses – clerical and lay, including the count – who charged them with lying.

The legate, like Henry, creates an atmosphere of danger as the backdrop for the letter's central message, in this case the events of the debate. The heretics are called 'false brethren' (*falsi fratres*), an echo of Galatians 2. 4 and II Corinthians 11. 26, who transform themselves into angels of light, although they are Satans, which recalls II Corinthians 11. 14. They deceive with poisoned preaching (*venenata praedicatione*) and diabolical deceit (*diabolica fraude*). Their refutation is compared with Daniel's confoundment of the elders of Israel, and is termed an uncovering of the 'poison of treachery'

---

[60] *PL*, CCIV, 240C: 'Cumque videremus quod nihil omnino praesumerent respondere, judicavimus praedictum Rogerum proditorem, haereticum et de violata pace episcopi et securitate perjurum, eum tanquam publica excommunicatione damnatum . . .'.

[61] On these two men who appear again at Lavaur in 1181, see Congar, pp. 22–3; and Maisonneuve, p. 133, n. 229, who identifies them as Cathar leaders. Raymond de Baimac was a 'perfect', later elected bishop of Val d'Aran; and Bernard Raymond was the bishop of Toulouse.

[62] *PL*, CCIV, 240D: 'Super haec autem omia praedictus comes sancti Aegidii coram populo civitatis praestito juramento firmavit, quod amodo nec prece nec pretio favebit haereticis nec eos in terra sua ulterius sustinebit.'

[63] *PL*, CCIV, 240C: 'Ecce amodo satis apparet quam grande et evidens ostium pater principibus Christianis, ut Christi ulciscantur injurias, ponantque desertum illud quasi hortum Domini, et solitudinem ejus in delicias paradisi.'

(*venenum perfidiae*). According to Peter, the simple have been 'imbued with their filth' (*illorum faeci . . . imbuti*).[64]

The legate puts aside the figures of pollution while he focuses on the doctrinal issues discussed, then takes them up again at the letter's close, as he recounts the sentence of excommunication, clinched by the heretics' refusal to take an oath. There he appeals to his audience to avoid Raymond, Bernard and their accomplices, to reject their preaching as false and contrary to the catholic and apostolic faith, and to expel them as heretics and forerunners of Antichrist.[65] Thus the letter closes on an apocalyptic note, just as it opened with the reference to angels of Satan pretending to be angels of light.

The doctrinal issues raised are consistent with other discussions of Cathar beliefs that interest heresiologists: the two principles, rejection of the Eucharist and transubstantiation, baptism and laying on of hands, sexual relations in marriage, oath-taking. Here Peter's remarks about the language of the debate are highlighted, one of the few known references to the linguistic problems that must have arisen when northern French and foreign preachers came to Occitania. Peter's comments also provide an example of the sense of cultural elitism present in the higher levels of the clergy.

The heretics, Peter explains, read the article of their faith from a written document. When the interrogators questioned certain suspect words (*verba quaedam . . . suspecta*) they asked for an explanation in Latin, because they 'did not know their language well enough, and because the Gospels and the Epistles with which they wanted to support their faith are known to be written in Latin'. One of the heretics attempted to speak in Latin, but failed, scarcely being able to 'join two words together'. The legate's irritation is apparent when he describes as rather absurd (*satis absurdum*) the necessity for the questioners to come down to the heretics' level (*nos illis condescendere*) to discuss the sacraments in the vulgar tongue because of their lack of learning (*imperitiam*).[66]

How the discussion proceeded despite the interrogators' incompetence in the vernacular is not explained in detail. It seems to have been a group effort, as the first person plural forms used in the letter refer to a collective 'we' and

---

[64] *PL*, CXCIX, 1120–1.
[65] *PL*, CXCIX, 1124B: '. . . tanquam excommunicatos et Satanae traditos cautius evitetis . . . praedicationem eorum tanquam falsam, et catholicae atque apostolicae fidei contrariam respuatis, et ipsos tanquam haereticos et Antichristi praeambulos a sinceritatis vestrae consortio, et vestris finibus longius expellatis.'
[66] *PL*, CXCIX, 1121D: 'quaesivimus, ut Latinis verbis respondentes, suam fidem defenderent: tum quia lingua eorum non erat nobis satis nota; tum quia Evangelia et Epistolae, quibus tantummodo fidem suam confirmare volebant. Latino eloquio noscuntur esse scripta. Cumque id facere non auderent, utpote qui linguam Latinam penitus ignorabant, sicut in verbis unius illorum apparuit, qui cum Latine vellet loqui, vix duo verba jungere potuit, et omnino defecit; necesse fuit, nos illis condescendere, et de ecclesiasticis sacramentis propter imperitiam illorum, quamvis satis esset absurdum, vulgarem habere sermonem.' English translations are mine.

not just to the legate himself. Other officials present would have known a language of the Midi. The count of Toulouse, for example, is named as present in St Etienne and St Jacques, where he denounced the two heretics as liars; and the bishop of Poitiers appears as an auditor in the church of St Etienne and attends the excommunication in the church of St Jacques.

The Third Lateran Council and afterwards

Henry, after refusing (later in 1178) election to the see of Toulouse and to the abbacy of Cîteaux, went to Rome for the Third Lateran Council, which met in the spring of 1179. There he was named cardinal bishop of Albano and consecrated by Alexander III at the same time as three others who would be the future popes Clement III, Celestine III and Gregory VIII.[67] A tale from Caesarius of Heisterbach describes Henry as initially lacking the learning to preach the crusade. The Cistercian calls upon the Virgin who inspires sufficient learning for preaching and being named cardinal.[68] While Henry's Latin does not measure up to Bernard's, there is no other evidence that he might have been deficient in his education.

Henry probably played a role in formulating Canon 27, which detailed measures for repressing heresy and codified the procedures for the 1178 mission. Canon 27 also resulted, however, from legislation of earlier twelfth-century councils (Toulouse, 1119; Rheims, 1157; Montpellier, 1162; Tours, 1163) moving toward a call for secular force to be used against heresy.[69] Nonetheless, as H. Maisonneuve pointed out, a real tribunal of inquisition had been functioning in the county of Toulouse for three months. The sanctions legislated at Tours – excommunication, exile, and confiscation of property – were not enough when a recalcitrant nobleman refused to persecute heretics. The Church sought a way to influence the secular authorities to take action. Maisonneuve further suggests that Henry of Clairvaux was named a legate after the Third Lateran Council to ensure the application of the council's sanctions in France.

The canon itself reads:

[67] See Congar, p. 27, n. 88; and Maisonneuve, pp. 133–5. Congar accepts Henry's probable influence on the canon's content but hesitates to accept the notion that Henry, not a canonist, actually wrote it. Maisonneuve states (p. 133): 'Comme la mission de 1145 avait reçu la consécration du concile de Reims, la mission de 1178 reçut la consécration du IIIe concile de Latran, canon 27.' Moore, *Formation*, p. 27, concludes that Henry 'inspired the Third Lateran Council to order that there should be no social or commercial dealings with heretics or their supporters, on pain of excommunication, and of the dissolution of the ties of homage and liability to confiscation of land and goods.'

[68] A. Hilka, *Die Wundergeschichten des Caesarius von Heisterbach*, 3 vols. (Bonn, 1933), III, 164.

[69] See Congar, p. 27; Maisonneuve, pp. 133–5.

Though ecclesiastical discipline contents itself with spiritual judgment and should avoid bloody punishments, it is, however, aided by the ordinances of catholic princes, for people often seek a salutary remedy for their souls only when they fear some severe corporal punishment will be imposed upon them. Wherefore, since in Gascony, in the territory of Albi, in Toulouse and its neighbourhood, and in some other places, the perversity of the heretics, whom some call Cathari, others Patarini, and others again Publicani, has assumed such proportions that they practise their wickedness no longer in secret as some do, but manifest their error publicly and attract the simple and the weak to their point of view, we decree that they and all who defend and receive them are anathematized, and under penalty of anathema we forbid that anyone give them shelter, admit them to his land, or transact business with them.[70]

Of particular interest to our study, the canon uses the public manifestation of error made by the heretics, that is preaching, to justify the declarations of anathema. This echoes somewhat Henry's observations in his Letter 11 and again in Letter 29. In Letter 11, he remarks in outrage that 'Now the heretics argue in public against the faith . . .', in contrast with the private unspeakable acts of which he accuses them.[71] In Letter 29, he expresses first his surprise and anger that the heretics have their own clerical structure and even their own evangelists who preach errors to the people. Later in the letter, however, he comments that the presence of orthodox preachers forced the heretics underground, like moles, and that they then gnawed the healthy plants at their roots.[72] Henry's language here follows a general pattern of the polemics against heresy: the dichotomy between open and concealed activity – the public and private domains – generally seems to be manipulated in whichever way the polemicists wish.

[70] The translation is modified from A. C. Shannon, *The Medieval Inquisition* (Collegeville, MN, 1984), p. 46. The Latin, cited in G. Gonnet, *Enchiridion fontium Valdensium*, I (Torre Pellice, 1958), pp. 29–30, from the *Corpus Iuris Canonici, Decretal. Gregor. IX*, Lib. V, Tit. VII, Cap. VIII, ed. Friedberg, II, col. 779–80. reads: 'Sicut ait beatus Leo, licet ecclesiastica disciplina, sacerdotali iudiciio, cruentas effugiat ultiones, catholicorum tamen principum constitutionibus adiuvatur, ut saepe quaerant homines salutare remedium, dum corporale metuerint super se supplicium evenire. Ea propter, quia in Vasconia, Albigesio et partibus Tolosanis, et aliis locis ita haereticorum, quos alii Catharos, alii Publicanos, alii Patarenos, et alii aliis nominibus vocant, invaluit damnanda perversitas, ut iam non in occulto, sicut alibi, nequitiam suam exerceant, sed errorem suum publice manifestent, et ad consensum suum simplices attrahant et infirmos, eos, et defensores et receptatores eorum anathemati decernimus subiacere, et sub anathemate prohibemus, ne quis eos in domo vel in terra sua tenere vel fovere, aut negotiationem cum eis exercere praesumat. Si autem in hoc peccato decesserit, neque sub privilegiorum nostrorum quibuscumque indultorum obtentu, neque sub alia quacunque occasione oblatio pro eo fiat, aut inter Christianos accipiat sepulturam.'

[71] *PL*, CCIV, 223D: 'Nam et haeretici in publico disputant contra fidem; et quod multi in occulto faciunt, et scribentis verecundiam, et in legentis laederet honestatem.'

[72] See n. 52 above.

They emphasize either what they see as suspicious and subversive secrecy or audacious and subversive openness.

The Waldensians

Henry, now cardinal bishop of Albano and legate appointed to southern France after the Third Lateran Council,[73] turned his attention to the Waldensians, a popular evangelical movement that advocated voluntary poverty and affirmed the right and responsibility of all believers to preach the gospel.[74] Henry held a council in the city of Lyons, probably in March of 1180 and on his way to southern France from the Third Lateran Council.[75] Valdes's 1173 conversion had initiated the movement in Lyons.[76] As legate, Henry's involvement in the Church's war against heresy was continuing and widening. It was he who accepted Valdes's profession of orthodoxy, along with Archbishop Guichard of Lyons, former Cistercian abbot of Pontigny, and Geoffrey of Auxerre, at that time abbot of Hautecombe, who reported on the abjuration and commented strongly on the usurpation of the preaching office by Valdes and his followers.[77] The three clerics – cardinal bishop (Henry), archbishop (Guichard), and abbot of Hautecombe (Geoffrey) – were all Cistercians with previous connections.[78]

[73] Gonnet dates his appointment as beginning in March of 1179, *Enchiridion*, p. 45; Congar, p. 30, posits late 1179 or early 1180 for the appointment.

[74] Scholars have debated the importance of poverty vs. preaching in the Waldensians' beliefs and eventual condemnation by the Church. M. Rubellin cites these debates and offers a fresh look at the several years before the Waldensians were persecuted in: 'Au temps où Valdès n'était pas hérétique: hypothèses sur le rôle de Valdès à Lyon (1170–1183)', in *Inventer l'hérésie?*, pp. 193–217.

[75] Gonnet, *Enchiridion*, I, p. 45, explains that Geoffrey of Auxerre, then abbot of Hautecombe, Henry of Albano and Guichard, all Cistercians, were present at the council. Guichard's death in July of 1180 is the *terminus ad quem* of the council. In his 'Le cheminement des vaudois vers le schisme et l'hérésie (1174–1218)', *Cahiers de Civilisation Médiévale* 19 (1976), 309–45 (p. 319), G. Gonnet suggests March 1180 as the date for the council, as does Congar, p. 32. Geoffrey of Auxerre's account of Valdes's profession of faith is the primary source we have for this event: *Apocalypsim*, pp. 179–80.

[76] Some date Valdes's conversion to 1170 or 1176. See Rubellin, 'Au temps où Valdès n'était pas hérétique', p. 202 and n. 31.

[77] See Congar, pp. 28–9, 31–3; Thouzellier, *Catharisme et Valdéisme*, pp. 25–35. J. Duvernoy challenges the view that the written text which has been considered Valdes's profession corresponds to this event. He holds that the text results from the profession made by Durand of Huesca in 1207, at the time of his reconciliation with Rome. Rubellin agrees with Duvernoy on the written text, but argues that Valdes did make an oral statement, which was not preserved in writing. See Rubellin, 'Au temps où Valdès n'était pas hérétique', p. 198 and n. 17; p. 214.

[78] See n. 66 above. Rubellin discusses with strong evidence the close ties between Henry of Albano and Geoffrey of Auxerre, and the probable conflicts between

According to Hélinand of Froidmont's *Chronicon*, Geoffrey of Auxerre was once a pupil of Abelard, then alongside Bernard of Clairvaux a fierce opponent of Abelard and Gilbert of Poitiers. Geoffrey later wrote against Joachim of Fiore as well.[79] After Geoffrey was forced to resign as abbot of Clairvaux in 1165, he was elected abbot of Fossanova, a daughter house of Hautecombe, with the support of Henry, then abbot of Hautecombe. When Henry moved to Clairvaux in 1176, Geoffrey then moved to Hautecombe serving as abbot there from 1176 to 1188. Hautecombe played an important role in the campaign against heresy, and Geoffrey added Joachim of Fiore to his list of targets.[80]

The 1180 council followed closely after the Third Lateran Council, which some Waldensians attended to seek approval for their preaching. The prevailing view holds that Guichard, archbishop of Lyons, prohibited it; a counter view asserts that Guichard supported Valdes and his followers so that they could assist him with his reforming efforts.[81] In any case, the Waldensians received the pope's blessing, but with the condition that they not preach without authorization.[82] The Waldensians did not heed the papal directive, and citing Acts 5. 29, they even asserted that obedience was owed to God alone and not to human authorities.[83] Furthermore, Waldensians commissioned translations of the Scriptures and other works into the vernacular to ensure that all their adherents could understand and proclaim the good news.[84] Women Waldensians were persecuted in Clermont around 1180, and protested publicly against the bishop,[85] Ponce of Polignac (d. 1189), abbot of Grandselve and then of Clairvaux, before his election in 1170 to the

Geoffrey and Guichard. Rubellin also sees Guichard as a supporter of Valdes and lay preaching; his arguments on the latter point are interesting but not wholly convincing. 'Au temps où Valdès n'était pas hérétique', pp. 213–16.

[79] Gastaldelli, *Apocalypsim*, pp. 16–17, proposes 1200 or 1210 for the date of Geoffrey of Auxerre's death, and mentions his writing against Joachim of Fiore. On Joachim and Geoffrey, see M. Reeves, *The Influence of Prophecy in the Later Middle Ages: A Study in Joachimism* (Oxford, 1969), pp. 14–15. In his *Chronicon*, Hélinand explains that Geoffrey of Auxerre was a student of Abelard and he describes his confrère's activities in the present tense. *PL*, CCXII, 1035A: 'Huius Petri aliquando discipulus fuerat Gaufridus Autissiodorensis, qui multo tempore notarius fuit beati Bernardi'; *PL*, CCXII, 1035D: 'Hic inter caetera de eodem Petro dicit . . .' ; and: 'Haec Gaufridus contra Petrum olim magistrum suum fortiter et catholice scribit.'

[80] On Geoffrey and Henry's connections, see *Apocalypsim*, pp. 15–16. On the importance of Hautecombe in the anti-heretical campaign, see Zerner-Chardavoine, 'Au temps de l'appel', pp. 133–4.

[81] This is Rubellin's thesis in 'Au temps où Valdès n'était pas hérétique', esp. pp. 209–17. Rubellin also reviews Guichard's career and the conflict in Lyons over his election, pp. 208–10. See also *Dictionnaire des auteurs cisterciens*, col. 310.

[82] Gonnet, *Enchiridion*, I, p. 29; 'Le cheminement des vaudois', pp. 314 and 319.

[83] On the issue of obedience, see Kienzle, 'Obedience', esp. pp. 259–63.

[84] On the translations, see Patschovsky, 'The Literacy of Waldensianism', pp. 112–36.

[85] See B. M. Kienzle, 'The Prostitute-Preacher: Patterns of Polemic against Waldensian Women Preachers', in Kienzle and Walker, pp. 99–113.

see of Clermont.[86] Archbishop Guichard's successor John Bellesmains, a collaborator with Henry of Albano in the 1181 preaching mission to Occitania,[87] expelled the Waldensians from Lyons around 1182/1183. They were then targeted in the decree *Ad abolendam*, issued in Verona in 1184 by Pope Lucius III and the Emperor Frederick Barbarossa, following the latter's reconciliation with the papacy after several years of schism (1159–77).[88] The Waldensians dispersed, taking to other regions their commitment to voluntary poverty and proclamation of the gospel. In 1199 Innocent III summoned Cistercian abbots to investigate Waldensian activities in the diocese of Metz, where lay women and men were meeting in secret to read the Scriptures and other texts, to discuss them, and to preach to one another.[89] A group of Waldensians led by Durand of Huesca reconciled with the papacy in 1208, took the name of the Poor of Lyons, and received authorization for preaching against heresy. Those who were not reconciled took refuge, mixed with and influenced other dissident groups.[90]

The Cistercians named above who played roles in the late twelfth-century controversy surrounding the Waldensians – Henry of Albano, Guichard of Lyons, Geoffrey of Auxerre, Ponce of Polignac – were joined by other clerics. Bernard, the Praemonstratensian abbot of Fontcaude, and Alan of Lille, a Paris master who became a Cistercian, composed influential anti-heretical treatises. Debates over the Waldensians' reclamation for evangelism reached Paris and the circle of intellectuals around Peter the Chanter, who might have encountered Henry of Clairvaux at the Third Lateran Council and learned about the Waldensians there. The Chanter's circle did not initially oppose lay preaching. In fact, in order to support it, they elaborated a distinction between exhortation (*exhortatio*), the sort of simple gospel-based preaching done by Waldensians, and preaching (*praedicatio*), the teaching of dogma in sermons authorized to clergy only.[91] While Innocent III allowed certain lay people to preach in order

---

[86] *Dictionnaire des auteurs cisterciens*, col. 576. See also Newman, p. 165, n. 122.

[87] On J. Bellesmains, see Rubellin, 'Au temps où Valdès n'était pas hérétique', p. 216; and the treatment of the mission below, pp. 132–3.

[88] See Gonnet, 'Le cheminement', pp. 325–9; Rubellin, 'Au temps où Valdès n'était pas hérétique', p. 203.

[89] On Innocent III's letters in this matter, see Kienzle, 'Obedience', pp. 259–78.

[90] On later events concerning the Waldensians, see works cited above: Gonnet, 'Le cheminement'; Kienzle, 'The Prostitute Preacher'; Patchovsky, 'The Literacy of Waldensianism'. Among the materials on the Waldensians up until the Reformation, see Lambert, *Heresy*, pp. 147–71; and P. Biller's excellent studies: 'The Preaching of the Waldensian Sisters', *Heresis* 30 (1999), 137–68; and 'What did Happen to the Waldensian Sisters?

[91] P. Buc, '*Vox clamantis in deserto?* Pierre le Chantre et la prédication laïque', *Revue Mabillon*, n.s. 4 (= t. 65) (1993), 5–47. Rubellin argues for adding Alexander III and Guichard of Lyons to the number of clerical supporters of lay preaching, 'Au temps où Valdès n'était pas hérétique', pp. 212–16. For a brief survey of debates over lay preaching, see Kienzle, 'Touchstone', pp. 32–5; and for an exhaustive treatment, see R. Zerfass, *Der Streit um die Laienpredigt* (Freiburg, 1974). A useful article on the

to combat heresy, the Council of Verona's condemnation of those who preached without authorization was repeated in the canons of the Fourth Lateran Council and then entered into canon law.[92]

The 1181 mission

Following Henry of Albano's involvement at the Third Lateran Council, his election as a cardinal, appointment as papal legate to France,[93] and presiding the council at Lyons in 1180, he crossed the line in the spring of 1181 between participating in a legation and leading an army. Accompanied by his ally, John Bellesmains, before his election as archbishop of Lyons,[94] Henry became the first papal legate to himself raise an army and lead an expedition into a Christian land. The castle of Lavaur was taken, probably in 1181, in an undertaking that has been termed a 'pre-crusade'.[95] Roger II, count of Béziers, was held up there, and we recall that Henry had not succeeded at capturing him in 1178 nor at persuading him to free the bishop of Albi. Henry's Letter 29 from 1178 described the resistance to orthodox preaching from the inhabitants of Roger II's castle, that is, Roger's wife and many others who were reportedly heretics or accomplices of heretics.[96] Their intransigence resulted in Roger's excommunication for heresy and Henry's determination to take Lavaur on his return to Occitania as papal legate. The *Chronicon Clarevallensis* credits a miracle for the success at Lavaur.[97] According to Congar, this implies that the taking of Lavaur was unexpectedly easy; he suggests that the complicity of Roger's wife, Adelaide, would have made that possible.[98]

Despite his military activity, Henry apparently still found time to preach.

---

twelfth-century question, which predates Buc's work, is J. M. Trout, 'Preaching by the Laity in the Twelfth Century', in *Studies in Medieval Culture 4.1*, ed. J. R. Sommerfeldt, L. Synergaard, and E. R. Elder (Kalamazoo, MI, 1975), pp. 92–108.

[92] The reconciled Waldensians, Poor of Lyons, and the Humiliati were allowed to do simple preaching in 1208 and 1201, respectively. On this and the canons, see Trout, 'Preaching by the Laity', p. 95. See also D. Pryds, 'Proclaiming Sanctity through Proscribed Acts. The Case of Rose of Viterbo', in Kienzle and Walker, pp. 159–72 on Rose of Viterbo, a lay woman who preached against heresy in thirteenth-century Italy.

[93] According to Gonnet, Henry was appointed legate to France shortly after Lateran III, beginning his legacy in March of 1179. *Enchiridion*, I, p. 45. Congar, pp. 38–41, describes the principal events of Henry's involvement in France before his return to Rome in 1182.

[94] See above, n. 87.

[95] Biget, 'Les Albigeois', p. 244.

[96] *PL*, CCIV, 239–40. See above, nn. 59–60.

[97] *Chronicon Clarevallensis*, *PL*, CLXXXV, 1250A.

[98] Congar, pp. 35–6. Congar states (p. 36): 'Henri s'empara du château par miracle, disent les documents cisterciens. Entendons d'une façon inespérée et sans qu'un assaut en règle fut nécessaire; en réalité, grâce à la complicité d'Adelaïde.'

Geoffrey of Auxerre reports the legate's success in 1181 at converting two heretics after bringing them to tears. This conversion took place on 15 September 1181 and the two convertees became canons of the cathedral of St Etienne in Toulouse. Geoffrey praises Henry's effective preaching and the chronicler Robert of Auxerre also testifies to the force of his word. Geoffrey states that the Holy Spirit moved the legate to such eloquence with his preaching that his words of grace brought the two to a heartfelt, tearful confession of their errors in the presence of a great and diverse crowd.[99] Robert describes Henry as: 'a man of eloquent tongue . . . who with the word of his preaching drew hoards of knights and soldiers from everywhere and combatted the aforesaid heretics'. The chronicler William of Puylaurens reports briefly on the taking of Lavaur and on the conversion of Bernard Raymond,[100] who was one of the two heretics sent by Henry to Peter of St Chrysogonus in Toulouse on the earlier failed expedition of 1178.

Henry seems to have occupied himself primarily at Rome for the next five years, that is, from the summer of 1182 onward.[101] He was a candidate for the papal elections of 1187, but he withdrew and instead offered the future Gregory VIII his services to preach the crusade to the Holy Land. Gregory died having spent only fifty-seven days as pope. Henry made the same offer to Clement III and then undertook preaching tours, which were recounted by the chronicler Giselbertus. In addition, an *exemplum* told by Caesarius of Heisterbach places Henry on horseback in Germany preaching the crusade to the Holy Land in 1188. In that tale, a lay brother, upon Henry's invitation to preach, tells a story in which St Benedict greets Henry at the gate of Heaven. Benedict, surprised by seeing a mitre on a monk, orders the door keepers to open Henry's stomach to see what he has eaten in life. Peas and simple food will allow him to enter with other monks; plump fish and worldly food will require him to remain outside. Henry reacts with amusement and praises the lay brother's tale.[102]

[99] *Apocalypsim*, p. 210: 'duos haeresiarchas . . . comprehensos novimus et oblatos venerabili patri nostro domino Henrico Albanensi episcopo, apostolicae sedis in Aquitania tunc legato. Quibus astantibus, dum idem pontifex ad copiossimam multitudinem diverse conditionibus et diversi ordinis adversus eandem haeresim sermonem faceret, prout Spiritus Sanctus dabat eloqui illi, praedicti haeresiarchae in verbis gratiae quae procedebant de ore eius, Domino inspirante, usque adeo sunt compuncti, ut secretas haeresis illius blasphemias et exsecrans abominationes cum multis lacrimis, audientibus omnibus, non distulerint confiteri.'

[100] Thouzellier, *Catharisme et Valdéisme*, p. 25, cites the passage from Robert of Auxerre's *Chronicon* (MGH SS SSVI, p. 245, 40: '. . . missus est ab Alexandro papa vir linguae diserte Henricis, ex abbate Clarevallis episcopus Albanensis, qui predicationis verbo militum peditumque copias undecumque contraxit, prefatos hereticos expugnavit.' Puylaurens, p. 28, includes the conversion episode. See also Congar, p. 38, nn. 119, 120; Thouzellier, *Catharisme et Valdéisme*, p. 39, nn. 95, 96.

[101] See Congar, p. 41.

[102] Caesarius, *Dialogus*, IV. lxxix, p. 247. See also Cole, *Preaching*, pp. 66–8.

Jerusalem fell on October 2, 1187 and the news reached Rome before the end of November. Exasperated with Henry II and Philip Augustus for failing to undertake the crusade, Henry wrote the final chapter of his *De peregrinante civitate Dei* late in 1188 and died not long afterwards on 1 January 1189 without having journeyed to the Holy Land.[103]

Since the treatise focuses on the Eastern crusade, it does not directly concern this study. However, it demonstrates the thought of a powerful man who was involved in shaping the crusading effort at home and abroad. We have already seen that Henry extended the idea of crusade from an excursion to the East to a holy war waged at home against heresy. In the treatise, Henry criticizes Christians who, he thinks, are not sufficiently concerned with the plight of the Holy Land. For Henry, they should have a sense of personal loss and see the desecration of sites in Jerusalem as a second crucifixion, considering Saladin a manifestation of the Devil and the crusade as a necessary step in the fight against evil.[104] The demonization of the Muslim corresponds to that of the heretic, as does the notion that fighting the named enemy, whoever it may be, contributes to a wider battle against the forces of evil. A similar conceptual framework lies behind Henry's calls for the crusade against Saladin and against heresy in Occitania.

How do we assess Henry's role in the campaign against heresy? Certainly his own writings from the campaign express an unambiguous commitment to the notion of a holy war. Moreover, they reveal highly charged rhetorical patterns that rely on Old Testament allusions and creatures that undergo metamorphoses. While the advocacy of holy war belongs to a developing militancy in the wider Church, some responsibility must lie with Henry himself. R. I. Moore attributes to the 1178 preaching mission the establishment of the last major component of the inquisitorial procedure: the accepting of denunciations.[105] When the Third Lateran Council issued its canons the following year, Henry influenced the drafting of Canon 27, which detailed measures for repressing heresy and denying rights to heretics. While Canon 27 followed from legislation of earlier twelfth-century councils moving toward a call for secular force to be used against heresy, Moore sees it as the final piece of the groundwork for the inquisition.[106] Finally, as Congar has pointed out, Henry himself set a lamentable precedent when he became the first papal legate to himself lead a military expedition in Christian lands at the siege of Lavaur in 1181.

---

[103] Congar, p. 43. According to Congar, Henry had begun the text at the Curia between 1185 and 1186.

[104] The text is found in *PL*, CCIV, 251–402, and is summarized by Congar, pp. 56–90, and Cole, *Preaching*, pp. 68–71.

[105] Moore, *Formation*, p. 26.

[106] Moore, *Formation*, p. 27.

CHAPTER FIVE

Innocent III's Papacy and the Crusade Years, 1198–1229: Weeding the Vineyard

Another phase of the Cistercian drive against heresy opened in January 1198, when Innocent III became pope,[1] and extended until 1208, when the murder of a Cistercian legate precipitated the advance toward armed intervention in Occitania. At the outset of his papacy, Innocent III undertook initiatives to effect a broad programme of reform, including a widespread crusade against the perceived enemies of Christendom. Although papal priorities stressed the crusade to the Holy Land, the fight against heresy intensified as well. In fact, the campaign against heretical Christians in Occitania reached for a time the status of the crusades to the Holy Land, with the awarding of plenary indulgences, the protection of crusaders, and various measures for recruiting and financing the expeditions.[2] Innocent III appealed strongly to the Cistercian Order to place qualified monks at his service for preaching. His persuasion began with a letter to the 1198 General Chapter and the failed but dramatic appearance there of his legate Fulk of Neuilly seeking to recruit Cistercians for preaching the Eastern crusade. By the 1201 General Chapter, Fulk had papal authorization to designate three Cistercian abbots as his assistants.[3] The same determination marked Innocent III's efforts to engage the Cistercians in preaching against heresy; his letters praise them and attempt to persuade them that the active life could be very profitable and useful.[4] Cistercians,

---

[1] On 21 April 1198, Innocent charged brother Rainier as legate for the problem of heresy in southern France. See Vicaire, 'Clercs', pp. 261–2. The legates from 1198 to 1241 are studied in detail by H. Zimmermann in his *Die päpstliche Legation in der ersten Hälfte des 13. Jahrhunderts vom Regierungsantritt Innocenz' III. bis zum Tode Gregors IX (1198–1241)* (Paderborn, 1913). On the earlier Cistercian preaching missions, see Chapters Three and Four of this book.

[2] R. Foreville examines carefully the crusade to the Holy Land as an ecclesiastical institution and traces the transfer of its components to the crusade against heretics. 'Innocent III et la croisade des Albigeois', in *Paix de Dieu et guerre sainte en Languedoc au XIIIᵉ siècle*, CaF 4 (Toulouse, 1969), pp. 184–217. See also Cole, *Preaching*, pp. 80–93; and Evans, 'Crusade', pp. 297–300.

[3] See Cole, *Preaching*, pp. 80–93; and for the 1198 letter, Canivez, *Statuta*, pp. 221–4.

[4] See, for example, the January 1205 letter, *PL*, CCX, 525–6, which speaks of the

including a 1206 delegation of abbots and numerous other monks, involved themselves in public preaching as never before. However diligently they endeavoured to convert the heretics, they failed. The assassination of the Cistercian legate Peter of Castelnau in 1208 epitomized the disaster and precipitated the crusade. Papal priorities shifted temporarily from the Holy Land to Occitania for several years.[5] Once the crusade began, some Cistercians who had been elected bishops, undertook military leadership. Preaching continued but served the additional tasks of recruiting and exhorting troops.

A brief overview of the crusade years will provide a chronological framework for the discussion of individual Cistercian leaders. The 1209–29 crusade generally is divided into six phases: (1) 1209–11, when the land belonging to the powerful Trencavel family was conquered; (2) 1211–13, when Toulouse and the surrounding area were subdued; (3) 1213, the year of the decisive battle at Muret, when allied forces under Peter of Aragon were defeated by Simon of Montfort's armies; (4) 1213–15, the period of Montfort's triumph and the Fourth Lateran Council, where the disposition of conquered territory was debated and Raymond VI was deprived of his lands; (5) 1215/16–1225, a decade of counter-attack and reassertion of southern lords; (6) 1225–29, the final phase when royal intervention conquered the southern forces and compelled Raymond VII's submission.[6] For the most part, these events constitute the backdrop for our focus on Cistercian preaching, but at times Cistercians influenced or were present at major military turning points.

Leaders of the Cistercian effort in Occitania included the legates Peter of Castelnau and Ralph of Fontfroide, appointed in 1203;[7] Arnaud Amaury, abbot of Grandselve (1198–1201), subsequently abbot of Cîteaux and archbishop of Narbonne (1212–25); Guy, abbot of les Vaux-de-Cernay and then bishop of Carcassonne (1212–23); and Fulk, abbot of Le Thoronet and then bishop of Toulouse. In the crusade years (1208/9–1229), the last three bishops along with other Cistercians wrote, preached, negotiated and held important sees in the region; furthermore, some even directed military efforts. All these endeavours exposed the Cistercians to danger. In addition to the well publicized murder of Peter of Castelnau, the abbot of Eaunes and a lay brother were slain during a journey undertaken to negotiate peace. Moreover, a preacher exhorting troops before battle could be struck from a long

---

necessity to leave the contemplative life of Rachel and Mary at times and to take on the burden of Leah or the service of Martha. Enduring tribulations and pressures in the active life will be profitable to oneself and others. The record of Innocent III's numerous letters to Occitan Cistercian monasteries is summarized very helpfully in E. Fachinger, 'Les cisterciens de Languedoc aux XIIIe et XIVe siècles, d'après les documents pontificaux', in *Cisterciens*, CaF, pp. 45–69, at 48–54.

[5] See Cole, *Preaching*, pp. 101–4.
[6] See Evans, 'Crusade', pp. 287–8.
[7] See Sibly, pp. 7–8.

Fig. 5. The Cistercian abbey of Fontfroide (Aude). The murder in 1208 of one of its monks, the papal legate Peter of Castelnau, precipitated the crusade.

distance by a crossbow.[8] Thus even apparently peaceful aspects of supporting the crusade, the *negotium fidei et pacis* as period sources call it,[9] entailed clear dangers.

Overall, few works for reconstructing the preaching of these Cistercians remain from the hand of the preachers themselves. Exceptional is one sermon preached in the vernacular by an unspecified Cistercian abbot to a lay audience at St Firmin in Montpellier and preserved in Latin by Alan of Lille.[10] Nonetheless, the major chronicle for the period – the *Hystoria Albigensis* – was composed by Peter of les Vaux-de-Cernay, nephew of the abbot Guy and eye-witness to many events in 1212–13, 1214, 1216 and 1218.[11] Not a work to be preached although it surely informed preachers, the *Hystoria Albigensis* goes beyond simple narrative to establish literary motifs and launch vehement propaganda against the dissidents. Moreover, the *Canso de la Crozada*, an

[8] See Sibly, 130, pp. 71–2; *Hystoria*, I, pp. 134–5, on the attack on the abbot of Eaunes, and below, n. 127, on Peter of Vaux-de-Cernay's narrow escape from a crossbow.

[9] For the phrase 'negotium fidei et pacis', see *Hystoria*, 67, I, p. 66; and Sibly, p. 38; Innocent III's letter in Sibly, p. 34.

[10] Newman, p. 330, n. 79, following M.-Th. d'Alverny, proposes Arnaud Amaury as the preacher. The sermon is discussed below.

[11] On Peter of les Vaux-de-Cernay's presence in the Midi, see Sibly, pp. xxiii–vi.

epic poem, makes numerous references to preaching and supplies material for rhetorical analysis. The tone of the struggle also emerges from Innocent III's letters, where the strife is cast as a stormy sea, or as the Lord's vineyard, ravaged by the little foxes. They consistently term heresy 'heretical perverseness' (*haeretica pravitas*) and depict it as resulting from contamination and spreading like disease.[12] Another source that provides crusade *exempla* that circulated in Cistercian circles is the *Dialogus miraculorum* by Caesarius of Heisterbach (*c.* 1180–1240), a Cistercian from the Rhineland.[13] A work written to instruct novices, it also belongs to the growing body of sermon literature that provided material for preachers (*materia praedicabilis*). Its episodes shed light on the Cistercian mentality surrounding the events.

Arnaud Amaury

We begin our examination of this crucial period with the most powerful and without doubt the most notorious of the Cistercians during the crusade: Arnaud Amaury, abbot of Cîteaux, formerly abbot of two other Cistercian monasteries, Poblet and Grandselve, and later archbishop of Narbonne from 12 March 1212 until his death in 1225. In close contact with Innocent III, his activities in Occitania ranged from preaching to leading armies. Generally, period sources recount his preaching along with that of other delegation members, but accord it scant attention. His military exploits, however, emerge boldly from the background events.[14]

Arnaud Amaury appears in the historical record in 1196, upon his election as abbot of Poblet, a Cistercian monastery in Catalonia. Various Spanish sources attest to his Catalonian origin.[15] Remaining at the Spanish monastery only a few years, he became abbot of Grandselve in 1198. At Grandselve, Arnaud Amaury denounced a crime of heresy to Raymond VI: a heretic reportedly defecated next to the altar in a church at Toulouse and wiped himself with the altar cloth. What is more, he said that a priest receiving the sacrament was taking an evil spirit into his body. The offender was not punished and, according to Peter of les Vaux-de-Cernay, Arnaud Amaury

---

[12] See below, n. 36.

[13] Caesarius, *Dialogus*. On Caesarius and the Albigensian Crusade, see J. Berlioz, '*Exemplum* et histoire: Césaire de Heisterbach (v. 1180–v. 1240) et la croisade albigeoise', *Bibliothèque de l'Ecole des Chartes* 147 (1989), 49–86.

[14] For Arnaud Amaury see: R. Foreville, *Gouvernement et vie de l'Eglise au Moyen-Age. Recueil d'études* (London, 1979), chapter XIV (which emphasizes his role at regional councils); and M. A. Cabrer, 'El *venerable* Arnaldo Amalarico (h. 1196–1225): Idea y realidad de un cisterciense entre dos cruzadas', *Hispania Sacra* 98 (1996), 569–91 (which adds Spanish sources to his analysis of this controversial Cistercian). For most dates, I have followed Alvira Cabrer's chronology, which in turn follows Foreville's. I am grateful to Alvira Cabrer for bringing his article to my attention.

[15] Cabrer, 'Idea y realidad', p. 570.

was still telling the story at the 1213 council at Lavaur. It became part of Cistercian anti-heretical lore and was recounted at the General Chapter and repeated in Caesarius of Heisterbach's *Dialogus miraculorum*.[16] In any case, Arnaud Amaury must have distinguished himself sufficiently to be chosen abbot of Cîteaux in 1200.[17] That position placed him as leader of about 600 abbeys and 10,000 monks, surely then, as M.-H. Vicaire observed, one of the most powerful men of his era.[18] Arnaud Amaury's ties to Innocent III at that time manifest themselves in a collection of sermons sent to Arnaud Amaury by the pope at the Cistercian's request and dedicated to him. Some of the sermons, preached to the clergy and the people, were delivered in Latin and others in the vernacular. In that same year (1200), Arnaud Amaury headed an important meeting of the Cistercian General Chapter which consolidated the order's statutes into one collection.[19]

Collaboration between Arnaud Amaury and the pope strengthened and grounded a key piece of the papal strategy for Occitania. An overview of correspondence from the early 1200s shows Innocent III hard at work and juggling priorities. Prior to Arnaud Amaury's abbacy, the Cistercians at the 1198 General Chapter had refused to cooperate with Fulk of Neuilly's appeal for their aid in preaching the crusade to the Holy Land. Innocent III

[16] Sibly, 40, p. 24; *Hystoria*, I, pp. 37–8. Any ambiguity about the man's action is eliminated by the second gesture: 'juxta altare cujusdam ecclesie purgavit ventrem et in contemptum Dei cum pallia altaris tersit posteriora sua.' Caesarius's version, *Dialogus* 5.21, pp. 302–3, reads a little differently: 'Juxta altare maioris ecclesiae ventrem suam purgavit, et palla altaris ipsas immunditias detersit,' Caesarius then relates an incident concerning sacrilegious damage to a crucifix: 'Ceteri furori furorem adiicientes, scortum super sacrum altare posuerunt, in conspectu crucifixi eo ibi abutentes. Postea ipsam sacram imaginem detrahentes, brachia ei praesciderent.' Both were relayed to the Cistercian general chapter by Cardinal legate Conrad of Urach, formerly abbot of Villers, Clairvaux and Cîteaux. A prayer for the Albigensian Crusade was subsequently introduced for the whole Cistercian order. Canivez, *Statuta*, 1221.25. See also Berlioz, '*Exemplum* et histoire', p. 67. Outrages committed by the Count of Foix and his mercenaries occupy chapters 199–203 of the *Hystoria*, I, pp. 200–6; Sibly, pp. 104–6. On Caesarius's version of the defecation tale, see Berlioz, '*Exemplum* et histoire', pp. 63–4.

[17] M. Mousnier, 'Grandselve et la société de son temps', in *Cisterciens*, CaF, p. 119.

[18] Vicaire, 'Clercs', p. 265.

[19] Daunou, M., 'Arnaud Amaury', in *Histoire littéraire de la France, XVII* (Paris, 1895), pp. 306–34 (pp. 306–7). The sermons are probably the same ones edited in *PL*, CCXVII, and prefaced by a letter from Innocent III to Arnaud Amaury (*PL*, CCXVII, 309–11). I am grateful to Katherine Jansen for this reference. Jansen posits that Innocent III had sermons from 1202 to 1204 collected and sent to Amaury, and that several other sermons were added to the collection later. K. L. Jansen, 'Innocent III and the Literature of Confession', in *Innocent III: Urbs et Orbis, Acts of the international conference commemorating the 800th anniversary of the accession of Innocent III to the papal throne, Rome 9–15 September 1998* (forthcoming). I am planning an article on these sermons from Innocent III as a source for heresiology. The *Sermones de tempore* contain the following direct references to heresy: Sermons II, 335C–D; VI, 344A; VIII, 349D; XII, 366–7, 370; XIII, 376B; XVI, 389–90, 396; XXI, 408.

later granted Fulk authority to recruit any monks or canons. The 1201 General Chapter witnessed a very different scene, where nobles attended and Fulk produced a papal letter designating three abbots as preachers for his mission. Innocent III was exerting strong pressure on the Cistercians, and Arnaud Amaury apparently did not resist. Instead he came to 'incarnate in word and deed the pope's executive power', to quote Raymonde Foreville.[20] The same pressure exerted to advocate the Eastern crusade was applied to persuade the Cistercians to preach in Occitania. All the while Innocent III was balancing the campaigns in the areas targeted for papal intervention.

One extant sermon from the early 1200s belongs to the period of pre-crusade Cistercian preaching and may voice the thoughts of Arnaud Amaury while he was abbot of Grandselve.[21] Sometime before Alan of Lille's death in 1203, he rendered into Latin a vernacular sermon delivered by an unspecified Cistercian abbot at the parish church of St Firmin in Montpellier. Alan was in Montpellier around 1200, working on theological texts.[22] He may have translated a written version of the sermon, or worked from existing Latin notes, or perhaps even taken the notes himself during the sermon. Vernacular sermons were commonly turned into Latin when preserved in writing.[23] The sermon, the only one exemplifying Cistercian preaching to the people against heresy during this period, demonstrates how the anti-heretical arguments and rhetorical patterns of clerical treatises and ecclesiastical correspondence appear after they have been simplified for preaching to the people. It also illustrates the high emotions surrounding the image of the Cross, focal point for the Cathars' rejection of traditional beliefs about the Crucifixion.

Simple in content and syntax, the sermon expounds the themes of imitation of Christ and spiritual vigilance against the Devil. It takes a paraphrase of Genesis 35. 3 as its theme: 'Come and let us go up to Bethel and build an altar to the Lord who brought us out of tribulation and was our

---

[20] R. Foreville, *Le Pape Innocent III et la France*, Päpste und Pappstum 26 (Stuttgart, 1992). I am grateful to Anne Brenon for this reference.

[21] Paris, Bibliothèque Nationale, MS Lat. 14859, fols. 233ra–234rb: *Sermo quem composuit abbas cisterciensis romanis verbis aput Montepessulanum in ecclesia beati Firmini quem postea magister Alanus transtulit in latinam.* M. Newman cites a short passage from the sermon in *Boundaries*, p. 330, and includes it for its reforming message. I am very grateful to her for sharing her notes and photographs of the manuscript with me. M.-Th. d'Alverny, *Alain de Lille: Textes inédits* (Paris, 1965), pp. 13–15, suggests the attribution to Arnaud Amaury, to whom one of Alan's pupils dedicated a work. Since the sermon apparently precedes the arrival of the delegation of abbots in 1206, that reduces the number of possible attributions, although none can be made with certainty.

[22] R. de Lage, *Alain de Lille: poète du XIIe siècle* (Paris, 1951), pp. 121; 42; 30, n. 59. See also Longère, *Prédication*, p. 88.

[23] On the connections between vernacular and Latin sermons, see *The Sermon*, pp. 971–4.

companion on the way.'[24] The preacher urges the audience to identify with the suffering of Christ and exhorts them to fight sin with virtues, good works and the sacrament of confession. At the sermon's core lies the statement that heretics do not believe in Christ's Incarnation and Passion and therefore represent enemies of the Cross. The same epithet was attached to Jews also and appears in the Cistercian *Statutes* of 1189 and 1190.[25]

The preacher strikes the concerns of lay people when he presents the Devil as a thief in the night who brings death and ruin by invading the household. To protect one's home and belongings, one must put the house in order and awake to the crowing of spiritual roosters – the prophets and apostles.[26] The abbot repeatedly exhorts the audience to rise from sin, represented by Jericho for sins of the flesh, Egypt for ignorance of sin, and Babylon for the confoundment of pride.[27] Similar to the thief, wickedness and sin creep up like gangrene and invade the whole body.[28] Like Jacob wrestling with the angel, Christians should resist the Devil by wrestling with Christ. They should return home as Jacob did to Bethel, the house of God. The command that Jacob received to reject other gods is interpreted as rejecting enmity to the Cross.[29]

Here the preacher defines what being an enemy of the Cross entails: speaking against the Incarnation, denying the Passion and holding contempt for the Cross. He then personalizes the attack on heresy. Heretics, he states, are enemies of the Cross because they object to the Cross and deny Christ's Passion. Intensifying the emotive aspect of the argument, the preacher exhorts his audience to glory in the Cross, as Paul proclaims (Galatians 6. 14), to cast out enmity to the Cross and to venerate Christ's Passion. They should contemplate the suffering Christ on the crucifix, the nail imprints on the hands, feet, and side, and the head that has no place to rest. The abbot exclaims that Christ's having no place to rest his head represents great lack of faith and iniquity.[30]

---

[24] The sermon reads: 'Venite et ascendamus in Bethel et edificemus altare Domino qui eripuit nos de tribulatione, qui fuit socius noster in via'; and Genesis 35. 3 reads: 'Surgite et ascendamus in Bethel ut faciamus ibi altare Deo qui exaudivit me in die tribulationis meae et fuit socius mei.'

[25] *Statuta*, p. 113: 1189.15; p. 121: 1190.14, refer to Jews as 'inimici crucis'.

[26] MS Lat. 14859, fol. 233ra: 'Surgamus ad sollicitudinem rei familiaris . . . Surgamus ad galli cantum. Galli spirituales sunt prophetae et apostoli qui ortum solis iusticie adventum Christi praeconati sunt.'

[27] MS Lat. 14859, fol. 233ra: 'Surgite ergo de Iericho, id est de carnis peccato . . . Surgite de Egipto, id est de ignorantie delicto . . . Surgite de Babilone, id est de superbie confusione . . . Sic pravum exemplum alios inficit et commaculat.'

[28] MS Lat. 14859, fol. 233rb: 'Surgere . . . ad luctandum cum angelo, id est, cum Christo . . . surgere etiam debemus cum Iacob ad revertendum . . . reverteri debemus in Bethel, id est, in domum Dei.'

[29] MS Lat. 14859, fol. 233va: 'Abiciamus deos alienos . . . dii alieni sunt inimicitia crucis'.

[30] MS Lat 14859, fol. 233va–vb: 'Inimicitia crucis est incarnationi Christi contradicere, passionem eius negare, crucem eius contempnere. Inimici ergo crucis sunt heretici

Thus denying Christ's humanity as symbolized by his Passion becomes equivalent to showing no compassion for his suffering, a refusal to find a place for Christ's head to rest. Framing that powerful accusation are the rhetorical patterns of demonization, pollution and threat to the social order, as well as motifs based on several polarities: sleep and vigilance, night and sunrise, darkness and light, the Devil and Christ, error and truth, black and white, war and peace, earth and Heaven, Babylon and Jerusalem. Listeners are asked to choose one over the other. Finally, the abbot emphasizes penance, practising good works and virtue over vice, and the sacrament of confession – a common anti-heretical theme.

The feeling that orthodox and dissident Christians represent friends and enemies of the Cross renders the polyvalent symbol of the Cross even more powerful. So crucial was the physical symbol of the Cross for crusaders to the Holy Land that the eager Christians listening to Bernard of Clairvaux's sermon at Vézelay in 1145 quickly exhausted the stock of cloth crosses for sewing on garments and the abbot tore his own robes to provide an additional supply.[31] Popular sentiment held that the cross protected the wearer; the *Hystoria Albigensis* reports that a knight at Lavaur (1211) was saved from a fire that consumed all his cloak except for the stitched-on cross. Before the battle of Muret, Fulk of Toulouse went among the troops to extend a crucifix to each for adoration until the bishop of Comminges seized it, worried about time constraints, and blessed all with the sign of the Cross.[32] Apparitions of the Cross also appear commonly in crusade literature. A miracle story from the *Hystoria Albigensis* centres on the power of such a vision of the Cross. A Cistercian abbot of Bonneval obtained a public apparition of the Cross to bolster his recruitment preaching. Addressing a crowd too large for the *castrum*'s church to accommodate it, the abbot exhorted his audience to take on the Cross against the Toulousan heretics, whereupon an enormous Cross appeared in the sky for all to see. Its appearance proclaimed the truth of his message, the penitential value of crusading, and the error held by the dissidents who rejected the symbol and were accused, like the Jews, of abusing it.[33] Crusade *exempla* from the *Hystoria Albigensis* recount episodes where

qui Christi cruci obviant, passionem negant. Simus ergo amici crucis cum apostolo dicentes: "Absit mihi gloriari nisi in cruce Dominis Iesu Christi [Galatians 6. 14]." Abiciamus ergo deos alienos, id est crucis inimicitias, et accedamus ad Christem per fidem, Christi venerantes passionem, considerantes quomodo caput inclinavit in cruce, nec invenit usquam reclinare. Unde ipse ait: "Vulpes foveas habent, et volucres coeli nidos: filius autem hominis non habet ut caput reclinet [Matthew 8. 20; Luke 9. 58]." Quanta infidelitas, quanta iniquitas, vix invenitur aliquis qui prebeat capiti Christi reclinatorium! Qui sustinentes in cruce ut nos reciperet . . . consideremus quomodo pedes Christi clavis ferreis fuerunt perforati. Consideremus quomodo perforatus fuit latus Christi.'

[31] See Cole, *Preaching*, p. 42.
[32] *Hystoria*, 229, p. 229, 461, pp. 151–2; Sibly, pp. 117–18, 209.
[33] Sibly, 298, p. 147; *Hystoria*, I, p. 292. See Chazan, *Stereotypes*, pp. 60–1, on mid-

soldiers supporting the heretics profane symbols, dismembering a crucifix in one case and in another, urinating in a chalice.[34]

Thus Cathar docetism in this sermon and elsewhere translates as contempt for the crucified Christ. The sermon illustrates how the theological debate over Christ's divine and human natures leads in popular preaching to the removal of humaneness from heretics. The twelfth century's growing humanization of Christ was accompanied by increasingly severe judgment of the Jews as killers of Christ;[35] turned against the Cathars, it brought similar accusations of indifference and even scorn for Jesus's death and passion. Finding such a profound lack of understanding between orthodoxy and heterodoxy, one more readily grasps both the outrage the Cistercians felt before the Cathars' beliefs and the Cathars' refusal to renounce their docetic tenets. The Cistercian missions' failure to persuade them is hardly surprising.

The year 1204 was pivotal for the preaching campaigns: Arnaud Amaury was appointed legate; the recruitment of preachers intensified; and various facets of the papal plan for Occitania sharpened. In January 1204, Innocent III wrote to Berenger, archbishop of Narbonne, reproaching him for his negligence in allowing the region to be 'infected with the blemish of heretical perverseness' and for his lack of assistance to the legates Ralph and Peter of Castelnau, monks of Fontfroide.[36] In 1203 the two legates succeeded brother Rainier, who had been charged by Innocent III on 21 April 1198 with the problem of heresy in southern France.[37] Peter of les Vaux-de-Cernay's history begins prior to Arnaud Amaury's appointment with the legates' work, frequently termed the 'business of the faith and peace' (*negotium fidei et pacis*). He contrasts the 'apostolic men' with their 'infected and diseased' listeners and stresses how the preachers urged the heretics many times to repent and exhorted the citizens of 'treacherous Toulouse' to drive out the heretics from their midst. Apparent success in December 1203, when the city's consuls and citizens swore to cast out heretics, proved an illusion. This initial

---

twelfth-century accusations of Jewish abuse of Christian symbols. Jessalyn Bird explores the cult of the Cross, particularly in connection with the crusades to the Holy Land, in her forthcoming dissertation 'Crusade and Reform in the Circle of James of Vitry' (to be submitted for Oxford D.Phil. in 2001).

[34] On the profanation *exempla*, see Berlioz, 'Exemplum et histoire', pp. 63–4. Peter of les Vaux-de-Cernay (*Hystoria*, 85, p. 87; Sibly, p. 49) relates an incident where a priest is assaulted, the chalice seized and urinated in. Sibly and Sibly interpret the action (*minxerunt in eo*) as urinating on the priest, not the chalice ('on him' versus 'in it'). Either is possible grammatically but I think interpreting the chalice as 'eo' is a better translation. Another example of sacrilegious behavior follows below, p. 153 n. 80.

[35] See Chazan, *Stereotypes*, pp. 88–9, on the humanization of Christ and the guilt attached to Jews for his death.

[36] *PL*, CCXV, 273–5: 'Labe igitur haereticae pravitatis provincia tua infecta . . .' *PL*, CCXV, 274B.

[37] Vicaire, 'Clercs', pp. 261–2.

phase of preaching failed, and the preachers experienced deep discouragement. Peter explains that the weary legates wanted to give up their preaching, because they had achieved no success in winning over the heretics. Whenever the churchmen tried to preach, the heretics countered with accusations about the worst lifestyles of some of the clergy, telling the legates to stop their preaching and concentrate on those clerics instead. Peter blames the campaign's demise on the corruption of the Toulousans, whom he covers with extreme language of pollution. Heresy, the 'ancient filth', spreads like a plague, rot on grapes, or mange on animals from the citizens of Tolouse, a 'nation of vipers', to neighbouring cities and towns. The chronicler interrupts his narrative with this portrait of an infected Toulouse and then elaborates the heretics' errors before resuming his account with events of 1206.[38]

Peter discusses Cathar dualism, emphasizing the 'absolute' tendency : the belief in two creators, one good and one evil, and the complete rejection of the Old Testament.[39] The 'mitigated' view receives only one sentence stating that some heretics thought that the creator had two sons. Various secondary myths colour the chronicler's account, such as the good god having two wives and Mary Magdalene being the concubine of Jesus. These points follow closely an anonymous source dated from 1208–13 that sets forth beliefs of Cathars and Waldensians and calls for their extermination by secular force.[40] Peter of les Vaux-de-Cernay portrays Cathar rejection of the Roman Church and its sacraments in terms of invective ascribed to the dissidents, such as the 'holy water of baptism was no better than river water'. Dietary practices, specifically the renunciation of meat, eggs and cheese are described accurately as is the centrality of the *consolamentum*, although its administration and functions are not portrayed exactly. Peter concludes with a few lines devoted to the 'less perverted' Waldensians.[41]

While the legates continued their preaching campaign, Innocent III stepped up his recruiting. The January 1204 letter to Archbishop Berenger addressed other ecclesiastics as well and urged Arnaud Amaury to recruit any qualified Cistercian monks to help the legates with their preaching. Arnaud Amaury, commissioned as legate himself in May 1204, joined the others at the end of

---

[38] *Hystoria*, 20, I, p. 22: '. . . injuncte sibi legationi pre tedio renuntiare volentes, eo quod nichil aut parum hereticis predicando proficere potuissent : quotienscunque enim vellent ipsis hereticis predicare, obiciebant eis heretici conversationem pessimam clericorum; et ita, si vellent clericorum vitam corrigere, oporteret eos a predicatione desistere.' Sibly, 10–19, pp. 10–15.

[39] Scholarly debate on the dualism of the Cathars is extensive. A. Brenon explains that radical dualism, attested only after the turn of the thirteenth century, developed gradually as Cathar thinkers systematized their beliefs in response to attack and to the scholastic milieu around them. Brenon also points out that the Cathars used the Psalms and Wisdom literature. See A. Brenon, *Les cathares. Vie et mort d'une église chrétienne* (Paris, 1996), pp. 124–9, 103.

[40] See WE, 37, pp. 230–5; and Duvernoy, *Religion*, pp. 17; 222, n. 8.

[41] *Hystoria*, 10–17, pp. 9–20; Sibly, pp. 10–14. See also WE, 38, pp. 235–41.

the month. The three were given full jurisdiction over the provinces of Aix, Arles, and Narbonne, and were charged with extirpating heresy in that area.[42] Unseating local prelates who were sympathetic to heretics constituted a high priority on the papal agenda. Accusing Archbishop Berenger of tolerating heresy, the legates set out to depose him and Raymond of Rabastens, bishop of Toulouse.[43] Both were replaced eventually by Cistercians: Arnaud Amaury became archbishop of Narbonne in 1212 and Fulk, abbot of Le Thoronet, assumed the Toulousan see in 1206. The legates were further charged with the power to grant indulgences equal to that given for crusades to the Holy Land,[44] which indicates the importance of the Occitanian mission in the eyes of the pope at that time, and illustrates how crusade ideology was applied to the Church's fight against heresy. In the 31 May 1204 bull *Etsi nostra navicula*, where Innocent III set out his orders to the legates and their powers, he also praised the order for the various qualities that made its men suited for confounding heretics: zeal, knowledge, strength of deed and word, speech more penetrating than a sword, harmony between what they preached and what they practised.[45] He would repeat such praises of the order as he tried to encourage the Cistercians and keep them to their task.

Innocent III repeatedly tried to boost the Cistercians' morale, sending a letter to the legate Peter of Castelnau in January 1205 and finally calling on Cîteaux for help in July 1206.[46] The January letter to Peter of Castelnau tries to strike a hopeful note, speaking first of the necessity at times to leave the

---

[42] Bull of 31 May 1204, *Etsi nostra navicula*, *PL*, CCXV, 360: 'Ut autem injunctae vobis, non tam nostrae quam divinae, legationis officium possitis melius et liberius exercere, plenam vobis in Aquensi, Arelatensi et Narbonensi provinciis, et vicinis etiam diocesibus, si quae sunt haereticorum labe pollutae, concedimus facultatem destruendi, disperdendi et evellendi, quae destruenda, disperdenda et evellenda fuerint, et plantanda sub interpositione anathematis prohibentes, ne qui pro ecclesiasticis sacramentis quidquam audeant extorquere, illos qui contra prohibitionem vestram venire praesumpserint canonice punituri.'

[43] Correspondence between Innocent III and the legates shows several letters demanding investigation of local clergy. Fachinger, 'Les documents pontificaux', pp. 49–51. J.-L. Biget observes that heresy probably offered Rome a way to rid itself of Occitan prelates whom it found undesirable. 'Les Albigeois', pp. 250–1. See also Daunou, 'Arnaud Amaury', pp. 307–8.

[44] *PL*, CCXV, 360C: '. . . cum illos, qui contra haereticos fideliter laborarint, eadem indulgentia gaudere velimus, quam in terrae sanctae subsidium transfretantibus indulgemus.'

[45] *PL*, CCXV, 358–60, esp. 359BC. *Etsi nostra navicula*, 31 May 1204, praises the order for various qualities that make its men suited for confounding heretics: zeal, knowledge, strength of deed and word, speech more penetrating than a sword, harmony between what they preach and what they practice. The theme of excellence in word and deed, *in opere et sermone*, was a standard one in the twelfth century. C. Bynum traces it in *'Docere Verbo et Exemplo': An Aspect of Twelfth-Century Spirituality*, Harvard Theological Monographs (Missoula, MT, 1979).

[46] *PL*, CCXV, 525–6 for January 1205 letter, *Debitum caritatis*; listed in Fachinger, 'Les documents pontificaux', p. 49. *PL*, CCXV, 940–1 for July 1206 letter.

contemplative life of Rachel and Mary and take on the burden of Leah or the service of Martha. The active life can be viewed as more useful and profitable both to oneself and others, because virtues increase by enduring tribulations and pressures, as Paul advises in Romans 5. 3–5: 'Suffering produces endurance, endurance produces character, character produces hope, and hope does not disappoint us.' The pope argues that the legate must not refuse the work enjoined on him, even though the people to whom he was sent seem hard and incorrigible, for the Lord has the power to raise the children of Abraham from stones. The legate must continue in his evangelical task and strive to fulfil his commission, hoping securely in Christ Jesus.[47]

In the summer of 1206, support arrived when Diego, bishop of Osma, and Dominic of Guzman, the future founder of the Dominican order, joined the company of the Cistercians. Peter of les Vaux-de-Cernay resumes his account of the preaching mission with a meeting between Diego, bishop of Osma and the three legates in Montpellier. Diego of Osma attempted to breathe new life into the disheartened preachers, advising them to follow the apostles' model, specifically to devote themselves with greater vigour to preaching, display humility in all their doings and follow Jesus's example in word and actions by travelling on foot and eschewing ornaments of gold or silver.[48] The Cistercians did not object but also hesitated to assume leadership for this new style of life; they preferred to follow someone else's direction. Diego of Osma offered to conduct them himself, aided by one companion, the future St Dominic. Diego and Dominic teamed up with two of the Cistercian legates while Arnaud Amaury returned to Cîteaux for general chapter with the intent of bringing back a group of abbots to assist with the preaching. During his absence, the preachers reportedly reaped success in Servian, after about a week of preaching and debating, and in Béziers after about two weeks there. In Carcassonne they spent about a week in sermons and debates; and in Montréal debates and evangelizing occupied two weeks. Peter of Castelnau left them after Béziers to pursue diplomatic missions; the chronicler reports that he was so hated that the other legates feared for his life.[49]

When Arnaud Amaury appealed to Cîteaux's General Chapter for assistance in summer 1206, Innocent III also addressed the abbots in a July 1206 letter. The pope frames his message with the imagery of the Church as a ship, navigating on stormy seas with its fishermen unable to cast their nets to catch fish. Evocation of sea monsters and Scylla and Charybidis heighten the atmosphere of danger. In this perilous situation, Innocent III asks for the

---

[47] *PL*, CCXV, 525–6.
[48] *Hystoria*, 21, I, p. 23: 'Memoratus episcopus adversus hujusmodi perplexitatem salubre dedit consilium, monens et consulens ut, ceteris omissis, predicationi ardentius insudarent et, ut possent ora obstruere malignorum, in humilitate procedentes, exemplo Pii Magistri facerent et docerent, irent pedites absque auro et argento, per omnia formam apostolicam imitantes.' Sibly, 21 and 24, pp. 17–19.
[49] *Hystoria*, 22–3, I, pp. 25–6; Sibly, pp. 18–19.

abbots' prayers and then, employing the agricultural imagery of the vineyard, he implores them both to eradicate the harmful plants from the Lord's vineyard and to take care in planting beneficial ones.[50]

The appeals were successful. Arnaud Amaury brought back a delegation of twelve abbots and numerous other monks. He joined the other legates at Montréal. Peter of les Vaux-de-Cernay praises the abbots as men of highest religious life, accomplished learning and incomparable holiness, modelling in life and in number the company of the apostles. They were always ready to defend the faith in disputes, the Cistercian chronicler observes – an essential quality for the model anti-heretical preacher. All the legates travelled on foot, as the bishop of Osma had recommended.[51] The chronicler Robert of Auxerre tells of their journey,[52] and Peter of les Vaux-de-Cernay explains how each one was assisted by two or three monks and charged with a specific region for 'pressing on with preaching and toiling in disputations'.[53] In the delegation was Guy of les Vaux-de-Cernay, Peter's uncle, who would later become the master of the preachers (1208). Another one of the twelve, Henry of Mont-Sainte-Marie, apparently remained in Occitania for a few years, because Peter of les Vaux-de-Cernay later mentions his preaching at a church near Pamiers.[54]

The band of preachers encountered many obstacles and much frustration – not only the opposition of the dissidents, but also resistance from feudal lords faithful to their subjects and from incumbent clergy who were accused of sheltering heretics. William of Puylaurens, chronicler for Fulk of Toulouse, reports that the preachers, 'God's blessed warriors', continued their efforts for around two years before appealing to Rome for relief upon the death of Peter of Castelnau.[55] William of Tudela, the author of the first section of the

---

[50] *PL*, CCXV, 941: 'De plenitudine vero gratiae nostrae securi, ad sanctae religionis cultum latius propagandum ferventius insistatis, et de vinea Domini Sabaoth, vestrae curae commissa, quae per cuius gratiam a mari usque ad mare palmite jam extendit, studeatis eradicare nociva, et utilia plantare curetis . . .'

[51] *Hystoria*, 47, I, p. 42: '. . . vir venerabilis abbas Cistercii, Arnaldus . . . abbates XII habens secum . . . et hi omnes, cum pluribus monachis, quos secum adduxerant, omnem sectantes humilitatem, juxta exemplar quod eis ostensum erat in Monte, id est secundum quod audierant de episcopo Oxomense, pedites procedebant . . .'; Sibly, p. 26. See also Thouzellier, *Catharisme et Valdéisme*, pp. 194–5.

[52] Thouzellier, *Catharisme et Valdéisme*, p. 199.

[53] *Hystoria*, 47, I, pp. 42–3: '. . . ab abbate Cisterciense longe lateque abbates singuli sunt dispersi et assignati sunt unicuique termini proprii, per quos discurrendo predicationi insisterent, disputationibus insudarent'; Sibly, pp. 25–6.

[54] Peter of les Vaux-de-Cernay cites him in the context of events from 1210 to 1211, although the dating for the episode is not clear. Certainly it occurs after the departure of the other abbots who left in 1206 after a few months. *Hystoria,* 201, I, pp. 203–4; Sibly, p. 105.

[55] Puylaurens, p. 54: 'Continuato itaque biennio et amplius hoc labore, cum accensum ignem per hanc viam extinguere non valerent benedicti Dei pugiles, attendentes quod res ista altiori consilio indigeret, clamare ad Sedem apostolicam sunt coacti.'

Canso, composed between 1210 and 1213, sings about the Cistercian preaching missions, praising Arnaud Amaury, whom he calls formulaically 'the one whom God loved so much', for his efforts at preaching conversion to the heretics:

> This very holy man went, he too, into the heretics' land; he preached to them and tried to convert them. But the more he pleaded, the more they mocked him, paying him no more heed than they would to any fool whatsoever. And yet he was the legate of the pope, who had given him extensive powers so that he could eliminate this faithless people. With brother Arnaud, the abbot of Cîteaux, at their head, the legates went about on foot or on horseback, disputing with the perfidious heretics, stubborn in their errors. They did not stop urging them strongly in their speeches; but the heretics paid them no heed and scorned them.

The poet also recounts in a later passage that Arnaud and Fulk, bishop of Toulouse, went out to preach daily, but that the crowds derided them and compared their voices to the buzzing of bees.[56]

What can we determine about the content and form of the Cistercians' preaching? The *Hystoria Albigensis* speaks of the preachers with the formulas 'predicando et disputando' or 'evangelizando et disputando'.[57] The two activities were closely linked. It seems that the Cistercians and their companions went about preaching until a bystander challenged them, whereupon the sermon, already in the form of an imagined dialogue, became a spontaneous debate, like the confrontations Bernard of Clairvaux met in 1145.[58] An anecdote told by Caesarius of Heisterbach records a conversation between a knight and a monk accompanying the delegation of abbots (1206). In this case, the monk sought out a potential heretic in order to unmask him in debate. Caesarius uses this *exemplum* to illustrate precisely what he has just summarized about the doctrines and sacraments that the heretics reject. The exchange seems to constitute an excerpt from an informal debate about reincarnation: the monk approaches the knight, engages him in discussion, sensing that he must be a heretic, and then proceeds to ask him questions designed to uncover heretical views. When questioned about his field and its revenues, the knight, well-off enough to have a horse and a ploughman, explains that the field is his, that he and his family live off its proceeds and give some of the surplus to the poor. Asked what good his alms-giving will bring, the knight replies that his spirit will go forth gloriously after his death (*gloriose pergat post mortem*). The monk asks where the knight's spirit will go (*Quo perget?*); and he answers that it depends

---

[56] *Chanson,* laisses 3–4, I, pp. 12–13, laisse 46, pp. 110–13. New edition, *La Chanson de la croisade albigeoise,* with translation by Henri Gougaud and introduction by M. Zink (Paris, 1989). Shirley, p. 32.

[57] See for example, *Hystoria*, I, 26–8, 43, 46.

[58] See Kienzle, 'Tending the Lord's Vineyard', pp. 56–7.

on his merit: if good, his spirit will delight within the body of some future prince or king, or some other prominent person; if not, it will suffer in the body of a poor, unfortunate person. Caesarius adds that the Albigensians believe the soul passes through various bodies, even those of animals and reptiles, in accordance with its merit (a common confusion resulting from the identification of Catharism with Manicheanism). The novice exclaims: 'Foul heresy!', and Caesarius does not report how the monk counters the knight's statement. We may imagine that the conversation continued. In any case, the *exemplum* suggests that such debates, even in dialogue or a small group, were taking place as the Cistercian preachers travelled the countryside.[59]

We recall that Peter of les Vaux-de-Cernay mentions preaching and debates in Servian, Béziers, Carcassonne, and Montréal. The Montréal dispute, which included two Cathar bishops, was scheduled and transcribed, whereas other debates probably arose spontaneously. According to the chronicler, the debate at Montréal extended over a fortnight. The arguments from both sides were written down and handed over to judges, but no record remains.[60] A disputation took place with the Waldensians at Pamiers, attended by Fulk of Toulouse and several abbots; it resulted in the conversion of Durand of Huesca and other Waldensians who formed the order of the Poor Catholics.[61] One disputation led to a reported miracle that preserved the notes Dominic took on his sources following the debate. The document, given to the heretics for study, survived three attempts to burn it. The dissidents were not persuaded by its resilience, but the miracle was reported to others by a knight who witnessed the event.[62]

Most confrontations were not as successful as that at Pamiers, nor did they lead to miracles. Generally the legates and their companions encountered failure. Furthermore, Diego of Osma returned to Spain and died there on 30 December 1207. Ralph of Fontfroide also died in 1207, and the other preachers went home disheartened, as did most of the abbots. The chronicler Robert of Auxerre describes their futile effort.[63] Peter of les Vaux-de-Cernay argues that the preachers were clearly persuasive, but admits that they were unable

---

[59] Caesarius, *Dialogus*, 1.5.21, p. 301.

[60] *Hystoria*, 26, I, p. 29: 'Protelata autem fuit disputatio per XV dies et redacta fuerunt in scriptum hinc inde proposita et tradita judicibus . . .'; Sibly, p. 20. Also *Hystoria*, 47, I, p. 41; Sibly, p. 26.

[61] *Hystoria*, 48, I, p. 43; Sibly, pp. 26–7.

[62] *Hystoria*, 54, I, pp. 47–9; Sibly, pp. 29–30.

[63] Thouzellier, *Catharisme et Valdéisme*, pp. 203–5; R. d'Auxerre, cited in Thouzellier, *Catharisme et Valdéisme*, p. 205, n. 108, says the efforts lasted only three months. The editors of the Latin edition of P. les Vaux-de-Cernay's history disagree, dating the recognized failure of the mission by a 17 November letter of Innocent III stating that the heretics 'were neither reached by reasoned propositions, nor frightened by warnings, nor softened by soft words' (*nec propositas rationes attendunt nec terrentur comminationibus nec possunt blanditiis deleniri*). *Hystoria*, I, p. 46, n. 2.

to convert the heretics, who were so stubborn in their wickedness that the preachers 'were able to achieve little or nothing by preaching or disputing'.[64]

Still some Cistercian preachers continued to evangelize and to debate, notably Arnaud Amaury, Guy of les Vaux-de-Cernay, and Fulk of Toulouse. William of Tudela, who compares the preachers' voices to buzzing bees, asserts that all the preachers did not give up their efforts, and that every day Arnaud Amaury and Fulk went out preaching to the local residents, who nonetheless refused to convert:

> The bishop of Toulouse, Fulk of Marseille, who has no equal in merit, and the abbot of Cîteaux concerted their efforts; every day they went out to preach to the people of the region, who showed little inclination to convert . . . Throughout the Agenais, the abbot made so many tours that he went as far as Sainte-Bazeille. But nothing of what they preached entered the ears of the people who said to them mockingly: 'Listen to the bee buzz.' May Faith come to my aid, it does not astonish me that they are destroyed, stripped and pillaged, nor that they are done violence to bring them to the good.[65]

The connection that the poet makes here between the heretics' mockery and the violence they endured comes disturbingly close to justifying the coming massacres of the crusade.

A turning point came in 1208 when the legate Peter of Castelnau was murdered. We recall that Peter had separated himself from the other preachers in 1206 to undertake diplomatic missions. Peter of les Vaux-de-Cernay recounts that the legate took refuge out of fear for his life. Castelnau had also pleaded with the pope to allow him to return to his monastery, leading to the January 1205 papal letter insisting that the legates persevere.[66] Now Innocent III was enraged at Castelnau's murder, and he called for armed intervention when he responded to the event in March 1208. A letter of 10 March to the archbishops of the region (Narbonne, Arles, Embrun, Aix and Vienne) and their suffragans announces Peter's murder and urges the continuance of the preaching campaign. The vineyard image figures strongly: Castelnau was one of the workers sent into the Lord's vineyard, entrusted to the pope's care. He and others were sent to uproot the useless plantings and propagate the useful, 'catching the little foxes that endeavour to ruin the vineyard itself'.[67] The count of Toulouse, called a minister of the

---

[64] *Hystoria*, 51, I, p. 46: 'Discurrentes igitur predicatores sancti hereticosque disputando manifestissime convincentes, set, quia obstinati erant in malicia, convertere non valentes, post multum temporis, cum parum aut nichil predicando sive disputando proficere potuissent, ad partes Gallie sunt reversi'; Sibly, p. 28.

[65] *Chanson*, laisse 2, I, pp. 8–11, laisse 46, I, pp. 110–13; Shirley, pp. 11–12, 32.

[66] See above, n. 46; Evans, 'Crusade', pp. 28–30; Lambert, *Heresy*, pp. 97–8; C. Thouzellier, *Catharisme et Valdéisme*, p. 196; Fachinger, 'Les documents pontificaux', p. 49.

[67] *PL*, CCXV, 1354: '. . . ut in dominicam vineam nostrae culturae commissam

Devil, was held responsible for the murder.[68] Another letter of the same day calls on Philip Augustus to follow the model of the two swords (Luke 22. 38),[69] joining the material with the spiritual sword to restore peace, to force the count of Toulouse's repentance, and to destroy the heresy, described in vehement language as plague and rabies.[70] In fact, the pope had already been appealing to Philip Augustus and all the barons and knights of France, promising indulgence as a reward for their intervention. His letter of 17 November 1207 does not mention preaching.[71] However, after Peter of Castelnau's death, Innocent issued a bull on 28 March 1208, repeating the exhortation of his 1204 bull, *Etsi nostra navicula*, and enjoining the legates to find men to preach. The 28 March 1208 bull charged Arnaud Amaury as chief legate and Guy of les Vaux-de-Cernay as master of the preachers. Earlier (17 March) Innocent III had congratulated Arnaud Amaury for his willingness to follow in Peter of Castelnau's footsteps and risk martyrdom in defence of the faith.[72]

Bishop Fulk departed for Rome sometime after the deaths of Peter of Castelnau, Diego of Osma and Ralph of Fontfroide. Peter of les Vaux-de-Cernay reports that the remaining preachers realized that their campaign had failed and decided to appeal to the pope for help. The chronicler does not include such a meeting in Rome but records that Innocent III responded by commissioning his notary Milon as legate.[73] However, William of Tudela depicts a scene in Rome involving Arnaud Amaury instead of Fulk, which reportedly was relayed to him by an eye-witness. According to the poet's account, Innocent III learns of Castelnau's murder and excommunicates the count of Toulouse in the presence of Arnaud Amaury and the notary Milon. The latter, 'who speaks Latin so well', was commissioned as a legate in March 1209. In Rome, according to the poet, the crucial decision was made that would result 'in the death of many and would order the destruction of any

operarios mitteremus. Attendentes ergo jamdudum quod in Provincia nimis creverant plantaria vitiorum, ne spuria vitulamina radices mitterent altiores, viros illuc idoneos destinavimus, qui de vinea Domini Sabaoth avellerent inutilia et utilia propagarent, capientes vulpeculas quae moliuntur ipsam vineam demoliri.' Listed in Fachinger, 'Les documents pontificaux', pp. 52–3.

[68] M. Roquebert goes as far as to implicate Amaury in a plot to assassinate Castelnau, claiming that Amaury had more to gain from the murder than did the count of Toulouse. If Raymond VI, he argues, could have gotten rid of someone, it would have been Amaury and not Peter of Castelnau. *L'épopée cathare*, 4 vols. (Toulouse, 1970–89), I, 216–19.

[69] The two swords' image figures in Henry of Clairvaux's Letter 11 of May 1178. See Kienzle, 'Henry of Clairvaux', pp. 68–9.

[70] *PL*, CCXV, 1358–9.

[71] *PL*, CCXV, 1246–8; see Thouzellier, *Catharisme et Valdéisme*, p. 204.

[72] See Thouzellier, *Catharisme et Valdéisme*, pp. 207–8, on the 28 March 1208 bull; and Fachinger, 'Les documents pontificaux', p. 53, on the 17 March letter, *Recepimus litteras*.

[73] *Hystoria*, 67, 69, I, pp. 65–9; Sibly, pp. 38–40.

that resisted it, from Montpellier to Bordeaux'. Arnaud Amaury, impatient to return to Occitania, stands erect next to a marble pillar and urges the pope 'to have his letters written in Latin' sent to southern France, and to have the indulgence proclaimed throughout the world. After the abbot of Cîteaux, called 'the wisest and most virtuous ever to have worn a mitre', expresses his opinion, all agree, and the pope instructs him to 'take the road to Carcassonne and Toulouse', to 'lead the armies against the perfidious people', to 'pardon the sins of the good catholics and to preach to them' on behalf of the pope, exhorting them to 'chase the heretics out from the good people'.[74] Peter of les Vaux-de-Cernay reports that Arnaud Amaury appealed to King Philip Augustus, who sent some of his barons to assist the crusade but would not come himself or send his son.[75]

William of Tudela then places Arnaud Amaury at Cîteaux, where the abbot returns for general chapter. In the presence of all, he celebrates a solemn mass and preaches; he then shows everyone present the papal bull, probably the one of 28 March 1208, advising them to preach the crusade and to make known the indulgence the pope would grant.[76] No indications of the sermon's content are specified, but the poet immediately describes a widespread and enthusiastic response to the indulgence. In formulaic style, he exclaims: 'Never in my life have I seen such a great assembly as that which was made against the heretics and the Waldensians.' Again in the style of epic poetry, a catalogue of names and arms follows.[77]

The crusade was launched and Peter of les Vaux-de-Cernay correlates the failure of the preaching missions with the subsequent violent measures against heresy. Just before the crusaders' arrival the *Hystoria Albigensis* comments that God had sent preachers to the heretics and their supporters 'not one, but many, not once, but often' and, echoing Matthew 21. 6–7, 'some of the preachers they heaped with abuse, others they even killed'.[78]

Once the crusade began, Arnaud Amaury figures in the sources primarily as the troops' leader. The best known and most damaging tale about Arnaud Amaury comes from the *Dialogus miraculorum* of Caesarius of Heisterbach, a Cistercian monk from the Rhineland. It concerns not the abbot's preaching but his fierceness at the sack and massacre of Béziers, which took place on 22 July 1209, shortly before the siege of Carcassonne (1–15 August 1209). At Béziers, when asked whether to kill both catholic Christians and heretics, and

---

[74] *Chanson*, laisses 5–8, I, pp. 16–23; *Shirley*, pp. 13–15. Amaury's presence in Rome at the time, March 1208, has been disputed by some but E. Martin-Chabot finds it plausible and feels that Amaury influenced the writing of the 10 March 1208 bulls concerning the repression of heresy and then returned to Occitania bearing the 28 March bull. *Chanson*, p. 17, n. 6.

[75] *Hystoria*, 71–2, I, pp. 71–2; Sibly, pp. 40–2.

[76] *Chanson*, laisse 8, pp. 22–3; *Shirley*, pp. 14–15.

[77] *Chanson*, laisse 8, I, pp. 24–5; *Shirley*, pp. 14–15.

[78] *Hystoria*, 81, I, pp. 80–1; Sibly, p. 46.

how to tell one from the other, Arnaud Amaury reportedly replied: 'Kill them all; God will recognize his own.'[79]

Caesarius's own view of heresy's threat to the social order stands out when he introduces the anecdote with a claim that the Albigensian heresy would have overrun all of Europe, had it not been repressed by the sword. It is clear that Caesarius finds the words attributed to Arnaud Amaury praiseworthy, for the Rhineland monk remarks:

> The Albigensian error was so strong that in a short period of time it would have infected as many as 1,000 cities, if it had not been repressed by the swords of the faithful. I think that it would have corrupted all of Europe.

Caesarius also considers the crusade significant enough that he expounds the heretics' beliefs, tracing them back to Mani and Origen's *Periarchon*. Furthermore, he recounts the crusade's major events from 1208/9 to around 1220 and includes several well-known *exempla*, some of them among the most notorious profanation stories. One involves an incident preceding the siege of Béziers, when heretics reportedly saw the crusaders coming, then grabbed a Gospel book and urinated on it before hurling it at the oncoming soldiers. Such episodes of sacrilege heighten the charge that the monk levels throughout these chapters, that heresy constitutes the work of the Devil. Furthermore, the discussion of heresy falls within a division of the *Dialogus* that concerns demons. Thus the rhetorical categories of demonisation, pollution and threat to the social order emerge strongly from Caesarius's treatment of heresy.[80]

Whether or not Arnaud Amaury uttered the infamous words that Caesarius attributed to him, all the inhabitants of Béziers were slaughtered by the army the Cistercian led, and he reported succinctly to Innocent III that 'neither age, nor sex, nor status had been spared, and nearly twenty thousand people perished'. The legate described the subsequent sack and burning of the city as 'divine revenge raging wondrously against it', and he termed the event a 'great miracle'.[81] In sharp contrast, the troubadour William Figuéiras

---

[79] 'Caedite eos. Novit enim Dominus qui sunt eius'. Caesarius, *Dialogus*, 1, 5.21, p. 302.

[80] 'In tantum enim Albiensium error invaluit, ut brevi intervallo temporis infecerit usque ad mille civitates, et si non fuisset gladiis fidelium repressus, puto quod totam Europam corrupisset.' Caesarius, *Dialogus*, 1, 5.21, pp. 301–2. Chapters 18–25 of Book Five, pp. 296–309, deal with heresy. Book 5.21, p. 302, contains the Gospel book story: 'In quorum [centum millia hominum] aspectu haeretici super volumen sacri Evangelii mingentes, de muro illud contra Christianos proiecerunt, et sagittis post illud missis clamaverunt: "Ecce lex vestra, miseri."' Berlioz, 'Exemplum et histoire', pp. 63–4, finds the story implausible because the Cathars revered the New Testament. In my view, if the culprits were in fact Cathar believers, the action could have represented the lack of respect for the Gospel message that they saw in the crusaders about to attack them.

[81] *PL*, CCXVI, 139CD: '. . . capta est civitas Biterrensis, nostrique non parcentes ordini, sexui, vel aetati, fere viginti millia hominum in ore gladii peremerunt; factaque hostium strage permaxima, spoliata est tota civitas et succensa, ultione divina in

blamed the massacre on Rome and Cîteaux, exclaiming bitterly: 'Rome, you wear a wicked hat, you and Cîteaux both, and you have committed astonishing butchery at Béziers.'[82] In Simon of Montfort's letter to the pope, primarily focused on Montfort's own deeds and appointment as viscount of Béziers and Carcassonne, he praises the abbot legate as 'more than others, faithful to God's affairs, disposed to action in all matters, steadfast in complete faith, counsel, deed and speech'.[83] Neither Arnaud Amaury's account nor Montfort's reveals any regret or misgivings for the murder of a reported 20,000 people, not even of the 'orthodox' who chose not to abandon their city to the crusaders. Many of those victims had taken refuge in the church of Sainte Marie-Madeleine, which was set ablaze. The Dominican scholar Marie-Humbert Vicaire noted too that the legate 'was not moved, nor troubled, nor even saddened at the thought of souls of the saved ('âmes d'élites') in danger'.[84] Arnaud Amaury's biographer in the *Histoire littéraire de la France* observes that nothing in the legate's character would make the story at Béziers unbelievable.[85]

William of Tudela, who consistently praises the abbot legate, does not tell the story related by Caesarius, nor do other accounts contain it.[86] William relates, as does Arnaud Amaury's letter to Innocent III, the effort made by the bishop of Béziers to persuade the people to allow the crusaders to enter without resistance. The poet describes the bishop's distress, but no such feelings from the abbot legate, who appears first at the gates of Béziers, followed by the crusaders. However, the poet attributes to the secular leaders the decision to destroy everything and everyone. William of Tudela also reports that no one escaped alive, and he describes the crusaders and their deeds as savagery: 'I do not think that such savage killing has ever been carried out or done since the time of the Sarrasins.'[87] After his first appearance, the abbot legate no longer figures in the events at Béziers which the poet narrates.

eam mirabiliter saevient. Disseminato ergo rumore tanti miraculi usque adeo territi sunt universi . . .'
[82] 'Roma . . . / Quar de mal capel / Etz vos e Cistel – qu'a Bezers fezetz faire / Mout estranh mazel.' 'Sirventès contre Rome', ed. R. Nelli, in *Ecrivains anticonformistes du Moyen Age occitan, II, Hérétiques et politiques* (Paris, 1977), p. 256.
[83] *PL*, CCXVI, 142BC: 'Venerabilem siquidem virum abbatem Cistercii prae caeteris negotio Dei fideliorem et proniorem in omnibus inveni, sermone, opere, consilio, fide integra constantiorem.'
[84] Vicaire, 'Clercs', p. 267. On the number of victims and its exaggeration, see Evans, 'Crusade', p. 289 n. 14, who states that the entire population of Béziers at that time was around eight to nine thousand.
[85] Daunou, 'Arnaud Amaury', p. 313.
[86] J. Berlioz points out that Caesarius is the only one to tell the story and examines the other accounts carefully. Berlioz also studies the possible scriptural bases for the statement. *'Tuez-les tous, Dieu reconnaîtra les siens' La croisade contre les albigeois vue par Césaire de Heisterbach* (Portet-sur-Garonne, 1994), pp. 74, 76–83.
[87] *Chanson*, laisse 20, I, pp. 58–9; *Shirley*, p. 21. My translation here.

Nonetheless, in the second part of the *Canso*, whose anonymous author often expresses outrage at the crusaders, Arnaud Amaury and Bishop Fulk of Toulouse accompany the cardinal legate, Bertrand, when he exhorts the crusaders to attack Toulouse in 1217 and murder its inhabitants. The cardinal legate's reported words reveal no mercy, and his call for slaughter constitutes a discourse somewhat parallel in content and situation to the speech attributed to Arnaud Amaury at Béziers:

> Next came the throng of great barons and commanders, the lord cardinal ahead of them all, bishop and archbishop in his train, with all their mitres, rings, crosses and croziers and missals. He addressed them, a learned man speaking: 'My lords, the spiritual king tells each one of you that the fires of Hell are in this town! It is brimming with guilt and sin, for there inside it is Raymond, their overlord. Whoever attacks this place will be saved before God. Recapture the town, seize every house! Let neither man nor woman escape alive, no church, no relics or hospice protect them, for in holy Rome sentence has been given: the sharp sword of death shall touch them. As I am a good and holy man, worthy and loyal, as they are guilty, wicked and forsworn, let sharp steel strike down each of them!'[88]

These ruthless words echo, by their call for slaughter and their disregard of sanctuary, the orders reportedly given by Arnaud Amaury at Béziers. In so doing, they argue for the plausibility that such an utterance issued from the archbishop legate's mouth.

While the tale itself has been considered suspect, a recent study reassesses it and brings to light a new source, concluding that the story is at least plausible, if not verifiable. Jacques Berlioz highlights and analyses details from six chapters (20–5) of the *Dialogus* that concern heresy during this period, a clear indication of Caesarius's concern and his conviction that the heretics' errors justified their repression.[89] In addition, Berlioz reviews contemporary reactions to the massacre at Béziers. The troubadour William Figuéiras harshly denounced it, as we noted above, blaming the collaboration of Rome and Cîteaux, while other poets condemned more generally the entire enterprise of the crusade, seeing it as a way to divert attention from the loss of the Holy Land.[90] Berlioz also brings to light the important story of a man returned from the dead, included in the encyclopaedia of the English cleric Gervase of Tilbury. Tilbury's work was composed between 1209 and 1214, and the anecdote, dated in 1211, takes place in the city of Beaucaire, on the right bank of the Rhône. The 'revenant' appears to a young girl in Beaucaire

---

[88] *Chanson*, laisse 187, II, pp. 12–13; *Shirley*, p. 131. The second part of the *Canso* takes up with laisse 131. The anonymous author writes in a completely different point of view from William of Tudela. On the beginning of the second part of the *Canso*, see M. Zink, 'Introduction', *Chanson* (1989 edn), p. 17.

[89] Berlioz, *'Tuez-les tous'*, pp. 11–22.

[90] Berlioz, *'Tuez-les tous'*, pp. 87–8.

who poses several questions, and the prior of Tarascon follows suit. The prior received from the Cistercian William Hélie, bishop of Orange (1200–21), a series of difficult questions directed expressly to the 'revenant', among them: 'Did the death or the massacre of the Albigensians please God?' The 'revenant' replied that nothing had pleased God as much, because God in his judgment wanted the good to be distinguished from the heretics. In fact, the good, although not tainted by heresy, still sinned by their tolerance of the heretics. The evil ones whose bodies were burned on earth, were burned even more harshly in mind after their deaths. Connections between this story and the massacre of Béziers are evident: notably the refusal of the 'orthodox' Christians in the city to yield to the crusaders, and the words attributed to Arnaud Amaury. Berlioz draws several conclusions from the anecdote: the massacre at Béziers had troubled public opinion enough that the bishop of Orange would send questions about it to the 'revenant'; the 'revenant''s message to him was reassuring; the dead man's words about the fate of the victims did not shock the prior, which shows the plausibility of the statement attributed to Arnaud Amaury; the tolerant catholic Christians were considered guilty for having tolerated heretics in their midst, which would make the massacre acceptable to people in the region; and the 'revenant' brought back a message from God, which demonstrated that God was on the side of the crusaders.[91] Berlioz's findings underscore both the plausibility of the statement attributed to Arnaud Amaury and its approval in some Cistercian circles.

There are some references in the *Canso* to the abbot legate's preaching during the crusade. One of those concerns Arnaud Amaury's conduct at Carcassonne in 1209 following the siege of Béziers. William of Tudela describes the Cistercian's role at the taking of that city. Before relating the troops' unopposed entrance into the city, the poet praises Arnaud Amaury as the one without whose advice 'nothing would have been done'. The abbot mounts a marble block to preach to the crusaders, while heralds run through the ranks crying: 'Come, for pardon! The abbot of Cîteaux wants to preach to you.' Rushing to assemble around Arnaud Amaury, the crusaders listen to a sermon, reported as follows:

> My lords! Listen to my words. You see now what miracles the King of Heaven does in your favour: There is no resistance. I command you, in the name of God, to take nothing of the goods in the city, not even the value of a piece of coal, or we will immediately punish you with excommunication. For all this we will give to a powerful lord who will govern the area to God's satisfaction, in order that the heretical traitors do not recover it.

What the poet calls a sermon here consists of a series of orders and instructions, the primary homiletic element being that of exhortation. All of

---

[91] Berlioz, *'Tuez-les tous'*, pp. 93–8.

course agree to the orders, in the poet's account. However, there is evidence that some crusaders were in fact excommunicated for taking part of the loot.[92] Shortly after this 'sermon', Arnaud Amaury reportedly preached about Christ's birth before he busied himself with finding a ruler for Carcassonne. The abbot legate, William of Tudela asserts, 'did not fall asleep' on the job.[93]

Another event indicative of Arnaud Amaury's character occurred in the summer of 1210, when the crusaders under Simon of Montfort took the town of Minerve, and Arnaud Amaury was delegated the decision over the fate of the heretics there. Montfort preferred to yield to the abbot legate's opinion as 'appointed leader of the whole of Christ's business'. Peter of les Vaux-de-Cernay recounts that Arnaud Amaury wished the death of the heretics as 'enemies of Christ', but as a monk and priest, he did not dare order them put to death. Consequently, he offered them freedom if they would abjure, knowing all the while that they would not. To Robert of Mauvoisin, a crusader who objected to any offer of freedom, the abbot legate replied: 'Forget your concern, I believe very few of them will accept conversion.'[94] At Minerve 140 Cathar Christians were burned.[95] It is difficult not to ascribe partial responsibility for their deaths to Arnaud Amaury: the chronicler's distinction ordering them put to death, on the one hand – and offering an alternative that assuredly would lead to their deaths, on the other – does little to convince this writer of his integrity as a monk and priest.

In 1211 a brutal episode occurred, where Arnaud Amaury played a disputed role. Unable to take Toulouse, Arnaud Amaury and Simon of Montfort separated the army into two groups. One group headed towards the castle at Les Cassès to besiege it and then took numerous prisoners, burnt them alive, and razed the castle. In the first part of the *Canso*, William of Tudela mentions the siege of Les Cassès but places the responsibility for the deaths there on Simon of Montfort. Abbot Arnaud, he says, stayed in Cahors begging the nobles of that area to support Montfort, and left the cloister there only when Montfort came to fetch him sometime before the company travelled north to Rocamadour.[96] The biography of Arnaud Amaury in the *Histoire littéraire de la France* reverses the roles, placing the troops who took Les Cassès under the abbot's direction.[97] Peter of les Vaux-de-Cernay reports that Simon of Montfort commanded the troops and that once the inhabitants

---

[92] *Chanson*, laisse 29, I, pp. 82–3; *Shirley*, p. 24. On the excommunication, see *Chanson*, p. 83, n. 2.
[93] *Chanson*, laisse 34, I, p. 85; *Shirley*, p. 26. J. Bird in her dissertation is studying later crusading sermons by Jacques of Vitry that deal with the Incarnation and heretics' differing views on Christ's dual nature ('Crusade and Reform').
[94] *Hystoria*, 232, I, pp. 231–2; Sibly, p. 120.
[95] Vicaire, 'Clercs', p. 267; *Hystoria*, 154, I, p. 158; Sibly, pp. 83–4.
[96] *Chanson*, I, laisses 84–5, p. 200; *Shirley*, p. 48.
[97] Daunou, 'Arnaud Amaury', p. 318, cites the *Histoire de Languedoc*, XXII, no. 4–5, 8.

surrendered, the bishops entered the *castrum* to preach to the heretics. Finding them unwilling to convert, the bishops abandoned the prisoners to the crusaders who burnt almost sixty 'with great rejoicing'. Peter does not account for Arnaud Amaury's whereabouts but states that Bishop Fulk was travelling with the army at that time.[98] It would seem then that Bishop Fulk was the responsible cleric and not Arnaud Amaury.

The following year, on 12 March 1212, Arnaud Amaury was elected archbishop of Narbonne, and in addition claimed secular power over the duchy of Narbonne – a bold move that neither previous nor subsequent archbishops, until the seventeenth century, dared to make. The pope was then asked to confirm this new disposition of power. Arnaud Amaury quarrelled continually with Simon of Montfort over control of the duchy, displaying a desire for temporal power which some historians ascribe to his descent from the lineage of the dukes of Narbonne.[99]

Later the same year and during the midst of the crusade, Arnaud Amaury left France, assembling some 100 knights and leading them into Spain to play a role in the victory at the battle of Las Navas de Tolosa (16 July 1212).[100] Arnaud Amaury sent an account of the battle from Spain to the Cistercian General Chapter of September 1212. Primarily a narrative of the expedition and battle, the letter nonetheless couches the report of victory in striking language: the Lord's grace rendered the victory, and the wrath of God would menace those who did not repent from their errors. The abbot legate directly warned that if the heretics of Occitania did not repent, they would face an end similar to that of the Muslims at Las Navas de Tolosa. He placed the victory in the framework of an enterprise against three types of plagues and enemies: schismatics from the east, heretics from the west and Saracens from the south.[101] The rhetoric of pollution and threat to the social order resonates loudly, as the three groups are called 'plagues to humanity and enemies of Christ's holy Church'. Arnaud Amaury's inclusion of Eastern Christians ('schismatics') among the enemies of the Church follows a pattern of lament over heresy, loss of the Holy Land and

---

[98] *Hystoria*, 232, I, pp. 231–2; Sibly, p. 120.

[99] See Cabrer, 'Idea y realidad', p. 588, and Foreville, *Gouvernement et vie*, chap. XIV, p. 131. Daunou, 'Arnaud Amaury', pp. 318–19, cites *Hystoria*, c. 82, *Histoire de Languedoc*, XXII, and *Gallia christiana nova*, t. VII.

[100] Vicaire, 'Clercs', p. 266; Daunou, 'Arnaud Amaury', p. 319.

[101] The letter found in *Recueil des historiens des Gaules et de la France*, ed. M. Bouquet *et al.*, 24 vols. (Paris, 1738–1904), XIX, 250–4, reads (at p. 253): 'Benedictus per omnia Dominus Jesus Christus, qui per suam misericordiam in nostris temporibus, sub felici apostolatu domini Papae Innocentii, de tribus pestilentium hominum et inimicorum ecclesiae sanctae suae, videlicet orientalibus schismaticis, occidentalibus haereticis, meridionalibus Sarracenis, victorias contulit catholicis christianis . . . Erat quippe quoddam castrum maurorum quod Tolosa nuncupatur, quod nunc in potestate nostra per Dei gratiam est redactum, ut indignationem Dei timeant similiter, nisi poenituerint, haeretici tolosani.'

schism. Innocent III employs it,[102] although such rhetoric contrasts with his order that leaders of the Fourth Crusade not fight against Eastern Christians. Guy of les Vaux-de-Cernay and Simon of Montfort defended the papal order against attacking the Christian city of Zara during the Fourth Crusade but the crusaders went on to sack Constantinople.[103]

The fear of an alliance between Western heretics and Muslims may relate to Joachim of Fiore's prophecies, particularly his commentary on Revelation, in which heretics and Saracens ally. A Cistercian himself before breaking away to found his own order, Joachim was interviewed by Adam of Perseigne in 1195, before Adam engaged in preaching the Fourth Crusade. Moreover, Innocent III was acquainted with Joachim's writings before condemning his notions of the Trinity at the Fourth Lateran Council.[104]

Hence the letter sheds light on Arnaud Amaury's attitudes, both by the few lines above, which illustrate the ideology, and by the bulk of it, which demonstrates a focus on military events. The threat to Occitan heretics would be consistent with reports on Arnaud Amaury's ruthless position at Béziers and Minerve. From it, one may surmise that Arnaud Amaury sought to frighten heretics in Occitania into submission. The abbot legate clearly saw a crusade in three parts, viewing the Eastern Church, the Muslim Saracens and the Christian heretics as one enemy.

Other motives for Arnaud Amaury's participation at Las Navas de Tolosa emerge from various additional sources. Caesarius of Heisterbach claims that the Albigensians called on the king of Morocco for help and provided him a pretext to invade.[105] Martín Alvira Cabrer raises several other possibilities: the Almohads' capture in 1211 of Salvatierra, seat of the military order of Calatrava, whose head was the abbot of Cîteaux;[106] the Cistercian General

---

[102] See for example, *PL*, CCXV, 453, 456; *De contemptu mundi*, Caput XLI, *PL*, CCXVII, 734C. On Innocent III and the Greek Church, see A. Luchaire, *Innocent III. La Question d'Orient*, 6 vols. (Paris, 1907), IV, esp. 22–75, 149–229. I am grateful to Jessalyn Bird for pointing out this topos, discussed in her dissertation ('Crusade and Reform').

[103] See D. E. Queller and T. F. Madden, *The Fourth Crusade. The Conquest of Constantinople*, 2nd edn (Philadelphia, 1997), pp. 74–93, *passim*. Foreville, 'Innocent III et la croisade des Albigeois', p. 187, also cites Innocent III's orders.

[104] B. McGinn notes Innocent III's appeal to Antichrist in his crusade propaganda and summarizes the view of Antichrist in Joachim's prophecies. *Antichrist*, pp. 140–3, 150. See also McGinn, *Visions of the End*, pp. 126–42, for translation from Joachim; and Reeves, *Influence of Prophecy*. I am grateful to Jessalyn Bird for suggesting the influence of Joachim here. Manselli, 'De la *persuasio* la *coercitio*', p. 184, points out that Joachim's opinion was not an isolated one, because a letter of Conrad of Porto echoes the same theme.

[105] Caesarius, *Dialogus*, 5. 21, p. 303: Berlioz, *Tuez-les-Tous*, pp. 18–19, explores the background of this claim.

[106] Pope Alexander III approved the knights of the Order of Calatrava as Cistercian warriors in 1164, which prompted the criticism of Isaac, abbot of Stella. On the knights see J. F. O'Callaghan, 'The Order of Calatrava and the Archbishop of Toledo,

---

Chapter's involvement in disseminating information about the Almohad invasion; Arnaud Amaury's sense of solidarity with the Spanish ruler because of his Catalan origin; his personal pride; and a political strategy to block Peter II of Aragon from aiding Raymond VI in Occitania.[107]

Given the range of Arnaud Amaury's possible reasons for intervening at Las Navas de Tolosa, his role there seems a logical and not surprising product of personal ambition and the crusade mentality. Furthermore, Innocent III was urging the crusade against Muslims in Spain. In January of 1212, he wrote Arnaud Amaury to bring about a truce in Occitania, while at the same time he declared a crusade against the Almohads, a project he valued more than the Albigensian Crusade. Recruiting for the crusade against Occitania dwindled for a time but was later renewed, only to be deflected again toward the Eastern crusade.[108]

In January 1214, Innocent III relieved the archbishop of his duties as legate and appointed Robert of Courçon and Peter of Benevento, who resumed the push for recruits. While Arnaud Amaury's power and influence on the crusade seems to decline, the 1218 and 1219 Cistercian statutes reveal concern to discipline Cathar and 'faidit' sympathizers.[109] Arnaud Amaury quarrelled repeatedly with Simon of Montfort for sovereignty over Narbonne, and after Simon was killed on 25 June 1218, the Cistercian formed an alliance with Simon's son, Amaury.[110] The archbishop died at Fontfroide on 29 September 1225, and was buried at Cîteaux.[111]

While Henry of Clairvaux/Albano departed markedly from his monastic role, Arnaud Amaury certainly surpassed him in this. The precedent for a churchman leading a military expedition had been set, but Arnaud Amaury extended it. There is no evidence of regret in his account of the massacre at Béziers in 1209, and his stance at Minerve in 1210 does him no credit either. Arnaud Amaury, by his conduct at Béziers, Minerve, and Las Navas de Tolosa strayed far from the limitations set by Bernard of Clairvaux, who had refused to ride at the head of an army, because he found such an action exceedingly far from his monastic vocation.[112] Arnaud Amaury's conduct, particularly at Las Navas de Tolosa, brings to mind the literary character of the warrior bishop, like Archbishop Turpin in the *Chanson de Roland*. For the poet and the poems' interpreters, Turpin personifies the crusade mystique,

---

1147–1245', in *Studies in Medieval Cistercian History Presented to Jeremiah O'Sullivan*, CS 1 (Spencer, MA, 1971), pp. 65, 83. On Isaac, see *Sermons*, III, ed. A. Hoste, G. Raciti, trans. G. Salet and G. Raciti, SC 339 (Paris, 1987), S. 48, pp. 158–60.

[107] Cabrer, 'Idea y realidad', p. 579, summarizes previous views on Amaury's motives, primarily those of Foreville, and adds his own reflections.

[108] See Cole, *Preaching*, p. 103; Evans, 'Crusade', pp. 297, 303, 308; and the January 1212 letter in *PL*, CCXVI, 744–5.

[109] Canivez, *Statuta*, pp. 489, 491, 510.

[110] Evans, 'Crusade', pp. 314–15; Daunou, 'Arnaud Amaury', pp. 322–7.

[111] *Dictionnaire des auteurs cisterciens*, 54.

[112] See Kienzle, 'Tending the Lord's Vineyard', pp. 59–61.

combining Christian and chivalric ideals.[113] Scholars agree in their negative view of Arnaud Amaury. The Dominican scholar Marie-Humbert Vicaire concluded that it is difficult to see Arnaud Amaury as a true monk ('un vrai religieux') motivated by strong faith and charity.[114] The biographer in the *Histoire littéraire de la France* describes Arnaud Amaury's life as 'turbulent, more military than ecclesiastic', offering 'only scandalous scenes' and 'un tissu d'intrigues, fourberies et attentats'.[115] Raymonde Foreville underscores the lack of pastoral activity during Arnaud Amaury's ten years as archbishop.[116] Martín Alvira-Cabrer concludes that one observes in the abbot, 'attitudes of extreme violence, cruelty and fanaticism'.[117]

I can only agree with those assessments and extend them to say that Arnaud Amaury demonstrated the worst of Cîteaux, an appalling contradiction of monastic spirituality and its ideals of humility, prayer and contemplation. His conduct should not be judged as representative of the order. Fortunately, most of Arnaud Amaury's Cistercian confrères did not follow his example. The abbots he brought to Occitania in 1206 to preach returned home in discouragement. His contemporary Guy of les Vaux-de-Cernay, who directed the preaching mission, did become a bishop, as did many other Cistercians at the time, but he remained much closer to his monastic vocation. Even Fulk, a controversial figure elected bishop of the key city of Toulouse, is credited with emphasizing the role of preaching and teaching over that of military direction.

Guy of les Vaux-de-Cernay

Guy, abbot of les Vaux-de-Cernay and then bishop of Carcassonne[118] played a leading role in Occitania at the same time as Arnaud Amaury. Abbot Guy became bishop of Carcassonne in 1212, the same year that Arnaud Amaury assumed the see of Narbonne. The uncle of the chronicler Peter of les Vaux-de-Cernay, Guy not surprisingly occupies a prominent role in his nephew's *Hystoria Albigensis*. A strong supporter of Simon of Montfort, Guy had ties to Montfort's family and the two men participated in the early part of the Fourth Crusade, defending the papal command not to attack Christian cities, urging

---

[113] See, for example, P. Le Gentil, *La chanson de Roland* (Paris, 1967), pp. 135–6. M. Zink points out that both authors of the *Canso* demonstrate familiarity with other vernacular epic poems; textual allusions to several appear in the *Canso*. 'Introduction', *Chanson* (1989 edn), p. 30.

[114] Vicaire, 'Clercs', pp. 266–7.

[115] Daunou, 'Arnaud Amaury', p. 330. Daunou also remarks that Amaury shows more knowledge of the military profession than one would expect from an archbishop.

[116] Foreville, *Gouvernement et vie*, chap. XIV, pp. 130, 133.

[117] Cabrer, 'Idea y realidad', p. 590.

[118] Guy's biography has been documented carefully by Zerner-Chardavoine, 'L'abbé Gui'.

the crusaders not to besiege Zara, and eventually leaving the redirected crusade before its lamentable conquest of Constantinople.[119] Guy of les Vaux-de-Cernay also had connections in Paris with intellectuals and preachers who formed part of the circle of Peter the Chanter.[120]

In 1181 Guy became abbot of les Vaux-de-Cernay, an abbey about 50 kilometres from Paris. In the same year, Simon IV of Montfort became lord of his family lands, which adjoined the abbey. Guy also formed ties to the royal government. Philip Augustus in an 1190 donation called him *virum religiosum dilectum et familiarem nostrum*. The abbot probably was, however, one of the clergy who distanced themselves from the king during the scandal which broke out in 1193 over the divorce and imprisonment of his wife, Queen Ingeburg of Denmark. Guy's opposition to the king's rejection of Ingeburg would have allied him with Peter the Chanter and with Hélinand of Froidmont, the trouvère become Cistercian monk, who composed his *Vers de la Mort* in part to chastise the bishops who supported the king's claim of consanguinity with Ingeburg.[121] Philip Augustus's displeasure with Guy of les Vaux-de-Cernay's stance probably accounts for the absence of donations to the abbey from the king between 1190 and 1209.[122]

Guy of les Vaux-de-Cernay had experience in crusade preaching; he was involved in the Fourth Crusade when Innocent III enjoined upon him and the abbot of Saint-Victor the responsibility for making arrangements for the crusade and imposing a tax ('quarantième') on ecclesiastical revenues. Fulk of Neuilly, the preacher charged in 1198 with propagating the Fourth Crusade, collaborated again with Guy of les Vaux-de-Cernay on propaganda for the Albigensian Crusade. In the chronicle of Villehardouin, which recounts events of the Fourth Crusade, the abbot of les Vaux-de-Cernay stands out for his opposition to the attack on Zara, a city held by the Christian king of Hungary, and the deviation of the crusade toward the conquest of Constantinople. A letter to the abbot of Cîteaux from Stephen of Tournai, with the agreement of the abbot of Saint-Victor and the cathedral chanter, requests that the abbot not send Guy, weakened in body and spirit by the Fourth Crusade, back to the Holy Land.[123] According to M. Zerner-Chardavoine, Guy was discouraged and also isolated by his failed opposition to the course of the Fourth Crusade. He was still busy at les Vaux-de-Cernay, however, and is cited five times in a collection of miracle stories. Five of the stories were told by Guy, and one was reported through him from the word of a countess of Leicester who became a nun at Canterbury. She was the widow of the maternal uncle of Simon of

[119] See n. 103 above and references to Queller and Madden, *Fourth Crusade*.
[120] The grid of connections between the latter two churchmen and the Cistercians is examined briefly below.
[121] On the Philip Augustus-Ingeburg controversy, see below, n. 112, and on Hélinand and the same affair, see Kienzle, 'Midi', pp. 37–67.
[122] Zerner-Chardavoine, 'L'abbé Gui', p. 187.
[123] Zerner-Chardavoine, 'L'abbé Gui', pp. 188–91, n. 22.

Montfort and died in 1208. Guy was also strengthening ties to the neighbouring lords, now returned from the crusade, who had supported his dissenting opinion. Four of those lords who were to play a role in the Albigensian Crusade made donations to the monastery between 1206 and 1210.[124]

The principal source for Guy's involvement in Occitania is the *Hystoria Albigensis*, the work of his nephew Peter. In November 1209, Innocent III and Arnaud Amaury asked Guy, one of the abbots who participated in the spring 1207 preaching mission, to assist the crusaders in Carcassonne. The *Hystoria* reports instances of his preaching and participation in various activities from building bridges to exhorting crusaders to battle.[125] For a time Guy served as vice legate and in 1212 he attended the siege of Renne in the Agenais. The chronicler records that Guy 'devoted himself to preaching and other duties connected with the siege'. Similarly, before the siege of Moissac, he laboured alongside William, archdeacon of Paris, who appears frequently in the *Hystoria* preaching to troops before battle, recruiting reinforcements and working as a very capable military adviser. Again before the siege of Casseneuil in 1214, Guy helped to prepare the attack and oversaw the building of a bridge. Such preparations for battle occupied Guy when he was present with the troops. His nephew describes another role of clergy at Carcassonne in 1214, where the bishop of Carcassonne (Guy) and other priests prayed and sang the 'Veni Creator Spiritus' while the soldiers fought. Guy worked with the soldiers after battles too; he led a contingent of crusaders to destroy the *castrum* of Montfort, whose inhabitants had already fled.[126]

Preaching before battles posed clear dangers, for the chronicler reports that mercenaries would fire their crossbows into the crowd listening to the bishop of Carcassonne's preaching. The author himself was nearly wounded during an exhortation on horseback to crusaders stocking the petraries (siege-engines) at Moissac. An arrow pierced his robe and fixed itself in his saddle.[127]

In contrast to the posture of Arnaud Amaury at the massacre of Minerve in the spring of 1210, Guy is cited for attempts to preach to the heretics confined in their houses.[128] Reportedly he heard a crowd of heretics gathered in one house and approached them, offering 'words of peace and admonishments for salvation' and desiring to convert them. They interrupted him and said with one voice:

> Why are you preaching to us? We don't want your faith. We renounce the Roman Church. You are working in vain. Neither life nor death will call us back from the belief [*secta*] we hold.

[124] Zerner-Chardavoine, 'L'abbé Gui', pp. 193–4.
[125] Zerner-Chardavoine, 'L'abbé Gui', p. 195, n. 35; p. 197, n. 41.
[126] Sibly, 324, p. 56; 342, p. 162; 346, p. 163; 351, p. 164; 520, 524, pp. 234–5; 526, p. 236. On William of Paris, see Sibly, 175, p. 93; 285, pp. 142, 150; 342, p. 162.
[127] Sibly, 346, p. 163; another battle exhortation in 351, p. 164.
[128] Zerner-Chardavoine points out that was his last attempt at preaching to the unconverted. 'L'abbé Gui', p. 196.

Guy then went to another house where women heretics were gathered, but he found them more obstinate and hardened than the others. Subsequently Simon of Montfort arrived, the fire was prepared, and about 140 people were burnt. The account in the *Hystoria Albigensis* makes no reference to any role of Guy of les Vaux-de-Cernay in the decision to burn the resistant Cathars, but identifies Arnaud Amaury as the one asked to make the decision.[129]

Since Simon of Montfort repeatedly needed reinforcements, Guy made trips northward from 1210 to 1215 to preach the crusade, as did Fulk, bishop of Toulouse. In 1210 Guy, Fulk, the abbot of Villelongue, and a Cistercian from Grandselve, Aimery of Solignac, were also preaching in Toulouse, along with Dominic.[130] The *Hystoria Albigensis* tells of two instances where knights influenced by Guy's preaching arrived to shore up Montfort's campaign. In the first, Robert of Mauvoisin, a neighbour of les Vaux-de-Cernay abbey, arrived during the summer of 1211 with about 100 knights who had taken the cross in response to appeals from the bishop of Toulouse and the abbot of les Vaux-de-Cernay. The second instance, dated at the beginning of 1213, concerns the pope's order for those preaching the Albigensian Crusade to direct their efforts towards the problem of the Holy Land. Only one preacher, Guy, then bishop of Carcassonne, continued to travel throughout France and devote all his energy to keeping alive the cause of the Albigensian Crusade. He returned after a year in the spring of 1214 with a large army, and the legate Robert of Courçon, who had diverted preachers toward the Eastern crusade, took the cross himself against the Toulousans and allowed other preachers to return to the preaching campaign against heresy. The following year, the king's son Louis arrived in Occitania as a crusader.[131]

Little is known about the final years of Guy of les Vaux-de-Cernay. A necrology from the cathedral of Carcassonne registers the date of his death as 21 March 1223, but he probably did not die in the city, which was abandoned by the French in January of the same year. The abbey of les Vaux-de-Cernay remained a centre of attraction for those involved in the Albigensian Crusade. For example, Thibaud of Marly, son of Bouchard of Marly, one of the most faithful companions of Simon of Montfort, entered the monastery in 1226, became abbot in 1235, and was eventually canonized.[132]

Guy of les Vaux-de-Cernay's character, as it emerges from his nephew's chronicle, differs markedly from that of Arnaud Amaury. The chronicle

---

[129] *Hystoria*, I, pp. 158–61 at 150, p. 160: 'Quid nobis predicatis? Fidem vestram nolumus. Romanam ecclesiam abdicamus. In vanum laboratis. A secta quam tenemus neque mors neque vita nos poterit revocare.' Translation is mine here. See above, p. 157 n. 94.

[130] Mousnier, 'Grandselve', p. 128; and M. H. Vicaire, *Histoire de Saint Dominique*, 2 vols. (Paris, 1957), I, 169.

[131] *Hystoria*, 494, 508, pp. 185–6, 202–4; Sibly, pp. 222 and 229. Zerner-Chardavoine, 'L'abbé Gui', p. 198, nn. 43–4.

[132] Zerner-Chardavoine, 'L'abbé Gui', p. 200, nn. 50–1.

depicts a churchman who continued his preaching efforts against heresy despite his fellow preachers' loss of interest. While some of his preaching was aimed at recruiting troops for Simon of Montfort and thus ultimately contributed to acts of violence, he did not, as far as we know, lead men into battle as did his contemporary Arnaud Amaury. He is depicted making preparations for sieges but not leading them. Of course, Arnaud Amaury did not have a nephew, as Guy did, or a personal chronicler, as Fulk of Toulouse enjoyed in William of Puylaurens, to transmit the record of his deeds.

Fulk of Toulouse

Fulk of Toulouse, that city's controversial bishop from 1206 to 1225, travelled north with Guy of les Vaux-de-Cernay to recruit crusaders during periods of exile from his see. The bishop aroused hostility for sharpening rivalries between the partisans of heresy and the supporters of orthodoxy in Toulouse. As part of his efforts to combat heresy, he established a company of preachers which provided the core for the founding of the Dominican order. A recent biography emphasizes the consistent importance he placed on preaching as the means to vanquish heresy.[133] In contrast, the anonymous author of the second part of the *Canso* paints an angry portrait of a bishop who participated in military planning, accepted military command, and supported the ruthless cardinal legate Bertrand of Saints John and Paul.

Fulk left his family and a successful career as merchant and poet to join the Cistercian monastery of Le Thoronet in 1195. In his vocational change from poet to Cistercian monk, he joined another troubadour, Bertran de Born, and a trouvère, Hélinand of Froidmont.[134] Fulk apparently turned his poetry to preaching just before entering the monastery. Among his twenty remaining poems, the last two are crusade songs and were described by a thirteenth-century commentator as being like sermons ('prezicansa'). Fulk was chosen as abbot of Le Thoronet in January 1199 and served in that office until he was elected to the see of Toulouse.[135]

Fulk arrived in Toulouse as its new bishop on 5 February 1206. The chronicler William of Puylaurens reports that in the cathedral that day

---

[133] See P. Cabau, 'Foulque, marchand et troubadour de Marseille, moine et abbé du Thoronet, évêque de Toulouse (v. 1155/1160–25.12.1231)', in *Cisterciens*, CaF, pp. 151–79. See also O. Pontal, 'De la défense à la pastorale de la foi: les épiscopats de Foulques, Raymond du Fauga, et Bertrand de l'Isle-Jourdain à Toulouse', in *Effacement du Catharisme? (XIIIe–XIVe s.)*, CaF 20 (Toulouse, 1985), pp. 175–97; and R. Lejeune, 'L'évêque de Toulouse Folquet de Marseille et la principauté de Liège', in *Mélanges Félix Rousseau. Etudes sur l'histoire du pays mosan au moyen âge* (Brussels, 1958), pp. 433–48; S. Stronski, *Le troubadour Folquet de Marseille, édition critique précédée d'une étude biographique et littéraire* (Cracow, 1910).

[134] See Paden, '*De monachis rithmos facientibus*', pp. 669–85, on Bertran and Hélinand.

[135] Cabau, 'Foulques', pp. 155–7.

Fulk preached on the Parable of the sower (Matthew 13. 4–9, 18–23),[136] a text well-suited for exercising the episcopal office of teaching and preaching against heresy. The parable's agricultural imagery of good and bad seeds could lend itself easily to establishing distinctions between true and false opinions and to asserting the bishop's role as cultivator of orthodoxy. When Bernard of Clairvaux preached on a similar text during his visit to Albi in 1145, he expounded the Parable of the tares (Matthew 13. 24–30, 36–52) against heresy, following a tradition that dates back at least to Augustine of Hippo, who used the same text against the Donatists.[137] One can imagine that Fulk used imagery similar to Augustine's and Bernard's to describe undertaking his work as bishop of Toulouse. William of Puylaurens claimed great success for Fulk's opening sermon, stating that 'from that time on, no one was to doubt that he, like Elijah, had been sent to revive the dead bishopric'.[138]

The confrontational dimension of preaching in this period and the brutality of the milieu emerge from an *exemplum* about Fulk. While the bishop was preaching to the Christians and warning them to beware of false prophets, he explained that the wolves in the biblical story represented the heretics and the sheep stood for the Christians. In the midst of the sermon, a heretic arose who had been disfigured by Simon of Montfort, reportedly in retaliation for doing similar things to Christians. The heretic, showing his mutilated face, said to the crowd: 'You have heard the bishop say that we are the wolves and you are the sheep. Have you ever seen sheep that would bite a wolf this way?' The bishop responded with a lengthy analogy that, in the view of the *exemplum*'s author, preserved the distinction between sheep and wolves and, therefore, the bishop's integrity as a preacher. Just as the Cistercian abbeys do not keep everything in the abbey, the bishop said, but place sheep in granges with guard dogs to protect them from the wolves, so the Church maintains granges and sheep outside Rome. For their protection, the Church sent a good strong dog, namely the count of Montfort, who bit the wolf in this way because he was eating Christians, the Church's sheep.[139] Introducing the dog into the story allowed the bishop to escape the heretic's challenge and avert the paradoxical conclusion that a wolf, the usual representation for a heretic, was deformed by a sheep, the symbol that the bishop first chose for an orthodox Christian. The *exemplum* does not record the heretic's reaction. One doubts that he found the bishop's ploy successful, given that his own mutilation proved the bishop's initial analogy wrong.

---

[136] Puylaurens, pp. 44–5.

[137] See Chapter Three in this book, p. 95 n. 64, on Bernard's sermon and the exegetical tradition.

[138] Puylaurens, p. 44: 'Quem missum ad episcopatum mortuum suscitandum, velut alterum Heliseum, iam nemo debeat dubitare.'

[139] A. Lecoy de la Marche includes this *exemplum* in: Etienne de Bourbon, *Anecdotes historiques, legendes et apologues*, ed. A. Lecoy de la Marche (Paris, 1877), pp. 23–4, n. 3. However, it comes from an anonymous collection.

Although the above confrontation probably took place in Toulouse, much of Fulk's preaching was done outside the city. He spent at least fifteen of his twenty-six years as bishop in exile. Three times he journeyed to northern France to recruit knights for the crusade in the south: in 1211, 1213 and 1217. On the second of those trips, he met James of Vitry in Liège. That friendship led to James's preaching the Albigensian Crusade and dedicating his *Vita* of Marie of Oignies to the bishop of Toulouse.[140]

To reinforce his preaching, Fulk was determined to establish a corps of diocesan preachers in Toulouse. To that end, he supported legislation at the Council of Avignon (Canon 1, 6 September 1209) specifying that bishops should enlist persons of virtue and discernment to preach against vices and advocate virtues.[141] Fulk also attended the Fourth Lateran Council and must have influenced Canon 10, which advises bishops to recruit preachers outstanding in deed and word for preaching and edifying the people. The canon further recommends that cathedrals and conventual churches institute corps of worthy people to assist with preaching and hearing confessions. In 1215 Fulk established brother Dominic and his companions as preachers in the diocese of Toulouse. They were to receive support from diocesan funds in order to preach the gospel in evangelical poverty, wearing no shoes. Furthermore, a master of theology was appointed at the cathedral in Toulouse, and Dominic and his companions attended his lectures (1215–17).[142]

Historians signal Fulk's establishment of the ill-fated White Confraternity for fighting usury and heresy, which provoked the formation of the opposing Black Confraternity and fostered civil war culminating in the first siege of Toulouse by Simon of Montfort in 1210–11. A glimpse of this preaching against usury appears in the first part of the *Canso*. William of Tudela praises the bishop and his preaching alongside Arnaud Amaury, although he also laments its failure:

> . . . a man of incomparable goodness [Fulk] took counsel with the abbot of Cîteaux. Both of them preached assiduously to audiences who remained wrapped in slumber, and they spoke against money-lending and usury. . . . Not one word of their exhortations did those people listen to. . . .

The poet then tells how the preachers' words were scorned like the buzzing of bees.

William of Puylaurens provides details about the civil conflict that the White Confraternity stirred up. He explains the formation of the confraternity by Fulk's desire to have his flock not be deprived of the indulgences which

---

[140] Cabau, 'Foulques', p. 177. *Vita Mariae Oigniacensis*, ed. D. Papebroeck, in *AASS, Iunius*, v, 5 (June 23) (Paris, 1867), cols. 542–72; *BHL* 5516; *The Life of Marie d'Oignies*, trans. with intro. and notes by M. H. King (Toronto, 1989), esp. pp. 16–17.

[141] Cabau, 'Foulques', p. 163.

[142] Cabau, 'Foulques', pp. 163–6.

were being granted to outsiders taking the cross. Members of the Confraternity, recruited from the Cité (under the bishop's jurisdiction) swore oaths and took the cross like crusaders; they were placed under the direction of knight officers, who forced usurers to appear before them. The Confraternity wrought conflict and destruction, and the citizens of the Bourg (under civil government) countered with their own confraternity. The chronicler reports that frequent battles took place between the two groups, complete with arms, standards and warhorses.[143]

William of Tudela, author of Part One of the *Canso* relates that Fulk, with Arnaud Amaury, was in military command of the count of Toulouse's castle on the road to Narbonne.[144] Fulk's intervention at Lavaur in 1211 recalls his predecessors' leadership of troops. With a reported 5,000 troops of the White Confraternity he intervened to aid Montfort at the siege of that town. The town was sacked; around 400 people were burned; the defender Aimery of Montréal and his knights were hung; and the lady of the castle, Geralda, was stoned to death at the bottom of a well. In contrast, an account of the royal crusade in 1227 credits Fulk with trying to aid the innocent. At the siege of Labécède, the king's army attempted to kill everyone, and Fulk tried to help women and children escape. The former story comes primarily from William of Tudela and Peter of les Vaux-de-Cernay, and the latter from William of Puylaurens, Fulk's own chronicler.[145] Another account from William records Fulk's clemency towards twelve people who had plotted against him.[146] Peter of les Vaux-de-Cernay mentions the bishop frequently. One episode concerns his role at the battle of Muret, where he stood in as legate for Arnaud Amaury. The bishop of Toulouse with other prelates escorted the army into battle, tried to reach a reconciliation beforehand, and afterwards attempted to persuade the defeated Toulousans to convert.[147] This course of activities reflects behaviour that contrasts with the bolder actions of Arnaud Amaury. In contrast to Arnaud Amaury's consistently belligerent profile, the portrait of Fulk contains episodes that depict the bishop of Toulouse, much like Guy of les Vaux-de-Cernay, aiding but not heading the troops.

Fulk's close alliance with Simon of Montfort allowed him to further his ecclesiastical agenda for Toulouse in the short run, but eventually his

---

[143] *Chanson*, laisse 46, I, pp. 110–11; *Shirley*, p. 32. Puylaurens, pp. 64–7. J. Bird deals extensively with preaching against usury in her forthcoming dissertation.

[144] *Chanson*, laisse 44, I, pp. 108–9; *Shirley*, p. 31.

[145] The siege of Lavaur is recounted in the *Chanson*, I, laisses 68–72, pp. 162–74; and the *Hystoria*, I, 214–28; and the siege of Labecède in Puylaurens, p. 126. Wakefield, *Crusade*, pp. 200–6, includes the translation of the relevant sections of the *Hystoria Albigensis*. See also Evans, 'Crusade', pp. 292–3; Costen, *Cathars and Albigensian Crusade*, p. 132. I am grateful to Anne Brenon for bringing Fulk's presence at these two events to my attention.

[146] Cabau, 'Foulques', p. 166; Pontal, 'De la défense', p. 184, n. 45, citing Puylaurens, p. 127.

[147] *Hystoria*, 470–1, 484, II, pp. 162–5, 176–8; Sibly, pp. 214–15, 217.

dependence on an alien and excessively harsh leader brought about the failure of the measures he tried to establish.[148] Moreover, his intervention at Lavaur doubtless led to great resentment from the people of the region, as his creation of the White Confraternity certainly did.

Bitterness toward Fulk issues from the early second part of the *Canso*, which depicts his attendance at the Fourth Lateran Council.[149] The anonymous author imagines a scene in Rome, where the pope hears testimony for and against the count of Toulouse's rights to his inheritance. The count of Foix, a vassal of the count of Toulouse, intervenes in the exchange, prompting the bishop of Toulouse to counter the count of Foix's defence of his suzerain. Fulk denounces Foix as a centre for heresy and mentions the famous Esclarmonde, Cathar 'perfecta' and the count's sister.[150] The count of Foix ripostes quickly and harshly, denouncing Bishop Fulk:

> And I tell you that the bishop, who is so violent that in all he does he is a traitor to God and to ourselves, has gained by means of lying songs and beguiling phrases which kill the very soul of any who sing them, by means of those verbal quips he polishes and sharpens, by means too of our own gifts through which he first became an entertainer, and through his evil teaching, this bishop has gained such power, such riches, that no one dares breathe a word to challenge his lies. Yet when he was an abbot and a cowled monk, the light was so darkened in his abbey that there was no goodness or peace there until he was removed. And once he was elected bishop of Toulouse, a fire has raged throughout the land that no water anywhere can quench, for he has destroyed the souls and bodies of more than five hundred people, great and small. In his deeds, his words, and his whole conduct, I promise you he is more like Antichrist than a messenger from Rome.[151]

In this vehement speech, the poet turns against Fulk some of the same rhetorical patterns that appear in the Church's denunciations of heretics: the bishops employs eloquent speech to deceive and overturn the social order; his actions are as dangerous as a raging fire; and he behaves like Antichrist.

The anonymous author of the latter part of the *Canso* also includes episodes where Fulk gives military advice or meets with military leaders. Once the poet portrays the bishop speaking in the rhetoric of a peace-maker, although the writer warns that Fulk and Montfort are hatching a secret plan, which the ecclesiastic's deceptive language obscures. Finally, Fulk forms part of the ecclesiastical assembly on two occasions when cardinal legate Bertrand

---

[148] Cabau, 'Foulques', pp. 166–7, 177.

[149] Pontal is highly critical of the portrait historians have drawn from the first translation of the *Canso*, which she considers a 'remake' and not a translation. 'De la défense', p. 183.

[150] On Esclarmonde, see Brenon, *Les femmes cathares*, pp. 108, 134, 139, 242; Wakefield, *Crusade*, p. 74.

[151] *Chanson*, laisse 145, II, pp. 52–55; *Shirley*, p. 75.

delivers an odious exhortation, calling on the troops to slaughter everyone in the city of Toulouse.[152] The bishop utters no words, but his presence at the cardinal's side implicates him in the speech's brutal message.

Fulk lived until 1235, witnessing the tenuous peace of 1229 and the submission of Raymond VII in Paris the same year. He continued his support of the Dominicans, awarding them land for a church in Toulouse, laying its cornerstone in 1229 and preaching on that occasion, and naming a Dominican, Raymond of Le Fauga, as his successor to the see of Toulouse. At the end of his life, in spite of the reestablishment of peace, Fulk still moved about with armed guards out of fear of local nobles who never accepted the northerners, nor his ties to them. Still he fared better than his successor, who, with other Dominicans, was expelled from Toulouse in a popular revolt against the Inquisition.[153]

Fulk's participation with Simon of Montfort in military affairs approaches Arnaud Amaury's lamentable conduct; one may compare Lavaur to Las Navas de Tolosa. However, Fulk's recognition of Montfort as secular sovereign of Toulouse in 1215–16 contrasts sharply with Arnaud Amaury's attempt to seize both secular and ecclesiastic power for himself in the duchy of Narbonne. Fulk's ambition did not reach the extremes of Arnaud Amaury's and did not extend as far beyond ecclesiastical affairs. Still he contributed significantly to the crusade by recruiting northern troops, partaking in military decisions, accepting military command and leading troops to Lavaur. Furthermore, he sharpened hostility in Toulouse by establishing the White Confraternity. Less bellicose and ambitious than Arnaud Amaury, Fulk of Toulouse nonetheless strayed far beyond Bernard of Clairvaux's restraint in military affairs. Apparently Fulk stepped into military matters more than his fellow Cistercian bishop, Guy of les Vaux-de-Cernay, but both appear to have been more concerned with preaching than was Arnaud Amaury.

The militance of Arnaud Amaury in particular and the order's aid to the crusade in general led to destructive attacks on Cistercian monasteries. Evidence records Grandselve's pillaging in 1211–12 by southern lords and their followers. Peter of les Vaux-de-Cernay describes the monks' anxiety that

---

[152] *Chanson*, laisses 189 and 207, III, pp. 26–31, 222–7; *Shirley*, pp. 136, 175; *Chanson*, laisse 175, II, pp. 226–31; *Shirley*, p. 111; *Chanson*, laisses 187, 207, III, pp. 10–13, 222–7; *Shirley*, pp. 131, 176.

[153] Cabau, 'Foulques', pp. 166–7, 177. Cabau observes that Fulk's solidarity with Montfort became 'the strength but also the weakness of his position'. She emphasizes that Fulk demonstrated 'un souci tout religieux' during this period. She concludes (p. 168) that Fulk's attempts at religious reform were 'trop étroitement liées à l'instauration du pouvoir d'un féodal étranger, puis à l'établissement de l'ordre politique de la royauté française pour être réellement acceptées de beaucoup de méridionaux'. On Fulk's successor and the expulsion from Toulouse, see the translation from William of Pelhisson's *Chronicle* in Wakefield, *Crusade*, pp. 220–1.

they would die under the sword if Montfort were killed, because the count of Toulouse and his men hated all Cistercians, especially those of Grandselve since Arnaud Amaury had been abbot there. The monasteries of Grandselve, its neighbour Belleperche, and daughter-house Candeil all received reparations from the 1229 treaty. The abbey's precise role during the conflict is difficult to ascertain; along with references to prayers for the crusaders, there are indications that it served as a base for assembling troops.[154] The record of damage to Grandselve's properties and fear for the monks' lives sheds light on the everyday consequences of Cistercian support for the crusade.

Conclusion

The three Cistercians whose crusade preaching has provided the core of this chapter – Arnaud Amaury, Guy of les Vaux-de-Cernay, and Fulk of Toulouse – all had ties, directly or indirectly, to the circle of Peter the Chanter. John Baldwin describes the Chanter's influence in terms of inner and outer circles: an inner circle of students and preachers and an outer circle of theologians.[155] Pope Innocent III studied in Paris and is considered a product of the Chanter's circle. Innocent III relied heavily on preachers who emanated from that same intellectual milieu, among them Fulk of Neuilly, James of Vitry, and Robert of Courçon.[156] Among the Cistercians we have studied, Arnaud Amaury felt Innocent III's influence strongly from papal letters and perhaps a sermon collection to use as a model. Guy, abbot of les Vaux-de-Cernay, had at least two friends in the circle of the Paris schools: Peter the Chanter himself, and Stephen of Tournai, abbot of Sainte-Geneviève who became bishop of Tournai in 1192.[157] Furthermore, Guy was residing in Paris in 1194, where he probably heard the preaching of Fulk of Neuilly and could have met James of Vitry.[158] Both those preachers belonged to the Chanter's inner circle and preached the crusade to the Holy Land and against Occitania. Fulk of Neuilly worked with and inspired several Cistercians on preaching campaigns, notably for the Fourth Crusade in 1198.[159] James

---

[154] See Mousnier, 'Grandselve', pp. 121–3.
[155] Baldwin, *Masters*, I, 6. J. Bird investigates links between the Cistercians and the circle of Peter the Chanter in her forthcoming dissertation.
[156] Fulk of Neuilly and James of Vitry have been mentioned above and are discussed below in more detail. On Robert of Courçon, see Cole, *Preaching*, p. 127; Evans, 'Crusade', pp. 300 and 303.
[157] See Zerner-Chardavoine, 'L'abbé Gui', p. 186.
[158] Zerner-Chardavoine asserts that it would have been impossible for Guy not to have been affected by preaching saturated with ideas diffused from that environment. See Zerner-Chardavoine, 'L'abbé Gui', p. 201.
[159] Fulk had papal authorization to recruit monks and canons (5 November 1198, from Innocent III). Among those who joined him were Eustace, the abbot of Flay (a Benedictine), the Cistercian abbots of Columba, Perseigne, and Guy, abbot of les

was perhaps in Paris at the same time as Guy of les Vaux-de-Cernay in 1194, and they may have known each other.[160] A certain and strong connection between James of Vitry and the Cistercians was evident in his friendship with Fulk of Toulouse. When Fulk came north to recruit for the southern crusade, the fame of Marie of Oignies, a founder of the Beguine movement and friend of James, brought the Toulousan bishop to her city, where James served as canon of the church of St Nicholas from at least 1211 to 1216. Fulk persuaded James to preach against Occitanian heresy, which he began to do in 1213.[161] James's preface to the *Vita* of Marie dedicates the work to Fulk and describes the *Vita*'s intended use as a model for preaching against heresy and living in opposition to it.[162]

Also in Paris in 1194 and part of the Chanter's outer circle was Alan of Lille, who was writing texts in the 1190s to promote the cause of anti-heretical preaching. Concerning the year 1194, the chronicler Othon de Saint-Blaise tells that Peter the Chanter, Alan and Prepositinus (of Cremona) were the outstanding teachers in the city.[163] According to Raynaud de Lage, Alan became a Cistercian during a mission in the Midi, possibly that of Peter of Castelnau in 1198.[164] Alan was in Montpellier around 1200, we recall, and died at Cîteaux in 1203.[165] During this last period of his life, he composed his *Summa quot modis*, dedicated to Ermengaud, abbot of Saint-Gilles and the

Vaux-de-Cernay. On Fulk of Neuilly, see Baldwin, *Masters*, I, 36–7, 266; II, 28, nn 235–6; Longère, *Prédication*, pp. 80–1; M. R. Gutsch, 'A Twelfth-Century Preacher – Fulk of Neuilly', in L. J. Paetow, ed., *The Crusades and Other Historical Essays Presented to Dana C. Monro* (New York, 1928), pp. 183–206; J. F. Hinnebusch, *The Historia occidentalis of Jacques de Vitry. A Critical Edition*, Spicilegium Friburgense 17 (Fribourg, 1972) , pp. 94–101; and J. M. O'Brien, *Fulk of Neuilly* (Los Angeles, 1961). On Fulk's anti-Jewish preaching, see Chazan, *Stereotypes*, pp. 107–8. The 1198 letter is *PL*, CCXIV, 375–6.

[160] Zerner-Chardavoine, 'L'abbé Gui', p. 201.

[161] Baldwin, *Masters*, I, 38–9. C. Muessig has studied some of Jacques of Vitry's sermons against the Cathars in 'Les sermons de Jacques de Vitry sur les cathares', in *Prédication*, CaF, pp. 69–83. In contrast to the lack of Cistercian sermons against heresy from the Albigensian Crusade, some of Jacques's remain among his *Sermones feriales et communes*. Six crusade sermons are extant also from Paris in 1226 and are described by N. Bériou, 'La prédication de croisade de Philippe le Chancellier et d'Eudes de Châteauroux en 1226', in *Prédication*, CaF, pp. 85–109.

[162] See above, n. 140. *Vita*, 546–9.

[163] *Chronicon* 40, *Monumenta Germaniae Historica*, SS. xx, p. 326, 17: '1194 . . . His temporibus Petrus Cantor Parisiensis et Alanus et Prepositinus magistri claruerunt.' Thouzellier, *Catharisme et Valdéisme*, pp. 81–2.

[164] R. de Lage, *Alain de Lille: poète du XIIe siècle* (Paris, 1951), pp. 121, 42, 30, n. 59. See also Longère, *Prédication*, p. 88.

[165] E. de Bourbon, *Anecdotes historiques*, 293, p. 246: '. . . cum magister Alanus legeret apud Montem-Pessulanum'; 426, p. 370: '. . . magister Alanus . . . apud Montem-Pessulanum ubi incipienti legere in theologia'; for his death at Cîteaux, see de Lage, *Alain de Lille*, pp. 12, 14, 42. References cited by Thouzellier, *Catharisme et Valdéisme*, p. 81, nn. 4–5.

Summa quadripartita, possibly written in Montpellier around 1190–1194, between periods of teaching in Paris.[166]

Connections between the Cistercians and the Chanter's circle illustrate the white monks' involvement in the ambitious programme of reform mandated by Innocent III. Preaching was a crucial tool to implement the papal agenda and the Cistercians were key players in campaigns for crusading to the Holy land and against heresy. An important study by Jessalyn Bird on reform and crusade in James of Vitry's circle extends the boundaries of this book into the thirteenth century and among secular clergy and mendicants. It underscores the continuing importance of preaching as the vehicle for spreading the reform message against vice in general, usury, heresy and prostitution. The Cistercians we examine here were laying the foundation for even broader reform efforts.[167]

Before we witness the waning of Cistercian involvement in Occitania, however, we shall investigate in the next chapter the role of Hélinand of Froidmont. Hélinand witnessed the crusade's end and will bring our coverage of the Cistercian preaching against heresy to a close. He too had ties to Peter the Chanter's circle and we shall discuss those further in Chapter Six.

---

[166] Thouzellier, *Catharisme et Valdéisme*, pp. 81–2, supports this with a lengthy note (p. 82, n. 7).

[167] Bird argues convincingly that anti-usury campaigns were tied to important measures taken in the Albigensian crusade, and that usurers, Jews and heretics suffered similar legal restrictions and prejudicial attitudes ('Crusade and Reform').

CHAPTER SIX

Hélinand of Froidmont: Planting Virtues in the Vineyard

Previous chapters have centred on Cistercian preachers, legates, bishops, an archbishop, and a cardinal – the foremost 'clerics of the crusade', as the Dominican historian M.–H. Vicaire[1] called them. The Cistercian role continued but diminished somewhat after the first decade or so of the crusade: Innocent III, who had urged the white monks toward action, died in 1216; Arnaud Amaury in 1225; Guy of les Vaux-de-Cernay in 1223. A few Cistercian legates were appointed after these men, but during the last years of the crusade, Romano of St Angelo served as legate and presided over the implementation of the 1229 treaty's provisions.[2] Bishop Fulk of Toulouse still held his see but had spent at least fifteen years in exile, including the period 1217–29.[3] As war drew to a close, the Cistercian abbot of Grandselve, Hélie Garin, helped the negotiations.[4] Then, at the termination of hostilities, another Cistercian came to centre stage: Hélinand of Froidmont, a former trouvère from the abbey of Froidmont in Beauvais. Poet, monk, historian, encyclopaedist, preacher and social critic, Hélinand joined the Cistercian campaign against heresy at its end and played a crucial role at a decisive moment: the events surrounding the Treaty of Paris/Meaux, confirmed on 12 April 1229.[5] Serving as neither military adviser nor legate nor bishop, Hélinand apparently came primarily

---

[1] Vicaire, 'Clercs de la croisade', pp. 260–80.

[2] The last Cistercian legates for the Albigensian Crusade during this period were Conrad of Urach, former abbot of Cîteaux, appointed in 1220, and Nicholas of Claromonte in 1223. On these and other legates, see Zimmermann, *Die päpstliche Legation*, pp. 76–7 on Conrad of Urach, 80 on Nicholas of Claromonte, 81 on Romano of St Angelo. A. Evans questions Zimmerman's dating of Romano's actual working in France as prior to 1225. Evans, 'Crusade', p. 315, n. 55. F. Neininger focuses on Conrad of Urach, Arnaud Amaury's successor at Cîteaux, in *Konrad von Urach (†1227). Zähringer, Zisterzienser, Kardinallegat* (Paderborn, 1994).

[3] Cabau, 'Foulque', pp. 151–79.

[4] See Mousnier, 'Grandselve', pp. 122–3, and Puylaurens, p. 133.

[5] See Thouzellier, *Catharisme et Valdéisme*, pp. 139–212. Groundwork for this study was laid in B. M. Kienzle, 'Deed and Word: Hélinand's Toulouse Sermons, I', and 'Erudition at God's Service, Hélinand's Toulouse Sermons, II', in *Erudition at God's Service*, ed. J. R. Sommerfeldt, *Studies in Medieval Cistercian History*, XI, CS 98 (Kalamazoo, MI, 1987), pp. 267–90.

Fig. 7. The cloister of the Eglise des Jacobins, the Dominican church in Toulouse whose construction began in 1230

to preach. He addressed two important assemblies in 1229, giving the inaugural sermon for the nascent university and delivering the opening and closing sermons for the synod that regulated the tenuous peace.

As with Hélinand's predecessors, we shall survey briefly what is known about his life and then look at his works to examine what light they shed on the Cistercian effort in Occitania, and particularly on preaching. We shall also ask why Hélinand represented the Cistercian order at this crucial point in history. Hélinand and the textual evidence for his activity in the campaigns against heresy recall the role of Bernard of Clairvaux more closely than that of his immediate predecessors: Hélinand's sermons include historical and doctrinal investigations of heresy, as well as the sermons preached *in situ*. Unlike any of the other Cistercian texts available for this book, some of Hélinand's extant sermons were actually preached in Occitania. Hélinand's preaching against heresy constitutes the last episode of Cistercian engagement in Occitania that we will examine. The Cistercians yielded the role of preaching against heresy to the Dominicans. However, their influence did not disappear completely from the region. They sold lands to Capetian lords during the thirteenth century, and in the fourteenth, the famous inquisitor, Jacques Fournier, was a Cistercian.[6]

---

[6] Higounet, 'Nouvelles réflexions sur les bastides 'cisterciennes', in *Cisterciens,* CaF, p. 134. See the Conclusion of this book pp. 211–12 for more on J. Fournier.

Hélinand was no stranger to political upheaval, and the evidence about his life and political connections may explain in part why he was the Cistercian spokesperson in 1229. Born in northern France, probably in the vicinity of Beauvais around 1160, Hélinand wrote that his father and uncle were exiled from Flanders following the assassination of Charles the Good in 1127. The two boys lost their father, who was probably punished on the wheel, and a sizeable inheritance.[7] Despite this reversal of fortune, the uncle had connections to royalty in France, which seem to have extended to his nephew. Hellebaud, the uncle, became the chamberlain of Archbishop Henry of Rheims,[8] who was the son of Louis VI, the brother of Louis VII and of Robert of France, the count of Dreux. Henry of Rheims, formerly a monk at Clairvaux, was a strong ally of Pope Alexander III, a supporter of Becket against King Henry II, and an associate of John of Salisbury, whose work Hélinand used heavily. The nephews of Henry of Reims, who were also the cousins of King Philip Augustus, were Philip and Henry of Dreux, bishops of Beauvais and Orléans respectively. Philip of Dreux and Hélinand enjoyed a friendship; Hélinand speaks of him with affection and tells stories about the bishop's visit to Froidmont while Hélinand was a monk there.[9] We know nothing more about the identity of Hélinand's family, but his relatives were probably embroiled in political conflicts during his lifetime, because a letter to Hélinand makes reference to his suffering on account of their constant danger.[10]

---

[7] 'In auctores sceleris acerimme vindicatum est a Ludovico Francorum rege Philippi filio; ita ut etiam nonnulli ad rotam damnati sint. Eorum progenies tota exsiliata est; et multi innocentes quae non rapuerant, exsoluerunt. Inter quos fuerunt pater meus Hermanus, et frater ejus Ellebaudus, qui pueri nobiles et pulcherrimi magnis haereditatibus perditis, de Flandriis in Franciam aufugerunt.' *PL*, CCXII, 1028D.

[8] 'De qua re [Virgilianus error de animabus defunctorum] certissimum referebat exemplum patruus meus Hellebaudus, Henrici quondam Remensis archepiscopi cubicularius. Dicebat enim: Dominus meus archiepiscopus mittebat me apud Atrebatum . . .': *PL*, CCXII, 733B (*De cognitione sui/Chronicon* liber VIII). On Henry of Rheims, see also his letters in *PL*, CXCVI; Newman, pp. 204–11; and *Apocalypsim*, p. 15.

[9] 'l'evesque cui je aim tant / Et qui toz jorz m'a tenu chier'. *Vers de la Mort*, XVI, ll. 2–3, 15. *PL*, CCXII, 730CD (*Chronicon* liber VIII): 'Audi ergo non fabulam, sed rem gestam de tuo Helinando. Philippus episcopus Belvacensis apud nos aliquando hospitatus est, non ut quidam, devorationis causa, sed devotionis. Jam enim ordinis nostri communis hospitalitas plures invenit, qui eam devorent; quam singularis sanctitas, qui eam honorent. Praecepit autem mihi praefatus episcopus, ut facerem missam matutinalem audire. Ad quem cum die crastina prima jam cantata venissem, inveni eum adhuc dormientem, et nemo vel de familia, vel de suis familiaribus eum excitare praesumebat. Ego autem accessi propius, et excitavi eum quasi jocando dicens . . .' On Philip of Dreux, see: H. Géraud, 'Le comte-évêque', *Bibliothèque de l'Ecole des Chartes* 5 (1843–4), 8–36 (pp. 33–4).

[10] 'Non ignoro, quantas ebibis amaritudines pro consanguineorum discrimine tuorum, qui in mortibus frequenter periclitantur, sed confide: potens est Deus diutinas inimicantium contumelias celeri sententia terminare, ita ut pax et

Like other Cistercians we have met thus far, Hélinand studied in a cathedral school, notably in Beauvais under the tutelage of Ralph of Beauvais, a former pupil of Abelard.[11] Ralph's work was noted for the reapplication of the study of authors to grammar, seen in the free use of illustrative quotations taken carefully from his own reading.[12] Hélinand also spent some time in Paris as a young man, possibly studying there also.[13] His first career was that of a trouvère,[14] and his poetry gained enough recognition that the public doubted the sincerity of his conversion.[15]

Hélinand's biographer states that he was inspired to enter the monastery by the sermons of Fulk of Neuilly and Eustache of Flay, the latter known not only for preaching the crusade, but also for campaigning in England against Sunday markets.[16] At the time that Eustache de St Germer was elected abbot

adversitas omnia tibi cooperentur in bonum.' Thomas de Froidmont (*c.* 1150–post 1225), *Lettre à H*, ed. E. Mikkers, 'Een onuitgegeven brief van Thomas van Beverley, monk van Froidmont', in *Cîteaux in de Nederlanden* (1956), pp. 245–63 (p. 258).

[11] 'Hujus etiam Petri Abaelardi discipulus fuit magister meus, qui me docuit a puero, Radulphus, natione Anglicus, cognomento Grammaticus, Ecclesiae Belvacensis, vir tam in divinis quam in saecularibus litteris eruditus.' *PL*, CCXII, 1035D. See B. M. Kienzle, 'Education in the Late Twelfth and Early Thirteenth Centuries: The Witness of Hélinand of Froidmont', in *Faith Seeking Understanding: Learning and the Catholic Tradition*, ed. G. C. Berthold, Selected Papers from the Symposium and Convocation celebrating the Saint Anselm College Centennial (Manchester, NH, 1991), pp. 77–88 (p. 88).

[12] R. W. Hunt, 'Studies in Priscian in the Twelfth Century II: The School of Ralph of Beauvais', *Medieval and Renaissance Studies* 2 (1950), 11–16.

[13] 'Olim cum adolescentior essem Parisius memini me ibi vidisse musicum quemdam quem violatorem vulgus appellat in arte violandi peritissimum cognominando asinum.' Paris, Bibliothèque Mazarine MS 1041, fol. 24va.

[14] 'Ipse quidem spectaculum factus est, et angelis et hominibus levitate miraculi, qui prius eis spectaculum fuerat levitatis; dum non scena, non circus, non theatrum, non ampitheatrum, non amphicircus, non forum, non platea, non gymnasium, non arena sine eo resonabat.' *PL*, CCXII, 748CD. See also F. McCulloch, 'The Art of Persuasion in Hélinant's *Vers de la Mort*', *Studies in Philology* 69 (1972), 38–54 (p. 39), on the *Roman d'Alexandre* where a certain Hélinand (Elinant) sings at the king's court.

[15] 'Nosti Helinandum, si quis novit hominem, si tamen hominem neque enim tam natus erat homo ad laborem, quam avis ad colandum [Job 7. 1], circumiens terram, et perambulans eam, quaerens que devoraret [1 Peter 5. 8] aut adulando, aut objurgando. Ecce in claustro clausus est, cui totus mundus solebat esse non solum quasi claustrum, sed etiam quasi carcer . . . Unde et tanta levitas, tam leviter mutata, apud plerosque nihil aliud quam quinquennis ejus conversatio vix facit alicui fidem de futuro. Nimirum quantum in se ipso experimentum dedit inconstantiae, tantum perseveraturae constantiae nunc debilitat argumentum.' *PL*, CCXII, 748–9. The letter to H also alludes to this: 'Novi conversationem tuam quidquid de te dicatur. Novi, inquam, quam compositum reddat corporus tui statum necnon et mentis, ut reor, habitum disciplina . . .' Thomas de Froidmont (c. 1150–post 1225), *Lettre à H*, 259.

[16] See J. L. Cate, 'The English Mission of Eustace of Flay (1200–1201)', *Etudes d'histoire*

of Flay, he was serving as secretary to Philip of Dreux.[17] The dates for
Hélinand's entrance into the monastery at Froidmont are uncertain; the
abbacy of Guillaume I (1181–93) has been suggested, whether around 1182,
when Hélinand was about twenty,[18] or later, when the poet was thirty-five.[19]
Hélinand's name appears in six charters from the Froidmont chartulary,
dated between 1190 and 1198, so we know that he had entered the abbey
before 1190.[20] Hagiography from the diocese of Beauvais and a reference in
Hélinand's sermons indicate that he was eventually ordained priest and that
he served as prior but refused an earlier election as abbot.[21]

Once a monk, Hélinand still kept his eye on the world: between 1193 and
1197, he composed the lengthy and influential poem, the *Vers de la Mort* (*Verses
on Death*).[22] Its satiric verses denounce the bishops who supported King Philip

---

dédiées à la mémoire de Henri Pirenne (Bruxelles, 1937), pp. 67–89. A. Sabatier, *Vie des
saints du diocèse de Beauvais* (Beauvais, 1866), pp. 42–8 (p. 44).

[17] Eustache's predecessor, Abbot Hugh III of St Germer, died 26 October 1200. Cate,
'English Mission', p. 69.

[18] Sabatier, *Vie des saints*, p. 44 (no exact date but reference to abbot Guillaume I). L.-E.
Deladreue, 'Notice sur l'abbaye de Froidmont', *Mémoires de la Société Académique
d'Archéologie, Sciences et Arts du Département de l'Oise* 7 (1870), 469–624; 8 (1871), 1–78
(7: 514, 521–9), under the abbacy of Guillaume I (1181–93). See also A. Dimier,
'Hélinand de Froidmont', *Dictionnaire des auteurs cisterciens*, 343–5.

[19] S. Lenssen, *Hagiologium Cisterciense* (Tilburg, 1948), I, 192: 'Cisterciense monaster-
ium Frigidi-Montis, triginta quinque annos antus, ingressus est . . .' The later date
would require moving Hélinand's birthdate later in order for the conversion to fall
under the abbacy of Guillaume I.

[20] W. D. Paden, 'Documents concernant Hélinant de Froidmont', *Romania* 105 (1984),
332–9.

[21] Abbot Sabatier's biography says that Hélinand was ordained priest, that he made
preaching tours ('allait au loin évangéliser les peuples'), and that because of his
preaching, several men entered religious life, including his brother Guillaume (a
conjecture based on the *De reparatione lapsi*, in the *Flores*, excerpts from the *Chronicon*
collected by Vincent of Beauvais). *Vie des saints*, pp. 44–5. I have found one passage
that refers to a preaching prior at Froidmont, supporting the suggestion made by
Lenssen that Hélinand held that post. Lenssen, *Hagiologium*, p. 193: 'Utique liberae
et apertae, fide maxime, caritate et zelo animatas, praecipue tum habuit, cum ad
Albigenses missus esset in oppidum Tolosanum. Domum redux, cum Prioris
probabiliter fungeretur officio, fratribus explanavit Regulam, cujus ad pium
animum colendum praestantiam apposite profitetur.' *PL*, CCXII, 559D: 'Auditorium
namque dicitur, ab officio discipuli, locutorium ab officio magistri, non quia ibi
passim omnes loqui debeant, sed quia ibi prior et abbas de necessariis disponunt.'

[22] Hélinand is credited with creating a famous poetic stanza, imitated in French
medieval literature. It appears for the first time in the *Vers de la Mort* and involves
twelve octosyllabic lines with the rhyme scheme: *aabaabbbabba*. A. Mary describes it
as a 'rythme savant et fort difficile où l'inventeur présumé a montré une indis-
cutable maîtrise'. *Anthologie poétique française: Moyen Age* (Paris, 1967), p. 281. The
poem was the subject of a 1987 symposium. See *Hélinand de Froidmont (Colloque et
Exposition) (Mai–Juin 1987)*, Cahiers de l'Abbaye de St-Arnoult 2 (Amiens, 1987).
Also in 1987, Hélinand's verses were adapted for the stage by Emile Lanc as the:
Triomphe de la Mort, presented at the Théâtre-Poème of Brussels. E. Lanc, 'L'adapta-

Augustus's effort to divorce Ingeburg of Denmark in 1193. Hélinand and Peter the Chanter, both natives of the Beauvais region, took a stand on the same side of the affair. The Chanter, appointed papal judge delegate in the divorce case, formed part of an 1196 commission that included the abbots of Clairvaux and Cîteaux (both named Guy). It was charged with persuading Philip to take back Ingeburg.[23] In case of failure, the commission was to call an assembly of the archbishops and suffragans to apply pressure on the king. Hélinand was therefore on the same side of the controversy as the Chanter and Guy of les Vaux-de-Cernay. The poet composed his *Vers de la Mort* in outrage at the bishops who yielded to the king's pressure.[24] Despite Cistercian engagement in the controversy, the poem's circulation provoked in part the Cistercian ban on monks' writing vernacular poetry, instituted among the statutes of 1199.[25]

Between 1199 and Hélinand's presence in Toulouse in 1229, we know little about his life. Between 1211 and 1223, he was working on his *Chronicon*, a world history and encyclopaedia, writing the eighth book between 1211 and 1217.[26] The only date that has been proposed for Hélinand's death is 3 February 1237, and it also marked his feast in the diocese of Beauvais.[27] The manuscript rubrics for one of his Palm Sunday sermons read that Hélinand died afterwards, but no further information appears.[28]

Ties to the nobility of Beauvais may explain in part Hélinand's involvement in Occitania. Philip of Dreux, bishop of Beauvais (1175–1217) and Hélinand's friend, participated in the Albigensian Crusade in 1210 and

---

tion scénique des Vers de la Mort', in *Hélinand de Froidmont (Colloque et Exposition)*, pp. 75–85; E. Lanc, *Le Triomphe de la Mort,* adaptation scénique des *'Vers de la Mort'* d'Hélinand de Froidmont, préface de M. Santucci, sérigraphies originales de R.-M. Balau (Brussels, 1987).

[23] Baldwin, *Masters,* I, 7–8, on Philip Augustus and Ingeburg; I, 266 on the Chanter's birthplace.

[24] See Kienzle, 'Midi'.

[25] For the dating and the controversy provoked by the poem, see Paden, 'De monachis'.

[26] J. N. Carman established the dates of 1211 and 1223 in: *The Relationship of the 'Perlesvaus' and the 'Queste del Saint Graal'* (Chicago, 1936), pp. 11–13. In consultation with Edmé Smits I established the period between 1198 (date of death for Henry of Orléans) and 4 November 1217 (date of Philip of Dreux's death). See Géraud, *Le comte-évêque*, 35, and Kienzle, 'The Witness of Hélinand of Froidmont', p. 85. The passage in question reads: 'Philippus episcopus Belvacensis apud nos aliquando hospitatus est, non ut quidam, devorationis causa, sed devotionis. . . . de qua Henricus Aurelianus episcopus nostri Belvacensis episcopi frater referre solebat rem valde mirabilem, quam ipse audierat ab illo qui viderat, scilicet Joanne Aurelianensis Ecclesiae canonico' (*PL*, CCXII, 730–1), where the usage of the imperfect tense implies that Henry was already dead, and the use of the perfect as well as the words 'nostri Belvacensi episcopi frater' indicate that Philip was still alive.

[27] Sabatier, *Vie des saints*, p. 42. His feast was celebrated in Beauvais on 3 February. A. Dimier, 'Elinando di Froidmont', in *Bibliotheca sanctorum IV* (Rome, 1964), 1073–4.

[28] 'Obiit Elinandus post sermonem istum.' *Sermo 8, PL*, CCXII, 544–54; incomplete in BN MS Lat. 14591, fols. 48vb–49vb.

again in 1215, at the age of sixty-two, with Prince Louis.[29] Some evidence for the bishop's companions on the crusade, and for Froidmont's gain from it, appears in an entry from the Froidmont chartulary, which records the gift of a vineyard to the monastery in 1210, when a certain Pierre of Hénu accompanied his bishop on the crusade.[30] Philip of Dreux's successor, Milon of Nanteuil, also took part in the crusade in 1226 with Louis VIII.[31] Hélinand could have composed anti-heretical works for his bishop as well as for Cistercian dossiers.

We have mentioned some of Hélinand's works already: the *Chronicon*,[32] the *Vers de la Mort*,[33] and the sermons. Sixty-nine Latin sermons are extant, twenty-eight of which were printed in the *Patrologia Latina*; the others are in two Paris manuscripts.[34] A few other Latin texts have been preserved,[35] and Hélinand also states in the *Chronicon* that he wants to write a Latin version of the Grail story, making it more plausible and beneficial (*verisimiliora et utiliora*) to readers.[36] There is no such extant text attributed to him, but his

[29] See Géraud, *Le comte-évêque*, 33; *Hystoria*, 174, 181, 184, 550, pp. 176, 184, 187, 243; Sibly, pp. 92, 96–7, 246.

[30] Deladreue, 'Notice sur l'abbaye de Froidmont', p. 521, cites the cartulary: 'iter arripiens apud Albigenses'.

[31] C. Delettre, *Histoire du diocèse de Beauvais*, 3 vols. (Beauvais, 1842–3), I, 248–9.

[32] The two manuscripts are: Vat. Reg. lat. 535 and London BL Cotton Claudius B IX. Books XLV–XLIX appear only in B. Tissier, *Bibliotheca Patrum Cisterciensium VII* (Bonofontae, 1669), pp. 206–306. See Smits, 'Editing the *Chronicon*', pp. 269–89. Numerous textual links between the *Chronicon* and the sermons promise to be established when the editions are completed. The *Chronicon* edition is in progress at the University of Gröningen. It was interrupted by the untimely death of Edmé Smits. See, for example: *In dedicatione*, Bibliothèque Nationale MS Lat. 14591, fol. 40 on the rainbow, and *Chronicon*, Liber IV, in Smits, 'Editing the Chronicon', p. 282.

[33] For a list of Hélinand's works, see A. Hoste, *Dictionnaire de Spiritualité* (Paris, 1969), VII, 141–4. Some works printed in Migne actually belong to the *Chronicon*: *De cognitione sui* (Book VIII of the *Chronicon*); and *De bono regimine principis*; *Liber de reparatione lapsi* in *PL*, CCXII, 721–35, 735–45, 745–60.

[34] Tissier, *Bibliotheca Patrum Cisterciensium VII*, pp. 206–306; *PL*, CCXII, 47–720. See J. B. Schneyer's list of 68 sermons, which is missing the text, *De uno martire*, Bib.Maz. 1041, fols. 74v–77va. *Repertorium der lateinischen Sermones des Mittelalters* (Münster, 1970), II, 618–22. The six sermons without a manuscript version are numbers 1, 6, 16, 17, 18 and 25 in *PL*.

[35] The other Latin works are probably part of the *Chronicon*. They include: E. Smits, 'An Unedited Correspondence between Hélinand of Froidmont and Philip, Abbot of Val Ste Marie, on Genesis 27.1 and the Ages of the World', in *Erudition at God's Service*, pp. 243–66; and in the *Flores*, a letter to Drogo, canon of Noyons, *PL* 212, 727C; and *Passio S. Gereonis*, *PL*, CCXII, 759–72; *Dictionnaire de spiritualité*, VII, 144. See also A. Bondeelle-Souchier, *Bibliothèques cisterciennes dans la France médiévale. Répertoire des Abbayes d'hommes* (Paris, 1991), p. 119.

[36] *Chronicon*, Liber 45: 'Hoc tempore in Brittania cuidam eremitae est mirabilis quaedam visio per angelum de sancto Joseph de curione, qui corpus Domini deposuit de cruce; et de cateno illo sive paropside, in quo Dominus coenavit cum discipulis suis, de quo ab eodem eremita descripta est historia quae dicitur de gradali. Gradalis autem sive gradale Gallice dicitur scutella lata, et aliquantulum

view on plausible and beneficial literature connects to Bishop Fulk's shame for his earlier vernacular compositions. We recall that Fulk undertook penance whenever he heard his troubadour compositions performed. Similarly, Hélinand warns about the vanity of love poetry in the *Vers de la Mort*.[37] Among Hélinand's works, the sermons receive the emphasis here, because several relate to heresy. Some reference will be made also to anti-heretical passages in the *Chronicon*, but a definitive analysis of its content awaits its complete edition.

When Hélinand addressed the 1229 synod in Toulouse, he was looking back at twenty years of war in Occitania and about eighty-five years of Cistercian involvement there. The last period of the crusade saw victories for a few years by southern forces at Castelnaudary, Agen, and Moissac (1221) and Carcassonne (1223–24). The deaths of Count Raymond VI in 1222, Raymond-Roger of Foix in 1223, and King Philip Augustus in 1223 led to a reversal of southern victories. When Louis VIII acceded to the throne, full royal intervention in Occitania ensued. After negotiations with Raymond VII and his excommunication in 1226, the king's army moved southward. After Louis VIII's death in November of the same year, his cousin, Humbert of Beaujeu, continued the campaign, under the urging of Blanche of Castile, who was serving as regent because her son, the future Louis IX, at the age of twelve was too young to assume the responsibilities of kingship. Humbert directed the systematic devastation of the area around Toulouse, which, along with pressure from Pope Gregory IX, forced the beginning of negotiations for peace, culminating in the treaty of Paris/Meaux in 1229.[38]

Such were the events preceding Hélinand's journey to Occitania. As part of his work on preaching, Hélinand probably used and certainly added to

profunda; in quo pretiosae dapes cum suo jure divitibus solent apponi gradatim, unus morsellus post alium in diversis ordinibus, et dicitur vulgari nomine graalz, quia grata et acceptabilis est in ea comedenti: tum propter continens, quia forte argentea est vel de alia pretiosa materia tum propter contentum, id est ordinem multiplicem pretiosarum dapum. Hanc historiam Latine scriptam invenire non potui, sed tantum Gallice scripta habitur a quibusdam proceribus, nec facile, ut aiunt, tota inveniri potest. Hanc autem nondum potui ad legendum sedulo ab aliquo impetrare. Quod mox ut potuero, verisimiliora et utiliora succinte transferam in latinum.' R. Molina, 'Hélinand de Froidmont, Hélinand de Perseigne et la Littérature du Graal', in *Hélinand de Froidmont (Colloque et Exposition)*, pp. 57–63, looks for links between Hélinand and Adam, abbot of Perseigne, where a manuscript of the Grail existed. J. B. Schneyer's repertorium of Latin sermons confused Hélinand of Froidmont with an Hélinand of Perseigne: Schneyer, *Repertorium*, II, 617. Molina explains this by possible contact between Adam and Hélinand, who would have stayed at Perseigne for a while to consult the Grail manuscript. Molina goes as far as to claim that Hélinand is the 'grand architecte du Corpus Lancelot-Graal composé dans les ateliers champenois entre 1215 et 1235'.

[37] See Chapter One, n. 55.

[38] Events are narrated in Evans, 'Crusade', pp. 315–22; Strayer, *Crusades*, pp. 123–42; Costen, *The Cathars and the Albigensian Crusade*, pp. 150–5.

Cistercian documentation supporting the anti-heresy campaigns. M.-H. Vicaire referred to a specific 'Cistercian dossier against heresy' at Cîteaux.[39] Hélinand's familiarity with the texts of his predecessors, notably Bernard of Clairvaux and Geoffrey of Auxerre,[40] and possibly others, builds a case for assuming that other monasteries in the north kept such files available for preachers.

Furthermore, Hélinand was not the only Cistercian involved in events surrounding the Treaty. Fulk was bishop until 1231. Another Cistercian, Hélie Garin, abbot of Grandselve, served as negotiator between the legate Romano, cardinal of St Angelo, and the count of Toulouse, Raymond VII. Abbot Hélie also recruited the masters for the University of Toulouse,[41] founded in 1229.[42] Hélinand delivered the inaugural sermon as well as the addresses for opening and closing the synod that met in November of 1229. According to P. Bonnassie and G. Pradalié, the collaboration of the cardinal legate, Bishop Fulk, and Hélinand shows clearly that 'the foundation of the University of Toulouse was part of a global project undertaken by the Roman Church.[43]

The Toulouse sermons

From the manuscript rubrics, four sermons are associated with Hélinand's stay in Toulouse; all were delivered in the church of St Jacques, presumably in the same year: 1229. The four sermons, extant in Paris, Bibliothèque Nationale MS Lat. 14591, include one for Rogation; another for the feast of the Ascension, identified as the inaugural address for the new university; and two sermons for the November synod.[44] A nineteenth-century historian of

---

[39] Vicaire, 'Clercs', p. 262: 'De toutes ses activités, Cîteaux a conservé le dossier dans ses Archives et l'expérience tactique et stratégique dans le savoir-faire de ses chefs.'

[40] Hélinand uses two *exempla* from the Revelation commentary of Geoffrey of Auxerre, both about Jean de Lyon: *Apocalypsim*, Sermo XVII, pp. 203–5, ll. 91–135, and *Chronicon*, liber 48, *PL*, CCXII, 548–9; *Apocalypsim*, Sermo XV, pp. 185–6 and *Chronicon*, IV, now being edited by Eric Saak. Text not available.

[41] See Mousnier, 'Grandselve et la société de son temps', pp. 122–3.

[42] P. Bonnassie and G. Pradalié, *La capitulation de Raymond VII et la fondation de l'Université de Toulouse 1229–1979: Un anniversaire en question* (Toulouse, 1979).

[43] Bonnassie and Pradalié, *La capitulation de Raymond VII*, p. 13.

[44] *Sermo fratris Elynandi in Rogationibus*. Apud Tolosam in ecclesia Beati Jacobi, BN MS Lat. 14591, fols. 35va–37va, ed. B. M. Kienzle, 'Cistercian Preaching Against the Cathars: Hélinand's Unedited Sermon for Rogation, BN MS Lat, 14591', *Cîteaux* 9 (1988), 297–314; In ascensione, BN MS Lat. 14591, fols. 2–8rb and *Sermo* 15, *PL*, CCXII, 595–611; Sermo in synodo, MS Lat. 14591, fols. 8rb–12ra; *Sermo* 26, *PL*, CCXII, 692–700; and *In synodo, Sermo* 28, *PL*, CCXII, 711–20, MS Lat. 14591, fols. 44vb–48va. The church of St Jacques, now the site of a car park outside the cathedral of St Etienne, was used for large assemblies. See J. de Lahondès, *L'Eglise Saint-Etienne* (Toulouse, 1890), pp. 37–8; R. Mesuret, *Evocation du vieux Toulouse* (Paris, 1960), p. 240; and J. Chalande, *Histoire des rues de Toulouse* (Toulouse, 1929), pp. 366–7.

Toulouse first suggested that Hélinand travelled to that city in the company of the papal legate, Romano of St Angelo, and university masters who were recruited from Paris for the new institution.[45]

The Rogation sermon

The Rogation sermon, structured in form and content around the three Rogation days, explains the history of the three-day observance, interprets its allegorical and moral meaning, and specifies the requests that should be made during the three days of litanies. The sermon's scriptural theme, 'Ask for peace in Jerusalem' (Psalm 121. 6), makes a clear connection to contemporary events and establishes implicit parallels between Toulouse and the Jerusalem that Jeremiah denounced for its betrayal (Jeremiah 3. 20) and Jesus rebuked for its crimes (Matthew 23. 37). Within that structural and thematic framework, Hélinand criticizes doctrines held by the Cathars, notably the belief that Satan created the material world and their rejection of the sacraments of confession and the Eucharist.[46]

After explaining that the name Rogation means asking and praying, Hélinand distinguishes the circumstances in which petitions are made: human beings petitioning God, and God making requests of humans. However, the Devil and other human beings also request things from humans. While other humans should be obeyed sometimes, the Devil never should. Heretics, Hélinand asserts, seek temporal goods from the Devil. He denounces this notion, exclaiming: 'Who are they who say this, the heretics who seek temporal goods from the Devil and eternal ones from God?' And he poses the question rhetorically: 'Is there an insult or a blasphemy more serious against God than to attribute the creation of the world to his adversary and not to Him?'[47] Hélinand demonstrates some knowledge of Cathar cosmology. Around 1190, therefore forty years earlier, the Italian Cathar bishop Nazarius had brought to Italy from Bulgaria the *Interrogatio Iohannis*, a mythical account of creation in which God forms the spiritual world and the angels, including

[45] A.-F. Gatien-Arnoult, 'Hélinand', *Revue de Toulouse et du Midi de la France* 22 (1866), 287–302, 345–6; 'Notes sur les commencements de l'Université de Toulouse', *Mémoires de l'Académie des sciences, inscriptions et belles-lettres de Toulouse* E.I (1857), 202–20; 'Histoire de l'Université de Toulouse', *Mémoires* G.IX (1877), 455–94. Y. Dossat agreed in 'Les premiers maîtres à l'Université de Toulouse: Jean de Garlande, Hélinand', in *Les Universités de Languedoc au XIIIe siècle*, CaF 5 (Toulouse, 1970), p. 200.

[46] For a full discussion of the sermon and the edited text, see B. Kienzle, 'Hélinand's Unedited Sermon for Rogation', in *Cîteaux: commentarii cistercienses* 3–4 (1988), 298–314.

[47] 'Qui hoc dicunt heretici qui a diabolo petunt bona temporis, a deo bona eternitatis? . . . Nam que maior iniuria potest Deo fieri, que maior blasphemia illi infieri, quam ut opus tante potencie, tante sapiencie, et tante bonitatis ut mundi creatio non ei attribuetur sed eius inimico?' BN MS Lat. 14591, fol. 36rb; Kienzle, 'Sermon for Rogation', p. 309.

Satan. The latter rebels; falls, taking away Heaven's inhabitants; and fashions the material world and human beings.[48] The notion of petitioning the Devil, however, does not correspond to Cathar beliefs and demonstrates the demonizing aspect of Hélinand's rhetoric. The Cistercian preacher presents arguments to counter the idea that Satan created matter, adducing Revelation 14. 7, that God make Heaven and earth, the sea and the sources of waters; and Matthew 5. 45, that God made the sun and causes the rain to fall. Both those scriptural verses appear as proof-texts in other anti-heretical writings. Alan of Lille in particular wrote against the view that Satan took all the inhabitants of Heaven with him, objecting that the dragon of Revelation 12. 4 dragged away only one third of the heavenly dwellers.[49]

Hélinand continues the association between heretics and Satan when he denounces those who display not the true peace of God, but the wicked and false peace of the Devil. Satan's peace is sly in traitors, he says, feigned in hypocrites, and flagitious in heretics and schismatics. Like Pilate and Herod (Luke 23. 12), heretics and schismatics become friends to each other but enemies of the Church. The identity of the schismatics to whom Hélinand was referring is uncertain, but they may be Waldensians.[50]

Speaking of asking for peace in Jerusalem (Psalm 121. 6), Hélinand explains that the Jerusalem in question is the one that Jeremiah denounced for its betrayal (Jeremiah 3. 20) and that Jesus rebuked for its crimes (Matthew 23. 37). The woman who spurns her lover in Jeremiah 3. 20 corresponds to the house of Israel's rejection of the prophet and by extension to the city of Toulouse's spurning Cistercian preachers, notably the city's bishop, Fulk, who returned for the reconciliation of Toulouse in 1229, after a period of exile that began in 1217.[51] Hélinand extends the image of being shut out of a city to Revelation 3. 20, 'I shall enter and I shall dine with him and he with me', interpreting that as Christ's knocking to enter and dine inside. Exhorting his listeners to open the door to Christ, Hélinand introduces the concept of consolation (*consolatio* or *consolo*) three times, undoubtedly evoking by contrast the Cathar sacrament of *consolamentum*, a ritual laying-on-of-hands that substituted for the traditional sacraments. Dining with Christ at the heavenly banquet table evokes an image that contrasts with the Cathars' rejection of the Eucharist, their docetism and denial that Christ ate while on earth, and their strict asceticism, which Hélinand criticizes elsewhere.[52] Hélinand also stresses confession here,

---

[48] See E. Bozóky's introduction to *Interrogatio Iohannis*, pp. 17–39.
[49] On the exegetical debates between Cathar and orthodox Christians, see Thouzellier, *Catharisme et Valdéisme*, pp. 81–106, who analyzes Alan of Lille's treatise against heresy and provides passages that do not appear in the version in *PL*, CCX. See also C. Thouzellier, *Un traité cathare inédit* (Louvain, 1961), pp. 70–1; and C. Thouzellier, 'La Bible des cathares', in *Cathares en Languedoc*, CaF 3 (Toulouse, 1968), p. 49.
[50] See Chapter Five, pp. 129–32, in this book.
[51] See Cabau, 'Foulques', cited in n. 3 above, and Chapter Five, pp. 167, 170.
[52] See below on Sermon 25, pp. 189–92, and on Cathar abstinence, Duvernoy, *Religion*, pp. 173–6.

reminding his audience that it washes all things. Confession was a standard topic of anti-heretical literature, because the Waldensians and the Cathars rejected the idea that a priest's absolution was necessary. The November synod would require confession to a priest and reception of the Eucharist three times per year as signs of orthodoxy.[53]

The Ascension sermon for the opening of the university

Hélinand delivered his Ascension Day sermon to an audience of students (*ad clericos scholares*) and probably the new university masters. The Treaty of Paris/Meaux mandated the creation of the university and required Raymond VII to establish a fund to pay the salaries of the masters.[54] The university's opening and hence Hélinand's inaugural sermon have been dated to 24 May 1229. A quarrel arose at the University of Paris in March of that year, and the university issued an ultimatum, demanding redress of its grievances within a month after Easter, that is, by 15 May 1229. Discontented students and masters, including the well-known poet John of Garland, began to leave Paris, and some journeyed to Toulouse. John of Garland recorded the events in the *De triumphis ecclesiae*, and there he mentions the legate and masters travelling together. A.-F. Gatien-Arnoult, a nineteenth-century historian, considered Hélinand's sermon to be the Church's reply to a letter issued by the university masters, who praised the freedom of thought possible at the new university, where even works banned in Paris, such as Aristotle's *Libri naturales*, would be read.[55] In contrast, Hélinand emphasizes that the pursuit of learning must be directed toward true knowledge that dwells with God. For a learned audience, Hélinand displays an extensive repertoire of preaching techniques, erudite and popular. In the first half of the sermon, he makes numerous plays on words and refers frequently to classical literature, including Horace, Quintillian, Statius, Terence, Cicero, Juvenal and Virgil. Divisions of material are complex and lengthy.[56]

About midway through the sermon, the preacher announces a change in style and technique:

> Now let us say a few things in simple speech for the simple, so that they may likewise ascend with us and, through God's grace in our sermon, be

[53] See Thouzellier, *Catharisme et Valdéisme*, pp. 89–90; and the council canons in J.-D. Mansi, *Sacrorum conciliorum nova et amplissima collectio*, 31 vols. (Florence, 1759–98), XXIII, cols. 192–204.

[54] Evans, 'Crusade', p. 321.

[55] See articles by Gatien-Arnoult cited in n. 45 above.

[56] The sermon's techniques and word-play are discussed in Kienzle, 'Erudition at God's Service : Hélinand's Toulouse Sermons II', pp. 282–3. This text's resemblance to inception sermons need further study. On that genre, see N. Spatz, 'Evidence of Inception Ceremonies in the Twelfth-Century Schools of Paris', in *History of Universities* 13 (1994), 3–19; and 'Imagery in University Inception Sermons', in *Sermons and Society*, pp. 329–42.

able to find the road and the means of transport, the lamp and the travelling-money.[57]

Hélinand then criticizes vain erudition and recounts three *exempla* dealing with the theme of ascension: one of Cistercian provenance concerning Bernard of Clairvaux and William of Grandselve; a second about a nobleman of Macon, and a third about St Dunstan, whose bed attempted to ascend to Heaven with him upon his death. The *exemplum* belongs to the domain of popular preaching and many incorporated by Hélinand were transmitted to later centuries through his works. There are no more references to classical literature in the second half of the sermon, and the divisions are shorter.[58]

The sermon does not illustrate preaching against heresy; it does, however, provide an indication of the frequency of Hélinand's preaching in Toulouse, when he remarks that he has been obliged to preach three times in the same week.[59] Furthermore, its critique of education, probably the best-known passage from Hélinand's works, clarifies the preacher's mentality:

> The clerics in Paris pursue liberal arts; in Orléans, authors; in Bologna, [copies of Justinian's] *Codex*; in Salerno, medicine boxes; in Toledo, magic; and nowhere, virtue.

Well acquainted with the Latin satirical tradition, Hélinand draws on it to attack erudition not centred on God. His lament prompted Jacques Le Goff's comment that 'Hélinand can in no way be considered an avant-garde thinker, because he was fifty years out of date',[60] and the judgment of Pierre Bonnassie and G. Pradalié that Hélinand, as the university's 'directeur de conscience', proposed an 'astonishingly retrograde programme' that favoured 'holy ignorance'.[61] One historian has assumed that Hélinand taught at the new university, but the only names registered as university masters are Dominicans.[62] Hélinand must have played some role in overseeing the curriculum, since he delivered the inaugural sermon, but exactly what he did remains uncertain. Objecting to the new trends in education and to the Platonism taught in the schools years earlier, Hélinand not surprisingly opposed heretical beliefs all the more. He inherited the scepticism expressed by Bernard of

---

[57] 'Sed nunc sermone simplici pauca loquamur ad simplices, ut et ipsi nobiscum pariter ascensuri, invenire possint per Dei gratiam in sermone nostro viam et vehiculum, lucernam et viaticum.' *PL*, CCXII, 603A.

[58] The three *exempla* are found in *PL*, CCXII, 603–10. Their content and sources are discussed in Kienzle, 'Erudition at God's Service', pp. 285–6. On Hélinand's *exempla*, see J.-Th. Welter, *L'exemplum dans la littérature religieuse et didactique du moyen âge* (Paris, 1929), *passim*.

[59] A. Lecoy de la Marche, *La chaire française au moyen âge* (Paris, 1886), p. 166.

[60] J. Le Goff, 'Les universités du Languedoc dans le mouvement universitaire européen au xiiie siècle', in *Les universités du Languedoc*, pp. 316–28 (p. 318).

[61] Bonnassie et Pradalié, *La capitulation de Raymond VII*, pp. 16–17.

[62] See article by Dossat cited in n. 45 above.

Clairvaux and other monks towards philosophy, and he equated philosophers, whether followers of Pythagoras, Plato, Epicurus, or the Stoics, with the
heretical lineage of Lucifer, Alexander, and Simon the Magician![63] This lineage
of heresy recalls our discussion of the medieval notions of heresy, one of them
being that heresy had an unchangeable essence, taking different forms across
the centuries, and another that medieval heretics descended from Simon
Magus in a sort of parody of the apostolic succession.[64]

The two synod sermons

We do not know how Hélinand occupied himself between the opening of the
university and the synod called to deal with the problem of heresy after the
termination of the Albigensian Crusade. The synod was convened sometime
in the fall (*post aestatem*),[65] after the signing of the Treaty of Paris and
Raymond VII's public capitulation, penance, and absolution by Romano
cardinal of St Angelo in the presence of Louis IX before the doors of Notre
Dame in Paris on 12 April 1229.[66]

The forty-five canons of the council, dated from November 1229, provided
not only for the foundation of the University of Toulouse but also for
searching out and interrogating heretics. Hence they constitute a landmark
in the history of the Inquisition and predate by only two years Pope Gregory
IX's 1231 letter, *Ille humanis generis*, commissioning the Dominican prior of
Regensburg as a judge delegate to travel in pursuit of heresy and appoint
other Dominicans to do the same. That letter was followed by Gregory IX's
instructions to the archbishops of Occitania in 1233, designating the Dominicans as inquisitors. The first inquisitors were appointed in the dioceses of
Toulouse, Cahors and Albi in 1233.[67] Precedents for their work had been set
in 1229. The first eighteen canons from 1229 deal with searching for heretics,
judging them, penalties for sheltering or hiding them, treatment of converts,
administration of an oath abjuring heresy, and required signs of faith:
confession and receiving the Eucharist three times per year. Canons 19–24
define ecclesiastic privileges such as freedom from taxation and tolls, and the
legal rights of clerics. Three canons (25–7) order attendance at church on
Sundays and feast days, requiring fines for absentees. Another seventeen

---

[63] *PL*, CCXII, 602B: 'Hanc artem nescivit obscurus ille Lucifer . . . Nescivit Simon
Magus pestifer . . . Nescierunt philosophi . . . et ab eis notarentur discipuli
Pythagorei, vel Platonici, Epicurei vel Stoici, et caetera hujusmodi.'

[64] See Chapter Three of this book, pp. 104–5.

[65] The council, its preparations, and the arrival of the legate after Pentecost are
described by Puylaurens, pp. 134–9. C. E. Smith, *The University of Toulouse in the
Middle Ages* (Milwaukee, 1958), pp. 37–8, dates the cardinal's arrival in the autumn.
Smith also argued for dating the university's opening the following year. His
suggestion did not gain acceptance.

[66] See Bonnassie and Pradalié, *La capitulation de Raymond VII*, p. 7.

[67] See Lambert, *Cathars*, pp. 116–28; Peters, *Inquisition*, pp. 51–7, at 55 (where he gives
the date of 1234); and Costen, *The Cathars and the Albigensian Crusade*, pp. 164–9.

concern preserving peace, punishing disturbers of the peace, dealing with stolen goods, the responsibilities of judges, and providing legal assistance to the poor. The final canon (45) declares that all the preceding canons are to set forth by the parish priests four times per year. After the synod, the legate adjudicated an inquest, carrying the records to Rome in an unsuccessful attempt to protect those who gave depositions against suspected heretics.[68]

To this important synod Hélinand preached two sermons, generally assumed to represent the opening and closing addresses. One, Sermon 28 in the *Patrologia Latina*, affirms the Church's power and calls for obedience; the other, Sermon 26 in the *Patrologia Latina*, addresses the clergy, elaborating on the familiar theme of righteousness in deed and word. The order in which the sermons appear in the *Patrologia Latina* is presumably the reverse of their delivery: Sermon 28 probably opened the synod and Sermon 26 closed it. However, both relate very closely to the circumstances of the council, so that arguments could be made for either to have opened or closed.[69]

The opening sermon (28)

In this sermon Hélinand justifies the legate's presence in the region and the purpose of the council. Hélinand employs the vineyard imagery now familiar to us: God as *pater familias* sends workers into the vineyard to guard against thorny vines, nettles and vipers – all obvious symbols in this context for heretics and their beliefs. Jeremiah represents the biblical model for ecclesiastical leaders: as cultivator of the Lord's vineyard, he was established over peoples and kingdoms to pluck out, destroy, spoil, build and plant (Jeremiah 1. 10). Legates are sent from the pope, Hélinand explains, to perform this evangelist's work (*opus evangelistae*). Virtues cannot be planted until vices are extirpated. The legate brings a hoe of discipline and numerous rules needed for eradicating the many thorns. Hélinand praises the current papal legate, Romano of St Angelo, alluding to the simplicity of his arrival, perhaps an indication that Hélinand did accompany the legate or arrived before him. Playing on the common theme of satirical literature, that Rome is the centre of greed, Hélinand continues: 'If I dare say it, he is not a Roman; that is, he does not chase after money or surrender himself to monetary treasures.' Adducing classical references, the preacher furthers says that the legate is not the type whose nostrils flair at the scent of gold, or who have a hundred arms like Briareus to grab silver. He then asserts strongly that the cardinal is not like some of the other legates, who in the past left the pope's side as if they were Satan coming straight from God to punish the Church, or the furies released from Hell to wreak havoc.[70] The legates are not named, so we do not know if

---

[68] Mansi, *Sacrorum conciliorum nova et amplissima collectio*, XXIII, cols. 192–204.

[69] In Kienzle, 'Midi', the sermons are treated in the *PL* order: 26 followed by 28. 28 is erroneously identified as the closing sermon.

[70] 'In summa si audeo dicere, romanus non est, id est non abiit post aurum, nec sperat in

Hélinand was criticizing a fellow Cistercian, Arnaud Amaury, for example, or the later legates, who after 1214 were not Cistercians.[71] Hélinand closes the sermon with a plea for obedience, without specifically attacking any heretical beliefs. While he utilizes the destructive agricultural imagery that we have observed in earlier chapters, he speaks of peace and the preacher's responsibility for planting it in the hearts of his listeners.

The closing sermon (26)

The closing sermon for the council addresses the clergy, emphasizing the theme of righteousness from Psalm 132. 9: 'Your priests are vesting in righteousness'. From the text printed in the *Patrologia Latina*, Hélinand's technique of distinguishing orthodox from heterodox priests is not as evident as it is in the manuscript, which contains additional material relating to heresy.[72] Hélinand's exhortations to the clergy on inner examination and a righteous way of life join a tradition following Gregory the Great's *De regulae pastoralis* and renewed vigorously by the Cistercians who advised many bishops on their responsibilities and encouraged their moral reform.[73]

Hélinand, like Bernard of Clairvaux before him, criticizes what he sees as excessive asceticism among the heretics and hypocrisy among their elect, who abstain completely from eating meat and from any sexual contact with women. These practices reflect Cathar beliefs accurately, and Hélinand is aware of the groups of *electi* and *credentes* among the Cathars. Hélinand heats up his rhetoric by claiming that the heretics sacrifice to demons when they teach by word and example (a play on the traditional theme of *verbo et exemplo*) the error that one should abstain from foods created by God expressly for nourishing the faithful and encouraging their thanksgiving:

> Heretics are much worse through apostasy than pagans through idolatry; they sacrifice themselves to demons whenever they teach through the blasphemy of their error and by word and example alike to abstain from foods that God created for the faithful to receive with thanks.[74]

thesauris pecuniae. Non est de legatis illis quos aliquando novimus sic egressos fuisse a latere domini papae ac si ad ecclesiam flagellandam egressus esset Sathan a facie Domini. Ita plerique versantur in ecclesiis in provinciis debachantur ac si ad tedas in facinus excitandas egressa sit ab inferis iuxta Claudianum, Thesiphone vel Megera. Ipse eos . . . nichil est nisi merces publica. Qui corrumpcior est muneribus etiam si moribus corruptior sit, in causa facilius obtinebit. Ubicumque nares eorum afflaverit auri odor, quod ut ait Comicus: transmaria et terras olet, statim illi . . . afferunt manus Briarei et spinarum unges, famem canis et sitim dipsadis, ventrem balenae et cor monedulae. De qua pulcre Cicero sic lusit in quaedam de talibus: "Non plus aurum tibi quam monedulae commitendum" [Cicero Pro L.Flacco Oratio, 76]. Non est iste de talibus. f. 48va. Amator est iustitiae, zelator animarum, pecuniae contemptor . . .'

[71] See Zimmermann, *Die päpstliche Legation*, pp. 58ff, 72ff.
[72] *Sermo in synodo*, MS Lat. 14591, fols. 8rb–12ra; Sermo 26, *PL*, CCXII, 692–700.
[73] On such Cistercian literature, see Newman, pp. 156–70.
[74] ' . . . aut sicut haeretici multo peiores per apostaciam quam gentiles per idolatriam,

Hélinand also asserts that the heretics teach their believers (*credentibus*) that all sexual activity with a woman is the same, whether it be with a spouse, a sister, a mother, or a daughter:

> Their elect seem to and perhaps are even ordered to abstain from eating meat and lying with women. Yet they attempt to persuade their believers that all intercourse with a woman is the same and that one should no more abstain from it with a sister or mother or daughter than with one's own wife.[75]

This exaggerated notion about Cathar views of sex and rejection of marriage echoes Bernard's Sermons 65 and 66 on the Song of Songs, where he attacks the heretics already established in the Rhineland and described by Everwin of Steinfeld. In fact, Hélinand quotes Bernard almost directly at one point and he employs the term *electi*, which Everwin uses but Bernard doesn't.[76] Hélinand is almost surely using a repertoire of anti-heretical materials. Furthermore, this criticism of excessive asceticism coming from a monk in a religious order renowned for its own rigour in ascetic practices seems to be rooted in a sort of mimetic rivalry and resentment of dissidents who claimed close imitation of the apostles without accepting the authority of the Church or the monastic rule.

Unlike the other anti-heretical writers we have examined, Hélinand makes observations that demonstrate some interest in the history of heresy. He states that the 'priests of the Devil' who were once the idolatrous priests of antiquity are now the heretics' bishops or elect.[77] In so doing, he shows some knowledge of the structure of the Cathar counter-church, its bishops and its division into elect and believers. In Hélinand's view, one does not find the truth of righteousness among the heretics' elect, but instead a false appearance of holiness and truth.[78] For him, the spirits of error, namely unclean demons, that speak now in the world through the heretics' teachers are the same that used to

qui semetipsos immolant daemonibus, quotiens per erroris sui blasphemiam docent verbo pariter et exemplo abstinere a cibis quos Deus creavit ad percipiendum cum gratiarum actione fidelibus': MS Lat. 14591, fol. 9v. Cf. *PL*, CCXII, 698C.

[75] 'Electi eorum abstinere videntur, et forte etiam jubentur, ab esu carnium a concubitu mulierum: et tamen credentibus suis persuadere conantur, indifferentem esse omnem cum muliere coitum; nec magis abstinendum esse a sorore vel matre vel filia, quam ab uxore propria.' MS Lat. 14591, fol. 11ra–11rb. Cf. *PL*, CCXII, 698C.

[76] *Sermo* 65.6 and 66.3–5: *SBOp*, II, 176 and 179–182. On foods, Hélinand states: 'abstinere a cibis quos Deus creavit ad percipiendum cum gratiarum actione fidelibus'; and Bernard had said: 'abstinent . . . a cibis quos creavit Deus ad percipiendum cum gratiarum actione.' I am grateful to Peter Biller for pointing out this direct parallel. See also Brenon, 'La lettre d'Evervin', and Chapter Three in this book, pp. 88–9.

[77] '. . . dictum est ad differentiam sacerdotum diaboli, qui olim dicti sunt sacerdotes idolorum, vel qui adhuc sunt episcopi hereticorum, vel eorum electi.' *PL*, CCXII, 697B.

[78] 'In quibus quamvis nulla inveniatur justitiae veritas; multa tamen invenitur sanctitatis et veritatis similtudo palliata.' *PL*, CCXII, 698D.

speak in Egypt through the idolatrous priests.[79] Thus Hélinand sees a continuous presence of the Devil. The heretics are demonized and accused of deceit, a clear threat to the social order. The preacher calls upon priests to clothe themselves with righteousness (Psalm 131. 9), not a pretence of it, like the former priests of falsehood and the current teachers of error.[80]

St Jerome is the first authority cited to support Hélinand's assertions. In Jerome's *Contra Jovinianum*, Jovinianus being a monk condemned in 393 as a Manichean, the Cistercian found Chaeremon the Stoic's description of the Egyptian priests known for an ascetic stance that refused eating not only meat but also eggs and cheese.[81] We know that the Cathars also refused to eat meat and eggs.[82] Hélinand moves next to Euripides' observations on the priests of Jupiter in Crete, and he then cites two examples that appear only in the manuscript: Ovid on pagan priests who abstained from sex, and the hierophants (high-priests) of Athens who were temporarily emasculated by drinking hemlock. For the Cistercian, both cases exemplify chastity that is not genuine. Finally, Hélinand refers to a letter from Porphyry, now lost but quoted by St Augustine in the *City of God*, X,11.[83] The letter, like the other

---

[79] 'Plane eadem simulatio est in haereticis nostri temporis. . . . O doctrina infernalis, a quibus tenebris emersisti? Patet ergo eosdem spiritus erroris, id est immundos daemones nunc loqui in mundo per magistros haereticorum, qui tunc loquebatur in Aegypto per sacerdotes idolorum.' MS Lat. 14591, fol. 11ra–11rb.

[80] 'Propterea dicitur: Sacerdotes tui induantur justitiam (Ps 131,9) quasi diceret, non simulationem justitiae, sicut olim induti sunt sacerdotes falsitatis et adhuc induuntur magistri erroris . . .' *PL*, CCXII, 698D.

[81] 'Refert Hieronimus in libro Contra Jovinianum, Chaeremontem stoicum scripsisse de antiquis Aegypti sacerdotibus quod mirae fuerint abstinentiae in victu, continentiae in concubitu, paupertatis in habitu, humilitatis in victu, gravitatis in incessu. Denique ex quo semel falsorum deorum cultui mancipati erant, nunquam postea parentes visitabant, nec etiam filios [filiasve] venire ante conspectum suum patiebantur. Semper a vino et carnibus abstinebant, nunquam mulieribus jungebantur; nec solem carnes horrebant, sed etiam ova et caseum. Quorum primum dicebant esse carnem liquidam, secundum sanguinem colore mutato. Super nudum humum jacebant, scabellum pro cervicali capiti suo suppontes.' MS Lat. 14591, fols. 10vb–11ra. The text is a paraphrase of Jerome, *Contra Jovinianum* II, 13 (*PL*, XXIII, 316). On Chaeremon, see: *Chaeremon, Egyptian Priest and Stoic Philosopher*, ed. P. W. van der Horst (Leiden, 1984). Fragments of Chaeremon's works were cited by Porphry, *Epistola ad Anebonem* II, etc. and *De abstinentia* of Eusebius.

[82] On Cathar dietary practices, see Duvernoy, *Religion*, cited in n. 52 above.

[83] 'Euripides sacerdotes Jovis in Creta dicit semper a coctis abstravisse cibis.' [*Adversus Jovinianum*, Lib. 2.14, *PL*, XXIII, 317, l. 25.] 'Therofantas Atheniencium, mox ut electi erant ad sacerdotium observandam fortius castitatem cicutae sorbitione castrabantur [*Adv.Jov.* I.49, *PL*, XXIII, 294, l. 39]. Similia scripsit poeta de Paelignis in libro Fastorum de sacerdotibus idolorum, dicens: ''Usus abest Veneris nec fas animalia mensis ponere, nec digitis anulus ullus inest [Ovid, *Fasti* 4.655].'' Usus, inquit, abest Veneris. Ecce castitatis non veritas sed umbra, nec fas animalia mensis ponere. Ecce abstincentie figura non veritas, nec digitis anulus ullus inest. Ecce humilitatis non verum documentum sed inane simulacru, Porfirius enim, Augustino teste, philosophorum doctissimus non immerito quaerit in epistola ad Anebontem Aegyptium,

191

sources just mentioned, describes the excessive sexual and dietary abstinence of idolatrous priests. Thus Hélinand develops a sort of genealogy of Catharism, tracing their abstinence to the priests of antiquity, before the Christian era. He does not limit himself to historical aspects of Catharism, however: more than once, he demonizes the heretics' priests, again expressing something like the belief in an unchangeable essence of heresy that took different forms over the centuries.

The ending of this synodal sermon takes a surprising turn. The dominant image is the sword, but not the sword of Romans 13. 4, which avengers a wrong-doer, making the one who yields it a servant of God. Bernard of Clairvaux alludes to that sword in his Sermon 66 on the Song of Songs. Nor does Hélinand's image echo the two swords of Luke 22. 38, representing the union of secular and ecclesiastical power which Henry of Clairvaux evoked in his Letter 11 of May 1178.[84] Hélinand evokes the sword that the prophet Ezekiel describes as Yahweh's sword, a sword 'of great slaughter' (Ezekiel 21. 3–14). Hélinand adapts the verses of this violent passage, asserting first that the slaughter is meagre when an evil custom is abandoned but evil action remains. In contrast, the sword doubles its blow when evil custom and perverse action are relinquished, and triples it when evil will is cut off at the root (Ezekiel 21. 14). The image undeniably brings to mind the slaughter of the crusade, but Hélinand turns the sword against the clergy and its vices. In the sermon's final words, the preacher affirms: 'Then we are truly priests of God when we strike our own body and soul with such a sword.' Hence, although the sword image arguably justifies the slaughter under the condition that the clergy embrace its responsibilities during the peace, Hélinand's closing sentence calls all present to an inner battle with themselves. In so doing, he returns to a fundamental monastic theme expressed in the Prologue of the *Rule of Benedict*: preparing oneself in body and soul by doing battle with vices under the command of obedience.[85]

---

quid est, quod sacerdotes idolorum a contactu rei veneriae prohibentur cum ad incertos quosque concubitus quemlibet ducere non morentur; quid est, quod ab animalibus abstinere jubentur, cum illorum sacrificia sanguine pecudum et carnium iudicibus celebrentur.' MS Lat. 14591, fol. 11r. Hélinand could have found mention of the hierophants also in John of Salisbury's *Policraticus*, ed. C. C. I. Webb, 2 vols. (Oxford, 1909), 7.11, II, 306, l. 3 (*PL*, CXCIX, 755D), which he knew well: 'ierophantias quoque Atheniensium diutissime cicutae sorbitione castrari et, postquam in pontificatum fuerint allecti, viros esse desinere.' On Hélinand and John of Salisbury, see See H. Hublocher, *Helinand von Froidmont und sein Verhältnis zu Johannes von Salisbury* (Regensburg, 1913).

[84] See Chapter Three, pp. 90, 104 and Chapter Four, p. 115, in this book.
[85] See *Rule of Benedict*, Prologue, cited above, p. 45, n. 23.

Other anti-heretical sermons

Several other sermons by Hélinand deal with heresy. We know little to nothing about the circumstances of their delivery, but they provide evidence for his strong interest in the subject and for his historical or encyclopaedic approach to it. Four sermons from Paris, Bibliothèque Nationale MS Lat. 14591 contain polemics against heresy, as do a few others.

A Purification sermon[86] discusses why Mary, considered the purest of women, would need to subject herself to rites of purification. Hélinand expands that question to apply his lesson against dissidents' rejection of the human nature of Christ and of Mary. He presents four reasons why the Virgin Mary wished to submit to purification rites. Her first concern was to demonstrate her humanity and her son's. This provides Hélinand the opportunity to trace the origins of docetism, beginning in his view with second-century gnostics – Valentinus, Marcion, Apelles – and extending to Mani and finally to Mohammed. He adds that certain contemporary Manicheans (*quidam manichaeorum*) also believe that Mary was not truly human but a fantastic being (*mulierem fantasticam*).[87] This statement suggests familiarity with the *Interrogatio Iohannis*, which contains the notion that Mary was an angel, sent before Christ to receive him.[88] It also brings to mind some of the expressions and arguments of Eckbert of Schönau's *Sermones contra catharos* (*c.* 1163), even though he does not raise the question of Mary's humanity. In his ninth sermon, *Contra nonam haeresim de humanitate Salvatoris*, Eckbert presents arguments for Christ's humanity and traces Mani's ideas from Valentinus and Apelles. Eckbert uses the words *phantasticum corpus* to capture their views on the nature of Christ. The same expression appears earlier in the work of Rupert of Deutz (*c.* 1070–1129/30), speaking of

---

[86] See B. M. Kienzle, 'Mary Speaks against Heresy: An Unedited Sermon of Hélinand for the Purification, Paris, B.N. ms. lat. 14591', *Sacris erudiri* 32 (1991), 291–308 (pp. 300–8).

[87] MS Lat. 14591, fol. 33rb–33va: 'Redduntur tamen a sanctis patribus et alie cause purgationum matries et filii, quarum prima est, ut veritas carnis in matre mirabiliter pariente et in filio mirabilius nascente monstrateur . . . Huius autem opinionis falsissime quod scilicet Christus fantasticam carnem habuerit, primus auctor fuit Valentinus, post, credo, Marcionis magister, qui fuerunt tempore Ygini pape, deinde Appeles, deinde Manicheus, deinde Mahometus. Nunc autem quidam manicheorum eciam hoc addunt : Mariam mulierem fantasticam fuisse. Previdens ergo Dominus diabolum huiusmodi Antichristum ad predicandam falsitatem missurum, festinavit eis occurrere, et ad repellendas falsitatis tenebras, lucem vere circumcisionis opposuit, per quam se verum hominem demonstraret. Hac eciam ratione baptisari se voluit, quia sicut legitur in libris quorundam sapiencium, nihil quod sit per fantasiam vel artem nigromanticam, virtutem potest retinere fantasticam postquam in aqua mersum est.'

[88] Bozóky, *Interrogatio*, p. 36.

Valentinus and Apelles, and in a ninth-century sermon on John's gospel by Héric of Auxerre (841–*c*. 876) when he explains Marcionite and Manichean beliefs about Christ's nature. Hélinand's near contemporary Alan of Lille refers to the heretical view that Mary was not truly human, but he does not use this phrase.[89] Hélinand expresses the view that the Lord foresaw that the Devil's sending Antichrist to preach falsehoods and therefore prudently decided to receive baptism and institute a new sacrament by sanctifying baptismal waters. Similarly, Jesus submitted to circumcision to testify to his humanity.[90] Hélinand's comments in the sermon again demonize heretics by linking them with the Devil and Antichrist, but he does not take up other patterns of defamatory rhetoric. Moreover, anything fantastic, according to some authorities, could not retain its strength in water, so that immersion in water was proof of Christ's humanity.[91]

Trinitarian disputes also surface in a Pentecost sermon, where Hélinand defends the doctrine of the Trinity and, above all, the equality of the Holy Spirit with respect to the Father and the Son. He includes an *exemplum* dealing with the interrogation of a certain archdeacon during a council presided by Hildebrand, the future reformer-pope Gregory VII (1073–85). The archdeacon, accused of 'Macedonian' heresy, denied the creator and claimed that the Holy Spirit was only a created being (*creatura*).[92] Hélinand

---

[89] Eckbert of Schönau: *PL*, CXCV, 96B: 'Nam si phantasticum corpus habuisset, ita ut non fuisset in eo vera caro, sed inanis et umbratilis quaedam carnis similitudo . . .' Rupert of Deutz, *Commentaria in evangelium sancti Iohannis*, CCCM IX (Turnhout, 1969), Lib. 6, p. 318: 'Fuerunt enim haeretici qui dominum nostrum non verum et solidum sed phantasticum corpus habuisse dicerent hoc argumento nimis infirmo abutentes quia super aquas ambulavit'; Lib. 10, p. 540: 'Iam quidem gratulamur non solum adversus arium qui noluit intelligere quod intellixistis vos in his verbis : ego et pater unum sumus verum et adversus valentinianum sive apellem qui verum esse hominem negaverunt dominum nostrum iesum christum asserentes eum non verum habuisse corpus sed phantasticum.' Heiricus Autissiodorensis, *Homiliae per circulum anni, Pars hiemalis, Hom.* 31, l. 238: 'Nec negavit matrem de qua carnem assumpserat, dicut insaniunt marcionistae et manichaei, qui eum dicunt non habuisse verum corpus sed phantasticum, sed spiritalem propinquitatem carnis praetulit consanguinitati, ut et nos doceret in causa Dei nullum de affectione carnis recognoscere'; *Pars aestiva, Hom.* 45, l. 232: 'Unde et ipse dominus a mortuis resurgens et ad discipulos clausis ianuis ingrediens, ne putarent ipsi non verum sed phantasticum se conspicere corpus, manducavit coram eis ac reliquias ciborum dedit illis.' See E. Jeauneau, *Studi medievali* 3 (1970), 943–55. Alan of Lille, *PL*, CCX, 335C: 'Alii vero haeretici dogmatizant Christum corpus coeleste assumpsisse, et beatam Virginem in coelo creatam fuisse, et de coelesti natura; et ita Christum de beata Virgine carnem coelestem assumpsisse: quod variis modis probare conantur.' Finally Isidore of Seville notes for Apelles: '. . . dixit, Christum non Deum in veritate, sed hominem in phantasia apparuisse.' *Etymologiae*, vol. 1, VIII.v, 12. I am grateful to Peter Biller for this last reference.

[90] Kienzle, 'Mary Speaks against Heresy', p. 302.

[91] See Russell, *The Devil*, p. 246, who notes that water was reputed to offer protection from the Devil who could not traverse it.

[92] *Sermo* 16, *PL*, CCXII, 616–17: ' In eo enim concilio archidiaconus quidam accusatus

cites here, at least indirectly, Augustine's work, *De haeresibus*, where the bishop explains that the Macedonians, called Pneumatomakous by the Greeks, did not accept that the Holy Spirit was of the same essence as the Father and the Son, affirming instead that the Spirit is a created being (*creatura*), exactly the word that Hélinand uses.[93] A similar *exemplum* reports that the archbishop of Lyons (instead of an archdeacon) was questioned by Hildebrand in 1057, after having been accused of simony (not heresy). When the archbishop could not utter the name of the Holy Spirit, he was deposed.[94] Hélinand's version of the *exemplum* focuses on heresy and ends with the dismissal of an archdeacon and not an archbishop.

The All Saints' sermons

In an All Saints' Day sermon, Hélinand emphasizes the importance of confession, apparently reacting against some (*quidam*) who affirmed that contrition alone suffices for receiving God's pardon. Both Waldensians and Cathars rejected the idea that a priest's absolution was necessary. Hélinand states that they interpret badly what Saint Ambrose said about the effectiveness of tears of contrition, because they conclude from it that if the heart's contrition is great, no other confession is necessary.[95] Alan of Lille discusses the same issue in his anti-heretical treatise and cites the passage from Ambrose, concluding that heretics are wrong because the Milanese bishop's words apply only to public penitence.[96]

Another All Saints' sermon contains a short passage against the teachings of Carpocrates, a second-century gnostic teacher from Alexandria, whom Hélinand identifies as a leader of the Cathars, also called gnostics. According to Hélinand, Carpocrates maintained that anyone desiring to achieve perfection could not avoid demons except by releasing them through misdeeds. Hélinand could have found information on Carpocrates in various works on

de haeresi macedoniana, quae Spiritum sanctum asserit esse creaturam, et negat creatorem, jussus a pontifice praesentari, adfuit.'

[93] 'Nam de patre et filio recte sentiunt quod unius sint eiusdemque substantiae vel essentiae, sed hoc de spiritu sancto nolunt credere, creaturam eum esse dicentes.' *Sancti Aurelii Augustini Opera*. Pars XIII,2, CCSL XLVI, *De haeresibus*, LII, pp. 322–3.

[94] See Bonizon of Sutri, *Liber ad amicum*, VI, in *Monumenta Germanica Historiae, Libelli de lite imperatorum et pontificum*, I, p. 592, cited by M. Lauwers, who discusses the simoniac version of the *exemplum* but does not mention Hélinand's in 'Excursus: Un écho des polémiques antiques? A Saint-Victor de Marseille à la fin du XIe siècle', in *Inventer l'hérésie*, p. 64.

[95] BN MS Lat. 14591, fol. 39ra: 'Unde Ambrosius: lacrimae lavant quod pudor est confiteri, id est quodlibet delictum etiam illud, quod nemo sine pudore maximo confitetur. Nichil enim efficacius ad tales maculas abluendas, hanc autem Ambrosii sententiam quidam male intelligunt, dicentes Ambrosium affirmasse quod tanta potest esse cordis contritio, ut non sit necesse aliam confessionem facere. Quod omnino falsum esse demonstrat Dominus in evangelio . . .'

[96] Ambrose, *Super Lucam*, L.X, no. 87, *PL*, XV, 1825–6; Alan of Lille, *Contra haereticos libri quatuor*, Liber 1, Cap. 52–3, *PL*, CCX, 356–7.

heresy that date back to Irenaeus. He does identify a source but states that these beliefs have their origin with philosophers who were predecessors of Porphyry, the third-century Alexandrian opponent of Christianity. Hélinand may again be relying on Augustine's *De civitate Dei* for Porphyry's ideas on demons; however, the bishop does not mention Carpocrates there but in other works on heresy. One of those, the *De haeresibus*, contains a reference to Cathars, explaining the derivation of their name from the Greek word *katharos*, pure.[97] That Hélinand mentions the gnostics and Carpocrates evidences again his interest in the history of heresy.

The Dedication sermon

Hélinand's Dedication sermon focuses on another sacrament that the Cathars did not accept in its traditional form of administration: baptism by water.[98] The circumstances of its preaching are not identified but some intra-textual references may, if Hélinand in fact lived until 1237, link it with the dedication in 1236 of the newly constructed abbey church at Froidmont.[99] Already in 1952, a Cistercian scholar examining the importance of the liturgy in Hélinand's sermons, suggested that this particular sermon was directed against the Cathar rite of *consolamentum*.[100] A close study of the text confirms that hypothesis: Hélinand, describing himself here as a teacher of the Church with the obligation to instruct,[101] implicitly attacks the *consolamentum*, as he and other polemicists understood it: a rejection of baptism with water and a sort of protection against sin. The Cathars did reject baptism with water, advocating instead a baptism with the Holy Spirit, administered through the

---

[97] 'O quam vehementer erravit olim Carpocrates haereticus! Catharorum, qui dicuntur Gnostici, dux dicens omnem hominem qui ad perfectionem sui mysterii, seu potius sceleris pervenire volebat, non aliter effugere posse hujusmodi principes scilicet daemones, vel declinare, nisi per quaedam facinora, quae ipse statuebat, solverentur. Hujus autem erroris tenebras prius sparserant quidam philosophi, quos Porphyrius Platonicus sequens dicebat, bonum Deum seu ingenium non posse inveniri in homine, nisi ante malus fuerit Placatus.' Sermo 25, *PL*, CCXII, 687D. Augustine discusses the views of Porphry on demons in *De civitate Dei*, IX.9–11. See n. 87 above. He refers to Carpocrates in *De haeresibus*, CCSL XLVI, pp. 292–3. On Carpocrates, see *The Earliest Christian Heretics. Readings from their Opponents*, ed. A. J. Hultgren and S. A. Haggmark (Minneapolis, 1996), pp. 49–55.

[98] BN MS Lat. 14591, fols. 40ra–44vb; *PL*, CCXII, 700–11.

[99] Sermo 27, *PL*, CCXII, 700–11; BN MS Lat. 14591, fols. 40ra–44vb. fol. 45ra: 'nostra domus dedicata est a filio virginis acceptari'; other less precise references: fol. 41 va, vb: 'ecclesia dedicanda;' fol. 41vb: '[ecclesia] munda et vacua'. On the date for the dedication, see Deladreue, *Cartulaire*, p. 536.

[100] Dumontier, 'Hélinand de Froidmont et la liturgie', *Collectanea ordinis Cisterciensium Reformatorum* 14 (1952), 133–9, 213–15, 295–300; 17 (1955), 49–56, 118–25 (17: 53).

[101] BN MS Lat. 14591, fol. 40vb: 'His autem, fratres karissimi, vobis dico litteratis, in ablucionem manuum vestrarum preeffusis, cibanda est eodem pane quem vobis apposui, sed fracto diminutus, edentula parvulorum esuries, quibus maxime tenetur omnis doctor ecclesiasticus, ut frangat eis panem dominicum, quippe cuius dentes necessarii non sunt eruditoribus ad frangendum.'

laying on of hands, as they found it described in the book of Acts. Those who received the *consolamentum* were expected to sin no more, leading to the impression among orthodox writers that the Cathars believed their sacrament protected them from sin.[102] The Cistercian preacher explains each element of the baptismal rite and emphasizes the symbolism of rejecting the Devil as well as the Devil's real lack of power and the necessity for doing penance after baptism.[103] Nowhere in this sermon does Hélinand denounce heretics directly, but the emphasis on baptism and renouncing the Devil implies that spurning traditional baptism entails not rejecting but even accepting the Devil. Such a conclusion would be consistent with Hélinand's repeated demonization of heretics.

Sermon I for Palm Sunday

The last sermon that we shall examine, one for Palm Sunday, contains the most violent attack against heretics that Hélinand makes anywhere. According to the manuscript rubrics, this is also Hélinand's last sermon and he delivered it in French, although the manuscript records only the Latin, and an incomplete version of the whole, as it appears in the *Patrologia Latina*.[104] The anti-heretical section of the sermon deals with addressing prayers to the saints, a frequent topic in polemical literature against heresy during the eleventh and twelfth centuries.[105]

After telling a story about John of Lyons, the first abbot of Bonneval and later the bishop of Valence, Hélinand remarks that the saints intercede for us in a friendly and effective manner. He asserts that those who claim that prayer to saints is worthless, tell only lies. He calls such people 'Albigensian dogs'. Forming a pun on *Albigenses* and *abigendi* (the nominative plural gerundive of *abigo* – having to be driven away), he calls for not only expelling the dogs with stones and sticks, but also treating them like rabid dogs who ought to be put to the sword or burned.[106] The violence of the rhetoric here surpasses that of Hélinand's predecessors and is not found elsewhere in his sermons.

Textual problems hinder identification of the circumstances for preaching

---

[102] On the *consolamentum*, see Y. Hagman, 'Le rite de l'initiation chrétienne chez les cathares et les bogomiles', *Heresis* 20 (1993), 13–31; and A. Brenon, 'Les fonctions sacramentales du *Consolamentum*', *Heresis* 20 (1993), 33–55.

[103] BN MS Lat. 14591, fols. 41v–43v.

[104] BN MS Lat. 14591, fols. 48vb–49vb; *PL*, CCXII, 544–54. This sermon, incomplete in the manuscript, is supposed to be Hélinand's last and delivered in the vernacular.

[105] M. Lauwers, '*Dicunt vivorum beneficia nihil prodesse defunctis*. Histoire d'un thème polémique (XIe–XIIe siècles)', in *Inventer l'hérésie*, pp. 157–92.

[106] *PL*, CCXII, 549: 'Erubescant igitur canes Albigenses, qui contra veritatem latrando, mentiuntur, eorum orationem nihil nobis prodesse; qui non solum tanquam canes improbi et importuni lapidibus et baculis abigendi sunt, sed etiam tanquam canes rabidi confodiendi gladiis, vel ignibus comburendi.' The plays on words here are clearly based on Latin and not French. One wonders what a French sermon would have said here.

this passage: in the extant manuscript of the sermon, the text ends before the passage appears; the edited version ends just after it. However, the *exemplum* about John of Lyons also appears in Book 48 of Hélinand's *Chronicon*. There the source for the *exemplum* is identified: the Revelation commentary of Geoffrey of Auxerre. Geoffrey does not draw anti-heretical remarks from it.[107] In contrast, Hélinand adduces the *exemplum* in the *Chronicon*, as in the Palm Sunday sermon, to prove the error of heretics who claim that addressing prayers to saints is useless. There he calls the heretics holding this view *Paterini*, that is *Manichaei* or *Publicani*, names often used for the Cathars. Hélinand, as we have seen him do before, explains the source of this notion. He says that it is common to the *Paterini* and *Bulgarii*, and that it derives from Vigilantius, whose ideas he knows from Jerome's *Contra Vigilantium*. The Cistercian cites a passage from Jerome who denounced the apocryphal book of Esdra, and he concludes:

> It is better to hear and read the Second Book of Maccabees . . . than that apocryphal book which deserves to be burned because it forbids prayer to the dead. And these things have been stated briefly against this detestable heresy.[108]

Numerous twelfth-century polemicists cite II Maccabees as a proof text in their arguments; generally, however, they do not refer to Jerome.[109] The *Chronicon* confirms Hélinand's knowledge of the *exemplum* told by Geoffrey of Auxerre and his concern for the issue of addressing prayers to the dead. The tone of the *Chronicon* passage is more in keeping with the anti-heretical comments noted in the other sermons. The exceedingly violent rhetoric of the Palm Sunday sermon remains an anomaly.

Book 8 of the *Chronicon*, where the John of Lyons *exemplum* appears, deals

---

[107] *Apocalypsim*, pp. 203–5.

[108] *Chronicon*, lib. 48, in Tissier, *Bibliotheca*, VII, 178–79; *PL*, CCXII, 1019–22: 'Hoc exemplum aperitissime et fortissime facit contra haereticos nostri temporis, qui dicuntur Paterini, id est Manichaei, sive Publicani. Qui dicunt vanas esse peregrinationes, et vanas esse eorum invocationes, nec nostras preces ad eorum pervenire notitiam, quibus iam nihil sit cum nostra vita commune, cum ipsi sancti coeli sint. . . . Hic error, qui modo generalis et communis est omnium Paterinorum et Bulgarorum, quos vulgari nomine Publicanos appellamus, olim specialis fuit Vigilantii Presbyterii, qui dicebat sacrilegium esse orationem facere ad sanctorum reliquias. . . . Haec Hieronymus. O quam melius est audire et legere librum illum II Machabaeorum, ubi scriptum est . . . [II Maccabees 12. 46], quam librum illum apocryphum combustione dignum, qui prohibet orare pro mortuis [*Contra Vig*, 6. *PL*, XXIII, 360]. Sed haec breviter dicta sunt contra hanc heresim detestandam.' Edition in progress by M. M. Woesthuis, to whom I am grateful for lending me his notes. The passage is mentioned but not cited in full in M. M. Woesthuis, 'History and Preaching in Hélinand of Froidmont', *Sacris erudiri* 34 (1994), 313–33 (pp. 317–18). See also Duvernoy, *Religion*, p. 256 on the later usage of the term Bulgarii and Chapter Four above, p. 119, n. 34.

[109] Lauwers, 'Histoire d'un thème polémique', p. 189, cites only one reference to Jerome in these polemical texts, the *Epistola ad Pammachium* and not the *Contra Vigilantium*.

with the soul and the afterlife. Hélinand draws on the theories of Macrobius, Hesiod, and Virgil and includes citations from Ovid, Persius, Seneca and Juvenal. Still he considers the authority of Gregory's *Moralia in Job* and Bernard's *De consideratione* as superior because both lead to self-knowledge and thus to knowledge of God. He praises Bernard of Clairvaux as greater than the ancients: Apollo, Demosthenes, Aristotle, Seneca and Plato![110] Hélinand, seemingly inheriting Bernard of Clairvaux's quarrels with the Platonistic school at Chartres, assimilates two groups in his defence of orthodoxy: Platonists and Cathars. For the Cistercian writer, both rejected the Christian view of life after death and favoured belief in reincarnation. Hélinand remarks sarcastically that numbers of his contemporaries support either Epicurus's idea that there is nothing after death, or Plato and Pythagoras's view, that after death, they will be animals. In another passage of Book 8, the chronicler attacks the theory that the human body was created by an angel, according to Plato, or by a devil, according to the Manicheans.[111]

Conclusion

In conclusion, Hélinand repeatedly associates heretics with the Devil. He describes them as the spokespersons for demons and agents for the Devil and Antichrist. In one sermon for the 1229 Toulouse synod, the preacher claims that the voice of unclean demons has been expressed through the mouths of heretical teachers over the ages. Hélinand associates heretics, clearly the Cathars, most closely with the Devil and Antichrist in the Purification sermon. His assertion, that the Lord foresaw the Devil's sending Antichrist to preach the heresy that neither Jesus nor the Virgin Mary was a human being, implies that Cathar preachers were fundamentally Antichrists, who operated as emissaries of the Devil. In the Dedication sermon, Hélinand underscores the importance of rejecting the Devil through the sacrament of baptism by water. The refusal of traditional baptism entails at the least not rejecting the Devil, and at the most, accepting the Devil. Although demonization is a recurrent feature of

[110] See Kienzle, 'The Witness of Hélinand of Froidmont'. E. Saak finds that Hélinand's knowledge of the theories of the school of Chartres was the basis for his attacks on them. He found Platonism suspicious, probably in part because of its influence on the early heretics he considered the ancestors of the Cathars. E. Saak, 'An Encyclopedist at Work: The *Chronicon* of Hélinand of Froidmont' (unpublished paper).

[111] 'O quanti sunt et hodie qui vellent post mortem aut reverti in nichilum, secundum Epicureum aut secundum Platonem aut Pitagoram in iumentum converti.' Lib. 8, c. 24, 173b; p. 39 type script, c. 9, *Epistola ad Drogonem*, 162b. Eric Saak provided these references from the edition of the *Chronicon* in progress at the University of Gröningen.

Hélinand's rhetoric, the categories of pollution and threat to the social order, which appeared often in the writings examined in previous chapters, are remarkably absent. Apocalypticism also figures less forcefully in Hélinand's language, with the exception of his assimilation of heretics to Antichrist.

How do we explain the relative absence of virulent rhetoric in the works of Hélinand compared to those of his predecessors? Can we conclude that his writings, particularly the sermons preached in 1229, reflect a post-crusade atmosphere? I lean towards an affirmative answer. It would be reasonable to assume that Hélinand would not direct virulent rhetoric against an audience in Toulouse, right after the termination of the war. Moreover, Hélinand's language, with the exception of the Palm Sunday sermon, is generally less inflammatory than that of his predecessors who were engaged in the crusade, or in pre-crusade preaching.

If we recall the categories of medieval attitudes towards heresy,[112] Hélinand seems closest to the view that heresy had a constant essence which appeared under various forms and facades through history. Hélinand develops this usually vague notion by linking certain aspects of heresy, such as excessive asceticism, to practices in antiquity. Although the Cistercian mentions Simon Magus at one point, he does not claim the notion of an heretical apostolic succession. One finds, in contrast, a historical filiation of ideas, especially docetism and severe asceticism. A striking interest in the history of heresy emerges from Hélinand's writings, both sermons and *Chronicon*. Indeed he is the only Cistercian author we have studied who demonstrates a sense that heresy indeed has a history. He traces the development of ascetical practices to the East whereas Henry of Clairvaux/Albano and Arnaud Amaury denounced an imprecise eastern influence as pernicious. His discussion of an oriental influence is more academic and historical than defamatory. Moreover, his interest in the ancient world leads him to search for concrete connections between heretics of old and his contemporaries. Hélinand compares specific dietary practices and reflects on theological reasons for not rejecting certain foods. Bernard of Clairvaux in contrast couches fairly accurate observations in invective, denouncing the heretics' rejection of specific foods as unclean and accusing them of being unclean and therefore to be rejected by the Church. Furthermore, Bernard's observation that the 'new' heretics have no professed leader serves primarily as a point of departure for invective, not as an element of analysis. He does not discuss the origins of heretical ideas at all. Similarly Bernard denounces Henry the monk's rejection of infant baptism and launches into vitriolic language, demonstrating no interest in the history of this view.[113] Even Peter of les

---

[112] Russell, *Dissent and Order*, p. 4.
[113] See Chapter Three in this book, pp. 58–9.

Vaux-de-Cernay, who does treat Cathar beliefs in some detail, reveals no interest in their affiliations or historical background.

Finally, Hélinand's portrayal of Cathar beliefs differs remarkably from that of his Cistercian predecessors because his is surprisingly correct. Bernard held fairly precise views of heretical doctrine but framed them with vituperation. He was aware, for example, that the Cathars rejected marriage but he devotes more space to denunciation of sexual immorality than to exposition of beliefs. Henry of Clairvaux/Albano's writings are more concerned with narration of events than explanation of doctrine; some glimpses of Cathar practices surface in his writings but invective predominates. From Arnaud Amaury one learns nothing of Cathar beliefs unless we attribute to him the sermon which was translated by Alan of Lille that focuses on the rejection of christological doctrines. On the other hand, Peter of les Vaux-de-Cernay's exposition of heretical tenets contains much accurate information but also misconceptions and much vituperation with *exempla* that preachers could use to ridicule their opponents.[114] In comparison to Peter, Hélinand employs demonizing emotive apostrophes more than invective.

In spite of the superior accuracy of Hélinand's discussion of heresy, he still accepted and echoed the Manichean filiation for Catharism which appears throughout polemical sources. Hélinand knew and cited the works of Augustine and Jerome and probably referred as well to those of his near contemporaries Bernard of Clairvaux and Eckbert of Schönau. On the other hand, this Cistercian observed accurately that: the Cathars believed that Satan created the material world; they rejected the humanity of Christ and the Virgin Mary; some did not consider the Holy Spirit as the equal of the Father and the Son; they rejected the sacraments of the Eucharist, baptism and confession, as well as the idea of praying to saints; they practised rigorous asceticism; their ecclesiastical structure involved believers, elect and bishops. Furthermore, for Hélinand, the Cathars had spiritual and intellectual ancestors in the priests of Egypt and the gnostics – a filiation that has been either claimed or rejected loosely in previous research and is now being examined more rigorously by scholars of Catharism.

---

[114] See Chapter Five in this book, pp. 140–3 and 144 on the sermon attributable to Arnaud Amaury and on Peter of les Vaux-de-Cernay's discussion of Cathar beliefs.

CONCLUSION

We have surveyed about eighty-five years of history pertaining to the Cistercian Order's preaching and other engagement against heresy in Occitania from 1145 to 1229. I first situated monastic preaching in the context of twelfth-century events and currents of thought and their impact on Cistercian thinking and action; and second, within the framework of monastic spirituality and literature. The vineyard image, appearing in a letter where Bernard of Clairvaux employs it to describe turning from the interior vineyard of the monastery to the exterior one of the Church and the world, serves as a unifying motif for the book's chapters.

This study has held to a twofold task: reconstructing the preaching of individual Cistercians and collaborative campaigns; and deconstructing the rhetoric of the same preaching to reveal the strategies that the monks utilized against their adversaries. Some attention is given as well to what can be learned about dissident beliefs and practices from the pens of their adversaries. Cistercian participation in anti-heretical campaigns differs in accordance with the agenda of individual preachers and prelates, and along a range from reluctant acceptance of papal commission, to ardent public preaching, to leading armies. Individual Cistercians varied in their stance along that spectrum, but the extant texts reveal hostile language that belongs to the rhetoric of persecution. The Conclusion reviews the history of Cistercian preaching against heresy in Occitania from 1145 to 1229, evaluates the order's involvement, reviews the book's reconstructive process as well as its deconstruction of rhetoric, and points to possibilities for future research on later Cistercians and on the evidence for voices of dissent within the order.

Bernard, abbot of Clairvaux, after first taking a prominent role in affairs outside the monastery during the 1130s, turned his attention in 1145 towards popular heresy in Occitania. An exchange of letters with Everwin of Steinfeld in 1143–44 reveals Bernard's outlook immediately prior to the preaching mission, which was directed generally against heresy and specifically at Henry the monk. Bernard expresses his movement outward with biblical language – a turning from the interior vineyard of the monastery to the exterior vineyard of the Lord: the Church and the world. He conceptualizes his involvement as a widening of responsibility, which I describe as extending his abbot's charge to assume leadership beyond the monastery.

Accordingly, Bernard expanded the audience for his sermons from the monastic community to a society that included the sites for his preaching mission but also stretched as far as his letters, functioning as epistolary

Fig. 7. The town of Fanjeaux (Aude), stronghold for Catharism and site of the first
community founded by Dominic of Guzman.

sermons, were disseminated. Extant texts, whether sermons (although none
remains from the 1145 campaign itself), hagiographic and chronicle accounts,
or letters allow for reconstructing Bernard's preaching. Sermons recorded at
Albi, Sarlat, and an unidentified location demonstrate the power of Bernard's
words and miracles, his reliance on traditional themes and imagery and his
impressive performative skill. An account from Verfeil reveals that in spite of
all that, he sometimes failed to persuade his audience and left town
unsuccessful.

Deconstructing the letters and other sources demonstrates how scriptural
texts and imagery, familiar from the Bible as well as patristic writings against
heresy, were exploited to strengthen the arguments countering heresy, which
grew in subsequent decades into a dossier of anti-heretical writings: a web of
highly charged symbols expanded into a polemical net designed to trap
heretics. Underlying the symbols are rhetorical patterns of demonization,
moral and physical pollution, threat to the social order and apocalypticism.
The dissident preacher, epitomized by Henry the monk among others, was cast
as an emissary of Satan, spreading by word and example the poison of false
doctrine and the immorality of false abstinence, and thus overturning the
monastic view of society grounded on obedience to hierarchical order and
signalling the possible coming of the end. Typological thinking transformed
contemporary dissidents labelled heretics into prototypes of Antichrist and

antitypes having a range of scriptural types, such as foxes, serpents, wolves in sheep's clothing, and, as in I Timothy 4.2, those who heed 'deceitful spirits and doctrines of demons' because of their rejection of marriage and certain foods.

Bernard's mission firmly established preaching as an instrument of outside intervention in another region's affairs and set legal precedents for depriving heretics and their supporters of rights. Yet Bernard's views hold contradictions. If his statements opened the door to armed intervention against heresy in Occitania, he did not unequivocally demand it. Like the chimera figure with which he described himself, torn between the monastery and the world, his stance on treatment of heretics moves in two directions. Scholars emphasize one or the other, and his Cistercian successors did likewise, preaching and negotiating, but also taking quasi-military roles, calling for secular force, and eventually returning to an emphasis on pen and pulpit, leaving the preaching fields open for the friars in the thirteenth century. Importantly, Bernard refused roles that his successors adopted; as abbot of Clairvaux he rejected appointment as bishop and as leader of the Third Crusade. When one of his monks became Pope Eugene III, Bernard warned him not to direct the Third Crusade, and Bernard refused to lead the crusading army himself.[1]

Stretching the monastic vocation brought Bernard doubt and anxiety. No such hesitations appear in extant material about Henry of Clairvaux/Albano and Arnaud Amaury of Cîteaux, who departed decisively from the cloister and radically shifted the Cistercian role in Occitania. Henry accompanied the papal legate, Peter of St Chrysogonus, on a preaching mission to Occitania in 1178, an intervention that set the precedent for accepting denunciations in an inquisitorial process. Henry then returned as legate himself in 1181, setting another lamentable milestone as the first papal legate to raise an army and lead an expedition into a Christian land. Between the two missions, Henry played an important role at the Third Lateran Council (1179), where he was named cardinal, and at the 1180 questioning of Valdes. At the Third Lateran Council he helped draft Canon 27 on repressing heresy and denying rights to heretics.

For reconstructing Henry's preaching, we rely on chronicle accounts, praises from Geoffrey of Auxerre in an exegetical sermon series, *exempla*, and letters which, like Bernard's functioned as sermons when they were undoubtedly read aloud. The deconstruction of the extant texts authored by Henry shows an unambiguous position on the call to arms against heresy and the extension of crusade ideology to combat heterodox movements on native soil. Where Bernard hesitated and wavered, expressing contradictory opinions, Henry unflinchingly adopted only one side of Bernard's view and

---

[1] The sources for Bernard's preaching are introduced in Chapter Three, p. 81; the analysis of his rhetoric is summarized at pp. 103–6; and the evaluation of his role is discussed on pp. 106–8.

proceeded determinedly to assume the place that Bernard had refused at the head of troops.

Henry's writings reveal the same patterns of polemic that marked Bernard's anti-heretical works: demonization, pollution, threat to the social order and apocalypticism. Key symbols or biblical types for heretics reappear, such as foxes in the vineyard, wolves and serpents; and agricultural imagery has a pronounced role as it did in Bernard's writings. Yet Henry's symbolic and associative net intensifies. The anti-heretical bestiary expands somewhat to encompass moths, moles, and leopards; and the motif of darkness and evil contrasted with light and truth accentuates the gulf between orthodoxy and heterodoxy.

Particularly significant and disturbing are the destructive images and types, and the arguments that underlie them. Henry calls for avenging wrongs as did Phinehas (Numbers 25) against worshippers of Baal, an epithet Hildegard of Bingen also employs against the Cathars. The two swords image of Luke 22. 38 serves to call for uniting spiritual and temporal powers. David's battle against Goliath and the Philistines provides a violent frame for representing the campaign against heretics, called an army of the perverse. Joseph's coat represents the Church: rent, spotted and dishonoured, like the robe that *Ecclesia* laments in Hildegard of Bingen's portrayal of her distress over corrupted clergy and their neglect of heresy. Henry connects the ever evil type of the serpent to Sodom and Gomorrah and then links the cities with contemporary heretics, adding a violently punitive dimension to accusations of sexual impurity aimed at heretics. The close connection that Henry makes between 1178 Cathars and dwellers in Sodom and Gomorrah implies a sort of genealogy of sexual behaviour and dissident belief, and an implicit call for destruction whose violent rhetoric surpasses the accusations of immorality that Bernard of Clairvaux made in his letters. Moreover, Henry expresses contempt for Eastern influence, because the serpent rises from that direction. Finally, Henry associates heretics with lepers, an image that appears frequently in anti-heretical literature but does not figure in Bernard's writings against Occitanian heretics.[2]

Joining Henry of Albano in suppressing the Waldensians and attacking the Cathars were other Cistercians – bishops, abbots and intellectuals. Ponce, abbot of Clairvaux before his appointment as bishop of Clermont, banished women Waldensian preachers from that city. Geoffrey of Auxerre, former secretary to Bernard of Clairvaux and then abbot of Clairvaux and Hautecombe himself, took up his pen against both the followers of Valdes and Joachim of Fiore. Geoffrey denounces heresy in his accounts of Bernard's

---

[2] Analysis of sources on Henry of Clairvaux appears on pp. 112–13. Bernard of Clairvaux's denunciations of sexual immorality among the dissidents are analyzed on pp. 87–8. Hildegard's visions are analyzed in Kienzle's articles, cited on p. 14, n. 12.

preaching in the Midi (in the *Vita prima*). His exegetical sermon series on Revelation contains praises of Henry of Albano and vehement denunciations of Waldensian preachers, particularly two women whom he compares to Jezebel, resuscitated as a prostitute-preacher. Such unauthorized preachers were ravaging the Lord's vineyard in France, according to Geoffrey. Alan of Lille, a former university master and leading writer who joined the Cistercian Order near the end of his life, authored the important *Summa de arte praedicatoria*, a foundational work in the history of preaching manuals and one which devotes attention to heretical preachers. Alan also composed a lengthy treatise against the Waldensians, Cathars, Jews, and Muslims, expanding the academic underpinnings of prejudice against all who did not embrace orthodox Christianity. Alan's works have appeared in the background of this study: we have no evidence that he actually preached against heresy in Occitania, but he certainly provided fuel for preachers, as did Geoffrey of Auxerre, whose *exempla* reappear in the sermons of Hélinand of Froidmont. Alan also translated another Cistercian's vernacular sermon into Latin. The former university master constructed a repertoire of anti-heretical arguments and rhetorical figures which, with other treatises, supplied thirteenth-century preachers and inquisitors with extensive materials.[3]

Following Henry of Clairvaux's engagement in the fight against heresy and the peak of Alan of Lille's and Geoffrey of Auxerre's writing, Arnaud Amaury, abbot of Grandselve and afterwards Cîteaux, then papal legate (1204–14) and the archbishop of Narbonne (1212–25), became the major Cistercian actor in Occitania. He followed and joined the Cistercian legates Ralph of Fontfroide and Peter of Castelnau, whose murder precipitated the crusade after the preaching missions failed. Arnaud Amaury preached, recruited preachers for the campaign and also appeared at the head of armies. As abbot of Grandselve, he may have preached the one extant sermon that shows us how theological debates in learned circles were translated into everyday terms for lay people. Arnaud Amaury's involvement as legate coincided with Innocent III's push for widespread reform and crusading against the church's enemies, in which the campaign against heresy occupied a key position. After the sack of Béziers in 1209, Amaury reported to Innocent III a massacre of staggering proportions, giving no indication of regret or that he or anyone else tried to stop the killing. Instead he claimed the city's taking as a 'great miracle' and the product of divine vengeance. In 1212 Amaury led a corps of knights from France into Spain to take part in the battle of Las Navas de Tolosa, boasting in his report to the pope that a three-part war was being waged against the heresy of southern France, Eastern schismatics and Islam. Arnaud Amaury, replaced as legate in 1214, spent the next decade as archbishop of Narbonne, attempting to wrest

---

[3] On Geoffrey of Auxerre, see Chapter Three (on the *Vita prima*, pp. 92–3); and Chapter Four, pp. 129–30. For Alan of Lille, see pp. 131, 172–3.

secular power away from Simon of Montfort and then Simon's son, Amaury, before his death at Fontfroide in 1225.[4]

More or less contemporaneous with Arnaud Amaury, other Cistercians continued the preaching campaign, notably Guy, abbot of les Vaux-de-Cernay and then bishop of Carcassonne, and Fulk, abbot of Le Thoronet appointed bishop of Toulouse. Guy appears in the sources as a preacher primarily, not a participant in military action. He had close ties to the Montfort family, whose land neighboured the abbey of les Vaux-de-Cernay in northern France. The abbey and its neighbours lent strong support to the crusade; and Guy and Simon served together in the Fourth Crusade before undertaking the campaign in Occitania. Fulk was much more controversial than Guy of les Vaux-de-Cernay. He worked at solidifying a corps of anti-heretical preachers, thereby supporting the early Dominicans, but he also led troops and aroused so much hostility in his own city that he had to move about with armed guards. Both Guy and Fulk conducted recruiting campaigns in northern France, and spent some of their tenure as bishop in exile.[5]

Both had sympathetic chroniclers to record their deeds, whereas Arnaud Amaury did not. His preaching and military deeds are reconstructed primarily from letters, his and Innocent III's. In contrast. the *Hystoria Albigensis* was authored by Peter of les Vaux-de-Cernay, Guy's nephew, and William of Puylaurens, Fulk's chronicler, left an invaluable resource for historians. Another source that sheds light on Arnaud Amaury and Fulk is the *Canso de la crozada*, an epic poem with two authors, the first of whom was sympathetic to the crusaders while the second opposed and denounced them vehemently. Caesarius of Heisterbach's *Dialogus miraculorum* provides some of the most notorious tales from the crusade, including the words attributed to Arnaud Amaury at Béziers, 'Kill them all . . .', and stories of sacrilegious abuse of Christian symbols. Because we have few sources from the pens of Arnaud Amaury, Guy and Fulk, there is more material overall for recon-struction of their activities than for deconstruction of their writings.

Henry of Clairvaux, Arnaud Amaury, Guy of les Vaux-de-Cernay and Fulk of Toulouse were somehow linked to the circle of Peter the Chanter in Paris – Henry, Guy and Fulk through personal acquaintances, and Arnaud Amaury at the least by his contact with Innocent III and the papal reform and crusade agenda, formed in part in Parisian circles. The conceptual interrelatedness of the crusade theatres and the crucial role of preaching in propagating crusade and reform needs underscoring again. A guide for preachers, the *Brevis ordinacio de predicacione crucis*, which pertains primarily to preaching the Eastern crusade, nonetheless contains *exempla* related to the Albigensian crusade and thereby demonstrates the ideological connection between the

---

[4] On Arnaud Amaury, see Chapter Five, pp. 138–61.
[5] On Guy and Fulk, see Chapter Five, pp. 161–71.

two as facets of one holy endeavour.[6] Moreover, several preachers engaged in proclaiming both causes.

Three of the four Cistercians whom we studied after Bernard of Clairvaux – Henry of Clairvaux/Albano, Arnaud Amaury and Guy of les Vaux-de-Clernay – were involved in more than one arena of crusade preaching. Bernard himself preached the crusade to the Holy Land after his mission to Occitania in the summer of 1145; news that Edessa fell reached Eugene III in the autumn of that same year. Response to the papal appeal for an expedition was poor until Bernard exerted his influence in 1147.[7] Henry extended Bernard's work: he composed a major treatise on the theology of crusading, expanding Bernard's notion of penance and opening oneself to the risk of martyrdom. Henry was granted permission to go to the Holy Land after preaching the Fourth Crusade, but died before the crusades' departure. Thus Henry established his reputation as a preacher in Occitania in 1178, was named cardinal bishop in 1179, and undertook preaching the Third Crusade in 1187–88, after the mission to France in 1181. Guy of les Vaux-de-Cernay's career moved in the opposite direction. He and Simon of Montfort worked together during the Fourth Crusade, and Guy then preached the Albigensian Crusade but did not wish to return to the Holy Land.

Meanwhile other Cistercians engaged in preaching the Eastern crusade. Baldwin of Ford, archbishop of Canterbury, made a preaching tour in Wales, then died in Acre in 1190. Martin, Cistercian abbot of Pairis (Alsace), also served as a crusade preacher under Innocent III.[8] Arnaud Amaury was not involved in preaching the crusade to the Holy Land, but he articulated the interrelatedness of the arenas of crusade preaching, and he engaged in the crusade against Muslims in Spain, to the point of leading an army himself into the battle of Las Navas de Tolosa.

These connections demonstrate how preaching against heresy formed part of the church's wider programme for crusade and reform. Historians generally agree on Innocent III's crucial role in formulating and impelling an agenda that incorporated crusading against dissidents and Muslims in Western Europe, the Balkans, and the Holy Land. Assessments of Innocent III vary according to reactions to his dogged push for a multi-faced crusade, but a consensus emphasizes the strong determination and organization of his programme. Given that usury constituted another important target for papal reform, Jews also suffered as a result of the papal agenda, because of both their association with money-lending and the extension of the crusades' hostile vengeance against those perceived as the enemies of Christen-

---

[6] On the Cistercians and Peter the Chanter's circle, see Chapter Four, p. 131; Chapter Five, pp. 162, 171–3; and Chapter Six, pp. 207, 209. Cole analyses the *Brevis ordinacio* in *Preaching*, pp. 110–11, 125.

[7] See Cole, *Preaching*, pp. 37–43.

[8] On Cistercians preaching the crusade to Jerusalem, see Cole, *Preaching*, pp. 40–61, 65–79, and *passim*.

dom.[9] Our study has highlighted Innocent III's agenda as the background for preaching against heresy, as well as the relentless pressure he exerted on the Cistercians throughout his papacy. It emerges as a driving force behind their engagement in southern France.

Yet Cistercian involvement in Occitania began more than fifty years before Innocent III's papacy and continued after it, first through bishops named during his tenure: Arnaud Amaury, archbishop of Narbonne; Guy of Carcassonne; and Fulk of Toulouse, for example. Fulk played different roles throughout the crusade years, as preacher, bishop, leader and recruiter of troops, and he acted as a bridge between the pre-crusade years of wider Cistercian preaching to the period of the royal crusade and treaty negotiations. He also facilitated the introduction of Dominican preaching and teaching against heresy in Toulouse. His role in making the transition from Cistercian to Dominican leadership was capped by his designation of a Dominican as the successor to his see.[10]

When the university was founded at Toulouse in 1229, according to the provisions of the Treaty of Paris/Meaux, Cistercians played key roles. Fulk returned form exile; Hélie, abbot of Grandselve, oversaw the appointing of the masters, who were recruited at Paris and among the early Dominicans; Hélinand of Froidmont issued the academic charge to the new students and masters and preached to the synod that met to promulgate legislation against heresy. He must have worked side by side for a time with the early Dominican masters at the new university, as did Fulk, and as past Cistercian legates preached with Dominic at the beginning of the thirteenth century. Like other Cistercians before him, Hélinand had ties to Peter the Chanter's circle and to the upper echelons of French nobility. Unlike some of his Cistercian predecessors, Hélinand took no part in military endeavours.

Hélinand's extant sermons preached at Toulouse provide substantial material for analysing what this Cistercian preacher thought about heresy and what sort of rhetoric he used. Of the four rhetorical patterns we have traced, he relies most heavily on demonization, with apocalyptic overtones when he associates heretical preachers with Antichrist. Language of pollution and threat to the social order does not figure as saliently as it does in the writings of his predecessors. Hélinand's interest in the history of heresy also differentiates him from earlier Cistercians; he traces the Eastern roots of severe asceticism instead of denouncing Eastern origins as pernicious and polluting. Hélinand constitutes the last major Cistercian figure to represent the order in the anti-heretical campaigns surrounding the Albigensian crusade.[11]

---

[9] See Chazan, *Stereotypes*, pp. 100–7. Among the many other views of Innocent III, see Grundmann, *Movements*, pp. 31–7; Cole, *Preaching*, pp. 139–41; Maier, *Mendicant Friars*, pp. 2–3, J. M. Powell, 'Innocent III and the Crusade', in *Innocent III*, ed. J. M. Powell (Washington, D.C., 1994), pp. 121–34.

[10] Raimund du Fauga, the Dominican provincial. See Biget, *Cisterciens*, CaF, p. 357.

[11] On Hélinand of Froidmont, see pp. 174–201.

The Cistercians passed the responsibility for public preaching against heresy and in favour of the crusades to the mendicant orders, chiefly the Dominicans but also the Franciscans. St Francis embarked to the Holy Land himself twice, as far as we know, before finally arriving at Damietta in July 1219. The Franciscan Order became involved in anti-heretical preaching later than the Dominicans but played an influential role, especially in Italy. St Dominic was a member of the papal legation against the Albigensian heresy from 1205 to 1215, and, as we have noted, received strong support from Fulk of Toulouse. Although no records establish that Dominic preached the crusade, he did not disassociate himself from the crusaders. In fact, some evidence indicates that he stayed at times with the crusading armies and his religious community of Prouille benefited from donations from crusaders, including Simon of Montfort. Dominic baptized Simon's daughter and performed the marriage of his son. One of Dominic's biographers, Gerard of Fracheto, teamed the two men in his remark that Simon fought with the 'material sword' and Dominic with the 'sword of the word of God'. Thirteenth-century popes recruited Dominicans and Franciscans for preaching the crusade to the Holy Land, the Baltic, and against heresy. Cistercians were also summoned at times, but the friars dominated the campaigns.[12]

After Innocent III's papacy, the legislative campaign to combat heresy was renewed by Honorius III (1216–27). Innocent III's inconsistent efforts in Italy were resisted strongly by the communes, but the migration of Occitanian Cathars into northern Italy increased the presence of the counter-church there and the papacy responded. The friars undertook influential preaching campaigns to swing public opinion toward enforcement of already existing legislation against heresy or enactment of new laws.[13] Concern with heresy remained relatively consistent in Germany, where the writings of the Cistercian prior, Caesarius of Heisterbach were widely disseminated. Attention to the Eastern crusade eclipsed the effort against heresy again in 1221, but Gregory VIII, Honorius's successor, resumed the legal assault on heresy, establishing Dominicans as inquisitors first in Germany with *Ille humani generis* (1231).[14]

A permanent tribunal of inquisition functioned first, however, in Occitania in 1233–34. In 1233 Gregory IX ordered that friars be sent to the archdioceses of Bourges, Bordeaux, Narbonne, and Auch to aid bishops in

---

[12] Maier, *Mendicant Friars*, p. 18. On early Dominican and Franciscan preaching, see Maier, *Mendicant Friars*, p. 9.

[13] See P. D. Diehl, 'Overcoming Reluctance to Prosecute Heresy in Thirteenth-Century Italy', in Waugh and Diehl, pp. 58–62, on preaching and legislation against heresy in thirteenth-century Italy. The dual affront of preaching and inquisition provoked popular revolts, but at the same time and in conjunction with papal pressure, Italian communes began to repress dissent, and enactment of laws against heresy continued into the fourteenth century.

[14] Peters, *Inquisition*, p. 55.

the battle against heresy. Accounts remain from this period for inquisitorial proceedings in Toulouse and Albi. Local protests against the inquisitors began shortly thereafter, and the townspeople of Narbonne reacted violently during the years 1234 to 1237. In at least two cases, the abbot of the Cistercian monastery of Grandselve was enlisted to investigate inquisitors' abuses.[15] Dominicans were expelled from Toulouse in 1235, but the city suffered persecution of the living and the exhumed dead from 1237 to early 1238. Occitanian nobles defied the French twice more in 1240 and 1242, but unsuccessfully. Meanwhile the inquisitors renewed their activities with fierce determination from 1241 onward at various sites. Acts of resistance to the inquisitors continued, and some were murdered at Avignonet in 1242. But the last strongholds of Cathar sympathizers were soon to fall, Montségur in 1244 and Quéribus in 1255.[16]

Under Innocent IV's papacy (1243–54), earlier procedures of inquisition were melded into formalized office, the 'inquisitor of heretical depravity'. A body of literature was assembled to provide manuals for inquisitors, including the noteworthy short manual from Carcassonne (1248–49) and extending to the lengthy manual of Bernard Gui (1323–14).[17]

Pope Alexander IV granted inquisitors broader powers in 1256. Although heresy was waning, the inquisitorial commissions continued, examining earlier proceedings and opening posthumous investigations. One of those concerned Peter Aymeric, accused of dying a heretic. Around 1297/98, his daughter enlisted the aid of Arnaud Nouvel, abbot of Fontfroide, who assisted in having the accusations overturned. The abbot, the uncle of Jacques Fournier, was named cardinal in 1310; he also intervened in other cases, notably one against the count of Foix, accused of heresy by a monk of Boulbonne in 1293.[18]

The inquisition found new interrogants when a revival of Catharism took place in Occitania during the early fourteenth century, after the return from Italy of the preacher Peter Authié. Under the papacy of John XXII, a Cistercian again assumed leadership in the anti-heretical campaign. Jacques Fournier, bishop of Pamiers and Mirepoix, conducted inquisitorial hearings from 1318 to 1325, leaving extensive registers that were edited by Jean Duvernoy and provided Emmanuel Le Roy Ladurie with the material for his *Montaillou: village occitan*.[19] A monk at the Cistercian abbey of Boulbonne,

---

[15] Mousnier, 'Grandselve', p. 123.

[16] Wakefield provides an excellent account of these events in *Heresy, Crusade, and Inquisition*, pp. 146–73.

[17] See Peters, *Inquisition*, pp. 58–60. Numerous excerpts from inquisitorial manuals are collected and translated in WE.

[18] F. J. Felten, 'Arnaud Nouvel, *doctor legum*, moine de Boulbonne, abbé de Fontfroide et cardinal († 1317),' in *Cistercians*, CaF, pp. 208–14.

[19] Wakefield, *Heresy, Crusade, and Inquisition*, pp. 188–9. Peters, *Inquisition*, p. 73. J. Duvernoy, ed., *Les registres d'inquisition de Jacques Fournier*, 3 vols. (Toulouse, 1965), E. L. R. Ladurie, *Montaillou: village occitan de 1294 à 1324* (Paris, 1978).

Fournier graduated as a master of theology from the Cistercian College of Saint Bernard in Paris, established in the mid-thirteenth century. He became abbot of Fontfroide in 1311, upon his uncle's election as cardinal. Elected bishop of Pamiers in 1317 and of Mirepoix in 1326, he was named cardinal in 1327, resided in Avignon and served as Pope Benedict XII from 1334 to 1342. Remembered also for his efforts at financial and educational reform, he authored a number of works, including sermons and treatises against heresy. A treatise he is known to have composed against the Fraticelli is not extant.[20]

By the end of the fourteenth century, Catharism had been eliminated. The year 1321 marked the burning of the last known Cathar perfect, William Bélibaste, in the town of Villerouge-Termenès, which now holds a medieval festival recalling that event.[21] The Cistercians retained a strong presence in Occitania and continued a course that has been characterized as 'anti-méridionale' and 'profrançais' in collaborating with Capetian lords who established the new towns called 'bastides' on Cistercian properties – forty-four of them between 1252 and 1328. Charles Higounet has scrutinized the transactions and concludes that the anti-Cathar stance of the Cistercians was converted into pro-French sentiment, explaining the high percentage of 'bastides' established on Cistercian land in Occitania and not elsewhere. Moreover, the white monks found in the exchange a solution to their economic problems.[22]

Medieval dissidence regained force in other areas during the fourteenth and fifteenth centuries, however, and Cistercians were not absent from those conflicts. From the time of Jacques Fournier at least, the university provided an entry for later medieval white monks into the debates over heresy. The Collège Saint Bernard was founded in 1224, followed by colleges at Montpellier and Estella in 1260–62, and Toulouse and Oxford in 1280. Benedict XII's reforming constitution, *Fulgens sicut stella*, organized the colleges in 1335, specifying that the best students be sent to Paris. When the Collège Saint Bernard was established, Cistercian students at Paris were entitled to the responsibilities and privileges of the mendicants, notably public preaching.[23] How that was exercised is a topic for further study. In any case, the university was a centre for involvement of fourteenth- and fifteenth-century Cistercians in debates over heresy. Two Cistercians at Oxford, Henry Crump and William Rymington, are remembered for their opposition to the teachings of John Wyclif – Crump for a sermon at St Mary's church against Wyclif's views and for subsequent accusations of heresy that Crump himself suffered during a quarrel with the mendicants. In fifteenth-century Prague,

[20] Lekai, *The Cistercians*, p. 238; *Dictionnaire des auteurs cisterciens*, pp. 98–9.
[21] In August 1996, I had the pleasure of speaking with Anne Brenon in Villerouge-Termenès.
[22] Higounet, 'Nouvelles réflexions', pp. 127–37.
[23] C. Obert-Piketty, 'Benoît XII et les collèges cisterciens du Languedoc,' in *Cisterciens*, CaF, pp. 140–1.

when the Hussites obtained control of the university, some Cistercians were expelled: notably in 1411 Matthew Steynhus of Königsaal (Bohemia), who then moved to Altzelle, helped to organize the Cistercian college at Leipzig and preached before the Council of Constance in 1417.[24] Generally, while some research has been done on these and other late medieval Cistercians,[25] their lives and writings largely have been overshadowed by their predecessors of the twelfth century. Although the friars dominated late medieval investigations and preaching against heresy, the Cistercians did not disappear entirely from the scene, and more work needs to be done on their role in the late Middle Ages.

After reviewing Cistercian activities against heresy from 1145 to 1229, the focal period for our study, and looking ahead somewhat to the end of the Middle Ages, we will now assess the reconstruction and deconstruction of the sources for this book.

For reconstructing Cistercian preaching during the period investigated here, I have relied on a variety of texts and not merely on sermons. In fact, sermons preached as part of these Cistercian anti-heretical campaigns are rarely extant. One preached in a church at Montpellier remains, as do four delivered in 1229 at Toulouse by Hélinand of Froidmont. The latter four, while anti-heretical, do not exemplify the sort of preaching in the field that one would wish to capture. In contrast, historians of preachers from the secular clergy and especially the mendicant orders have many more resources extant and the available material has not yet been mined extensively.[26]

Still, even when the desired type of sermon is extant, scholars need to consult sources beyond the sermons themselves in order to reconstruct the sermons' environment: the rhetorical circumstances of its delivery and the wider world of its author. Sermonists currently investigate sermon texts in various phases of redaction, such as summaries, outlines, *reportationes* or transcriptions in note form, and model sermons – expanded outlines designed to be converted into the spoken word. They also adduce related evidence from synodal statutes, canonization proceedings, university

---

[24] Lekai, *Cistercians*, p. 240; on Crump, see *Dictionary of National Biography*, ed. L. Stephen and S. Lee, 64 vols. (London, 1885–1900), V, 262–3; and on Steynhus, 'Matthieu de Zbraslav', *Dictionnaire des auteurs cisterciens*, col. 488. Rymington is mentioned for his argument with Wyclif in A. Hudson, 'John Wyclif', in *Dictionary of the Middle Ages*, ed. J. R. Strayer, 13 vols. (New York, 1982–9), XII, 709.

[25] T. Falmagne, 'Les instruments de travail d'un prédicateur cistercien. À propos de Jean Vilers (mort en 1336 ou 1346)', in *De l'homélie au sermon. Histoire de la prédication médiévale. Actes du Colloque International de Louvain-la-Neuve (9–11 juillet 1992)*, ed. J. Hamesse and X. Hermand (Louvain-la-Neuve, 1993), pp. 183–238.

[26] See N. Bériou, 'La prédication de croisade de Philippe le Chancellier et d'Eudes de Châteauroux en 1226', in *Prédication*, CaF, pp. 85–110; and C. Maier, *Crusade Propaganda and Ideology. Model Sermons for the Preaching of the Cross* (Cambridge, 2000), pp. 21, 222–7.

records, chronicles, *exempla* collections, hagiographical narratives, and other compilations that furnished material for preachers. Recognizing that medieval genres possessed fluid boundaries, sermonists also probe treatises, letters, and commentaries, which often stand close to the sermon genre, separated only by marks of performance, such as any recorded audience interjection, and signs of orality like exhortation and direct address. Evidence indicates that authors often composed in more than one genre and readily transposed passages from one to another of their works. Hence writing a history of preaching does not mean relying solely on sermons.

After the preceding discussion of the methodology of sermonists, in as far as it concerns the multiplicity of sources, we shall look now at the reconstructive work on the sources for this book. I reconstructed Bernard of Clairvaux's preaching against heresy from epistolary sermons written Everwin of Steinfeld; a hagiographical text – the *Vita prima*; *exempla* found within a sort of hagiographic chronicle – the *Exordium magnum*; letters that surely served for public reading; and a later chronicle by William of Puylaurens. A picture of the preaching done by Henry of Clairvaux/ Albano emerges from piecing together similar sources: letters written by Henry and his colleague, some of which must have been designed for public reading; chronicle accounts; *exempla*, including some from the *Exordium magnum*; passages within Geoffrey of Auxerre's exegetical sermons on Revelation; and the canons of the Third Lateran Council (1179), which Henry doubtless had a hand in drafting. A chronicle, the *Hystoria Albigensis*, by Peter of les Vaux-de-Cernay serves as the primary source for reconstructing the preaching done by early thirteenth-century legates to Occitania and by the leading figures Arnaud Amaury, Guy of les Vaux-de-Cernay and Fulk of Toulouse. The epic poem, *Canso de la crozada*, supplements that material, as do other chronicles, and letters and reports written by Arnaud Amaury. Caesarius of Heisterbach's *Dialogus miraculorum* sheds important light on the Cistercian mentality by illustrating the types of crusade stories that circulated. Writings from other ecclesiastical figures, notably Innocent III and Alan of Lille, elucidate the struggles behind the scenes and the conceptual framework for extant texts. Finally, for Hélinand of Froidmont's preaching, we benefit from actual sermons as well as cross-references to his *Chronicon*.

In sum, as a historian of preaching, I have first woven together many diverse threads to assemble the tapestry of the preaching that the Cistercians carried out between 1145 and 1229 in Occitania. The deconstruction of these varied texts aims to unravel the same cloth in a different fashion, not by generic categories of texts or comparison of events narrated, as in the first reconstructive task, but by common rhetorical patterns: threads beneath the coherent appearance of the surface. These may derive from earlier texts, scriptural authorities, or current ideas and experiences. They give the text its tenor, and when unravelled, reveal the depth of its messages and the strategies utilized to convey them.

We traced four overarching rhetorical patterns that reappear in anti-heretical texts: demonization, pollution, threat to the social order and apocalypticism. All converge to portray heretics in general, and unauthorized preachers in particular, as allies of the Devil, contaminated as if with a highly contagious disease, threatening to overturn established order and usher in the fearful era preceding the end of time. Within the bounds of these four patterns, more specific accusations appear. These follow certain polarities, usually contradictory, as when heretics are depicted as menacing for their simultaneous stupidity and astuteness, or for spreading their doctrines both privately or publicly. They include the opposite elements of: learning and ignorance, urban and rural, elite and popular, public and private, and West and East. Within the rhetorical patterns and the more specific accusations, we find recurrent images and authorities, primarily from Scripture. Anti-heretical authors portray their targets with images and animals such as foxes (Song of Songs 2. 15), serpents (Psalm 9. 29), dogs (II Peter 2. 22), wolves in sheep's clothing (Matthew 7. 15), and the like. Scriptural authorities that emerge frequently include passages referring to the preceding animals as well as: the Parable of the tares (Matthew 13. 24–30, 36–52); I Timothy 4. 2, those who heed 'deceitful spirits and doctrines of demons'; and II Timothy 2. 17, on words that spread like gangrene. Furthermore, typologies of good and evil loom large in some of the texts, as does military imagery, derived from real life and from scriptural citations to the Israelites and their enemies. For Henry of Clairvaux/Albano, Arnaud Amaury and Fulk of Toulouse, this militant imagery spilled over into real life as well.

All these patterns, images, and authorities combine to create a hostile and often violent rhetoric that launches verbal weapons at dissidents. Coupled with the reality of the persecutions that took place, it seems unavoidably to have contributed to the deaths of heretics. Some writers more than others utilize inflammatory rhetoric, and a few surpassed it by undertaking military actions.

In contrast, some evidence points to Cistercians who sympathized with the Cathars or with the southern lords, the 'faidits'. The Cistercian *Statutes* in 1218 refer to discipline against monks at Boulbonne who supported the count of Foix, and against the abbot of Belperche who argued for the orthodoxy of the count of Toulouse and his son (Raymond VI and VII). Another statute from 1218 prescribes punishment for monks or lay brothers who protect heretics. Such legislation indicates that dissenters, protectors or sympathizers of the Cathars must have existed. Unfortunately, we know little more than that.[27]

---

[27] Canivez, *Statuta*, p. 489, 1218.24; p. 491, 1218.35; p. 510, 1219.36. See J. Duvernoy, 'Boulbonne et le Lauragais au XIIIe siècle', in *Le Lauragais, Histoire et Archéologie* (Montpellier, 1983), pp. 110–13. D. Baker points out evidence for heretical monks at

Apart from Bernard of Clairvaux's striking contradictions, the voices of the hesitant Cistercians left us little in the way of written documents. Moreover, the everyday life of Occitanian Cistercian houses during this period has been lost to us, for the most part. Some abbeys prospered from crusaders' donations: donations to les Vaux-de-Cernay and Froidmont are cited among our sources. Nonetheless, destructive consequences and fears also beset Cistercian abbeys because of the order's support for the crusade; these surface from the documents of Grandselve. One wishes for more records of the legates' pleas to return to the monastery, for a transcription of the deliberations from the general chapters, for the thoughts of the abbots who returned home from the 1206 preaching mission. Further research may one day locate documents that could identify dissenting Cistercian voices and clarify doubts that lay behind or even contradicted the strident voices we have retrieved. The existing record at least demonstrates that this period of intense activity outside the monastery was not the norm for a contemplative order founded on a charter of charity, whose greatest writers sang of divine love and exalted human friendship.

To simplify the overall pattern that emerges from analysis of the Cistercian role in public preaching against heresy and related endeavours, we observe fluctuations that end with Hélinand of Froidmont's preaching in a university and synodal context, while public preaching and inquisition were consigned to the friars. After the initial tension and contradiction apparent in Bernard of Clairvaud, we witness the headlong plunge into action with Henry of Clairvaux/Albano, followed by hesitation, then renewed preaching, under pressure from Innocent III. Deeper engagement in military action also ensues under Arnaud Amaury, but evidence of hesitation surfaces with the abbots who went back to Cîteaux discouraged. Bishop Fulk of Toulouse, while sometimes taking a military role, emphasizes preaching and assists the foundation of the Dominican order. The return to an emphasis on influential preaching alone occurs with Hélinand of Froidmont in 1229, the end of the crusade. Hélinand's Toulouse sermons point to a model for future Cistercians based on the mendicants' teaching and preaching in the university context, but not on their popular preaching and inquisitorial leadership.

Recourse to the defamatory and persecutory rhetoric that we have heard and analysed springs from the authors' convictions that the targeted persons deserve to be classified as heretics. This may occur from prior prejudice or be set in motion by conclusions based on elements of belief and practice, notably: the Trinity and the nature of Christ; the role of the sacraments; the role of the saints and the dead; ascetically practices; the role and responsibility for evangelism; morality and the interpretation of the virtues of

the abbey of Gondon in the 1230s. 'Heresy and learning in early cistercianism', in *Schism, Heresy and Religious Protest*. Papers Read at the Tenth Summer Meeting and the Eleventh Winter Meeting of the Ecclesiastical History Society, ed. D. Baker (Cambridge, 1972), pp. 93–108.

poverty, chastity, obedience and humility. Although I have not focused on the retrieval of dissidents' beliefs from texts written by the opposition, some observations on heretical tenets and practices emerge from the writings of Bernard of Clairvaux, Henry of Clairvaux/Albano, Peter of les Vaux-de-Cernay and especially Hélinand of Froidmont. The latter's view of Cathar beliefs lies fairly close to the information that historians glean from actual Cathar texts.

Readers may quite legitimately ask what the heretics had to say about the orthodox polemicists. Most extant texts of dissident origin, apart from the Cathar–Bogomil visionary works, date from the later Middle Ages and not from the focal period of this book. Anne Brenon has edited Waldensian sermons and supplemented René Nelli's translations into French of extant Cathar works in Latin and Occitan. The available sources show some of the same images as in orthodox texts and a dominating typology of good and evil, but these are reversed and function defensively and not offensively, that is, not linked to extending and maintaining power but to coping with persecution. Fifteenth-century sermons from Waldensians taking refuge from the Inquisition in the Piedmontese Alps accuse the Roman Church of being a persecutor as pitiless as the Antichrist. A Cathar treatise denounces the Roman Church for its attempted domination of pagans, Jews and foreigners ('pagans e Judios e gentils'). Its priests claim to be sheep, the Cathar author writes, but act like wolves. Unlike the Cathar treatise, the Waldensian author shares the prejudices of orthodox medieval writers, grouping Jews and Muslims together as murderous persecutors. Cathar and Waldensian texts ground themselves on Acts 14. 21: one reaches the kingdom of God only by enduring persecution. A Waldensian treatise ascribes a penitential value to suffering and concludes that persecution distinguishes the good from the evil: clearly the evil persecute the good. Cathar opinions join the Waldensian in observing that the true church has been persecuted since the time of Christ (John 15. 20); the sheep have had to deal with wolves (Matthew 10. 16). Both groups stress that the wheat will be separated from the tares at the last Judgment; on earth no Christian should take up arms against anyone. Despite the prejudices in the Waldensian text and differences in theology on the penitential value of suffering, the Judgment and the existence of the Antichrist, the overriding impression of these texts from the dissidents is that they, like their orthodox Catholic opponents, considered themselves true Christians. The harsh reality of persecution only confirmed that view. Dissidents found parallels between their suffering at the hands of persecutors and that of the early Christians. Thus the dissidents' reasons for calling the inquisitors wolves relates to their persecution and not to accusations of deception and the like; the images serve to strengthen their resoluteness in the face of persecution and not to launch, incite, or even support real assaults on their opponents. For that reason, I distinguish between the dissidents' defensive use of rhetoric and the orthodox clergy's offensive rhetorical attack. Surely words spoken from a position of power with the capacity to actualize them wield more force in their day than those uttered by the powerless.

After numerous pages probing the complexities of the Cistercians' role in the anti-heretical campaigns, the dissidents' words, particularly the Cathar plea for tolerance of all persons, haunt us with their simplicity and their sharp distinction between persecutors and persecuted. I close with Peter Authié's words that 'one church takes possession and flays, the other takes refuge [cf. Matthew 10. 23] and forgives'.[28]

---

[28] A. Brenon, 'Christianisme et tolérance dans les textes cathares et vaudois du bas moyen âge', in *Ketzerei und Ketzerbekämpfung in Wort und Text*, ed. P. Blumenthal and J. Kramer (Stuttgart, 1989), pp. 65–77. Cathar treatise, 'L'Eglise de Dieu', in *Ecritures cathares*, ed. and trans. R. Nelli, new edn, ed. A. Brenon (Monaco, 1995), pp. 274–88. P. Authié in *Ecritures cathares*, p. 330.

BIBLIOGRAPHY

Unpublished primary sources

London, British Library, Cotton Claudius B IX.
Paris, Bibliothèque Nationale, MS Lat. 14591
Paris, Bibliothèque Nationale, MS Lat. 14859
Paris, Bibliothèque Mazarine, MS 1041
Rome, Vatican Library, Reg. lat. 535
Toulouse, Bibliothèque Municipale, MS 609

Published primary sources

Acta Iohannis, ed. E. Junod and J.-D. Kaestli, Corpus Christianorum, Series Apocryphorum (Turnhout, 1983).
'Acts of Peter', in The *Ante-Nicene Fathers VIII*, ed. A. Roberts, J. Donaldson and A. C. Coxe (Grand Rapids, MI, 1951).
Adam of Perseigne, *The Letters of Adam of Perseigne*, trans. G. Perigo, Cistercian Fathers 21 (Kalamazoo, MI, 1976).
Alan of Lille, 'Rhythmus alter', *PL*, CCX, 579.
Alan of Lille, 'Summa quadrapartita (Summa contra haereticos)', *PL*, CCX, 303–430.
Augustine of Hippo, *Commentaire de la Première Epître de S. Jean*, trans. P. Agaësse, SC 75 (Paris, 1984).
Augustine of Hippo, *Love One Another, My Friends. St Augustine's Homilies on the First Letter of John*, trans. J. Leinenweber (San Francisco, 1989).
Augustine of Hippo, *On Christian Doctrine,* trans. D. W. Robertson, Jr (Indianapolis, 1958).
Augustine of Hippo, *Sancti Aurelii Augustini Opera.* Pars XIII, 2, CCSL XLVI, *De haeresibus* (Turnhout, 1969).
Bede the Venerable, *Bedae Homiliae evangelii*, ed. D. Hurst, CCSL CXXII (Turnhout, 1955).
——*Homilies on the Gospels*, trans. L. T. Martin and D. Hurst, 2 vols. Cistercian Studies 110–11 (Kalamazoo, MI, 1991).
Bernard of Clairvaux, *Five Books on Consideration: Advice to a Pope*, Cistercian Fathers 37 (Kalamazoo, MI, 1976).
——*The Letters of St Bernard of Clairvaux*, trans. B. S. James, with new introduction by B. M. Kienzle (Stroud, 1998).
——*On the Song of Songs, III*, trans. K. Walsh and I. M. Edmonds, Cistercian Fathers 31 (Kalamazoo, MI, 1991).

Bernard of Clairvaux, *Sancti Bernardi Opera*, ed. J. Leclercq, H.-M. Rochais, and C. H. Talbot, 8 vols. (Rome, 1957–77).

—— *Selected Works*, trans. G. R. Evans (New York, 1987).

—— *Sermons for the Summer Season. Liturgical Sermons from Rogationtide and Pentecost*, trans. with Introduction by B. M. Kienzle, additional translations by J. Jarzembowski, Cistercian Fathers 53 (Kalamazoo, MI, 1991).

—— *Treatises II: The Book on Loving God*, trans. M. A. Conway; *The Steps of Humility and Pride*, trans. R. Walton, Cistercian Fathers 13 (Kalamazoo, MI, 1980).

—— *Treatises III: In Praise of the New Knighthood*, trans. C. Greenia, Cistercian Fathers 19 (Kalamazoo, MI, 1977).

Bernard of Fontcaude, 'Adversus Waldensium sectam', *PL*, CCIV, 795–840.

Caesarius of Heisterbach. *Dialogus Miraculorum*, ed. J. Strange, 2 vols. (Cologne, 1851).

Chaeremon, Egyptian Priest and Stoic Philosopher, ed. P.W. van der Horst (Leiden, 1984).

La Chanson de la croisade albigeoise, ed. E. Martin-Chabot, 3 vols. (Paris, 1931).

La Chanson de la croisade albigeoise, new edn, with translation by H. Gougaud and introduction by M. Zink (Paris, 1989).

'Chronicon Clarevallensis', *PL*, CLXXXV, 1247–51.

Eckbert of Schönau, 'Sermones contra Catharos', *PL*, CXCV, 11–102.

Écritures cathares, ed. and trans. R. Nelli, new edn by A. Brenon (Monaco, 1995).

Etienne de Bourbon, *Anecdotes historiques, légendes et apologues*, ed. A. Lecoy de la Marche (Paris, 1877).

Everwin of Steinfeld, 'Epistola 182', *PL*, CLXXXII, 676–80.

Exordium magnum cisterciense sive narratio de initio cisterciensis ordinis, ed. B. Griesser (Rome, 1961).

Decretum Magistri Gratiani, ed. E. Friedberg, Corpus Iuris Canonici 1 (Leipzig, 1879).

Geoffrey of Auxerre, *Super Apocalypsim*, ed. F. Gastaldelli, Temi e Testi 17 (Rome, 1970).

—— 'Vita prima', *PL*, CLXXXV, 301–68.

Gregory the Great, *Forty Gospel Homilies*, trans. D. Hurst, Cistercian Studies 123 (Kalamazoo, MI, 1990).

—— *Homiliae in Hiezechihelem prophetam*, ed. M. Adriaen, CCSL CXLII (Turnhout, 1971).

—— 'Homiliae XL in evangelia', *PL*, LXXVI, 1075–312.

—— *S. Gregorii Magni Moralia in Iob* Libri I–IX, ed. Marcus Adriaen, CCSL CXLIII (Turnhout, 1979).

Guillaume de Puylaurens, *Chronique, Chronica magistri Guillelmi de Podio Laurentii*, ed. and trans. J. Duvernoy (Paris, 1976).

Hélinand of Froidmont, 'Chronicon', *PL*, CCII, 771–1082.

—— 'Sermones', *PL*, CCXII, 47–720; B. Tissier, *Bibliotheca Patrum Cisterciensium VII* (Bonofontae, 1669), pp. 206–306.

—— *Les Vers de la Mort*, ed. F. Wulff and E. Walberg (Paris, 1905).

Henry of Clairvaux, 'Epistolae 11, 28–9', *PL*, CCIV, 223–5, 234–40.

Hildegard of Bingen, *Epistolarium* I, ed. L. Van Acker, CCCM XCI (Turnhout, 1991).

—— 'Expositiones evangeliorum', ed. J.-B. Pitra, in *Analecta S. Hildegardis*, Analecta sacra 8 (Rome, 1882), pp. 245–327.

Idung of Prufening, *Cistercians and Cluniacs: The Case for Cîteaux. A Dialogue between Two Monks, An Argument on Four Questions*, trans. J. O'Sullivan, J. Leahey and G. Perrigo, Cistercian Fathers 33 (Kalamazoo, MI, 1977).

Innocent III, 'Epistolae', *PL*, CCXV, 273–5, 358–60, 525–6, 940–1, 1246–8, 1358–9.

—— 'Sermones de tempore', *PL*, CCXVII, 309–450.

Isaac of Stella, *Sermons*, I, ed. A. Hoste and G. Salet, SC 130 (Paris, 1967).

—— *Sermons*, III, ed. A. Hoste, G. Raciti, trans. G. Salet, G. Raciti, SC 339 (Paris, 1987).

Isidore of Seville, *Etymologiarum sive originum Libri XX,* ed. W. M. Lindsay, 2 vols. (Oxford, 1911).

James of Vitry, *The Historia occidentalis of Jacques de Vitry. A Critical Edition*, ed. J. F. Hinnebusch (Fribourg, 1972).

—— *The Life of Marie d'Oignies*, trans. with introduction and notes by M. H. King (Toronto, 1989).

—— *Vita Mariae Oigniacensis*, ed. D. Papebroeck, in *Acta Sanctorum, Iunius*, v. 5 (June 23) (Paris, 1867).

Jerome, 'Adversus Jovinianum', *PL*, XXIII, 221–352.

—— 'Contra Vigilantium', *PL*, XXIII, 353–68.

John of Salisbury, *Policraticus*, ed. C. C. I. Webb, 2 vols. (Oxford, 1909).

Julien of Vézelay, *Sermons*, ed. D. Vorreux, 2 vols., SC 192–3 (Paris, 1972).

Le livre secret des Cathares. Interrogatio Iohannis, apocryphe d'origine bogomile, ed. and trans. E. Bozoky (Paris, 1980).

Origen, *De Principiis*, H. Crouzel and M. Simonetti, *Origène: Traité des principes*, I, SC 252 (Paris, 1978).

Peter of Celle, 'Epistola 167', *PL*, CCII, 610.

Peter of St Chrysogonus, 'Ad universos fideles', *PL*, CXCIX, 1119–24.

Peter the Venerable, *Tractatus contra Petrobrusianos*, ed. J. Fearns, CCCM X (Turnhout, 1968).

Pierre des Vaux-de-Cernay, *The History of the Albigensian Crusade*, trans. W. A. and M. D. Sibly (Woodbridge, 1998).

—— *Hystoria Albigensis*, ed. P. Guébin and E. Lyon, 3 vols. (Paris, 1926–39).

Rabanus Maurus, 'De universis', *PL*, CXI, 9–614.

Robert of Auxerre, *Chronicon, MGH.SS*, 26 (Hannover, 1882), pp. 219–76.

The Rule of St Benedict, trans. with introduction and notes by A. C. Meisel and M. L. del Mastro (New York, 1975).

Rupert of Deutz, *Commentaria in evangelium sancti Iohannis*, CCCM IX (Turnhout, 1969).

The Song of the Cathar Wars, trans. J. Shirley (Aldershot, 1996).

Thomas of Froidmont, *Lettre à H*, ed. E. Mikkers, 'Een onuitgegeven brief van Thomas van Beverley, monk van Froidmont', in *Cîteaux in de Nederlanden* (1956), pp. 245–63.

The Twelfth-Century Cistercian Hymnal, ed. C. Waddell, 2nd edn, Cistercian Liturgical Series 2 (Trappist, Kentucky, 1984).

Secondary sources

Angleton, C. d'Autremont, 'Two Cistercian Preaching Missions to the Languedoc in the Twelfth Century, 1145 and 1178' (unpublished Ph.D. dissertation, Catholic University of America, 1984).

Ardura, B., *Prémontrés: Histoire et Spiritualité* (Saint-Etienne, 1995).

Armengaud, A. and Lafont, R., *Histoire d'Occitanie* (Paris, 1979).

Auerbach, E., 'Figura', in *Scenes from the Drama of European Literature* (New York, 1959), pp. 1–29.

Baker, D., 'Heresy and Learning in Early Cistercianism', *SCH* 9 (1972), pp. 93–108.

——'Popular Piety in the Lodèvois in the Early Twelfth Century: The Case of Pons de Léras', *SCH* 15 (1978), 39–47.

Baldwin, J. W., *The Language of Sex. Five Voices from Northern France around 1200* (Chicago, 1994).

——*Masters, Princes and Merchants: The Social Views of Peter the Chanter and his Circle*, 2 vols. (Princeton, NJ, 1970).

Bec, P., *Nouvelle anthologie de la lyrique occitane au moyen âge* (Avignon, 1972).

Benson, R. L., and Constable, G., with Lanham, C., eds., *Renaissance and Renewal* (Cambridge, MA, 1982).

Benveniste, E., *Problems in General Linguistics*, trans. M. E. Meek, Miami Linguistics Series No. 8 (Coral Gables, FL, 1971).

Berger, D., 'The Attitude of St Bernard of Clairvaux toward the Jews', *Proceedings of the American Academy for Jewish Research* 40 (1972), 89–108.

Bériou, N., 'La prédication de croisade de Philippe le Chancellier et d'Eudes de Châteauroux en 1226', in *La prédication en Pays d'Oc (XIIe–début XVe siècle)*, ed. J.-L. Biget, CaF 32 (Toulouse, 1997), pp. 85–109.

Berlioz, J., '*Exemplum* et histoire: Césaire de Heisterbach (v. 1180–v. 1240) et la croisade albigeoise', *Bibliothèque de l'Ecole des Chartes* 147 (1989), 49–86.

——'*Tuez-les tous, Dieu reconnaîtra les siens'. La croisade contre les albigeois vue par Césaire de Heisterbach* (Portet-sur-Garonne, 1994).

Berman, C., *Medieval Agriculture, the Southern French Countryside, and the Early Cistercians. A Study of Forty-three Monasteries*, Transactions of the American Philosophical Society 76:5 (Philadelphia, 1986).

Biget, J. L., '"Les Albigeois": remarques sur une dénomination', in *Inventer l'hérésie?*, pp. 219–55.

——ed., *La prédication en Pays d'Oc (XIIe–début XVe siècle)*, CaF 32 (Toulouse, 1997).

Biller, P., 'Cathars and Material Women', in *Medieval Theology and the Natural Body*, ed. P. Biller and A. J. Minnis, York Studies in Medieval Theology 1 (Woodbridge, 1997), pp. 61–108.

——'The Cathars of Languedoc and Written Materials', in Biller and Hudson, pp. 48–58.

——'Heresy and Literacy: Earlier History of the Theme', in Biller and Hudson, pp. 1–18.

——'The Preaching of the Waldensian Sisters', *Heresis* 30 (1999), 137–68.

——'What *did* Happen to the Waldensian Sisters? The Strasbourg Testimony', in

Studi in onore del Prof. Jean Gonnet (1909–1997), ed. F. Giacone, *Protestantesimo* 54 (1999), 222–33.

——'William of Newburgh and the Cathar Mission to England', in *Life and Thought in the Northern Church c. 1100–1700. Essays in Honour of Claire Cross*, ed. D. Wood, *SCH S* 12 (Woodbridge, 1999), pp. 11–30.

——and Hudson, A., eds., *Heresy and Literacy, 1000–1530*, Cambridge Studies in Medieval Literature 23 (Cambridge, 1994).

Bird, J., 'The Religious's Role in a Post-Fourth-Lateran World: Jacques de Vitry's *Sermones ad status* and *Historia occidentalis*', in *Medieval Monastic Preaching*, ed. C.A. Muessig (Leiden, 1998), pp. 209–30.

Bolton, B. M., *Innocent III: Studies on Papal Authority and Pastoral Care* (Aldershot, 1995).

——'The Cistercians and the Aftermath of the Second Crusade', in *The Second Crusade and the Cistercians*, ed. M. Gervers (New York, 1992), pp. 131–40.

——'Poverty as Protest: Some Inspirational Groups at the Turn of the XIIth Century', in *The Church in a Changing Society* (Uppsala, 1978), p. 28–32.

Bondeelle-Souchier, A., *Bibliothèques cisterciennes dans la France médiévale. Répertoire des Abbayes d'hommes* (Paris, 1991).

Bonnassie, P. and Pradalié, G., *La capitulation de Raymond VII et la fondation de l'Université de Toulouse 1229–1979: Un anniversaire en question* (Toulouse, 1979).

Bornstein, D. E., 'Introduction' to A. Vauchez, *The Laity in the Middle Ages. Religious Belief and Devotional Practices*, trans. M. J. Schneider (Notre Dame, IN, 1993).

Boswell, J., *Christianity, Social Tolerance, and Homosexuality: Gay People in Western Europe from the Beginning of the Christian Era to the Fourteenth Century* (Chicago, 1980).

Bouchard, C., *Holy Entrepreneurs: Cistercians, Knights, and Economic Exchange in Twelfth-Century Burgundy* (Ithaca, NY, 1991).

Bounoure, G., 'L'archevêque, l'hérétique et la comète', *Médiévales* 14 (1988), 113–28; 15 (1988), 73–84.

——'Le dernier voyage de saint Bernard en Aquitaine', *Bulletin de la Société Historique et Archéologique du Périgord* 115 (1988), 129–35.

——'Saint Bernard et les hérétiques du Sarladais', *Bulletin de la Société Historique et Archéologique du Périgord* 116 (1989), 277–92.

Bozóky, E., 'Introduction' in *Le livre secret des cathares. Interrogatio Iohannis. Apocryphe d'origine bogomile. Edition critique, traduction, commentaire* (Paris, 1980).

Bredero, A. H., *Bernard of Clairvaux: Between Cult and History* (Grand Rapids, MI, 1996).

Brenon, A., *Les Cathares. Pauvres du Christ ou apôtres de Satan?* (Paris, 1997).

——*Les cathares. Vie et mort d'une Église chrétienne* (Paris, 1996).

——'Christianisme et tolérance dans les textes cathares et vaudois du bas moyen âge', in *Ketzerei und Ketzerbekämpfung in Wort und Text*, ed. P. Blumenthal and J. Kramer (Stuttgart, 1989).

——*Les femmes cathares* (Paris, 1992).

——'Fin'amors et catharisme. L'exemple de Peire Vidal en Lauragais et de Raymond de Miraval en Carcasses, avant la croisade contre le Albigeois', in *Peire William de Luserna e lo tems dals trobaires*. Atti del convegno Storico

Internazionale, 4 e 5 maggio 1991 in Luserna, ed. V. Cognazzo and G. Mocchia di Coggiola (Cuneo, 1994), pp. 139–58.

—— 'Les fonctions sacramentales du *Consolamentum*', *Heresis* 20 (1993), 33–55.

—— 'Les hérésies de l'an mille', *Heresis* 24 (1995), 21–36.

—— 'La lettre d'Evervin de Steinfeld à Bernard de Clairvaux de 1143: un document essentiel et méconnu', *Heresis* 25 (1995), 7–28.

—— *Le vrai visage du Catharisme* (Toulouse, 1990).

—— 'The Waldensian Books', in Biller and Hudson, pp. 137–59.

Brouette, E., Dimier, A., and Manning, E., eds., *Dictionnaire des auteurs cisterciens*, La documentation cistercienne (Paris, 1979).

Brown, R. E., 'Hermeneutics', in *The New Jerome Biblical Commentary*, ed. R. E. Brown, J. A. Fitzmyer and R. E. Murphy (Englewood Cliffs, NJ, 1990), LXXI, 46–7.

Brundage, J., 'St. Bernard and the Jurists', in *The Second Crusade and the Cistercians*, ed. M. Gervers (New York, 1992), pp. 25–34.

Buc, P., '*Vox clamantis in deserto?* Pierre le Chantre et la prédication laïque', in *Revue Mabillon*, n.s., 4 (= t. 65) (1993), 5–47.

Bynum, C. W., '*Docere Verbo et Exemplo': An Aspect of Twelfth-Century Spirituality*, Harvard Theological Monographs (Missoula, MT, 1979).

—— *Jesus as Mother: Studies in the Spirituality of the High Middle Ages* (Berkeley, CA, 1982).

Cabau, P., 'Foulque, marchand et troubadour de Marseille, moine et abbé du Thoronet, évêque de Toulouse (v. 1155/1160–25.12.1231)', in *Cisterciens*, CaF, 151–79.

Cabrer, M. A., 'El *venerable* Arnaldo Amalarico (h. 1196–1225): Idea y realidad de un cisterciense entre dos cruzadas', *Hispania Sacra* 98 (1996), 569–91.

Canivez, J., ed., *Statuta Capitulorum Generalium Ordinis Cisterciensis ab anno 1116 ad annum 1786, I (1116–1220)* (Louvain, 1933).

Carman, J. N., *The Relationship of the 'Perlesvaus' and the 'Queste del Saint Graal'* (Chicago, 1936).

Carruthers, M., *The Book of Memory. A Study of Memory in Medieval Culture* (Cambridge, 1990).

Casey, M., *Athirst for God. Spiritual Desire in Bernard of Clairvaux's Sermons on the Song of Songs*, Cistercian Studies 77 (Kalamazoo, MI, 1988).

Cate, J. L., 'The English Mission of Eustace of Flay (1200–1201)', in *Etudes d'histoire dédiées a la mémoire de Henri Pirenne* (Bruxelles, 1937), pp. 67–89.

Chalande, J., *Histoire des rues de Toulouse* (Toulouse, 1929).

Châtillon, J., 'La Bible dans les écoles du XIIe siècle', in *Le Moyen Âge et la Bible*, ed. P. Riché and G. Lobrichon, La Bible de tous les temps 4 (Paris, 1984), pp. 179–186.

Chazan, R., *Medieval Stereotypes and Modern Antisemitism* (Berkeley, CA, 1997).

—— *The Year 1096 and the Jews* (Philadelphia, 1996).

Chenu, M.-D., *Nature, Man and Society in the Twelfth Century*, ed. and trans. J. Taylor and L. K. Little (Chicago, 1968).

Clark, A., *Elisabeth of Schönau: A Twelfth-Century Visionary* (Philadelphia, 1992).

Clark Wire, A., *The Corinthian Women Prophets: A Reconstruction through Paul's Rhetoric* (Minneapolis, 1990).

Cole, P., *The Preaching of the Crusades to the Holy Land, 1095–1270* (Cambridge, MA, 1991).

Congar, Y., 'Henri de Marcy, abbé de Clairvaux, cardinal-évêque d'Albano et légat pontifical', *Analecta Monastica,* Series 5, Studia Anselmiana 43 (1958), 1–90.

Constable, G., *Letters and Letter Collections*, Typologie des sources du moyen âge occidental 17 (Turnhout, 1976).

——'Papal, Imperial and Monastic Propaganda in the Eleventh and Twelfth Centuries', in *Preaching and Propaganda in the Middle Ages: Islam, Byzantium, Latin West. Penn-Paris-Dumbarton Oaks Colloquia III, Session of October 20–25, 1980*, ed. G. Makdisi, D. Sourdel and J. Sourdel-Thoumine (Paris, 1980), pp. 180–99.

——*The Reformation of the Twelfth Century* (Cambridge, 1996).

——'The Second Crusade as Seen by Contemporaries', *Traditio* 9 (1953), 213–79.

——*Three Studies in Medieval Religious and Social Thought* (Cambridge, 1995).

Costen, M., *The Cathars and the Albigensian Crusade* (Manchester, 1997).

Cracco, G., 'Bernardo e I movimenti ereticali', in *Bernardo Cistercense: Atti del XXVI convegno Storico Internazionale, Todi, 8–11 ottobre 1989*, ed. E Menesto, Academia Tudertina. Centro di studi sulla spiritualità medievale dell'università degli Studi di Perugia 3 (Spoleto, 1990), pp. 165–86.

Crouse, R. D., 'Origen in the Philosophical Tradition of the Latin West: St Augustine and John Scotus Eriugena', in *Origeniana Quinta*, ed. R. Daly (Leuven, 1992), pp. 564–9.

Curtius, E. R., *European Literature and the Latin Middle Ages*, trans. W. R. Trask, Bollingen Series 36 (Princeton, 1973).

Czeski, A., 'Aspects de la vie quotidienne à Montségur, révélés par les témoins archéologiques', in *Montségur: La Mémoire et la Rumeur 1244–1994*, ed. C. Pailhes (Saint-Girons, 1995), pp. 65–86.

Dahan, G., *Les intellectuels chrétiens et les juifs au moyen âge* (Paris, 1990).

Daley, B., 'Origen's *De Principiis*. A Guide to the Principles of Christian Scriptural Interpretation' in *Nova et vetera*, ed. J. Petruccione (Washington, DC, 1998), pp. 3–21.

D'Alverny, M.-T., *Alain de Lille: Textes inédits* (Paris, 1965).

——'Translations and Translators', in *Renaissance and Renewal*, pp. 421–62.

Daunou, M., 'Arnaud Amaury', in *Histoire littéraire de la France* XVII (Paris, 1895), pp. 306–34.

D'Avray, D., *The Preaching of the Friars. Sermons diffused from Paris before 1300* (Oxford, 1985).

de Lage, R., *Alain de Lille: poète du XIIe siècle* (Paris, 1951).

de Lahondès, J., *L'Eglise Saint-Etienne* (Toulouse, 1890).

de Lubac, H., *Medieval Exegesis, I*, trans. Mark Sebanc (Grand Rapids, MI/ Edinburgh, 1998).

de Rougement, D., *Love in the Western World*, trans. M. Belgion (Greenwich, CN, 1956).

de Vogüé, A., *The Rule of Saint Benedict: A Doctrinal and Spiritual Commentary*, trans. J. B. Hasbrouck, Cistercian Studies 54 (Kalamazoo, 1983).

de Waal, E., *Seeking God. The Way of St Benedict* (Collegeville, MN, 1984).

Deladreue, L.-E. 'Notice sur l'abbaye de Froidmont', *Mémoires de la Société*

Académique d'Archéologie, Sciences et Arts du Départment de l'Oise, 7 (1870), 469–624; 8 (1871), 1–78.

Delcorno, C., 'Medieval Preaching in Italy (1300–1500)', in *The Sermon*, ed. B. M. Kienzle, Typologie des sources du moyen âge occidental 81–83 (Turnhout, 2000).

Delettre, C., *Histoire du diocèse de Beauvais* 3 vols. (Beauvais, 1842–43).

Dessí, R. M., and Lauwers, M., eds., *La parole du prédicateur Ve–XVe siècle*, Collection du Centre d'Études Médiévales de Nice 1 (Nice, 1997).

Diehl, P. D., 'Overcoming Reluctance to Prosecute Heresy in Thirteenth-Century Italy', in Waugh and Diehl, pp. 47–66.

Dimier, A., 'Elinando di Froidmont', in *Bibliotheca sanctorum IV* (Rome, 1964).

—— 'Hélinand de Froidmont', in *Dictionnaire des auteurs cisterciens*, ed. E. Brouette, A. Dimier and E. Manning, La documentation cistercienne (Paris, 1979).

Dossat, Y., 'Les premiers maîtres à l'Université de Toulouse: Jean de Garlande, Hélinand', in *Les Universités du Languedoc au XIIIe siècle*, CaF 5 (Toulouse, 1970), pp. 179–203.

Douglas, M., *Purity and Danger. An Analysis of the Concepts of Pollution and Taboo* (London, 1984).

Dronke, P., 'Profane Elements in Literature', in *Renaissance and Renewal*, pp. 569–92.

Dumontier, 'Hélinand de Froidmont et la liturgie', *Collectanea ordinis Cisterciensium Reformatorum*, 14 (1952), 133–9, 213–5, 295–300; 17 (1955), 49–56, 118–25.

Duvernoy, J., 'Boulbonne et le Lauragais au XIIIe siècle', in *Le Lauragais, Histoire et Archéologie* (Montpellier, 1983), pp. 105–13.

—— *Le Catharisme: L'histoire des Cathares* (Toulouse, 1979).

—— *Le Catharisme: la religion des Cathares* (Paris, 1976).

—— 'Le Catharisme: l'unité des églises', *Heresis* 21 (1993), 15–27.

—— 'La prédication dissidente', in *La prédication en Pays d'Oc (XIIe–début XVe siècle)*, ed. J.-L. Biget, CaF 32 (Toulouse, 1997), pp. 111–24.

—— ed., *Les registres d'inquisition de Jacques Fournier*, 3 vols. (Toulouse, 1965).

Eagleton, T., *Literary Theory* (Minneapolis, 1983).

Evans, A. P., 'The Albigensian Crusade' in *A History of the Crusades*, ed. R. L. Wolff and H. W. Hazard, 4 vols. (Philadelphia, 1962), II, 277–324.

Evans, G. R., *The Language and Logic of the Bible. The Earlier Middle Ages* (Cambridge, 1991).

Fachinger, E., 'Les cisterciens de Languedoc aux XIIIe et XIVe siècles, d'après les documents pontificaux', in *Cisterciens*, CaF, pp. 45–69.

Falmagne, T., 'Les instruments de travail d'un prédicateur cistercien. À propos de Jean de Vilers (mort en 1336 ou 1346)', in *De l'homélie au sermon. Histoire de la prédication médiévale. Actes du Colloque International de Louvain-la-Neuve (9–11 juillet 1992)*, ed. J. Hamesse and X. Hermand (Louvain-la-Neuve, 1993), pp. 183–238.

Felten, F. J., 'Arnaud Nouvel, *doctor legum*, moine de Boulbonne, abbé de Fontfroide et cardinal (†1317)', in *Cisterciens*, CaF, pp. 208–14.

Fernández, E. Mitre, 'Animales, vicios y herejías (sobre la criminalización de la disidencia en el Medievo)', in *Cuadernos de Historia de España LXXIV en memoria de don Claudio Sánchez-Albornoz* (Buenos Aires, 1997), pp. 257–83.

Fichtenau, H., *Heretics and Scholars in the High Middle Ages 1000–1200*, trans. D. A. Kaiser (University Park, PA, 1998).

Foreville, R., *Le Pape Innocent III et la France*, Päpste und Pappstum 26 (Stuttgart, 1992).

—— *Gouvernement et vie de l'Église au Moyen Âge. Recueil d'études* (Ashgate, 1979).

—— 'Innocent III et la croisade des Albigeois', in *Paix de Dieu et guerre sainte en Languedoc au XIIIe siècle*, CaF 4 (Toulouse, 1969), pp. 184–217.

Gatien-Arnoult, A.-F., 'Hélinand', 'Histoire de l'Université de Toulouse', *Mémoires de l'Académie des sciences, inscriptions et belles-lettres de Toulouse* G.IX (1877), 455–94.

—— *Revue de Toulouse et du Midi de la France* 22 (1866), 287–302, 345–6.

—— 'Notes sur les commencements de l'Université de Toulouse', *Mémoires de l'Académie des sciences, inscriptions et belles-lettres de Toulouse* E.I (1857), 202–20.

Géraud, H., 'Le comte-évêque', *Bibliothèque de l'École des Chartes* 5 (1843–4), 8–36.

Gervers, M., ed., *The Second Crusade and the Cistercians* (New York, 1992).

Giddens, A., 'Hermeneutics and Social Theory', in *Hermeneutics: Questions and Prospects*, ed. G. Shapiro and A. Sica (Amherst, MA, 1984), pp. 215–30.

Ginzburg, C., *The Cheese and the Worms* (Baltimore, 1992).

Girard, R., *The Girard Reader*, ed. J. G. Williams (New York, 1996).

Gonnet, G., 'Le cheminement des vaudois vers le schisme et l'hérésie (1174–1218)', *Cahiers de Civilisation Médiévale* 19 (1976), 309–45.

—— *Enchiridion fontium Valdensium*, I (Torre Pellice, 1958).

Grégoire, R., *Homéliaires liturgiques médiévaux. Analyse de manuscrits* (Spoleto, 1980).

Grundmann, H., 'Litteratus-illiteratus. Der Wandel einer Bildungsnorm vom Altertum zum Mittelalter', *Archiv für Kulturgeschichte* 40 (1958), 1–65.

—— *Religious Movements in the Middle Ages: The Historical Links between Heresy, the Mendicant Orders, and the Women's Religious Movement in the Twelfth and Thirteenth Century, with the Historical Foundations of German Mysticism*, trans. S. Rowan, with an Introduction by R. Lerner (Notre Dame, IN, 1995).

Gutsch, M. R., 'A Twelfth-Century Preacher – Fulk of Neuilly', in *The Crusades and Other Historical Essays presented to Dana C. Monro*, ed. L. J. Paetow (New York, 1928), pp. 183–206.

Hagman, Y., 'Le catharisme, un neo-manichéisme?' *Heresis* 21 (1993), 47–59.

—— 'Le rite de l'initiation chrétienne chez les cathares et les bogomiles', *Heresis* 20 (1993), 13–31.

Hamesse, J., Kienzle, B. M., Stoudt, D. L. and Thayer, A. T., eds., *Medieval Sermons and Society: Cloister, City, University*, FIDEM Textes et Études du Moyen Âge, 9 (Louvain-la-Neuve, 1998).

Hamilton, B., 'Wisdom from the East: The Reception by the Cathars of Eastern Dualist Texts', in Biller and Hudson, pp. 38–60.

Häring, N. M., 'Commentary and Hermeneutics', in *Renaissance and Renewal*, pp. 190–4.

Haskins, C. H., *The Renaissance of the Twelfth Century* (New York, 1963).

Head, T. and Landes, R., eds., *The Peace of God: Religious Responses to Social Turmoil in France around the Year 1000* (Ithaca, NY, 1992).

Hélinand de Froidmont (Colloque et Exposition) (Mai-Juin 1987). Cahiers de l'Abbaye de St-Arnoult 2 (Amiens, 1987).

Higounet, C., 'Le milieu social et économique languedocien vers 1200', in *Vaudois languedociens et Pauvres Catholiques*, CaF 2 (Toulouse, 1967), pp. 15–9.

——'Nouvelles réflexions sur les bastides 'cisterciennes', in *Cisterciens*, CaF, pp. 127–38.

Hilka, A., *Die Wundergeschichten des Caesarius von Heisterbach* 3 vols. (Bonn, 1933).

Holdsworth, C., 'Bernard, Chimera of his Age', in *Essays in Honor of Edward B. King* (Sewanee, 1991), pp. 147–63.

Hublocher, H., *Helinand von Froidmont und sein Verhältnis zu Johannes von Salisbury* (Regensburg, 1913).

Hultgren, A. J., and Haggmark, S. A., *The Earliest Christian Heretics. Readings from their Opponents* (Minneapolis, 1996).

Hunt, R.W., 'Studies in Priscian in the Twelfth Century II: The School of Ralph of Beauvais', *Medieval and Renaissance Studies* 2 (1950), 11–16.

Iogna-Prat, D., 'L'argumentation défensive: de la polémique grégorienne au *Contra Petrobrusianos* de Pierre le Vénérable (1140)', in *Inventer l'hérésie?*, pp. 87–118.

Jaeger, C. S., *The Envy of Angels. Cathedral Schools and Social Ideals in Medieval Europe, 950–1200* (Philadelphia, 1994).

Jansen, K. L., 'Innocent III and the Literature of Confession', in *Innocent III: Urbs et Orbis, Acts of the international conference commemorating the 800th anniversary of the accession of Innocent III to the papal throne, Rome 9–15 September 1998* (forthcoming).

Kaelber, L., *Schools of Asceticism. Ideology and Organization in Medieval Religious Communities* (University Park, PA, 1998).

——'Weavers into Heretics? The Social Organization of Early Thirteenth-Century Catharism in Comparative Perspective', *Social Science History* 21 (1997), 111–37.

Kelly, A., *Eleanor of Aquitaine and the Four Kings* (Cambridge, MA, 1950).

Kennan, E. T., 'Introduction' to *Five Books on Consideration: Advice to a Pope*, Cistercian Fathers 37 (Kalamazoo, MI, 1991).

Kienzle, B. M., 'Cistercian Preaching Against the Cathars: Hélinand's Unedited Sermon for Rogation, B. N. Ms. Lat, 14591', *Cîteaux* 9 (1988), 297–314.

——'Cistercian Views of the City in the Sermons of Hélinand of Froidmont', in *Medieval Sermons and Society: Cloister, City, University*, ed. J. Hamesse, B. M. Kienzle, D. L. Stoudt and A. T. Thayer, FIDEM Textes et Études du Moyen Âge 9 (Louvain-la-Neuve, 1998), pp. 165–82.

——'The Conversion of Pons of Léras and the True Account of the Beginning of the Monastery at Silvanès: Analysis and Translation of the Latin Text in Dijon, Bibliothèque Municipale', *Cistercian Studies Quarterly* 30 (1995), 218–43.

——'Deed and Word: Hélinand's Toulouse Sermons, I', and 'Erudition at God's Service, Hélinand's Toulouse Sermons, II', in *Erudition at God's Service*, ed. J. R. Sommerfeldt, *Studies in Medieval Cistercian History, XI*, Cistercian Studies 98 (Kalamazoo, MI, 1987), pp. 267–90.

——'Defending the Lord's Vineyard: Hildegard of Bingen's Preaching against the Cathars', in *Medieval Monastic Preaching*, ed. C. A. Muessig (Leiden, 1998), pp. 163–81.

——'Education in the Late Twelfth and Early Thirteenth Centuries: The Witness of Hélinand of Froidmont', in *Faith Seeking Understanding: Learning and the Catholic Tradition. Selected Papers from the Symposium and Convocation celebrating the Saint Anselm College Centennial*, ed. G. C. Berthold (Manchester, NH, 1991), pp. 77–88.

——'Exegesis on Luke 10:38 around 1100: Worcester MS F.94, f.1r–2r, A Tribute to James E. Cross', *Medieval Sermon Studies* 40 (Autumn 1997), 22–8.

——'Hélinand de Froidmont et la prédication cisterciènne dans le midi, 1145–1229', in *Prédication*, CaF 32, pp. 37–67.

——'Hélinand's Unedited Sermon for Rogation', *Cîteaux: commentarii cistercienses* 3–4 (1988), 298–314.

——'Henry of Clairvaux and the 1178 and 1181 Missions', *Heresis* 28 (1997), 63–87.

——'Hildegard of Bingen's Gospel Homilies and Her Exegesis of the Parable of the Prodigal Son', in *Im Angesicht Gottes suche der Mensch sich selbst* (forthcoming).

——'Holiness and Obedience: Denouncement of Twelfth-Century Waldensian Lay Preaching', in *The Devil, Heresy and Witchcraft in the Middle Ages. Essays in Honor of Jeffrey B. Russell*, ed. A. Ferreiro (Leiden, 1998), pp. 259–78.

——'The House of the Lord: Hélinand on Superfluous Monastic Construction', *Proceedings of the PMR Conference* 11 (1986), 135–41.

——'Mary Speaks against Heresy: An Unedited Sermon of Hélinand for the Purification, Paris, B.N. ms. lat. 14591', *Sacris erudiri* 32 (1991), 291–308.

——'*Operatrix in vinea domini:* Hildegard of Bingen's Preaching and Polemics against the Cathars', *Heresis* 26–27 (1996), 43–56.

——'Preaching as Touchstone of Orthodoxy and Dissent', *Medieval Sermon Studies* 42 (1999), 18–53.

——'La prédication: pierre de touche de la dissidence et de l'orthodoxie', in *La prédication sur un mode dissident: laïcs, femmes, hérétiques (XIe–XIVe)*, I, *Heresis* 30 (1999), 11–51.

——'The Prostitute-Preacher: Patterns of Polemic against Waldensian Women Preachers', in B. M. Kienzle and P. J. Walker, *Women Preachers and Prophets through Two Millennia of Christianity* (Berkeley, CA, 1998), pp. 99–113.

——ed., *The Sermon*, Typologie des sources du moyen âge occidental fasc. 81–3 (Turnhout, 2000).

——'Tending the Lord's Vineyard: Cistercians, Rhetoric and Heresy, 1143–1229. Part I: Bernard of Clairvaux, the 1143 Sermons and the 1145 Preaching Mission', *Heresis* 25 (1995), 29–61.

——'The Twelfth-Century Monastic Sermon', in *The Sermon*, pp. 271–323.

——'The Works of Hugo Francigena: *Tractatus de conversione Pontii de Laracio et exordii Salvaniensis monasterii vera narratio; epistolae*. Dijon, Bibliothèque Municipale MS 611', *Sacris erudiri* 34 (1994), 287–317.

——, Dolnikowski, E. W., Hale, R. D., Pryds, D., and Thayer, A. T., eds., *Models of Holiness in Medieval Sermons*. Proceedings of the International Symposium at Kalamazoo, 4–7 May 1995, ed., FIDEM Textes et Études du Moyen Âge, 9 (Louvain-la-Neuve, 1996).

——and Shroff, S., 'Cistercians and Heresy: Doctrinal Consultation in Some Twelfth-Century Correspondence from Southern France', *Cîteaux: commentarii cistercienses* 41 (1990), 159–66.

——and Walker, P. J., *Women Preachers and Prophets through Two Millenia of Christianity* (Berkeley, CA, 1998).

Kuttner, S., 'The Revival of Jurisprudence', in *Renaissance and Renewal*, pp. 299–323.

Ladurie, E. L. R., *Montaillou: village occitan de 1294 à 1324* (Paris, 1978).

Lambert, M. D., *Cathars* (Oxford and Malden, MA, 1998).

——*Medieval Heresy. Popular Movements from the Gregorian Reform to the Reformation*, 2nd edn (Oxford, 1992).

Lampe, G. W. H, 'The Exposition and Exegesis of Scripture: To Gregory the Great', in *The Cambridge History of the Bible, II: The West from the Fathers to the Reformation*, ed. G. W. H. Lampe (Cambridge, 1969), pp. 165–6.

Lanc, E., 'L'adaptation scénique des Vers de la Mort', in *Hélinand de Froidmont (Colloque et Exposition) (Mai–Juin 1987)*. Cahiers de l'Abbaye de St-Arnoult, 2 (Amiens, 1987), 75–85.

——*Le Triomphe de la Mort*, adaptation scénique des '*Vers de la Mort*' d'Hélinand de Froidmont, préface de M. Santucci, sérigraphies originales de R.-M. Balau (Brussels, 1987).

Lauwers, M., 'Dicunt vivorum beneficia nichil prodesse defunctis', Histoire d'un thème polémique (XIe–XIIe siècles)', in *Inventer l'hérésie?*, pp. 157–92.

——'Excursus: Un écho des polémiques antiques? À Saint-Victor de Marseille à la fin du XIe siècle', in *Inventer l'hérésie?*, pp. 37–66.

Leclercq, J., 'Études sur S. Bernard et le texte de ses écrits', *Analecta Cisterciensis* 9 (1953), 55–62.

——'L'hérésie d'après les écrits de S. Bernard de Clairvaux', in *The Concept of Heresy in the Middle Ages (11th–13th C.). Proceedings of the International Conference, Louvain, 13–16 May 1973*, ed. W. Lordaux and D. Verhelst (Leuven, 1976), pp. 12–26.

——*The Love of Learning and the Desire for God*, 3rd edn, trans. C. Misrahi (New York, 1982).

——'Monasticism and Asceticism II. Western Christianity', in *Christian Spirituality: Origins to the Twelfth Century*, ed. B. McGinn, J. Meyendorff and J. Leclercq (New York, 1988), pp. 113–24.

——'Saint Bernard's Attitude toward War', in *Studies in Medieval Cistercian History, II*, ed. J. R. Sommerfeldt, Cistercian Studies 24 (Kalamazoo, MI, 1976), pp. 1–39.

——'Le témoignage de Geoffroy d'Auxerre sur la vie cistercienne', *Analecta monastica*, Studia Anselmiana 31 (1953), 174–201.

——and Rochais, H., 'La tradition manuscrite des sermons liturgiques', *Scriptorium* 15 (1961), 240–84.

Lecoy de la Marche, A., *La chaire française au moyen âge* (Paris, 1886).

Le Gentil, P., *La Chanson de Roland* (Paris, 1967).

Le Goff, J., *The Birth of Purgatory* (Chicago, 1984).

——'Les universités du Languedoc dans le mouvement universitaire européen au xiiie siècle', in *Les universités du Languedoc au XIIIe siècle*, CaF 5 (Toulouse, 1970), pp. 316–28.

Lejeune, R., 'L'évêque de Toulouse Folquet de Marseille et la principauté de Liège', in *Mélanges Félix Rousseau. Etudes sur l'histoire du pays mosan au moyen âge* (Brussels, 1958), pp. 433–8.

Lekai, L., *The Cistercians, Ideal and Reality* (Kent, OH, 1977).

Lenssen, S., *Hagiologium Cisterciense* (Tilburg, 1948).

Lerner, R., 'Les communautés hérétiques (1150–1500)', *in Le Moyen Âge et la Bible*, ed. P. Riché and G. Lobrichon, La Bible de tous les temps 4 (Paris, 1984).

Lipton, S. G., *Images of Intolerance. The Representation of Jews and Judaism in the* Bible moralisée (Berkeley, CA, 1999).

—— 'Jews, Heretics, and the Sign of the Cat in the Bible moralisée', *Word and Image* 8 (1992), 362–77.

Little, L., *Religious Poverty and the Profit Economy in Medieval Europe* (Ithaca, NY, 1978).

Longère, J., 'La prédication d'après les statuts synodaux du Midi au XIIIe siècle', in *La prédication en Pays d'Oc (XIIe–début XVe siècle)*, ed. J.-L. Biget, CaF 32 (Toulouse, 1997).

—— *La prédication médiévale* (Paris, 1983).

Loos, M., *Dualist Heresy in the Middle Ages* (Prague, 1974).

Luchaire, A., *Innocent III. La Question d'Orient*, 4 vols. (Paris, 1904–8).

Luz, U., *Das Evangelium nach Matthäus 2, Mt 8–17* (Zürich, 1990).

Mack, B., *A Myth of Innocence: Mark and Christian Origins* (Philadelphia, 1988).

—— *Rhetoric and the New Testament* (Minneapolis, 1990).

Magnou-Nortier, E., *La société laïque et l'Église dans la province ecclésiastique de Narbonne (zone cispyrénéenne) de la fin du VIIIe à la fin du XIe siècle* (Toulouse, 1974).

Maier, C., *Crusade Propaganda and Ideology. Model Sermons for the Preaching of the Cross* (Cambridge, 2000).

—— *Preaching the Crusades. Mendicant Friars and the Cross in the Thirteenth Century* (Cambridge, 1994).

Maisonneuve, H., *Études sur les origines de l'inquisition*, 2nd edn (Paris, 1960).

Maloney, L. M., 'The Pastoral Epistles', in *Searching the Scriptures, II: Feminist Commentary*, ed. E. Schüssler Fiorenza (New York, 1994), pp. 361–80.

Manselli, R., 'De la *persuasio* à la *coercitio*', in *Le* Credo, *la Morale et l'Inquisition*, CaF 6 (Toulouse, 1971), pp. 175–97.

Mansi, J. D., ed. *Sacrorum conciliorum nova et amplissima collectio*, 31 vols. (Florence, 1759–98).

Markus, R. A., *Gregory the Great and His World* (Cambridge, 1997).

Martin, L. T., 'The Two Worlds in Bede's Homilies: The Biblical Event and the Listener's Experience', in *De Ore Domini: Preacher and Word in the Middle Ages*, ed. T. L. Amos, E. A. Green and B. M. Kienzle (Kalamazoo, MI, 1989), pp. 27–40.

Martin, R. P., '1, 2 Timothy and Titus', in *Harper's Bible Commentary*, ed. J. L. Mays (San Francisco, 1988), pp. 1237–44.

Mary, A., *Anthologie poétique française: Moyen Âge* (Paris, 1967).

Matter, E. A., *The Voice of My Beloved: The Song of Songs in Western Medieval Christianity* (Philadelphia, 1990).

McCulloch, F., 'The Art of Persuasion in Hélinant's *Vers de la Mort*', *Studies in Philology* 69 (1972), 38–54.

McGinn, B., *Antichrist: Two Thousand Years of the Human Fascination with Evil* (San Francisco, 1994).

—— *Apocalypticism in the Western Tradition* (Aldershot, 1994).

—— *The Presence of God: A History of Western Christian Mysticism*, 4 vols. (New York, 1996).

—— *Visions of the End: Apocalyptic Traditions in the Middle Ages* (New York, 1979).

——, Meyendorff, J. and Leclercq, J., eds., *Christian Spirituality: Origins to the Twelfth Century* (New York, 1988).

McGuire, B. P., *The Difficult Saint. Bernard of Clairvaux and His Tradition*, Cistercian Studies 26 (Kalamazoo, MI, 1991).

McGuire, B. P., *Friendship and Community*, Cistercian Studies 95 (Kalamazoo, MI, 1988).

——'La présence de Bernard de Clairvaux dans l'*Exordium magnum cisterciense*', in *Vies et légendes de Saint Bernard: Création, diffusion, réception (XIIe–XXe siècles). Actes des Rencontres de Dijon, 7–8 juin 1991*, ed. P. Arabeyre, J. Berlioz and P. Poirrier, *Cîteaux: Commentarii Cistercienses*, Textes et Documents 5 (Cîteaux, 1993), pp. 63–83.

McNamara, J., *Sisters in Arms. Catholic Nuns through Two Millennia* (Cambridge, MA, 1996).

Mesuret, R., *Évocation du vieux Toulouse* (Paris, 1960).

Meyvaert, P., Review of Francis Clark, *The Pseudo-Gregorian Dialogues*: 'The Enigma of Gregory the Great's Dialogues: A Response to Francis Clark', *Journal of Ecclesiastical History* 39 (1988), 377–81.

Molina, R., 'Hélinand de Froidmont, Hélinand de Perseigne et la Littérature du Graal', in *Hélinand de Froidmont (Colloque et Exposition) (Mai–Juin 1987)*. Cahiers de l'Abbaye de St-Arnoult 2 (Amiens, 1987), pp. 57–63.

Moore, R. I., 'À la naissance d'une société persécutrice: les clercs, les cathares et la formation de l'Europe', in *La persécution du Catharisme. Actes de la 6e session d'histoire médiévale, 1er–4 septembre 1993*, Heresis 6 (hors série) (Carcassonne, 1996), pp. 11–37.

——*The Birth of Popular Heresy*, Documents of Medieval History 1 (London, 1975).

——*The Formation of a Persecuting Society. Power and Deviance in Western Europe, 950–1250* (Oxford, 1987).

——'Heresy as Disease', in *The Concept of Heresy in the Middle Ages (11th–13th C.). Proceedings of the International Conference, Louvain, 13–16 May 1973*, ed. W. Lordaux and D. Verhelst, Medievalia Lovanensia, ser. 1, studia 4 (Leuven, 1976), pp. 1–11.

——'Literacy and the Making of Heresy, *c.* 1000–*c.* 1150', in Biller and Hudson, pp. 19–37.

——*The Origins of European Dissent* (London, 1977).

Morey, J. H., 'Peter Comestor, Biblical Paraphrase, and the Medieval Popular Bible', *Speculum* 68 (1993), 6–35.

Mousnier, M., 'Grandselve et la société de son temps', in *Cisterciens*, CaF, pp. 107–26.

Muessig, C. A., ed., *Medieval Monastic Preaching* (Leiden, 1998).

——'Les sermons de Jacques de Vitry sur les cathares', in *La prédication en Pays d'Oc (XIIe–début XVe siècle)*, ed. J.-L. Biget, CaF 32 (Toulouse, 1997), pp. 69–83.

Mumford, L., *The City in History* (New York, 1961).

Mundy, J. H., 'Urban Society and Culture. Toulouse and its Region', in *Renaissance and Renewal*, pp. 229–47.

——'Village, Town and City in the Region of Toulouse', in *Pathways to Medieval Peasants*, ed. J. A. Raftis, Pontifical Institute of Medieval Studies, Papers and Studies 2 (Toronto, 1981), pp. 119–40.

Murphy, J. J., *Rhetoric in the Middle Ages. A History of Rhetorical Theory from St Augustine to the Renaissance* (Berkeley, CA, 1974).

Neininger, F., *Konrad von Urach (†1227). Zähringer, Zisterzienser, Kardinallegat* (Paderborn, 1994).

—— 'Die Zisterzienser im Albigenserkreuzzug', in *Die rheinischen Zisterzienser. Neue Orientierungen in rheinischen Zisterzen des späten Mittelalters*, ed. N. Kuhn and K. P. Wiemer (Cologne, 1999), pp. 67–83.

Nelli, R., ed., *Écrivains anticonformistes de Moyen Âge occitan, II, Hérétiques et politiques* (Paris, 1977).

—— *Le phénomène cathare* (Toulouse, 1964).

—— *Le roman de Flamenca. Un art d'aimer occitanien du XIIIe siècle* (Carcassonne, 1966).

Newman, M., *The Boundaries of Charity. Cistercian Culture and Ecclesiastical Reform, 1098–1180* (Stanford, 1996).

Nirenberg, D., *Communities of Violence. Persecution of Minorities in the Middle Ages* (Princeton, NJ, 1996).

Obert-Piketty, C., 'Benoît XII et les collèges cisterciens du Languedoc', in *Cisterciens*, CaF, pp. 139–50.

—— 'La promotion des études chez les cisterciens à travers le recrutement des étudiants du collège Saint-Bernard de Paris au moyen âge', *Cîteaux: commentarii cistercienses* 39 (1988), 65–77.

O'Brien, J. M., *Fulk of Neuilly* (Los Angeles, 1961).

O'Callaghan, J. F., 'The Order of Calatrava and the Archbishop of Toledo, 1147–1245', in *Studies in Medieval Cistercian History Presented to Jeremiah O'Sullivan*, Cistercian Studies 13 (Spencer, MA, 1971), pp. 63–87.

O'Malley, J. W., *The First Jesuits* (Cambridge, MA, 1993).

Pacaut, M., *Les moines blancs. Histoire de l'ordre de Cîteaux* (Saint-Amand-Montrond, 1993).

Paden, W. D., Jr, *'De monachis rithmos facientibus*. Hélinant de Froidmont, Bertran de Born, and the Cistercian General Chapter of 1199', *Speculum* 55 (1980), 669–85.

—— 'Documents concernant Hélinant de Froidmont', *Romania* 105 (1984), 332–9.

Pagels, E., *The Origins of Satan* (New York, 1995).

Paolini, L., 'Italian Catharism and Written Culture', in Biller and Hudson, pp. 83–103.

Paravy, P., 'Waldensians in the Dauphiné (1400–1530): From Dissidence in Texts to Dissidence in Practice', in Biller and Hudson, pp. 160–75.

Paterson, L., *The World of the Troubadours. Medieval Occitan Society, c. 1100–c.1300* (Cambridge, 1993).

Patschovsky, A., 'The Literacy of Waldensianism from Valdes to *c.* 1400', in Biller and Hudson, pp. 112–36.

Pennington, B., 'The Religious World of the Twelfth Century III. The Cistercians', in *Christian Spirituality: Origins to the Twelfth Century*, ed. B. McGinn, J. Meyendorff and J. Leclercq (New York, 1988), pp. 205–8.

Perelman, C. and L. Olbrechts-Tyteca, *The New Rhetoric: A Treatise on Argumentation*, trans. J. Wilkinson and P. Weaver (Notre Dame, IN, 1969).

Peters, E., *Heresy and Authority in Medieval Europe* (Philadelphia, 1980).

—— *Inquisition* (Berkeley, CA, 1988).

Piazzoni, A. M., 'Le premier biographe de Saint Bernard: Guillaume de Saint-Thierry', in *Vie et légendes de Saint Bernard de Clairvaux: Création, diffusion, réception (XIIe–XXe siècles). Actes des Rencontres de Dijon, 7–8 juin 1991*, ed. P. Arabeyre, J. Berlioz and P. Poirrier, Cîteaux: Commentarii Cistercienses, Textes et Documents 5 (Cîteaux, 1993), pp. 3–18.

Picard, A. and Boglioni, P., 'Miracle et thaumaturgie dans la vie de Saint Bernard', in *Vie et légendes de Saint Bernard de Clairvaux: Création, diffusion, réception (XIIe–XXe siècles). Actes des Rencontres de Dijon, 7–8 juin 1991*, ed. P. Arabeyre, J. Berlioz and P. Poirrier, Cîteaux: Commentarii Cistercienses, Textes et Documents 5 (Cîteaux, 1993), pp. 36–59.

Pontal, O., 'De la défense à la pastorale de la foi: les épiscopats de Foulques, Raymond du Fauga, et Bertrand de l'Isle-Jourdain à Toulouse', in *Effacement du Catharisme? (XIIIe–XIVe s.)* CaF 20 (Toulouse, 1985), pp. 175–97.

Powell, J. M., *Innocent III. Vicar of Christ or Lord of the World?* 2nd edn ed. J. M. Powell (Washington, D.C., 1994), pp. 121–34.

Pryds, D., 'Proclaiming Sanctity through Proscribed Acts. The Case of Rose of Viterbo', in B. M. Kienzle and P. J. Walker, *Women Preachers and Prophets through Two Millennia of Christianity* (Berkeley, CA, 1998), pp. 159–72. pp. 159–72.

Queller, D. E. and Madden, T. F., *The Fourth Crusade. The Conquest of Constantinople*, 2nd edn (Philadelphia, 1997).

Recueil des historiens des Gaules et de la France, ed. M. Bouquet *et al.*, 24 vols. (Paris, 1738–1904).

Reeves, M., *The Influence of Prophecy in the Later Middle Ages: A Study in Joachimism* (Oxford, 1969).

Riché, P., 'Instruments de travail et méthodes de l'exégète à l'époque carolingienne', in *Le Moyen Âge et la Bible*, ed. P. Riché and G. Lobrichon, La Bible de tous les temps 4 (Paris, 1984), pp. 147–61.

Rigier, A., *Trobairitz. Der Beitrag der Frau in de altokzitanischen höfischen Lyrik. Edition des Gesamtkorpus* (Tubingen, 1991).

Riley-Smith, J., *The First Crusade and the Idea of Crusading* (Philadelphia, 1986).

Roberts, P., 'Medieval University Preaching: The Evidence in the Statutes', in *Medieval Sermons and Society: Cloister, City, University*, ed. J. Hamesse, B. M. Kienzle, D. L. Stoudt and A. T. Thayer, FIDEM Textes et Études du Moyen Âge 9 (Louvain-la-Neuve, 1998), pp. 317–28.

Roquebert, M., 'Le catharisme comme tradition dans la 'familia' languedocienne', in *Effacement du Catharisme? (XIIIe–XIVe s.)*, CaF 20 (Toulouse, 1985), pp. 221–42.

——*L'épopée cathare*, 4 vols. (Toulouse, 1970–89).

Rouse, R., 'Cistercian Aids to Study in the Thirteenth Century', in *Studies in Medieval Cistercian History II*, ed. J. R. Sommerfeldt, Cistercian Studies 24 (Kalamazoo, MI, 1976), pp. 123–34.

——, and Rouse, M., '*Statim invenire*: Schools, Preachers, and New Attitudes to the Page', in *Renaissance and Renewal*, pp. 201–25.

Rubellin, M., 'Au temps où Valdès n'était pas hérétique: hypothèses sur le rôle de Valdès à Lyon (1170–1183)', in *Inventer l'hérésie?*, pp. 193–217.

Russell, J. B., *The Devil: Perceptions of Evil from Antiquity to Primitive Christianity* (Ithaca, NY, 1977).

——*Lucifer: The Devil in the Middle Ages* (Ithaca, NY, 1984).

——*Dissent and Order in the Middle Ages: The Search for Legitimate Authority* (New York, 1992).

Sabatier, A., *Vie des saints du diocèse de Beauvais* (Beauvais, 1866).

Schaeffer, J.-M., *Qu'est-ce qu'un genre littéraire* (Paris, 1989).

Schneiders, S. M. 'Hermeneutics', in *The New Jerome Biblical Commentary*, ed. R. E. Brown, J. A. Fitzmyer and R. E. Murphy (Englewood Cliffs, NJ, 1990), 71:65.

Schneyer, J. B., *Repertorium der lateinischen Sermones des Mittelalters für die Zeit von 115–1350*, in progress (Münster, 1969–).

Schüssler Fiorenza, E., *Bread Not Stone: The Challenge of Feminist Biblical Interpretation* (Boston, 1984).

——*But She Said. Feminist Practices of Biblical Interpretation* (Boston, 1992).

——*In Memory of Her* (New York, 1983).

Scopello, M., 'Le renard symbole de l'hérésie dans les polémiques patristiques contre les gnostiques', *Revue d'Histoire et de Philosophie Religieuses* 71 (1991), 73–88.

Shannon, A. C., *The Medieval Inquisition* (Collegeville, MN, 1984).

Smalley, B., *The Gospels in the Schools c. 1100–c. 1280* (London, 1985).

——*The Study of the Bible in the Middle Ages*, 1st edn (Oxford, 1952).

Smetana, C., 'Paul the Deacon's Patristic Anthology', in *The Old English Homily and its Backgrounds,* ed. with an Introduction by P. E. Szarmach and B. F. Huppé (Albany, 1978).

Smith, C. E., *The University of Toulouse in the Middle Ages* (Milwaukee, 1958).

Smits, E., 'Editing the *Chronicon* of Hélinand of Froidmont: The Marginal Notes', *Sacris erudiri* 32 (1991), 269–89.

——'Hélinand of Froidmont, Science and the School of Chartres', in *Knowledge and the Sciences in Medieval Philosophy. Proceedings of the Eighth International Congress of Medieval Philosophy, Helsinki 24–29 August 1987*, III, Annals of the Finnish Society for Missiology and Ecumenics 55 (Helsinki, 1990), pp. 522–30.

——'An Unedited Correspondence between Hélinand of Froidmont and Philip, Abbot of Val Ste Marie, on Genesis 27.1 and the Ages of the World', in *Erudition at God's Service*, ed. J. R. Sommerfeldt, *Studies in Medieval Cistercian History, XI*, Cistercian Studies 98 (Kalamazoo, MI, 1987), pp. 243–66.

Southern, R., *Western Society and the Church in the Middle Ages* (Harmondsworth, 1970).

Spatz, N., 'Evidence of Inception Ceremonies in the Twelfth-Century Schools of Paris', *History of Universities*, 13 (1994), 3–19.

——'Imagery in University Inception Sermons', in *Medieval Sermons and Society: Cloister, City, University*, ed. J. Hamesse, B. M. Kienzle, D. L. Stoudt and A. T. Thayer, FIDEM Textes et Études du Moyen Âge 9 (Louvain-la-Neuve, 1998), pp. 329–42.

Stephen, L., and Lee, S., eds., *Dictionary of National Biography*, 64 vols. (London, 1885–1900).

Stock, B., *The Implications of Literacy. Written Language and Models of Interpretation in the Eleventh and Twelfth Centuries* (Princeton, NJ, 1983).

——*Listening for the Text. On the Uses of the Past* (Baltimore/London, 1990).

Strayer, J. R., *The Albigensian Crusades*, with a new epilogue by C. Lansing (Ann Arbor, 1992).

——ed., *Dictionary of the Middle Ages*, 13 vols. (New York, 1982–9).

Stronski, S., *Le troubadour Folquet de Marseille, édition critique précédée d'une étude biographique et littéraire* (Cracow, 1910).

Sumption, J., *The Albigensian Crusade* (London, 1978).

Thouzellier, C., 'La Bible des cathares', in *Cathares en Languedoc*, CaF 3 (Toulouse, 1968), pp. 42–58.

Thouzellier, C., *Catharisme et Valdéisme en Languedoc à la fin du XIIe et au début du XIIIe siècle. Politique pontificale – Controverses*, 2nd edn (Paris, 1969).

——*Un traité cathare inédit* (Louvain, 1961).

Torjesen, K. J., '"Body", Soul and "Spirit" in Origen's Theory of Exegesis', *American Theological Review* 67 (1985), 17–30.

Trout, J. M., 'Preaching by the Laity in the Twelfth Century', in *Studies in Medieval Culture 4.1*, ed. J. R. Sommerfeldt, L. Syndergaard and E. R. Elder (Kalamazoo, MI, 1975), p. 92–108.

Van Engen, J. H., 'The Christian Middle Ages as an Historiographical Problem', *American Historical Review* 91 (1986), 519–52.

Vauchez, A., *The Laity in the Middle Ages. Religious Beliefs and Devotional Practices*, ed. and intro. D. E. Bornstein, trans. M. J. Schneider (Notre Dame, IN, 1993).

Verger, J., 'Jean XXII et Benoît XII et les universités du Midi', in *La papauté d'Avignon et le Languedoc (1316–1342)*, CaF 26 (Toulouse, 1991), pp. 199–219.

——'La prédication dans les Universités méridionales', in *La prédication en Pays d'Oc (XIIe–début XVe siècle)*, ed. J.-L. Biget, CaF 32 (Toulouse, 1997), pp. 275–94.

Vicaire, M.-H., ed., *Les Cisterciens de Languedoc (XIIIe–XIVe s.)*, CaF 21 (Toulouse, 1986).

——'Les clercs de la croisade', in *Paix de Dieu et guerre sainte en Languedoc au XIIIe siècle*, CaF 4, ed. M.-H. Vicaire (Toulouse, 1969), pp. 260–80.

——*Histoire de Saint Dominique*, 2 vols. (Paris, 1957).

——, ed., *Paix de Dieu et Guerre Sainte en Languedoc au XIIIe siècle*, CaF 4 (Toulouse, 1969).

Wailes, S. L., *Medieval Allegories of Jesus' Parables* (Berkeley, CA, 1987).

Wakefield, W., *Heresy, Crusade and Inquisition in Southern France, 1100–1250* (Berkeley, CA, 1974).

——and Evans, A. P., *Heresies of the High Middle Ages. Selected Sources Translated and Annotated*, Records of Western Civilization Sources and Studies 81 (New York, 1991).

Waugh, S. L. and Diehl, P. D., *Christendom and its Discontents. Exclusion, Persecution and Rebellion, 1000–1050* (Cambridge, 1996).

Welter, J.-T., *L'exemplum dans la littérature religieuse et didactique du moyen âge* (Paris, 1929).

Werblowsky, R. J. Zwi, 'Introduction', *In Praise of the New Knighthood.* in Bernard of Clairvaux: *Treatises III*, Cistercian Fathers 19 (Kalamazoo, MI, 1977).

Wild, R. A., 'The Pastoral Letters', in *The New Jerome Biblical Commentary*, ed. R. E. Brown, J. A. Fitzmyer and R. E. Murphy (Englewood Cliffs, NJ, 1990), pp. 891–902.

Wildhaber, B., 'Catalogue des établissements cisterciens de Languedoc au XIIIe et XIVe siècles', *Cisterciens*, CaF, pp. 21–44.

Wiles, M., *Archetypal Heresy. Arianism through the Centuries* (Oxford, 1996).

Wilmart, A. 'Les homélies attribuées à S. Anselme', *Archives d'histoire doctrinale et littéraire du moyen âge* 2 (1927), 5–29, 339–41.

Woesthuis, M. M, 'History and Preaching in Hélinand of Froidmont', *Sacris erudiri*, 34 (1994), 313–33.

Wolff, P., *Histoire du Languedoc* (Toulouse, 1967).

Zerfass, R., *Der Streit um die Laienpredigt* (Freiburg, 1974).

Zerner, M., ed., *Inventer l'hérésie? Discours polémiques et pouvoirs avant l'Inquisition*, Collection du Centre d'Etudes Mediévales de Nice 2 (Nice, 1998).

——'Question sur la naissance de l'affaire albigeoise', in *Georges Duby. L'Écriture de l'Histoire*, ed. C. Duhamel-Amado and G. Lobrichon, Bibliothèque du Moyen Âge 6 (Brussels, 1996).

Zerner-Chardavoine, M., 'L'abbé Gui des Vaux-de-Cernay, prédicateur de croisade', in *Cisterciens*, CaF, pp. 183–204.

——'Au temps de l'appel aux armes contre les hérétiques: du *Contra Henricum* du moine Guillaume aux *Contra hereticos*', in *Inventer l'hérésie?*, pp. 119–56.

Zimmermann, H., *Die päpstliche Legation in der ersten Hälfte des 13. Jahrhunderts vom Regierungsantritt Innocenz' III. bis zum Tode Gregors IX (1198–1241)* (Paderborn, 1913).

INDEX

Note: Page numbers in italics indicate photographs. References to the major topics of the book – Cistercians, heresy, and preaching – are extensive but not exhaustive. Individual chapters should be consulted carefully.

Abelard, Peter 32, 33, 34, 35, 80, 91, 130, 177
Acre 208
Acts of the Apostles 14, 99, 197
  5. 29, 130
  8. 9–24 119
  13. 51 99
  14. 21 217
Acts of Peter see Peter
Ad abolendam see inquisition
Adam of Perseigne 34, 38, 159, 181
Adelaide of Béziers 132
Adversus Waldensium sectam liber see
  Bernard of Fontcaude
Agen 181
agricultural imagery 95, 122, 147, 166, 189, 205
Aimery of Montréal 168
Aimery of Solignac 164
Aix, region of 145, 150
Alan of Lille 5, 34, 35, 45, 54, 131, 172–3, 201, 206, 214
  against Cathar beliefs 184, 194, 195
  and name Cathar 119
  speculum image 67
  translation of vernacular sermon 137, 140, 201
Alberic of Ostia, legate 82, 93
Albi 91, 100, 101, 105, 106, 124, 128, 132, 166, 187, 203, 211
Albigensian crusade *see* crusade
Alexander III, pope 44, 65, 114, 115, 119, 127
Alexander IV, pope 211
Alexandria 63, 64, 67, 195
  see also exegesis
allegory *see* exegesis
Almohads 159, 160
Amaury of Montfort 160, 207
Ambrose of Milan, St 64, 121 n. 41, 195
Anacletus (Peter Leonis), antipope 80

Andrew of St Victor 66
animals, images of 87, 94, 120, 123, 215
  see also dog, fox, mole, serpent, sheep, wolf
Anonymous of Passau 119
Anselm of Canterbury, teacher at monastery of Bec, archbishop of Canterbury 65 n. 41
Anselm of Laon 65
Antichrist 14, 126, 169, 194, 199, 200, 203, 209, 217
antithesis 76
antitype 18, 68, 204
  see also typology
Apelles 193, 194
apocalypticism 3, 11, 104, 109, 126, 200, 203, 205, 209, 215; *see also* rhetoric
apocryphal literature, Christian *see* Peter, *Acts of Peter*; *Virtutes apostolorum*
apostles, apostolic models 7, 99, 100, 102, 106, 143, 146
  and Cistercians 7, 103, 147
  and dissidents 84, 87, 100, 103, 190
  and lay movements 5, 9, 15, 42
Arabic language 35
Archenfred, Master, letter to 100; *see also* Geoffrey of Auxerre; *Vita prima*
Ardura, B. 7 n. 23
Arianism, Arians, Arius 13, 92, 96, 103, 116, 117, 121, 124
Arles and archbishop of 91, 145, 150
Arnaud Amaury, abbot of Grandselve, Cîteaux, legate, and archbishop of Narbonne 5, 6, 10, 54, 163, 164, 165, 167, 168, 170, 171, 174, 189, 200, 201, 204, 206, 207, 208, 209, 214, 215, 216
  during Albigensian Crusade 152–61
  pre-Crusade 136–52
Arnaud Nouvel, abbot 211
Arnold of Brescia 43

Arnoldists 44
Arnulf of St Martin of Troarn, abbot 70
    n. 66
Arras 110
Ascension, sermon of Hélinand 185–7
asceticism 13, 104, 216; *see also* Cathars
Assize of Clarendon *see* inquisition
Auch 210
Auerbach, Eric 67 n. 54
Augustine, St, bishop 9, 18, 74, 100, 166,
    191, 196, 201
    De doctrina christiana 63 n. 28, 64, 67
Authié, Peter (Autier) 211, 218
authority 19, 84, 87
    see also preaching, authorization
Avignon 212
Avignonet 211

Baal 115, 205
Babylon, image of 9, 54, 56, 141, 142, 205
Baker, Derek 30–1 n. 20, 215–16 n. 27
Baldwin of Ford abbot, archbishop of
    Canterbury 208
Baldwin, John 28–9 n. 11, 117 n. 30, 118,
    171, 172 nn. 159, 161, 179 n. 23
baptism *see* sacraments
Beaucaire 155
Beauvais 35, 174, 176, 177, 178, 179
Bec, Pierre 36 n. 50, 50 n. 104
Bede, Venerable 68, 74
beguine movement 172
Bélibaste, William 212
Belleperche, abbot of 215
    Cistercian monastery 171
Benedict of Aniane 58 n. 3
Benedict XII *see* Fournier, Jacques
Benedict of Nursia 56, 133
Berengar of Tours 32
Berenger of Narbonne, archbishop 143,
    144, 145
Berger, David 108
Bergerac 91
Bériou, Nicole 172 n. 161, 213 n. 26
Berlioz, Jacques 143 n. 34, 153 n. 80, 154
    n. 86, 155, 156, 159 n. 105
Berman, Constance 2 n. 2, 41 nn. 67–8
Bernard of Clairvaux, St 29, 31, 33, 34,
    60, 73, 121 n. 41, 175, 182, 186, 189,
    200, 201, 202, 214, 217
    as abbot 61, 69
    attitude toward use of force vs heresy

85, 90, 106–08, 109, 122, 170, 204,
    214
    biography 30, 80–1
    canonization 99, 112
    chimera image 30, 81, 107, 204
    and inquisitorial process 52
    and interpretation of Scripture 18, 62,
        69
    and the Jews 107–08
    leadership of Cistercian order 54
    miracles *see* miracles
    preaching mission (1145) 3, 10, 15, 21,
        28, 40, 55, 81, 82, 90–106, 148, 166,
        202, 203, 204
    and the Second Crusade (1147) 72, 74,
        80, 81, 142, 208
    in *Vita prima* 97, 98, 99, 100, 106
    Works 62 n. 62
    *Five Books on Consideration: Advice to a
        Pope (De consideratione)* 5, 199
    Letters 205
        241 81, 93–5, 106
        242 81, 85, 93, 95–7, 106, 121
        250 30 n. 19
        256 106
        326 30 n. 19
        394 81
        544 106
    *In Praise of the New Knighthood (Liber
        ad milites Templi)* 30 n. 19, 80, 109
        n. 2, 115 n. 21
    Sermons *On the Song of Songs* 8, 10,
        64, 75, 78, 81, 82, 85–90, 190, 192,
        214
    Sermons for the Summer Season 31 n. 24,
        119 n. 36, 122 n. 48
Bernard Gui 211
Bernard of Fontcaude 122 n. 48, 131
Bernard Raymond 113 n. 13, 125, 126,
    133
Bernard of Tiron 43
Benveniste, Emile 16
Bertran de Born, converted troubadour
    28, 37, 165
Bertran of Ventadorn, converted
    troubadour 37
Bertrand of Sts John and Paul, cardinal
    legate 155, 165, 169–70
Besançon 44
Béziers 5–6, 146, 149, 152, 153–4, 155,
    156, 159, 160, 206, 207

Biget, Jean-Louis 21, 22 n. 19, 96 n. 66, 114, 132 n. 95, 145 n. 43
Biller, Peter 44 n. 85, 47 n. 94, 48, 49 n. 100, 50 n. 105, 89 n. 39, 110 n. 4
Bird, Jessalyn 29 n. 11, 143 n. 33, 157, 159, 173
Blanche of Castille 181
boar, image 94
Boglioni, Pierre 99 n. 73
Bogomils, and Cathars 46, 47, 55, 217
Bologna 36, 186
Bonneval, abbot of 142, 197
Bolton, Brenda 7 nn. 24, 26, 8 n. 28, 65 n. 43, 106
Bonizon of Sutri 195 n. 94
Bonnassie, Pierre 182, 186
Bordeaux 91, 92, 152, 210
Bornstein, Daniel 42 n. 74
Bourges 210
Boswell, John 27 n. 6, 117, 118, 119 n. 33
Bouchard, Constance 41 n. 68
Bouchard of Marly 164
Bounoure, Gilles 3 n. 9, 91, 92 n. 53, 97–8 n. 71, 98, 100
Bozóky, Edina 184 n. 48
Bredero A. H. 4 n. 13, 81 n. 6
Brenon, Anne 37 n. 53, 44 n. 84, 47 n. 94, 49 n. 103, 50 n. 105, 82 n. 11, 85 n. 19, 144 n. 39, 169 n. 150, 190 n. 76, 197 n. 102, 217
Brown, Raymond 18 n. 7, 63 n. 31, 64 n. 39, 69 n. 59
Brundage, James 85 n. 21, 106
Buc, Philippe 131 n. 91
Bulgaria 46, 183
Bulgarii 198
Bynum, Caroline Walker 25 n. 1, 145 n. 45

Cabau, Patrice 165 nn. 133, 135; 167 nn. 140, 141, 142; 168 n. 146, 169 n. 148, 170 n. 153, 174 n. 3, 184 n. 51
Cabrer, Martín Alvira 138 nn. 14, 15, 158 n. 99, 159, 160 n. 107, 161
Caesarius of Heisterbach 5–6, 127, 133, 138, 139, 148, 149, 152, 153, 154, 159, 207, 210, 214
Cahors 91, 92, 187
Calatrava, order of 159
Candeil, Cistercian monastery 171
canon law 52, 119, 132

Canso de la Crozada 6, 137–8, 155, 157, 165, 167, 168, 169, 207, 214
see also William of Tudela
Canterbury, nun of *see* Leicester, countess of; *see also* Baldwin of Canterbury
Carcassonne 40, 154, 164, 211
and Albigensian Crusade 152, 156, 157, 163, 181
site of preaching and debates 146, 149
see also Guy of les-Vaux-Cernay
Carman, J. N. 179 n. 26
Carpocrates 195–6
Casseneuil 163
Castelnaudary 181
Catalonia 138, 160
Cate, J. L. 177–8 n. 16, 178 n. 17
Casey, Michael 34 n. 35, 60 nn. 14, 16
Cathars 4, 51, 62, 71, 87, 92, 111, 120, 164, 183, 206
beliefs and practices 47, 50, 110, 140, 144, 149, 183–5, 189–92, 193, 195–7, 199–202
asceticism 184, 189, 190, 200, 201, 209
consolamentum 13, 47, 144, 184, 196–7
docetism 13, 47, 140, 143, 184, 193, 200, 201
dualism 111, 144, 183–4
rejection of traditional sacraments 13, 47, 50, 84, 110, 111, 144, 183, 185, 190, 195, 196–7, 199, 201
structure of church 46, 55, 123, 128, 189, 190, 201
believers (*credentes*) 46, 189, 190, 201
bishops 46, 110, 123, 149, 183, 190, 201
electi 189, 190, 201
perfectae 14, 169
perfecti 40
communities, *castrum* and city 39, 40, 48, 54
and economic growth 41
literacy 48–9
liturgy 47
in Occitania 46, 47–9, 96, 98, 103
outside Occitania: England, Germany, France 52, 109, 110, 111
see also Arras; Cologne; Eckbert of Schönau; Elisabeth of Schönau;

Cathars *(cont.)*
  Everwin of Steinfeld; Hildegard of
    Bingen; Oxford
  name given to them 103, 128
  name used by themselves 46, 110
  preaching 123–4, 128
  social class of 40, 47–8
  and troubadours 49–51
  see also Interrogatio Iohannis; Publicani
Celestine II, pope 91
Celestine III, pope 127
Chaeremon the Stoic 191
Chalande, J. 182 n. 44
Chanson de la croisade albigeoise see *Canzo
  de la crozada* 6, 148
Charlemagne 28
Charles the Good 176
Chartres 34, 199
Châtillon, J. 32 n. 28, 65 nn. 41, 42, 43;
  66 nn. 45, 46, 48, 49
Chazan, Robert 11 n. 36, 21 n. 18, 27 n. 6,
  51 n. 108, 68 n. 57, 105 n. 91, 108
  n. 99, 120 n. 37, 142 n. 33, 143 n. 35,
  172 n. 159, 208 n. 9
Chenu, Marie-Dominique 18 n. 4, 31
  n. 23, 67
Christ *see* Jesus Christ
chronicles, as source for history of
  preaching 10–11, 203, 204, 214
  see also specific titles
Chronicon Clarevallensis 132
Cistercian Order
  abbots 44, 108, 135, 136, 137, 147, 148,
    161, 202, 207, 216
  see also monasticism, abbot
  aesthetics 76
  agriculture 40
  bishops 5, 29, 54, 136, 145, 174, 209
  see also specific names
  countryside, settlement of the 40–1
  and economic growth 38, 40–1, 54
  exegesis 18
  expansion in Occitania *see* Occitania
  foundation and early history 1, 4, 53–4
  General Chapter 7, 114, 124, 135, 139,
    140, 146, 152, 158, 159–60
  and inquisition *see* inquisition
  and lay spirituality 42
  literature *see* monasticism, literature
  and reform movement 4, 29–31, 33,
    53–4, 189
  see also reform

preaching
  compilation of reference works 35, 45
  missions against heresy *see* preaching,
    by Cistercians; Bernard of
    Clairvaux; Henry of Clairvaux/
    Albano; Arnaud Amaury; Guy of
    les-Vaux-de-Cernay; Fulk of
    Toulouse; Hélinand of Froidmont
  statutes 45 n. 88, 139 n. 16, 141, 160,
    179, 213, 215
  and troubadours 37
  and 'Twelfth-Century Renaissance'
    33–5
  in Occitania 36–8
  and the university 33, 209, 212–13
    Collège Saint Bernard 212
  and Waldensians *see* Waldensians
  worldview 76, 138
  see also Eugene III; Innocent III
Cîteaux 34, 138, 139, 145, 146, 152, 154,
  155, 159, 160, 161, 172, 182, 206
  see also Cistercian Order
Clark, Ann 4 n. 12
classics, classical authors 32, 62, 185,
  186, 188, 199
Clement III, pope 127, 133
Clermont 130
Cluny and Cluniacs 28, 29, 30, 43, 80; *see
  also Dialogue between a Cluniac and a
  Cistercian*; Gregorian Reforms;
  reform
Cole, Penny 2 n. 4, 7 n. 25, 29 n. 12, 45
  n. 88, 72 n. 77, 112 n. 11, 133 n. 102,
  134 n. 104, 135 nn. 2, 3; 136 n. 5, 142
  n. 31, 160 n. 108, 209 n. 9
Cologne 4, 72, 82, 83, 110
Comminges, bishop of 142
Congar, Yves 5 n. 15, 8 n. 33, 108 n. 100,
  109, 111 nn. 10, 11; 114, 115 n. 21,
  116, 119 n. 35, 121, 125 n. 61, 127
  nn. 67, 69; 129 nn. 73, 77; 132, 133
  nn. 100, 101; 134
Conrad of Eberbach 91 n. 48, 102 n. 85,
  103
Conrad of Urach 139 n. 16, 174 n. 2
Constable, Giles 11 n. 36, 25 n. 2, 29
  n. 14, 30 n. 19, 41 n. 68, 45 n. 89, 72
  nn. 73, 74, 76; 80 n. 2, 85 n. 21
Constantinople 159, 162
Corinthians, First Letter of Paul to the
  10. 6, 63
  11. 27–30 98
  15. 32 119

Corinthians, Second Letter of Paul to the
3. 6 62
11.14, 11. 26 125
Costen, M. 1 n. 1, 165 n. 145, 181 n. 38
Council of Avignon (1209) 167
Council of Chartres (1150) 106
Council of Constance (1417) 213
Council of Lombers (1165) 71, 110
Council of Lyons (1180) 132
Council of Montpellier (1162) 127; *see also* inquisition
Council of Pisa (1135) 3, 91
Council of Rheims (1148) 34 (1157) 110, 127
Council of Sens (1140) 43
Council of Toulouse 1119 127; (1229) *see* Toulouse, synod
Council of Tours (1163) 60, 127; *see also* inquisition
Council of Verona (1184) *see* inquisition, *Ad abolendam*
Cracco, Giorgio 82 n. 12
Crete 191
cross, and crucifixion, symbol and theology of 140–3
Crouse, R. D. 63 n. 29
Crump, Henry 212
crusade 1, 2, 45, 135, 192
  Albigensian 1, 2–3, 15, 39, 45, 53, 136, 138, 139 n. 16, 153, 160, 162, 163, 164, 167, 170, 172, 173, 174, 179, 187, 192, 200, 207, 209, 210
  anti-Jewish propaganda 45
  Baltic 208, 210
  First 29
  Fourth 159, 161–3, 171, 207, 208
  Holy Land 2, 7, 29, 74, 80, 112, 133–4, 135, 139, 140, 142, 155, 160, 164, 171, 173, 207, 208, 209, 210
  ideology 112, 115, 134, 145, 160, 204, 207–08
  Second 5, 74, 81, 107
  Third 106, 204, 208
  see also Bernard of Clairvaux; Cistercian Order; Guy of les-Vaux-de-Cernay; Henry of Clairvaux/Albano; heresy; preaching
Curtius, Ernst R. 32 n. 27
Czeski, A. 48 n. 96

Dahan, Gilbert 11 n. 35, 39 n. 62, 68 n. 56, 94 n. 60

Dalon, Cistercian monastery 37
Daley, Brian 63 n. 9, 64 nn. 32, 34
d'Alverny, Marie-Thérèse 35 n. 44, 137 n. 10, 140 n. 21
Damietta 210
Daniel, prophet 125
d'Autremont Angleton, C. 41 n. 67, 91 n. 46
David *see* Goliath
d'Avray, David 46 n. 90
de Lage, Raynaud 140 n. 22, 172
de Lahondès, J. 182 n. 44
Delettre, C. 180 n. 31
de Lubac, Henri 62 n. 27, 63 n. 29, 64 n. 34
deconstruction *see* methodology
Decretum see Gratian
Delcorno, Carlo 16 n. 2
demonization, rhetoric of 1, 11, 84, 96, 104, 134, 142, 153, 184, 189, 191, 197, 199, 201, 203, 205, 209, 215
de Rougemont, Denis 49 n. 101
Devil 82, 120, 134, 140, 141, 142, 151, 153, 183, 184, 190, 191, 194, 197, 199, 215
de Vogüé, Adalbert 58 n. 5, 59 nn. 7, 10, 11, 12; 61 n. 22, 62 nn. 23, 24
de Waal, E. 56 n. 2
Dialogue between a Cluniac and a Cistercian 58
Dialogus miraculorum see Caesarius of Heisterbach
Diego of Osma, bishop 147, 149, 151
Diehl, P. D. 210 n. 13
Dimier, A. 178 n. 18, 179 n. 27
disobedience 12
disputation 83, 86
distinctiones see preaching, techniques and tools
dog, dogs 87, 94, 104, 166, 197, 215
Dominic of Guzman St 6, 7, 146, 167, 209, 210
Dominican order 2, 7, 46, 146, 165, 170, 175, 186, 187, 207, 209, 210, 216
  see also Fulk of Toulouse; inquisition; mendicant orders; Toulouse
Dordogne, river 91
Dossat, Yves 183 n. 45
Douglas, Mary 12 n. 37
Dronke, Peter 32 n. 27
Dumontier, Cistercian scholar 196 n. 100
Dunstan, St 186
Durand of Huesca 129 n. 77, 131, 149

Duvernoy, Jean 45 n. 86, 47 n. 94, 119
n. 34, 129 n. 77, 144 n. 40, 184 n. 52,
191 n. 82, 198 n. 108, 211, 215 n. 27

Eagleton, Terry 19, 23
East *see* West
Eastern (Orthodox) church 158, 159, 206
Eaunes, abbot of 136
Eglise des Jacobins, Toulouse *175*
Eckbert of Schönau, *Sermones contra
Catharos* 4, 103, 110, 193
see also Elisabeth of Schönau,
Hildegard of Bingen
Edessa 209
Egypt 141, 191, 201
Elijah, prophet 166
Elisabeth of Schönau 4, 110
Elisha, prophet 119, 120
Embrun 150
Engelberg, Benedictine abbey 73
England 3, 4, 34, 46, 70 n. 66, 72 n. 72,
109, 110, 112, 114, 177
see also Oxford
Epicurus 199
Ermengaud of St Gilles, abbot 172
Ernaldus, biographer 33
Esclarmonde of Foix, *perfecta* 169
Esdra, book of 198
Estella 212
Etienne of Bourbon 166 n. 139, 172 n. 165
Eucharist 14, 32, 47
see also Cathars, beliefs and practices
Eugene III, Pope 5, 30, 91, 106, 204, 208
Euripides 191
Eustache of Flay 177–8
evangelism 13, 27, 62, 131, 216
see also preaching
Evans, Austin P. 1 n. 1, 168 n. 145, 174
n. 2, 135 n. 2, 136 n. 6, 150 n. 66,
154 n. 84, 160 nn. 108, 110, 181 n. 38,
185 n. 54
Evans, Gilian R. 32 n. 26
Everwin of Steinfeld, prior, and letter to
Bernard of Clairvaux on heresy 4,
15, 82–4, 85, 86, 88, 89, 90, 93, 103,
190, 202, 214
exegesis 9, 17, 18, 62–9, 104
see also monasticism, exegesis;
typology
exemplum, exempla 10–11, 105, 112, 133,
138, 142, 148, 149, 153, 166, 186, 194,
195, 201, 204, 206, 208, 214

Exordium magnum cisterciense 81, 101,
102, 103, 105, 106, 112 n. 12, 214
Ezekiel
prophet 192
21. 3–14 192

Fachinger, E. 136 n. 4, 145 nn. 43, 46;
150 n. 66, 151 nn. 67, 72
faidits 2, 160, 215
Falmagne, Thomas 213 n. 25
Fanjeaux 48, *203*
Felten, F. J. 211 n. 18
Fernández, E. Mitre 8 n. 33
Fichtenau, Heinrich 25 n. 1, 32 nn. 28,
29
Flanders 176
florilegia 70
see also monasticism, literature
Foix, and count of 36, 39 n. 16, 169, 211,
215
Fontcaude, Praemonstratensian Abbey
of *111*
Fontevrault, double monastery 43
Fontfroide, Cistercian Abbey of 2, 40,
137, 143, 160, 207, 208, 211, 212
Foreville, Raymonde 135 n. 2, 138 n. 14,
140 n. 20, 158 n. 99, 159 n. 103, 161
Fournier, Jacques, abbot, bishop, Pope
Benedict XII 2, 175, 211, 212
foxes 8, 9, 78, 82, 85, 86, 87, 89, 103, 110,
120, 122, 123, 124, 138, 150, 204, 215
Francis of Assisi, St 210
Franciscan order 2, 46, 210
see also mendicant orders
Frederick I Barbarossa, Emperor 44, 52,
115, 131
friars *see* Dominicans; Franciscans;
mendicant orders
Froidmont, Cistercian abbey of 178, 180,
196, 216
see also Hélinand of Froidmont
Fulk of Neuilly 135, 139–40
Fulk of Toulouse, troubadour, abbot of
Le Thoronet, bishop 6, 15, 28, 37,
38, 45, 48, 51, 54, 98, 99, 136, 142,
145, 147, 148, 149, 150, 151, 155, 157,
161, 164, 165–71, 172, 174, 181, 182,
184, 207, 209, 210, 214, 216

Galatians, Letter to the
2. 4 125
6. 14 141, 142 n. 30

Garin of Bourges 121
Garnier of Rochefort, bishop of Langres 35
Gascony 3, 97, 128
Gatien-Arnoult, A. F. 183 n. 45, 185
Gaucelin of Lodève, bishop 71, 110
Genesis, book of 35. 3 140
Geoffrey of Auxerre 33, 34, 60, 73, 112, 133, 182, 198, 204, 205, 206, 214
    In apocalypsim 70, 75, 113 n. 14, 133 n. 99, 182, 198
    Vita prima 87, 92, 93, 97, 98, 99, 100, 101, 105, 116–17
    and Waldensians 129, 130, 131
Geoffrey of Chartres, bishop 91, 97
Gerald of Wales 41
Geralda of Lavaur 168
Gerard of Fracheto 210
Géraud, H. 176 n. 9, 179 n. 21, 180 n. 29
Germany 46, 110, 133, 210
    see also Cologne; Rhineland
Gervase of Tilbury 155
Giddens, Anthony 21 n. 16
Gilbert of Poitiers, bishop 33, 34, 130
Ginzburg, Carlo 22
Girard, René 12 n. 38, 22–3, 103
Giselbertus, chronicler 133
Glossa ordinaria 64, 66
    see also exegesis
gnosticism, gnostics 193, 195, 196
Goliath, and David 122, 205
Gonnet, Giovanni 128 n. 70, 129 nn. 73, 75; 130 n. 82, 131 nn. 88, 90; 132 n. 93
Grail, story 38, 180
Grandselve, Cistercian monastery of 40, 41, 170–71, 211, 216
    see also Aimery of Solignac; Arnaud Amaury; Hélie Garin, William of Grandselve
Gratian, *Decretum* 36, 52
Greece 13, 84
Greek language 35
Grégoire, Réginald 64 n. 38
Gregory the Great, pope 17 n. 3, 74, 121 n. 41, 189
    Moralia in Job 199
    De regulae pastoralis 189
Gregory VII, pope 28, 194; *see also* Gregorian reforms
Gregory VIII, pope 127, 133, 210
Gregory IX, pope 181, 187, 210

Gregorian reforms 25, 28, 29, 31, 38, 42, 51, 54, 80; *see also* reform movements
Grundmann, Herbert 27 n. 5, 42, 46 n. 90, 48 n. 96, 51 n. 109, 87 n. 26, 92 n. 54, 209 n. 9
Guichard of Lyons, abbot, archbishop 5, 129, 130, 131
Guillaume I, abbot 178
Gutsch, . '. R. 172 n. 159
Guy of les-Vaux-de-Cernay, abbot, bishop of Carcassonne 6, 15, 136, 137, 147, 150, 151, 159, 161–5, 168, 170, 172, 174, 179, 207, 208, 209, 214

Hadrian IV, pope 43
Hagman, Ylva 47 n. 94, 197 n. 102
Halley's Comet (1145) 3, 91
Hamilton, Bernard 46 n. 91, 47 n. 94, 48 n. 99
Häring, N. M. 32 n. 26
Haskins, Charles Homer 25 n. 1
Head, Thomas 39 n. 59
Hebrews, Letter to the 5. 4 85
Hélie Garin, abbot 6, 174, 182, 209
Hélinand of Froidmont 35, 38, 54, 130, 173, 214, 217
    life and works 162, 165, 176–81
    and Peter Comestor 66
    preaching in Toulouse 6, 8, 10, 36, 53, 182–92, 209, 216
    sermons against heresy (not in Toulouse) 193–99, 206, 213
    on Virgin Mary and elephant 69
Hellebaud, uncle of Hélinand 176
Henry II, king 30, 110, 112, 114, 120, 134, 176
Henry of Clairvaux/Albano, abbot, cardinal legate 5, 8, 10, 15, 88, 109, 112–34, 192, 200, 201, 204, 206, 207, 208, 214, 215, 216, 217
    De peregrinante civitate Dei 112, 134
    1178 mission 112, 113–29
    1181 mission 131, 132–3
    Letters
        11 112, 113, 115, 119–21, 128, 134, 192
        28 112, 113, 114, 116
        29 112, 113, 116, 121–5, 128, 132
    see also crusade; homosexuality; Lateran Council, Third; Waldensians

Henry of Dreux, bishop of Orléans 176
Henry the monk 3, 43, 52, 91, 92, 93, 94, 95, 98, 101, 200, 202, 203
Henry of Mont-Ste-Marie, abbot 147
Henry of Rheims 176
heresy
  and accusations of sexual immorality *see* sexual immorality; homosexuality
  and apostolic ideal *see* apostolic models
  and ignorance 51, 89, 126
  'intellectual' vs. 'social' 3
  and leprosy 120, 205
  medieval views 13–15, 104–5, 187, 190–2, 200, 209
  persecution by ecclesiastical and secular forces 54, 113, 114, 115, 121
  stereotype of the heretic 51, 104
  and treason 52–3, 116, 184
  twentieth-century views 20–3
  see also Apelles; Arianism, Arians; Cathars; gnostics; Manicheans; Marcion; Waldensians; inquisition; persecution; pollution; rhetoric; specific preachers by name
Héric of Auxerre 194
Herod 184
hierarchy, ecclesiastical 12, 15, 28, 47, 203
  see also Gregorian reforms
hierophants, priests of Athens 191
Higounet, Charles 40 n. 64, 175 n. 6, 212
Hildebert of Le Mans, bishop 43
Hildefonsus, count of St Gilles and Toulouse 93
Hildegard of Bingen 4, 52, 64, 72, 74, 110, 120, 205
Hilka, A. 127 n. 68
Histoire littéraire de la France 154, 157, 161
historiography
  feminist rhetorical 30
  of Catharism 21–2
  of persecution and heresy 20–3
  structuralism 20–1
Holdsworth, Christopher 30 n. 19
homosexuality 88, 117, 118, 119
Holy Land *see* crusade, Holy Land
Honorius III, pope 210
'hook-word' *see* monasticism, literature
Hublocher, H. 192 n. 83

Hugh Francigena, monk 71
Hugh of St Victor, *Didascalion* 66
Humbert of Beaujeu 181
Humbert of Silva Candida 28
Humiliati 44, 132 n. 92
Hungary 161
Hunt, R. W. 177
Hussites 213
Hystoria Albigensis 137, 142, 148, 152, 161, 163, 164, 207, 214
  see also Peter of les-Vaux-de-Cernay

Idung of Prufening 58 n. 4
Ingeburg of Denmark, queen, wife of Philip Augustus 162, 179
Innocent II, pope 5, 43, 80, 91
Innocent III, pope 8, 15, 28, 44, 131, 210, 214
  Albigensian Crusade 150, 151, 154
    see also crusade
  and circle of Peter the Chanter 171, 173
  and Cistercians 7, 8, 30, 54, 135, 138, 139–40, 143–46, 151, 160, 174, 209, 216
    see also Arnaud Amaury; Guy of les-Vaux-de-Cernay; Peter of Castelnau; Peter of les-Vaux-de-Cernay
  crusade to the Holy Land and Spain 136, 139–40, 160, 162
    see also crusade
  and Fourth Lateran Council 28, 159
  and inquisitorial procedures 52, 53
    see also Lateran Council, Fourth
  and reform agenda 206, 207, 208
    see also Arnaud Amaury; crusade; Guy of les-Vaux-de-Cernay; Peter the Chanter
Innocent IV, pope 211
Inquisition 1, 2, 51, 52, 55, 170, 211, 217
  development of procedures 15, 51–3, 55, 107, 127, 134, 204
  Ad abolendam (1184) 44, 52, 131
  Assize of Clarendon (1166) 52, 110
  Cum ex officii (1207) 53
  Ille humani generis (1231) 187, 210
  Vergentis in senium (1199) 52, 116
  see also Dominican Order; Fournier, Jacques; mendicant orders; Toulouse, synod of
integumentum see exegesis

Interrogatio Iohannis 47, 111 n. 8, 183, 193
involucrum see exegesis
Iogna-Prat, Dominique 7 n. 22, 43 n. 80, 83 n. 15, 86 n. 24, 87 n. 31
Isaac of Stella 34
Isidore of Seville 123 n. 50
Italy 3, 4, 35, 46, 110, 183, 210

James of Vitry 167, 171, 172, 173
Jaeger, C. Stephen 32 nn. 25, 27
Jansen, Katherine Ludwig 139 n. 19
Jeremiah, prophet 183, 184
  1. 10 188
  3. 20 183, 184
Jerome, St 9, 64, 85, 191
  Contra Jovinianum 191
  Contra Vigilantium 198
Jerusalem 109, 134, 142
  biblical 183, 184
  heavenly 9, 56, 59–60
  see also *Urbs Ierusalem beata*
Jesus Christ 11, 31, 62, 69, 98, 99, 122, 140, 141, 142, 144, 146, 183, 184, 216
  and meditation 59, 60
  nature, divine vs human 13, 47, 92, 94, 142, 143, 193, 194, 201
  see also Cathars, beliefs and practices
Jews
  and Christian exegetes 65, 66
  and heretics 120, 141
  medieval persecution of 22, 39, 107, 108, 208
  in Occitania 39
  polemics against 68, 94, 141, 142, 143, 206, 208
Jezebel 206
Joachim of Fiore 130, 159, 205
John Bellesmains, bishop 121 n. 43, 127, 131, 132
John Cassian 56 n. 2
John, Gospel of
  2.10 82
  6 98
  10.12 104
  15. 20 217
John of Garland, *De triumphis ecclesiae* 185
John of Lyons 197, 198
John of Salisbury 176, 192
Joseph, coat of 116, 205
Julien of Vézelay 73
Justinian Code 36

Kaelber, 40 nn. 64–5, 47 n. 93, 48 nn. 95, 96, 98
Kienzle, Beverly Mayne 4 n. 12, 6 n. 20, 20 n. 14, 31 n. 20, 44 n. 84, 64 n. 37, 69 n. 60, 70 nn. 64, 66; 71 nn. 67, 68, 69, 70; 72 n. 71, 73 nn. 78, 80; 74 n. 81, 75 nn. 86, 87; 100 n. 78, 120 n. 39, 130 nn. 83, 85; 131 nn. 89, 90, 91; 132 n. 92, 148 n. 58, 151 n. 69, 160 n. 112, 162 n. 121, 174 n. 5, 177 n. 11, 179 nn. 24, 26; 183 nn. 46, 47; 185 n. 56, 186 n. 58, 188 n. 69, 193 n. 86, 194 n. 90, 199 n. 110
Kings, Books of 119, 122
Knighthood 80, 81
Knights Templar 80, 107
Kuttner, S. 36 n. 45

Labécède 168
laity, spirituality of *see* preaching, lay; twelfth century, lay literacy and spirituality
Lambert, Malcolm 1 n. 1, 43 nn. 76–9, 81; 44 nn. 83, 85; 46 n. 91, 47 n. 94, 48 nn. 96, 97, 99; 50 n. 105, 52 n. 112, 95 n. 62, 111 n. 7, 131 n. 90, 150 n. 66, 187 n. 67
Lampe, G. W. H. 69 n. 58
Lanc, Emile 178 n. 22
Landes, Richard 39 n. 59
Lanfranc, teacher at monastery of Bec, archbishop of Canterbury 65 n. 41
Languedoc *see* Occitania
Laon 65
Lateran Councils
  Second (1139) 43
  Fourth (1215) 8, 28, 52, 55, 132, 136, 159, 167
  Third (1179) 5, 52, 55, 58, 88, 109, 112, 117, 118, 119, 127, 134, 204
    Canon 27 112, 113, 127–8, 130, 132, 134, 204, 214
Latin language 48, 49, 126, 137, 139, 140, 151, 152, 206, 217
Lauragais 46
Lauwers, Michel 22 n. 19, 195 n. 94, 197 n. 105, 198 n. 109
Lavaur 6, 125, 132, 133, 134, 139, 142, 168, 169, 170
Leclercq, Jean 21 n. 17, 25 n. 3, 56 n. 1, 58 n. 3, 59 n. 10, 60 n. 14, 62 n. 25, 64 n. 36, 70 n. 63, 72 n. 71, 73 nn. 79,

Leclercq, Jean (*conts.*)
80; 76 n. 89, 80 n. 5, 81 nn. 9, 10;
107 n. 97, 108 n. 100
lectio divina 74
Lecoy de la Marche, A. 186 n. 59
Le Gentil, P. 161 n. 113
Le Goff, Jacques 25 n. 1, 186
Leicester, countess of 162
Lejeune, Rita 165 n. 133
Lekai, Louis 2 n. 2, 212 n. 20, 213 n. 24
Leipzig 213
Le Mans 3, 91
Lenssen, Seraphin 178 nn. 19, 21
leopard 123, 205
leprosy 119
Lerner, Robert 13 n. 42
Le Roy Ladurie, Emmanuel 211
Les Cassès 157
les-Vaux-de-Cernay, Cistercian abbey of
164, 207, 216
see also Guy of les-Vaux-de-Cernay;
Peter of les-Vaux-de-Cernay
Le Thoronet, Cistercian abbey of 6, 37,
145, 165, 207
Liège 167
Lipton, Sarah G. 39 n. 62
literacy 15, 37
Little, Lester 27 n. 4, 41 n. 68
Lobrichon, Guy 22 n. 19, 65 n. 43
Lombers 48
see also Council of Lombers
Longère, Jean 27 n. 7, 46 n. 90, 140 n. 22,
172 nn. 159, 164
Loos, Milan 46 n. 91
Louis VI 176
Louis VII, 113, 114, 120, 176
Louis VIII 180, 181
Louis IX, St 181, 187
Louis the Pious 56 n. 3
Luchaire, Achille 159 n. 102
Lucius II, pope 91
Lucius III, pope 44, 131
Luke, Gospel of
9. 5 99
9. 58 142
10. 38 75
22. 38 115, 192, 205
23. 12 184
see also swords, image of two
Luz, Ulrich 100 n. 80
Lyons 3, 5, 129, 131, 132, 195

Maccabees, Second Book of 198
Macedonian heresy, 195
Machaut, Guillaume 22
Mack, Burton 19, 95 n. 65
Madden, T. F. *see* Queller, D. E.
Magnou-Nortier, E. 31 n. 22
Maier, Christoph 46 n. 90, 209 n. 9, 210
n. 12, 213 n. 26
Mainz 44
Maisonneuve, Henri 1 n. 1, 107 n. 98,
125 n. 61, 127
Maloney, L. M. 104 n. 89
Mani 153, 193
Manicheans, Manicheanism 43 n. 74, 88,
89, 92, 101, 110, 112, 149, 191, 193,
194, 198, 199, 201
Manselli, Raoul 51 n. 110, 92–3 n. 54,
107 n. 96, 159 n. 104
Marcion, Marcionites 193, 194
Marie of Champagne 34, 38
Marie of Oignies, and *vita* of 167, 172
Mark, Gospel of
6. 11 99
8. 1–9 75
16. 5 14
Markus, R. A. 64 n. 38
marriage *see* sacraments
Martin of Pairis, abbot 208
Martin, Lawrence T. 69 n. 58
Martin, R. P. 104 n. 89
Mary, André 178 n. 22
Mary, Virgin 69, 193–4, 199, 201
Mary Magdalene 73, 144
Matter, E. Ann 60 n. 18
Matthew, Gospel of
5. 45 184
7. 15 87, 93, 96, 97, 104, 215
7. 18 95, 104
8. 20 142
10. 4 99
10. 16 217
10. 23 218
10. 27 87
13. 4–9, 18–23 166
13. 24–30, 36–42 95, 100, 104, 105, 166,
215
21. 6–7 152
23. 37 183, 184
McCulloch, Florence 177 n. 14
McGinn, Bernard 12 n. 39, 25 n.1, 159
n. 104

McGuire, Brian Patrick 4 n. 13, 25 n. 1, 81, 102
McNamara, Jo Ann 88 n. 32
mendicant orders 33, 35, 36, 46, 173, 175, 204, 207, 209, 210, 211, 212, 213, 216
 see also Dominican Order; Franciscan Order
metamorphosis 124, 134
methodology
 agency 21
 deconstruction 10, 16, 23, 202, 203, 204, 207, 213, 214
 discourse analysis 16
 explication de texte 16–17
 feminist rhetorical historiography, 20
 literary criticism 17, 19
 reconstruction 10, 202, 207, 213, 214
 reception of text 17
 rhetorical criticism 11, 19–20
 sermons and related texts 213–14
 social critical interpretation 19–20, 23
 structuralism 10, 20–2
 sub-text 10, 17, 23
Metz 44, 131
Milan 44
Milo, notary, legate 151
Milon de Nanteuil, bishop 180
mimetic rivalry 103–04, 190
Minerve 157, 159, 160, 163
miracles
 of Bernard of Clairvaux 97, 98, 99, 101, 103, 106, 203
 as confirmation of preaching 97, 98, 99, 100, 105
Mirepoix 2, 211, 212
Mohammed 193
Mohrmann, Christine 76 n. 90, 79
Moissac 163, 181
mole 123, 124, 128, 205
Molina, R. 181 n. 36
monastery
 and heavenly Jerusalem 59–60
 schola Christi 31
monasticism
 abbot 61, 69, 76
 humility *see* virtues
 literature 56
 genres 70
 exegesis 56, 58, 62–70, 71, 74, 76, 77; *see also* typology
 letter 70, 71–3
 sermon 59, 70, 71, 72, 73–5

 see also Song of Songs
 imagery 75, 76
 body 60–1, 76
 heavenly Jerusalem *see* Jerusalem, heavenly
 military 60, 215
 and Scriptures 56, 58, 59, 62, 70, 71, 74, 75
 see also exegesis
 liturgy *see* Rule of Benedict
 obedience *see* virtues
 order 61, 76, 77
 see also social order
 spirituality 9, 58
 contemplation 59
 meditation and *lectio divina* 59, 74, 75
 style 76
 word association 76
 hook-words 75–6
 reminiscence 75
 and urban model 60
 work 62, 76
 see also Christ; Jerusalem, heavenly; *Rule of Benedict*; Scripture
Montfort, *castrum* of 163
Montpellier 36, 39, 137, 140, 146, 152, 172, 173, 212, 213
Montségur 48, 211
Moore, R. I. 1 n. 1, 4 n. 10, 12 n. 37, 15, 21, 27 n. 6, 29 n. 16, 43, 44 n. 82, 51 nn. 198, 109; 52 nn. 112, 113, 114; 89 n. 39, 91, 92 nn. 51, 52; 92–3 n. 54, 95 n. 62, 107, 110 nn. 3, 4, 5, 6; 111 nn. 7, 8; 113 n. 13, 117 n. 30, 120, 121 n. 44, 127 n. 67, 134
Moralia in Job see Gregory the Great
Morey, J. H. 34 n. 40
moth 120–1, 205
Mousnier, M. 139 n. 17, 164 n. 130, 174 n. 4, 182 n. 41, 21 n. 15
Muessig, Carolyn 172 n. 161
Muret, battle of (1213) 136, 142, 168
Mumford, Lewis 60 n. 15
Mundy, John H. 29 n. 13, 37, 47, 48 n. 95, 93 n. 54
Murphy, J. J. 19 n. 9, 32 nn. 27, 29
Muslims 158, 159, 160, 206, 208

Naaman 120
Narbonne 39, 145, 158, 160, 168, 170, 210, 211

Narbonne (*cont.*)
  archbishop of 44, 138, 150
  see also Arnaud Amaury; Berenger of
    Narbonne
Navas de Tolosa, Las (1212) 5, 158, 159,
    160, 170, 206, 208
Nazarius, Cathar bishop 183
Neininger, Falk 2 n. 3, 174 n. 2
Nelli, René 49, 50 n. 104, 106, 217
Neoplatonism 34, 186, 199
  and spiritual meaning of texts 17–18
Newman, Martha 1 n. 1, 29 n. 17, 30
    n. 18, 41 n. 68, 58 n. 4, 60 nn. 17, 18;
    61 n. 19, 72 n. 72, 80 n. 3, 83 n. 15,
    91 n. 47, 107 n. 98, 112 n. 9, 131
    n. 86, 137 n. 10, 140 n. 21, 176 n. 8,
    189 n. 73
New Testament 13, 18, 64, 68, 69, 98,
    110
  scholarship on 19–20
  see also scripture; typology
Nicholas of Clairvaux 34
Nicholas of Claramonte 174 n. 2
Nicholas of Trois Fontaines 65
Nirenberg, David 21 n. 16
Norbert of Xanten 43
Numbers, book of 25. 6–9 115, 205

Obert-Piketty, C. 33 n. 31, 212 n. 23
obedience *see* virtues
O'Callaghan J. F. 159 n. 106
Occitania 26
  boundaries 3 n. 7
  and Cistercians 2, 3, 5, 8, 25, 27, 28,
    202, 204, 206, 207, 208, 209, 214, 216
    expansion 28, 30–1, 40–1, 54
    see also Cistercian Order
  and economic growth in city and
    countryside 39–40
  and Gregorian reforms 31
  and heresy 25, 27, 28, 30, 31, 44, 46,
    47, 48, 49, 50, 107, 202, 204, 205, 206
    see also Cathars; Waldensians
  and inquisition 51, 210–12
    see also inquisition
  and 'Twelfth-Century Renaissance'
    35–8
  troubadours 36–8
  see also Bernard of Clairvaux; Henry
    of Clairvaux/Albano; Arnaud
    Amaury; Guy of les-Vaux-de-
    Cernay; Fulk of Toulouse; Hélinand
  of Froidmont; names of specific
    places; Toulouse
Odo of Ourscamp 34
Olbrechts-Tyteca, L. 12 n. 36, 19
Old Testament 13, 18, 64, 68, 134, 144
  see also scripture; typology; books of
    by name
O'Malley, John W. 33 n. 30
opus Dei see monasticism, liturgy
Origen 153
  on spiritual interpretation 63–4, 67
Orléans 186, bishop of 176
Othon de Saint-Blaise, chronicler 172
Ovid 191, 199
Oxford 110, 212

Pacaut, Marcel 29 n. 17, 58 n. 4
Paden, William D. 37 n. 54, 38 nn. 55–6,
    165 n. 134, 178 n. 20, 179 n. 25
Pagels, Elaine 12 n. 36
Pamiers 2, 147, 149, 211, 212
Paolini, Lorenzo 49 n. 100
Parable of the sower 166
  see also Matthew, Gospel of
Parable of the tares 95, 166
  see also Matthew, Gospel of
parallelism 76
Paravy, P. 44 n. 85
Paris 5, 28, 32, 33, 121, 131, 162, 170,
    171, 172, 177, 186, 187, 193, 212
  circle of Peter the Chanter 34, 35, 54,
    66, 162, 171, 172, 173, 207
  exegesis in schools 65, 66
  University quarrel 183, 185, 209
  see also Alan of Lille; Peter the
    Chanter; Peter Comestor; Saint-
    Victor, Abbey of; Treaty of Paris/
    Meaux; William of Paris
Patarini, Paterini 128, 198
Paterson, Linda 3 n. 7, 25 n. 3, 30 n. 20,
    48 n. 96, 49 n. 102
Patschovsky, A. 44 n. 84, 130 n. 84, 131
    n. 90
Paul, St 62, 63, 64, 93, 98, 120, 141, 146
Peace of God 38
Pelagius 110
Pennington, Basil 58 n. 4
Périgueux 92
Perelman, Chaim 12 n. 12, 19
persecution *see* inquisition; heresy; R. I.
    Moore; rhetoric
Perseigne, Cistercian abbey of 38

Peter, St 105, 117, 119, 120
  Acts of Peter 119
  Feast of St Peter in chains 100
Peter of Aragon 136, 160
Peter of Benevento 160
Peter of Bruys 43
  see also Petrobrusians
Peter of Castelnau, legate, monk of
    Fontfroide 6, 8, 54, 136, 143, 145,
    150, 151, 172, 206
Peter of Celle 34, 71 n. 67
Peter the Chanter 34, 35, 54, 66, 131, 162,
    171–3, 179, 207, 209
  and Cistercians 171–3
  and homosexuality 117
  and Third Lateran Council 117, 118
Peter Comestor, *Historia scholastica* 34,
    66
Peter of les Vaux-de-Cernay 137, 138,
    143, 144, 147, 149, 150, 152, 157,
    161, 163, 168, 170, 200–01, 207, 214,
    217
  see also Hystoria Albigensis
Peter Lombard, *Sententiae* 65
Peter Maurand 122, 124
Peter of St Chrysogonus 8, 112, 113, 114,
    115, 119, 120, 121, 122, 124, 125–7,
    133, 204
Peter, Second Letter of 2. 22 94, 104, 215
Peter the Venerable 7, 43, 52
Peters, Edward 1 n. 1, 12 n. 38, 28 n. 10,
    44 n. 83, 51 nn. 108, 110, 111; 53
    nn. 115, 116, 117, 118; 104 n. 90, 187
    n. 67, 210 n. 14, 211 n. 17
Petrobrusians 7, 52, 98
Philip Augustus (Philip II), king 134,
    151, 152, 162, 176, 178–9, 181
Philip of Dreux, bishop of Beauvais 176,
    178, 179, 180
philosophy, philosophers 34, 187
Phinehas 115, 205
Piazzoni, A. M. 99 n. 75
Picard, André 99 n. 73
Pierre of Hénu 180
Pilate, Pontius 184
Plato 34, 199
Platonism *see* Neoplatonism
Poblet 138
Poitiers 92
  see also John Bellesmains
polemical literature, polemics 9, 11, 14,
    17, 20, 23, 27, 100, 128, 197, 205

pollution, rhetoric of 11, 89, 90, 95, 96,
    97, 104, 109, 116, 121, 126, 138, 142,
    144, 151, 153, 158, 200, 203, 205, 209,
    215
Ponce of Polignac, abbot, bishop of
    Clermont 5, 130–01, 205
Pons of Léras 42
Pontal, O. 165 n. 133, 168 n. 146, 169
    n. 149
Poor Catholics 149
'Poor of Lyons' 131, 132 n. 92; *see also*
    Waldensians
Porphyry 191, 196
poverty *see* virtues
Pradalié, Georges 182, 186, 187 n. 66
Prague 212
Praemonstratensian order 4, 7, 32, 43, 82
  see also Bernard of Fontcaude
preacher, unauthorized 12, 45, 96, 97,
    203
  see also preaching
preaching
  authorization for 27, 45, 46, 54, 100,
    130, 131
  by Cathars 40, 45, 112, 123–4, 126, 128
  by Cistercians 1–3, 4, 5–8, 9, 10–11,
    14–15, 21, 25, 27–8, 29, 30, 33, 35, 44,
    54–5, 56, 77, 135–8, 143–52, 171–3,
    174, 175, 182, 202–09, 212–16
    see also Bernard of Clairvaux;
    crusade; Henry of Clairvaux/
    Albano; Arnaud Amaury; Guy of
    les-Vaux-de-Cernay; Fulk of
    Toulouse; Hélinand of Froidmont
  crusade to the Holy Land 2, 7, 29, 46,
    80, 133, 135, 139, 142, 143, 159, 162,
    164, 171, 173
  historiography and use of sources
    10–11, 74, 213–14
    see also chronicles; *exemplum*; letters;
    names of specific preachers;
    statutes; treatises
  by lay people 14, 15, 27, 43–6, 62,
    131–2
  mendicant orders *see* mendicant
    orders
  and miracles *see* miracles
  monastic, prohibitions against 1, 45,
    85
    see also monasticism, sermons
  public, popular 2, 6, 11, 14, 35, 45, 46,
    54, 103, 128, 136, 140, 212

preaching (*cont.*)
and reform 4, 7, 28, 30, 56, 173, 205
see also crusade, Albigensian
techniques and tools 27, 35, 45, 46,
148–9, 185–6
see also Alan of Lille; Bernard of
Clairvaux; *distinctiones*; *exemplum*;
Hélinand of Froidmont
unauthorized 12, 45, 46, 60, 85, 95–7,
99 n. 6, 100, 130–2
vehicle for Church's teaching 1, 27,
28, 35
by Waldensians 14, 15, 45, 54, 100,
130–2
by women 44, 130
see also evangelism; sermons
Prepositinus of Cremona 172
prototype 68; *see also* typology
Prouille, monastery of 210
Proverbs, book of 25. 2 87
Pryds, Darleen 132 n. 92
Psalms, book of
9. 29 96, 104, 215
62. 12 102
121. 6 183
131. 9 191
132. 9 189
Publicani 110, 128, 198
see also Cathars
purgatory 87
Purification, sermon of Hélinand of
Froidmont 193–4
Pythagoras 199

Queller, D. E. 159 n. 103, 162 n. 119
Quéribus 211

Rabanus Maurus 121 n. 41, 123 n. 52
Rainier, legate 143
Ralph, Cistercian monk 45
Ralph of Beauvais 35, 177
Ralph d'Escures 70 n. 66
Ralph of Fontfroide, papal legate 6, 136,
143, 149, 151, 206
Ralph of Laon 65
Raymond of Baimac 113 n. 13, 125, 126
Raymond V, count of Toulouse 36, 114,
120
Raymond VI, count of Toulouse 36, 136,
138, 160, 181, 215
Raymond VII, count of Toulouse 36
Raymond of Le Fauga 170

Raymond of Miraval, troubadour 37
Raymond of Rabastens, bishop of
Toulouse 145
Raymond Roger, count of Foix 181
reason (*ratio*), appeal to 82, 86, 90
reconstruction *see* methodology
Reeves, Marjorie 130 n. 79, 159 n. 104
reform movements 15, 28–9, 51, 53, 135,
173
see also Gregorian reforms; twelfth-
century, reform movements
Regensburg 44, 187
reincarnation 199
reminiscence *see* monasticism, literature
Renne 163
Revelation book of 3. 20, 12. 4, 14. 7 184
Rheims 111; *see also* Council of Rheims
rhetoric
circumstantiae, classical theory of 16
n. 2
defensive vs offensive 217–18
New Rhetoric, The, Perelman and
Olbrechts-Tyteca 19
patterns 9, 11, 14, 81, 104, 109, 134,
140, 169, 200, 203, 205, 209, 214, 215
of persecution 20–1, 22–3, 202, 218
see also apocalypticism,
demonization, pollution, threat to
the social order
Rhineland, heresy in 3, 4, 52, 82, 103,
109, 138
Riché, Pierre 32 n. 25, 64 n. 38
Rigier, A. 49 n. 102
Riley-Smith, Jonathan 25 n. 2, 29 n. 12
Robert of Arbrissel 43
Robert of Auxerre, chronicler 113, 133,
147, 149
Robert of Courçon 160, 164, 171
Robert of France, count of Dreux 176
Robert of Mauvoisin 157, 164
Robert of Molesme 4
Roberts, Phyllis B. 36 n. 47
Rocamadour 157
Rochais, Henri 73 n. 79, 81 n. 9
Rogation, sermon of Hélinand of
Froidmont 183–5
Roger II, count of Béziers 124–5, 132
Roger of Howden 112–13
Romano of St Angelo, cardinal legate
174, 182, 183, 187, 188
Romans, Letter to the
5. 3–5 146

5. 1 63
10. 15 85
13. 4 90, 104, 192
Rome 14, 44, 51, 55, 110, 127, 133, 134,
    147, 151, 154, 155, 166, 169, 188
Roquebert, Michel 48 n. 98, 151 n. 68
Rouse, Mary 35 n. 43
Rouse, Richard 35 n. 43
Rubellin, M. 129 nn. 74, 76, 78; 130 n. 81,
    131 nn. 87, 88, 91
Rule of Benedict 7, 9, 56–62, 70, 73, 74, 75,
    103, 192
    see also monasticism; virtues
Rule of the Master 56 n. 2
Rupert of Deutz 193
Russell, Jeffrey Burton 1 n. 1, 3 n. 6, 11
    n. 36, 12 n. 36, 28 n. 9, 29 n. 15, 42
    nn. 70–1, 43 nn. 76, 78, 79, 81; 44
    n. 83, 51 nn. 108, 110; 52 n. 112, 104,
    105 n. 91, 117 n. 28, 194 n. 91, 200
    n. 112
Rymington, William 212

Saak, Eric 199 nn. 110, 111
Sabatier, Agathon 178 nn. 18, 21; 179
    n. 27
sacraments 13, 67, 100, 141, 142, 144,
    195, 196–7, 199, 200, 201, 216
    baptism 84, 87, 94, 194, 196–7, 199,
        200, 201
    marriage 47, 50, 88, 110, 190, 201, 204
    rejection of 47, 87, 93, 94, 110, 111,
        126, 183, 184, 185, 195
    see also Cathars, beliefs and
        practices
Saint Félix de Caraman 110
Saint Paul-Cap-de-Joux 91
saints, intercession 13, 197, 201, 216
Saint Victor, Abbey of 32, 34, 66, 67, 162
    see also Andrew of St Victor; Hugh of
        St Victor
Saladin 134
Salerno 36, 186
Salvatierra 159
Santa Clara, Cistercian monastery
    (Lerida) 37
Sarlat 97, 98, 100, 101, 102, 105, 203
Satan 11, 94, 99, 126, 183, 184, 188, 201,
    203
Schaeffer, J.-M. 16 n. 2
schism
    of 1130 5, 30, 91

of 1159–77 52, 115, 131
Schneiders, S. 19 n. 12, 63 n. 30, 64
    nn. 32, 34, 38
Schneyer, Johannes Baptist 180 n. 34,
    181 n. 36
Schüssler Fiorenza, Elisabeth 20
Scopello, M. 8 n. 33
Scripture 13, 18, 59, 83, 87, 111, 114, 122,
    126, 131
    see also books by name; exegesis;
        monasticism; New Testament; Old
        Testament; typology
sermons
    against heresy 97, 106, 139, 213
        see also preaching, by Cistercians;
            Bernard of Clairvaux; Henry of
            Clairvaux/Albano; Arnaud
            Amaury; Guy of les-Vaux-de-
            Cernay; Fulk of Toulouse;
            Hélinand of Froidmont; Song of
            Songs
    and related texts 72–3, 74–5, 81–2,
        202–03, 204, 206, 213–14
    monastic 73–7
        see also monasticism, sermons;
            preaching, by Cistercians
    reported 97–103, 113, 133, 148, 156,
        163, 166, 167
    vernacular 137, 140–43
        see also methodology; preaching
serpent 94, 96, 104, 116, 123, 204, 205,
    215
Servian 146, 149
sexual immorality, accusation of 84, 88,
    116, 117, 118, 121, 201, 205
Shannon, A. C. 128 n. 70
sheep 87, 93, 96, 97, 104, 124, 166, 204,
    215, 217
Shroff, Susan 71 n. 69
Sibly and Sibly 143 n. 34
    see also Hystoria Albigensis
Simon Magus 105, 117, 119, 120, 187, 200
Simon of Montfort 37, 99, 136, 154, 158,
    159, 160, 161, 162, 163, 164, 165, 166,
    167, 168, 169, 170, 171, 207, 210
Simonetti, M. 64 n. 32
Smalley, Beryl 25 n. 1, 62 nn. 26, 27; 64
    nn. 33–4, 35, 38; 65 n. 44, 66 nn. 46,
    47, 48; 68 n. 55
Smith, Cyril E. 187 n. 65
Smits, Edmé 33 n. 33, 34 n. 40, 66 n. 50,
    179 n. 26, 180 nn. 32, 35

social order 12, 51, 90, 122, 169
  see also monasticism, order; threat to
    the social order
Sodom 116, and Gomorrah 117, 118, 205
Song of Songs
  exegetical sermon series 60 n. 18, 103
    see also Bernard of Clairvaux
  and little foxes in the vineyard (2. 15)
    8, 78, 82, 85, 96, 103, 104, 215
    see also foxes; vineyard
Southern, Richard 27 n. 3
Spain 5, 35, 110, 149, 158, 160, 208
Spatz, Nancy 185 n. 56
Spirit, Holy 194–5, 196
statutes *see* Cistercians
Stephen Harding, abbot 65
Stephen Langton, exegete, archbishop of
    Canterbury 66
Stephen of Tournai, bishop 162, 171
Steynhus, Matthew 213
Stock, Brian 7 n. 27, 18, 27 n. 5, 32 n. 29,
    51 n. 109, 52 n. 112, 69 n. 61, 104
    n. 9
Strayer, J. 1 n. 1, 3 nn. 5, 7
Stronski, S. 6 n. 19, 165 n. 133
sub-text *see* methodology
swords, image of two (Luke 22. 38) 115,
    116, 121, 151, 192, 205
  see also Luke, Gospel of; Henry of
    Clairvaux/Albano
Switzerland 73
Sylvanès, Cistercian abbey of 42, 71, 72
  see also Hugh Francigena; Pons of
    Léras
symbolist mentality 56, 66–67

Talbot, C. H. 81 n. 9
Tarascon, prior of 156
Theodosian Code 52
Thessalonians, First Letter to 5. 8 121
Thibaut of Marly 164
Thomas Becket 30, 112
threat to the social order, rhetoric of 11,
    94, 95, 96, 104, 109, 116, 121, 142,
    153, 158, 191, 200, 203, 205, 209
Thouzellier, Christine 112 n. 10, 113
    n. 15, 129 n. 77, 133 n. 100, 147
    nn. 51, 52; 149 n. 63, 150 n. 66,
    151 nn. 71, 72; 172 nn. 163, 165;
    173 n. 166, 174 n. 5, 184 n. 49, 185
    n. 53

Timothy, First Letter to
  2. 3 85 n. 22
  4. 1–3 82–3, 88
  4. 2 93, 204, 215
Timothy, Second Letter to
  2. 16 89
  2. 17 96, 215
Toledo 186
Torjesen, Karen Jo 64 n. 32
Toulouse 6, 10, 37, 40, 52, 127, 138,
    165, 168, 171, 179, 209, 211, 212,
    214
  during Albigensian Crusade 136, 152,
    155, 157, 164, 167, 170, 181
  and Bernard of Clairvaux 73, 81, 91,
    92, 93, 95–7, 101, 103, 107, 121
  bishop of *see* Fulk of Toulouse;
    Raymond of Rabastens
  cathedral of St Etienne 112, 127, 133
  church of St Jacques 112, 127, 182
  Confraternity, Black 167–8
  Confraternity, White 167–8, 169, 170
  counts of 36, 37, 45, 52, 94, 127, 150,
    151, 168, 169, 182, 215; *see also*
    specific names
  and Dominicans 167, 170, 187, 209
  economic change 39
  and Hélinand of Froidmont's
    preaching 181, 182–92
  heresy in 47, 96, 103, 123, 128, 142,
    143, 144
  1178 preaching mission 122, 123, 124,
    125, 127, 133
  Synod or Council of (1229) 8, 53, 175,
    181, 187–92, 199
    see also Council of Toulouse (1119)
  University of 6, 15, 36, 175, 182–3,
    185–6, 209
treatise, as source for history of
    preaching 10–11
Treaty of Paris/Meaux (1229) 6, 15, 53,
    171, 174, 181, 182, 185, 187, 209
Trencavel family 136
Trinity, doctrine of 194
troubadours 36–8, 49–51
Trout, J. 132 n. 91
Turpin, archbishop 160
type 68; *see also* typology
typology 18, 63, 64, 67, 68, 69, 203
twelfth century
  economic growth 25–6, 38–41
  lay literacy and spirituality 25, 42–6, 53

reform movement 25, 28–31
'renaissance' 25, 31–8, 65

universal salvation 47
  see also Cathars, beliefs and practices
Urban V, pope 29
urban expansion 15
Urbs Ierusalem beata, hymn 59
  see also Jerusalem, heavenly

Valdes (Peter Waldo) 5, 44, 112, 129,
  130, 204, 205
Valentinus 193, 194
Van Engen, John H. 25 n.1
variables
  rhetorical categories 12–13
  beliefs or practices 13–14
Vauchez, André 42, 43 n. 75, 47 n. 94
Veni Creator Spiritus 163
Verfeil 48, *79*, 91, 98–100, 105, 203
Vergentis in senium see inquisition
Verger, J. 36 n. 49
vernacular 25, 37, 48, 49, 126, 137, 139,
  140, 197, 206, 217
Vézelay 73, 80, 110, 111, 142
Vicaire, Marie-Humbert 2 n. 3, 30 n. 20,
  135 n. 1, 139, 143 n. 37, 154, 157
  n. 95, 158 n. 100, 161, 164 n. 130,
  174, 182
vices *see* virtues and vices
Victorines *see* Saint Victor, abbey of
Vienne 150
Vigilantius 198
  see also Jerome, St
Villelongue, Cistercian Abbey of *57*, 164
Villerouge-Termenès 212
vineyard, image of 8, 9, 11, 21, 55, 56,
  78, 80, 82, 96, 103, 104, 107, 110,
  114, 138, 147, 150, 188, 202, 205,
  206
  see also Song of Songs; foxes
virtues 13, 31, 141, 142
  charity 60
  chastity 13, 69, 216
  humility 13, 59, 60–1, 62, 161, 216
  obedience 13, 44, 54, 58, 60, 62, 130,
    189, 192, 203, 216
  poverty 7, 13, 42, 99, 131, 167, 216
  and vices 167, 188, 192
Virtutes apostolorum 99
Vita prima 3 n. 8, 81, 87, 91, 92, 105, 116,
  206, 214

see also Bernard of Clairvaux; Geoffrey
  of Auxerre

Wadislaus of Bohemia, duke 72
Wailes, Stephen L. 95 n. 64, 100 n. 80
Wakefield, Walter L. 45 n. 86, 100 n. 5,
  113 n. 13, 144 nn. 40, 41; 168
  n. 145, 169 n. 150, 170 n. 153, 211
  nn. 16, 19
Waldensians 44–5, 51, 52, 54, 62, 70, 84,
  87, 100, 129–32, 144, 149, 152, 184,
  185, 205, 206, 217
Wales 208
Walter Map 41
weavers 87, 89, 92, 103
  see also Cathars
Welter, J.-Th. 186 n. 58
Wends 81
Werblowsky, R. J. Zwi 80 n. 4
West, vs East 13
Wild, R. A. 104 n. 89
Wildhaber, B. 40 n. 66
Wiles, M. 92 n. 53
William, monk 92
William of Fécamp, abbot 70 n. 66
William Figuéiras, troubadour 153, 155
William of Grandselve 186
William Hélie, bishop 156
William of Newburgh, chronicler 110
William of Paris, archdeacon 163
William of Pelhisson, chronicler 170
  n. 153
William of Poitiers 91
William of Puylaurens, chronicler 81, 91,
  98, 99, 105, 113, 133, 147, 165, 166,
  167, 168, 207, 214
William of Tudela 6, 147, 151, 154, 157,
  167, 168
  see also Canso de la Crozada
Wilmart, André 71 n. 66
Wire, Antoinette Clark 19 n. 12
Woesthuis, Martinus M. 198 n. 108
wolf, wolves 87, 93, 96, 97, 104, 124, 166,
  204, 205, 215, 217
women
  and Cathars 14, 111
  heretics 20, 164
  Waldensian preachers 14, 44, 130, 206
word-association *see* monasticism,
  literature
Wyclif, John 212

Zara 159, 162

Zerfass, R. 131 n. 91

Zerner-Chardavoine, Monique 21, 22
n. 19, 92 n. 52, 130 n. 80, 161 n. 118,
162, 163 nn. 124, 125, 128

Zimmermann, H. 135 n. 1, 164 nn. 131,
132; 171 nn. 157, 158; 172 n. 160, 174
n. 2, 189 n. 71

Zink, Michel 155 n. 88, 161 n. 113

YORK MEDIEVAL PRESS: PUBLICATIONS

God's Words, Women's Voices: The Discernment of Spirits in the Writing of Late-Medieval Women Visionaries, Rosalynn Voaden (1999)

Pilgrimage Explored, ed. J. Stopford (1999)

Piety, Fraternity and Power: Religious Gilds in Late Medieval Yorkshire 1389–1547, David J. F. Crouch (2000)

Courts and Regions in Medieval Europe, ed. Sarah Rees Jones, Richard Marks and A. J. Minnis (2000)

Treasure in the Medieval West, ed. Elizabeth M. Tyler (2000)

Nunneries, Learning and Spirituality in Late Medieval English Society: The Dominican Priory of Dartford, Paul Lee (2000)

New Directions in Later Medieval Manuscript Studies: Essays from the 1998 Harvard Conference, ed. Derek Pearsall (2000)

York Studies in Medieval Theology

I *Medieval Theology and the Natural Body*, ed. Peter Biller and A. J. Minnis (1997)

II *Handling Sin: Confession in the Middle Ages*, ed. Peter Biller and A. J. Minnis (1998)

York Manuscripts Conferences

Manuscripts and Readers in Fifteenth-Century England: The Literary Implications of Manuscript Study, ed. Derek Pearsall [Proceedings of the 1981 York Manuscripts Conference]

Manuscripts and Texts: Editorial Problems in Later Middle English Literature, ed. Derek Pearsall [Proceedings of the 1985 York Manuscripts Conference]

Latin and Vernacular: Studies in Late-Medieval Texts and Manuscripts, ed. A. J. Minnis (1989) [Proceedings of the 1987 York Manuscripts Conference]

Regionalism in Late-Medieval Manuscripts and Texts: Essays celebrating the publication of 'A Linguistic Atlas of Late Mediaeval English', ed. Felicity Riddy (1991) [Proceedings of the 1989 York Manuscripts Conference]

Late-Medieval Religious Texts and their Transmission: Essays in Honour of A. I. Doyle, ed. A. J. Minnis (1994) [Proceedings of the 1991 York Manuscripts Conference]

Prestige, Authority and Power in Late Medieval Manuscripts and Texts, ed. Felicity Riddy (2000) [Proceedings of the 1994 York Manuscripts Conference]

Prophecy and Public Affairs in Later Medieval England, Lesley A. Coote (2000)

Problem of Labour in Fourteenth-Century England, ed. James Bothwell, P. J. P. Goldberg and W. M. Ormrod (2000)

Cistercians, Heresy and Crusade in Occitania, 1145–1229: Preaching in the Lord's Vineyard, Beverly Mayne Kienzle (2001)